LARGEMOUTH BASS

An In-Fisherman Handbook of Strategies

LARGEMOUTH BASS

An In-Fisherman Handbook of Strategies

Al Lindner
Ron Lindner
Jim Lindner
Doug Stange
Steve Quinn
Dan Sura
Dave Csanda
Larry Dahlberg
Ralph Manns

Published by
In-Fisherman

LARGEMOUTH BASS

Compiled by *Steve Grooms*
Cover Art by *Larry Tople*
Back Cover Art by *Joe Tomelleri*
Edited by *Doug Stange, Joann Phipps, Steve Quinn, Dave Csanda*
Layout and design by *Scott Pederson*
Litho Prep and Printing by *Bang Printing*

Acknowledgements:
Joe Tomelleri: species illustrations
Tom Seward: technical illustrations and ideas shared as a contributor to *In-Fisherman* magazine
Rich Zaleski: lake illustrations and ideas shared as a contributor to *In-Fisherman* magazine
Greg Meyer: super-tuning reels
Doug Hannon: ideas shared as a contributor to *In-Fisherman* magazine
Ralph Manns: lake illustrations and ideas shared as a contributor to *In-Fisherman* magazine, and author of chapter 8

ISBN: 0-929384-11-3 (Volume 7)

In-Fisherman

"Handbook of Strategies" Book Series

One of the

(F) Fish + (L) Location + (P) Presentation = (S) Success℠

Educational Services

visit our Web site: www.in-fisherman.com

A PRIMEDIA Publication
Published by In-Fisherman
7819 Highland Scenic Road, Baxter Minnesota 56425

20 19 18 17 16 15 14

For . . . People of Good Passion, Doing Not For Money But As A Daily Offering Of Selves As Living Sacrifices Feeding the Spirit Lake That Sustains Art In Many Forms From Generation To Generation As It Flows From God As A Token Of His Love.

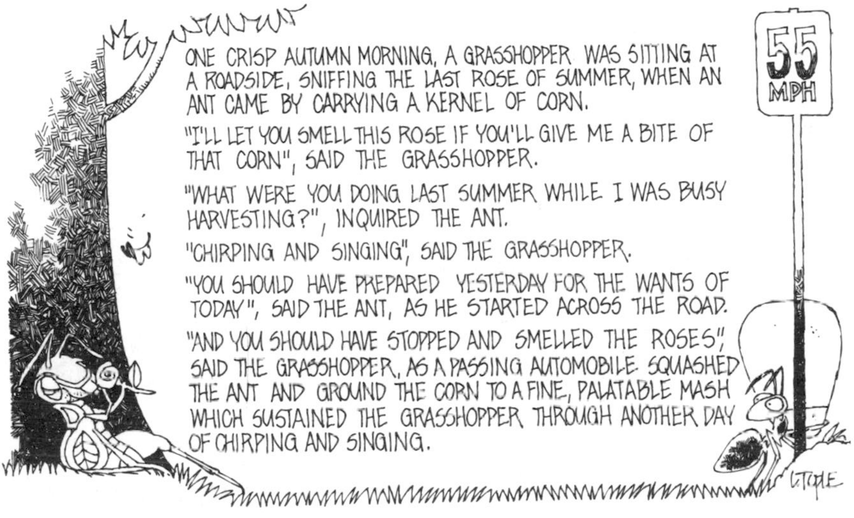

ONE CRISP AUTUMN MORNING, A GRASSHOPPER WAS SITTING AT A ROADSIDE, SNIFFING THE LAST ROSE OF SUMMER, WHEN AN ANT CAME BY CARRYING A KERNEL OF CORN.

"I'LL LET YOU SMELL THIS ROSE IF YOU'LL GIVE ME A BITE OF THAT CORN", SAID THE GRASSHOPPER.

"WHAT WERE YOU DOING LAST SUMMER WHILE I WAS BUSY HARVESTING?", INQUIRED THE ANT.

"CHIRPING AND SINGING", SAID THE GRASSHOPPER.

"YOU SHOULD HAVE PREPARED YESTERDAY FOR THE WANTS OF TODAY", SAID THE ANT, AS HE STARTED ACROSS THE ROAD.

"AND YOU SHOULD HAVE STOPPED AND SMELLED THE ROSES", SAID THE GRASSHOPPER, AS A PASSING AUTOMOBILE SQUASHED THE ANT AND GROUND THE CORN TO A FINE, PALATABLE MASH WHICH SUSTAINED THE GRASSHOPPER THROUGH ANOTHER DAY OF CHIRPING AND SINGING.

Presents
LARGEMOUTH BASS

*A Time For Every Purpose Under Heaven…
Including Fishing For Bass.*

The In-Fisherman® Staff
August 1990

TABLE OF CONTENTS

Minnesota Historical Society

Chapter 1

BASS FISHING IN AMERICA

In The Beginning

Colonists arrived in the New World in mass in the 18th Century. Although these colonists fished for food and sport, bass fishing didn't achieve its present popularity for over 200 years.

British colonists settled most of what is now the United States. Based on their experience in the old country, these colonists knew two classes of fish: the highly valued trout and salmon, and less valued "coarse" fish like pike and carp.

The sunfish family, of which the largemouth bass is a member, originally existed only in North America, so British colonists were unfamiliar with them. Bass were obviously "coarse," though, and therefore second-class denizens of colonial waters. An early writer described the native brook trout as "a thing of beauty and a joy forever," while the largemouth bass was a "blackguard and tough." Others suggested that catching a 15-pound bass in sluggish alligator-infested waters didn't equal catching even a small trout from clear waters in pristine surroundings.

Also, most early settlements were located in that portion of the eastern seaboard blessed with trout, but lacking bass. A leisure class developed much later in the lower Atlantic states where bass were plentiful.

In Kentucky, however, early in the 19th century, wealthy sportsmen wanted to fish closer to home than New England, where great trout waters were located. Bass were readily available in Kentucky. When Kentucky watchmakers invented the "Kentucky" reel around 1810, it spurred more interest in bass fishing. The reel was designed to cast live bait on the long slow-action rods of the day. Bass fishing was becoming "sporty."

Anglers in other parts of the country were already taking bass seriously when prominent physician and sporting writer Dr. James A. Henshall published his *Book of the Black Bass* in 1881. Appearing in this book is Henshall's famous praise for the fighting qualities of bass, "inch for inch and

Book of the Black Bass *(1881) by Dr. James A. Henshall was the first prominent book to discuss fishing for black bass.* More About Black Bass *followed in 1889.*

pound for pound the gamest fish that swims." Henshall prophesied that the bass would become the leading gamefish in America. But his was a minority opinion for decades. Trout had clout.

Henshall also led the trend to shorter rods. Rods were 10 feet or longer when Henshall began popularizing 8-footers. As artificial lures gained popularity in the early 1900s, shorter and stiffer rods were built for casting artificials. James Heddon began making plugs around 1896; the Johnson Silver Minnow spoon was invented in 1920; and even soft plastic lures, albeit poor ones, were around in 1920.

The next great advance in bass fishing came after World War II, with the development of plastics technology. The creation of inexpensive fiberglass fishing rods soon followed. Monofilament line was invented just as a new type of reel, the spinning reel, was imported from Europe. Spinning equipment finally gave average anglers access to affordable equipment that was easy to use. Then came . . .

SONAR

The first sonar units for fishing appeared in the late 1950s. They weren't popular immediately because many were troublesome and all were expensive. In 1958, a Lowrance Fish LO-K-TOR cost as much as a Browning shotgun. But Carl Lowrance's portable sonar, which began as a red box and later became the famous "green box," worked well enough to become commercially successful. Others followed.

Before sonar, the surface of the water stood between the world of fish and the world of fishermen. Except in clear water where anglers could see shallow underwater objects, the surface boundary hid the world of fish. Deeper water remained unknown territory.

An early version of Carl Lowrance's "Lowrance Fish LO-K-TOR." A red box (left) gave way to the famous portable "green box."

Early sonar units were only depth indicators, but improvements quickly appeared. Anglers learned they could determine bottom types—mud, rocks, sand—from the type of signal their sonars displayed. Sonar gave anglers underwater eyes. Bass fishing, which had been limited to visible cover objects, could move into deeper water when sonar made underwater cover visible.

MODERN WRITERS

For most of the 20th century, the fishing authorities were outdoor writers, especially fishing editors based in the Northeast. Most of them regarded bass as inferior to trout and fished for bass only out of professional curiosity.

Jason Lucas, fishing editor for *Sports Afield* from the early 1940s to the early 1960s, was an important exception. He was a bass fisherman. Though he fished for trout, he preferred bass and wasn't afraid to say so. Lucas became the most important spokesman for bass.

Lucas's disdain for livebait fishing created a legacy that lives today. He was a lone wolf and a fishing machine. Lucas often fished 12 hours a day, six or seven days a week—clearly no armchair authority. His book, *Lucas On Bass*, became extremely popular. It was revised in three major editions from 1947 to 1962.

Sports Afield

Jason Lucas, fishing editor for Sports Afield *during the 1940s and 1950s, was the "pioneer of modern bass fishing." Zack Taylor explained it this way in a* Sports Afield *article entitled "Evangelist of Bass Fishing: Jason Lucas."*

"When Lucas took command as angling editor of Sports Afield *in the early '40s, trout were the revered gamefish in America. When he stepped into retirement some 20 years later, bass were the favorites. And as much as any man who lived those years, Jason Lucas brought this change. It was an end of an era and the beginning of another, and, of course, Lucas was assisted in his campaign to anoint the bass as the 'great American gamefish' by the demise of the wild trout and the introduction of those paltry, hatchery-reared trout."*

When Lucas stepped from his post at *Sports Afield*, the world of bass fishing had changed. Buck Perry had created a new type of trolling called "speedtrolling." Anglers were taking sensational strings of bass on jigs and pork eels. Lucas disapproved of some of these new techniques.

But bass fishermen had "come out of the closet." By 1962, America's favorite fish was the largemouth bass. Henceforth, fishing editors of the "Big Three" magazines (*Outdoor Life, Sports Afield,* and *Field and Stream*) would be bass men.

ELWOOD "BUCK" PERRY

Elwood Lake "Buck" Perry invented the Spoonplug after traveling and fishing the South in the 1940s. The deep-diving metal lure functioned as a bottom mapping device. By trolling rapidly with Spoonplugs, Perry determined the shape and composition of the lake bottom. And when sonar became available, he incorporated it into his system.

Elwood "Buck" Perry, the "father of structure fishing," spurred bass anglers to abandon fishing only visual cover objects in favor of bottom changes discovered by trolling with Spoonplugs. Many an ardent bass angler in the 1950s spent time arguing who was the best bass angler, Lucas or Perry.

Perry came to the attention of the national fishing press in the late 1950s, mostly through the efforts of Chicago writer Tom McNally. McNally reported that Perry caught awesome stringers of bass by spoonplugging. At first spoonplugging meant trolling a certain pattern with Spoonplugs, but later the term was broadened to describe fishing the bottom systematically to eliminate unproductive water.

Perry was a maverick who made startling claims backed with fantastic catches. His statement "deep water is the home of the bass" persuaded bass chasers to abandon shoreline plugging and concentrate on offshore areas. Some of Perry's theories seemed scientific; some dogmatic. Later research has proven him wrong on some points, but he was often right and always thought-provoking. Perry probably presented the first logical theory for locating and catching fish. Certainly his theories gave others something to argue about. Perry provoked productive thinking.

While few people fish with Spoonplugs today, the Perry legacy endures. He put the proper emphasis on eliminating dead water, locating fish, and concentrating on productive areas. He was also the first fishing authority to talk about the importance of *structure*—the shape of the bottom and its fish-holding features. He was responsible for turning attention from the surface to features of the underwater world that concentrate bass. Perry said that bass live in schools. He led anglers to fish deeper water and taught the importance of identifying the right depth to find fish.

BILL BINKELMAN

In 1964, Bill Binkelman, an avid bass angler, was managing a large Milwaukee hardware store. Binkelman was fascinated by reports of Perry's fishing, because Perry was the first fishing authority whose advice matched Binkelman's experience.

Binkelman briefly became a spoonplugger. He also bought cases of spoonplugs to satisfy his customer's demands. To promote the Spoonplugs, Binkelman held fishing meetings in his store and published a newsletter, the "Fishing News." His newsletter crackled with the excitement of all the "fishing secrets" suddenly being discovered.

Binkelman found he hated motor trolling, however, so he abandoned spoonplugs. Throughout his life, he promoted structure fishing with refined

Al Lindner, Bill Binkelman, and Ron Lindner, men the public perceived primarily as walleye experts, each made important discoveries in and contributions to fishing for bass.

livebait presentations. Binkelman combined Perry's concentration on underwater structure with advanced livebait presentations he'd learned in trout fishing. Though he became famous for his walleye fishing, Binkelman admitted that he'd learned all his walleye techniques by catching bass.

At one of his store meetings in the early 1960s, Binkelman met two young Chicago anglers, Ron and Al Lindner. Binkelman remembered, "Al was just a kid, but he and Ron were already skilled fishermen, especially with plastic worms." A friendship formed that lasted until Binkelman's death in 1989.

Binkelman left the hardware store to begin *Fishing Facts* magazine. The Lindners became frequent contributors to the publication, the first magazine to deal seriously with structure fishing.

Fishing Facts became extremely influential, the first all-fishing magazine and the first publication to print underwater side views and contour maps. It generated excitement—hunger—for new techniques.

Binkelman left a legacy. He initiated one of the first all-fishing magazines and one of the first all-fishing television shows. Unlike Perry who was a loner, Binkelman collaborated in his efforts. He helped form several major fishing concepts, including the calendar of seasons. Probably most important, however, Binkelman expanded and reinterpreted Perry's rigid system, adapting it to livebait angling. With his unique and effective writing, Binkelman became one of the first fishing educators.

THE '60s AND '70s

At this point, bass fishing history becomes confusing because so much happened at once. A sport that sat dormant for 200 years blossomed in the late 1960s and early 1970s at a rate almost too fast to record.

- Manmade impoundments across the country reached their fishing peaks.
- The first hydrographic lake maps showed general underwater features. Sonar then let anglers fish these features more efficiently and effectively.
- The Bass Anglers Sportsman Society (B.A.S.S.) became the most influential force in the bass fishing world.
- Tournament fishing became popular.
- The success of tournaments and the publicity they offered led manufacturers to produce better fishing tackle adapted to newly developed techniques. Space-age fibers led to an affordable "graphite" rod with fine performance characteristics.
- Tournaments fostered the development of better baits. The old Shannon Twin Spin was refined into today's spinnerbait. Soft plastics multiplied as anglers devised countless ways to fish them.
- The bass boat was refined into a fast, comfortable, safe, efficient "fishing platform."
- A new fixture, the bass fishing pro, became influential.
- Scuba diving revealed underwater secrets of bass behavior.
- Major biological studies of black bass began, spurred by the increasing economic importance of bass fishing. New technologies allowed radio tracking of individual fish.

The increasing popularity of bass tournaments produced wide-reaching effects. Before tournaments, the best anglers were well known in local areas, but didn't usually fish a wide variety of waters. Most fishermen were one-lake or one-technique specialists.

Tournaments gave visibility to skilled anglers from across the country. Historically, winners had known a particular lake or had mastered one technique. Now a few tournament anglers became versatile multitechnique professionals who could win on any water. As professional fishermen grew in skill and stature, so did the sport of bass fishing.

Tournament publicity covered who won and lost, but behind the scenes, tournaments were educating a new generation of anglers. Tournaments weren't just contests, but showcases of bass fishing theories and techniques. The better anglers used tournaments as graduate level courses in angling.

Anglers were also learning more about how bass respond to their changing environment. Tournaments were held on all kinds of water during all kinds of weather. Someone always found a way to catch fish. When they did, other anglers took notes and added the new information to their growing awareness of bass and how to catch them.

When bass anglers became aware of how bass responded to environmental influences, the gap between science and the recreational angler narrowed. Luck faded as a factor in major tournaments as anglers recognized biological reasons for bass behavior. Bass movements and responses to lures followed certain patterns.

Tournaments fueled a hotbed of competing theories as the best bass anglers discussed fresh data. In just over a decade, this incredibly rich learning environment pushed bass fishing into the modern age.

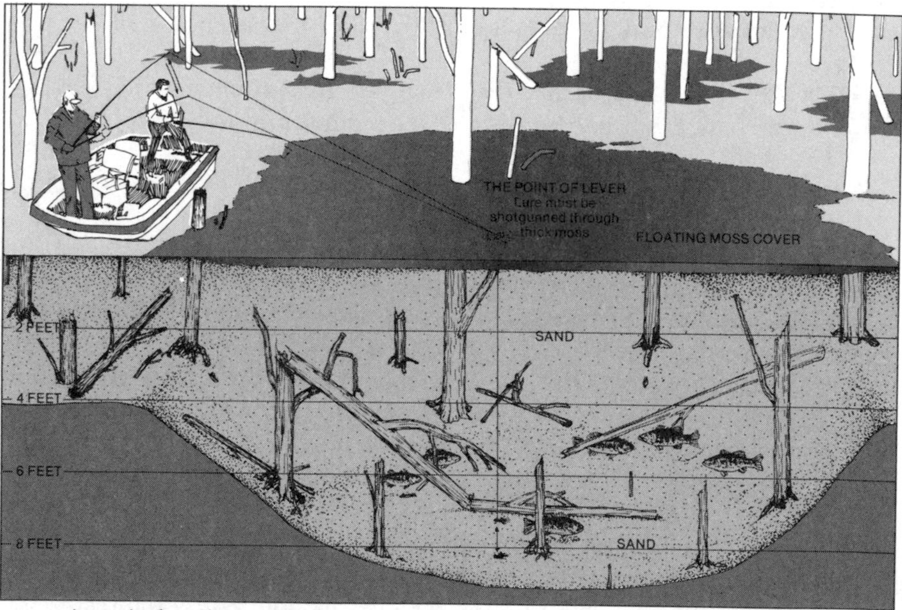

A typical early In-Fisherman *illustration, in this case describing the hot new flippin' technique, a product of tournament fishing in 1977.*

A FLIPPING CLINIC

No better example exists of how tournaments expedited angling education than the 1977 Texas Invitational B.A.S.S. tournament at Toledo Bend. Water temperatures were in the high 40s, with many prespawn bass shallow in murky water. Heavy catches seemed likely. But the tournament opened after the water cleared and a cold front dropped temperatures in the shallows, shutting down the bass.

Despite generally slow fishing, California's Dave Gliebe won the event with 20 bass averaging over 4 pounds. Gliebe found a heavily timbered flat with several deeper (8-foot) holes. Dead weeds had piled up to form huge matted "umbrellas" of cover 8 inches thick, offering overhead protection from the sun.

Gliebe found fish and knew how to extract them from dense cover. He'd learned "flipping" from his mentor, fellow Californian Dee Thomas, and he'd won two earlier tournaments by flipping heavy jigs in timber.

The winning trick was a flipping variation Gliebe called "lever-jigging." Using flipping tackle, he fired a 5/8-ounce jig to penetrate the matted weeds. He then let the jig fall to the bottom; his line bent at an angle by the surface mat. Working the jig up and down for up to five minutes on a cast, he waited for a negative bass to strike.

The national press were there and were impressed by how effective flipping could be when other methods didn't produce. Both flipping and "lever-jigging" had worked on California tule lakes, where flipping presentations were called "tule-dipping" or "doodle-socking," but they weren't known elsewhere.

Following the tournament, Gliebe demonstrated the technique for some of his fellow tournament contestants—Al and Ron Lindner and Roland Martin. Those anglers soon spread the word.

Roland Martin is now more identified with flipping than the technique's original enthusiasts, Gliebe and Thomas. Ron predicted that "there might be many other situations when this basic (lure) delivery system could be used."

Although the days of major fishing breakthroughs are now behind us, techniques are modified and systems from one region can be applied successfully to fishing situations elsewhere. Even as early bass tournaments were productive laboratories for the advance of fishing education, tournaments today remain proving grounds and laboratories for new equipment and techniques.

In 1977, Ron Lindner wrote the first instructional account of flippin' in InFisherman Segment 2, Study Report 2.

THE IN-FISHERMAN

Bass fishing began for Al and Ron Lindner when as kids they joined their parents on family fishing vacations to Wisconsin. Al avidly read Jason Lucas, the only national figure writing much about bass. And while bass weren't the only fish the Lindners sought, bass were important to the development of the two young anglers. Al remembers those days:

"We fished a lot on a little lake outside Hayward, Wisconsin, when I was about five years old. Ron and I didn't have a boat, so we ran around in swim suits fishing lily pads and deadfalls from shore. We usually fished with frogs on weedless hooks. Later we used all sorts of artificials.

"I remember two particular big bass. One was a huge fish Ron hooked on a Johnson Silver Minnow, while I held the boat with oars. We finally lost it, but I think that bass was 7 or 8 pounds, one heck of a fish for northern waters.

"Another time, on the same lake, I tied into one on a Burke plastic worm with propellers. I lost it in shallow pads. Figure it was a 10. Even if I'm wrong, it was huge!

"That lake turned me on to bass fishing. We fished for other species, but bass were exciting. I was pretty good with a jig and worm when I was 10, long before worms were popular in the North."

From the start, Ron and Al showed traits of their future as fishing educators. Ron was fascinated by theory. To catch fish was never enough; Ron had to know *why*. He frustrated hundreds of partners by fishing in screwball ways to test new theories.

Al was always an aggressive, result-oriented angler. He'd listen to any theory and apply it, *if* it helped him catch fish. But for Al, the proof was in

The early days on Sam Rayburn (left) and Toledo Bend.

the catching. A realist and a dreamer working together to probe the frontiers of fishing in a way no single personality could.

A major development in Al's bass angling career occurred in 1970. Having discovered how lean times get for a guide in the north during the ice season, he travelled to Sam Rayburn Lake in Texas to begin guiding. Rayburn had been created five years before and was just hitting its productive peak. So Al guided on Rayburn during its glory days in the early 1970s.

Although Al was an accomplished bass angler, he faced the challenge of learning the ways of winter bass in a huge southern reservoir. He learned how important timber and creek channels were to bass location. With the help of guides from Missouri and Arkansas, Al mastered deep-water jigging. Through this association with Rayburn, Al and Ron learned the effectiveness of lures that hadn't yet reached north.

By 1975, although they had accumulated extensive experience in fishing and the fishing industry, Al and Ron were almost out of money and without jobs. In these circumstances, *In-Fisherman* magazine began. Ron's original idea was to create a correspondence course for a select few serious angling subscribers. The magazine evolved to be much more than Ron had envisioned, assuming most of its current look in the 1980s. Radio shows and a television series were part of the network, too. Gradually In-Fisherman Inc. grew to the powerful and unique center for fishing education it is today.

What makes In-Fisherman unique?

• In-Fisherman has always been a collaborative effort, encouraging great fishing minds to work together to produce authentic and useful fishing information.

• In-Fisherman was never limited to one species, region, technique, or theory. Instead, In-Fisherman has always sought insight into all aspects and species of freshwater fishing.

• In-Fisherman developed *general* principles to help anglers understand fish and their world. Without such principles, fishing can become a mass of confusing and conflicting "tips" and "secrets."

• From the beginning, In-Fisherman presented a more comprehensive picture of angling than had been the norm. While other magazines concentrated on hot lakes and deadly baits, excluding fish behavior and environmental variables that affect fish location, In-Fisherman's F+L+P=S℠ formula covered a total angling concept.

• In-Fisherman used scientific research to help anglers understand fish and their environment.

• From the beginning, In-Fisherman brought together recreational anglers, scientists, and fisheries managers. It was inevitable that In-Fisherman would assume a leadership role in teaching sound conservation and wise fish management principles, as well as in teaching how-to fishing.

NEW AGE BASS FISHING

Where is bass fishing today? Unquestionably, the biggest boom in bass fishing popularity lies behind us. Yet bass fishing continues to be extremely

Pre-In-Fisherman days. Ron Lindner (left), Al Lindner, and Bud Olson with a catch from a Minnesota lake in the early 1970s.

popular, and interest in competitive fishing is increasing. In fact, bass fishing is becoming more competitive and challenging for two reasons:

(1) *Habitat*—Reservoir and pond construction have slowed. Older reservoirs are losing cover and silting in, becoming less productive bass habitat. Natural lakes are losing habitat to housing development and pollution (man-induced eutrophication).

(2) *Fishing pressure*—Fisheries regulations are playing a catchup game with increasing fishing pressure. America's 17 million bass anglers are challenging the ability of the resource to regenerate itself. Consider Texas, where about a million and a half bass anglers fish about a million and a half acres of water.

This pressure is changing the nature of bass fishing. In the past, knowing important facts about how bass operate in their world and the environmental influences affecting them let fishermen find and catch bass. Now you also must know a lake's history of fishing pressure and the regulations enacted to sustain good fishing.

More intensive management measures are also being implemented to protect or restore good-quality bass fishing. State agencies have moved beyond "quick fix" solutions. And results of earlier research are beginning to show. Partly because of this better management, bass fishing has improved in some regions. In recent years, many record bass have been caught and bigger fish are showing up in tournament catches.

Reservoir aging promises to be one of the most significant changes to hit bass fishing. Timber cover in older reservoirs has deteriorated. Complex woody structure has become "pole timber," which doesn't provide adequate cover for bass. Growth rates of bass in older reservoirs have declined also.

Recently, however, many reservoirs have been invaded by Eurasian milfoil, hydrilla, and other aquatic weed species. Milfoil and hydrilla are aggressive weeds that have quickly rooted, spread, and choked out native weeds. Milfoil and hydrilla have moved from lake to lake in livewells, on boat propellers, or on boat trailers. Originally imported for aquarium decoration, they're considered nuisances, but they have revitalized bass fishing in many aging reservoirs.

Rayburn is one example. Al Lindner recently returned to fish the old winter holes he guided on in the 1970s. "The holes weren't worth zippedy doo dah!" Al said. "The fish just aren't there any more. The bass are relating to weeds, not timber. Bass still use bends in creek channels, but the good bends were once near timber; now they're near weeds."

Following a period of being all but "dead," Rayburn has come roaring back. Al caught more big fish there than he'd taken in the 1970s.

More than ever, with the help of *In-Fisherman* magazine and other periodicals, the best anglers are coordinating wisdom and techniques from across the country into versatile bass fishing strategies. These remain exciting and challenging times for bass anglers.

Joe Tomelleri

Chapter 2

LARGEMOUTH BASS — STATUS SYMBOL

America's Most Important Fish

The largemouth bass is the most important fish in North America. According to a mass of recent survey data:

- More U.S. anglers fish for bass than for any other species group; panfish were second, catfish third, based on the 1985 survey by the U.S. Fish and Wildlife Service.
- Bass were tops in number of days anglers spent fishing for various species. Bass fishing accounts for 24 percent of all angler days (discounting Great Lakes fishing). Panfish and catfish tally about 20 percent each.
- According to the Sport Fishing Institute, about 44 percent of *all* fishing activity is directed toward black bass.
- In 1983, a Neilson study found that 14 percent of the *total American public* fished for bass. One American in seven was a bass angler.
- An In-Fisherman survey of state fisheries agencies showed that 33 of the 42 agencies that had data listed bass as the most popular or second most popular species. Trout placed second with 19 top-two finishes.
- In southern states, most anglers fish for bass. In Louisiana, for example, 63 percent of all anglers are bass fishermen. One out of five bass fishermen fishes tournaments.

• The Bass Anglers Sportsman Society (B.A.S.S.) totals half a million members. This membership comes from 52 countries and 50 states, including Alaska, which has no bass.

• Two separate calculations estimated there are 17 to 20 million bass fishermen in the United States.

So much for statistics. The popularity of the largemouth bass can be judged in other ways. Consider visible evidence: the infinite number of national, state and local bass tournaments; bass fishing videos; magazine articles on bass fishing; boats built for bass fishing; rods marketed as bass fishing tools; special publications for bass anglers; lures marketed for bass fishermen; books on bass fishing; television shows featuring bass . . .

Yes, trout and salmon dominate in some regions. Walleyes, too. And panfish and catfish fans are numerous, more so than you'd guess by the meager media attention they get. Ultimately, however, the American angler's love affair with largemouth bass can't be denied.

THE FISH THAT LAYS THE GOLDEN EGGS

Anglers rarely think about their sport in monetary terms, but the largemouth bass is uniquely important in supporting the U.S. fishing industry, an industry accounting for a revenue of about $3 billion each year. The largemouth bass is the single most important fish making all those cash registers ring. If bass fishing stopped, the American tackle industry would suffer.

More guides base their work on bass than any other fish; and bass account for tremendous sales of other marine gear, boats and motors. Marinas, resorts, and other tourist-related businesses would falter without revenue from bass fishermen. Bass tournaments alone generate tremendous economic activity. Major bass tournaments may generate up to $300,000 in expenditures in a local community.

Consider the fishing gear developed and marketed for bass. How many of the most significant tackle innovations—rods, reels, lines, and lures—were inspired by bass? How many were inspired by fish other than bass?

We talked to several major tackle manufacturers about the importance of bass. A spokesman for a rod and reel company said, "Our company is dependent on bass fishing and bass fishermen. Products like affordable graphite rods and magnetic-spool baitcasting reels were developed directly for bass fishing." According to a spokesman for a monofilament line manufacturer, "No single species is as important to the fishing tackle industry as the largemouth bass."

Diverse opinions exist on the reasons for bass popularity. Some observers note that bass anglers have particular characteristics. In the words of a major line manufacturer, "The bass angler is an avid fisherman willing to invest in fine-quality equipment."

Avid? You bet! A California study showed over 25 percent of bass fishermen fish more than 30 times a year. Another manufacturer characterized the bass angler as "technique-hungry" and "result-oriented," tackle-industry lingo for saying the bass angler is a good customer. In sheer

National Fishing Surveys

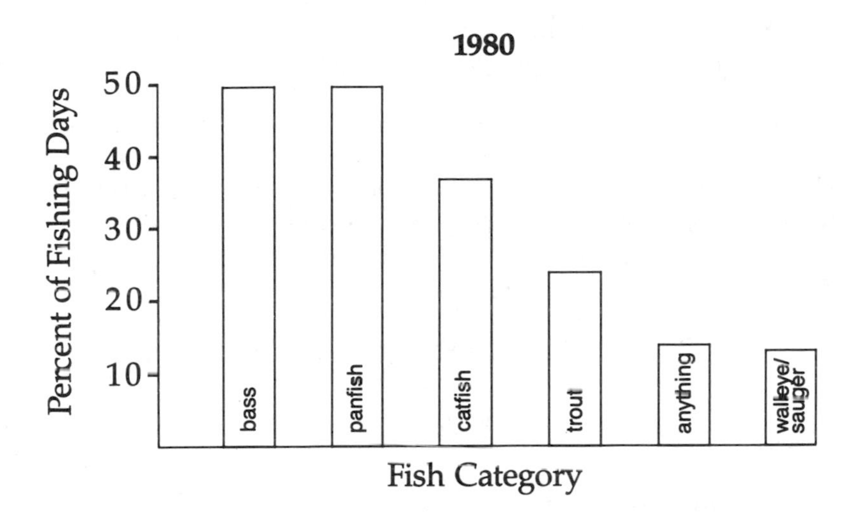

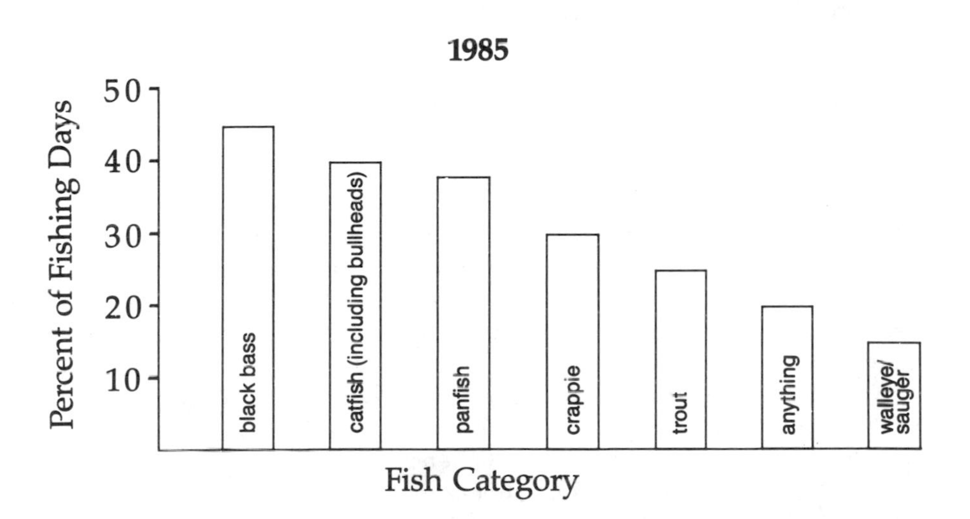

Every five years, the U.S. Fish and Wildlife Service in conjunction with the Bureau of the Census conducts a national survey of fishing-, hunting-, and wildlife-associated recreation. Results show trends in economic, sociological and angling characteristics of American fishermen.

These graphs illustrate data from 1980 and 1985. In 1985, the catfish category included bullheads, while they were included in the "panfish" category in 1980. Similarly, crappie were included in "panfish" in 1980.

The 1980 "bass" category represents the same group of fish as the 1985 "black bass" category. Apparently, the category name was changed to assure that fish such as the striped bass, white bass, and rock bass, weren't included in the category.

abundance and per capita tackle purchases, the bass angler is the world's most important fishing tackle consumer.

Largemouth bass have characteristics that make them economically important. No fish is better known for hitting a wide variety of artificial lures, from surface twitch baits to bottom-bumping jigs. Bass eat livebait, too, of course, but fish that are predominantly caught on livebait can't match the dollars generated by those that smash $5 crankbaits. Moreover, as bass become conditioned to lures they see often, they bite them less eagerly, which motivates manufacturers to develop new lures.

The tackle industry, however, isn't as reliant on bass as it was 15 years ago. Tackle manufacturers have welcomed walleye, crappie, and striper tournaments. These species now shoulder more of the economic burden traditionally carried by bass. But they still trail far behind bass in their economic impact.

In sum, no gamefish holds as much economic clout as the largemouth bass, the fish that lays golden eggs.

BASS ARE EASY TO LIKE

Largemouths are easy to like. They're "sporty." They jump. They plunge. Other fish fight harder "inch for inch, pound for pound" than bass, but bass are justifiably known for scrappy and showy fights. They're simply fun.

Because largemouths hit artificials and because they're often found in shallow water, they're the ultimate fish for anglers who prefer to cast. For many folks, casting is part of the fun of fishing. Even when the catching is slow, moving along a shoreline, pegging casts within inches of dock posts or stumps is fun. When you're bass fishing, you can always be doing something.

People also enjoy bass fishing because of the type of water bass inhabit. Imagine you're trolling with dowriggers miles offshore on one of the Great Lakes. You catch a 3-pound bass. Big thrill, huh? But fire a spinnerbait through a narrow gap between two tree trunks and catch that bass in two feet of water. That's more like it!

Bass often spend time in shallow water near visible objects; so bass location is easy to visualize. Areas often look "bassy." Fishing becomes first a test of location theories, then the challenge of presenting lures to entice bites and land fish, often from thick cover.

Many people like bass fishing because bass can be caught so many different ways: Walk the dog. Buzz the shallows. Crank the breaks. Slow-roll timber. Flip bulrushes. Bass anglers typically change tackle and presentation several times a day, switching tackle for the kind of water they're working. Variety is part of bass appeal.

Perhaps the most interesting lesson tournaments teach is that there's *always* a way to catch bass. Many tournaments take place under difficult fishing conditions. Sometimes great bass anglers are defeated. But someone always puts it together. Someone always analyzes the situation and finds a way to catch bass. Bass fishing is a thinking game, because there's always a way to catch bass. Finding that way is the challenge.

State By State Records

LARGEMOUTH BASS

State	Weight	Angler	Water	Year
Alabama	16 lbs. 8 oz.	Thomas Burgin	Mountain View Lake	1987
Alaska	None			
Arizona	14 lbs. 8 oz.	Alex Atamanchuk	Roosevelt Lake	1988
Arkansas	16 lbs. 4 oz.	Aaron Madris	Lake Mallard	1976
California	21 lbs. 3⅕ oz.	Raymond Easley	Lake Casitas	1980
Colorado	10 lbs. 6¼ oz.	Sharon Brunson	Stalker Lake	1979
Connecticut	12 lbs. 14 oz.	Frank Domurat	Mashapaug Lake	1961
Delaware	10 lbs. 5 oz.	Tony Kaczmarczyk	Andrews Lake	1980
Florida	20 lbs. 2 oz.	Fritz Friebel	Big Fish Lake	1923
*Georgia	22 lbs. 4 oz.	George Perry	Montgomery Lake	1932
Hawaii	8 lbs. 0 oz.	Earl Vito	Kilauea, Kauai	1977
Idaho	10 lbs. 15 oz.	Mrs. M. W. Taylor	Anderson Lake	Unknown
Illinois	13 lbs. 1 oz.	Edward J. Waibel	Stone Quarry Lake	1976
Indiana	11 lbs. 11 oz.	Curt Reynolds	Ferdinand Reservoir	1968
Iowa	10 lbs. 12 oz.	Patricia Zaerr	Lake Fisher	1984
Kansas	11 lbs. 12 oz.	Kenneth M. Bingham	Farm Pond	1977
Kentucky	13 lbs. 10¼ oz.	Dale Wilson	Woods Creek Lake	1984
Louisiana	12 lbs. 0 oz.	Harold C. Dunaway	Farm Pond	1975
Maine	11 lbs. 10 oz.	Robert Kamp	Moose Pond	1968
Maryland	11 lbs. 2 oz.	Rodney L. Cockrell	Farm Pond	1983
Massachusetts	15 lbs. 8 oz.	Walter Bolonis	Sampson Pond	1975
Michigan	11 lbs. 15 oz.	Wm. J. Malone	Big Pine Is. L.	1934
Minnesota	8 lbs. 9.5 oz.	Timothy Kirsch	Fountain Lake	1986
Mississippi	14 lbs. 12 oz.	Perry Reed	Tippah Co. Lake	1987
Missouri	13 lbs. 14 oz.	Marvin Bushong	Bull Shoals	1961
Montana	8 lbs. 2½ oz.	Juanita Fanning	Milnor Lake	1984
Nebraska	10 lbs. 11 oz.	Paul Abegglen Sr.	Sandpit	1965
Nevada	11 lbs. 0 oz.	H. P. Warner	Lake Mohave	1972
New Hampshire	10 lbs. 8 oz.	G. Bullpitt	Lake Potanipo	1967
New Jersey	10 lbs. 14 oz.	Robert A. Eisele	Menantico Pond	1980
New Mexico	12.58 lbs.	Danny Lee Cummins	Bill Evans	1988
New York	11 lbs. 4.16 oz.	John L. Higbie	Buckhorn Lake	1987
North Carolina	14 lbs. 15 oz.	Leonard Williams	Santeetlah Reservoir	1963
North Dakota	8 lbs. 7½ oz.	Leon Rixen	Nelson Lake	1983
Ohio	13 lbs. 2 oz.	Roy Landsberger	Farm Pond	1976
Oklahoma	13 lbs. 8 oz.	Paul Tasker	Lake Fuqua	1990
Oregon	11 lbs. 4.6 oz.	Joe Pool	Lost Creek Lake	1988
Pennsylvania	11 lbs. 3 oz.	Donald Shade	Birch Run Reservoir	1983
Rhode Island	10 lbs. 5 oz.	Tim Stedman	Wordens Pond	1987
South Carolina	16 lbs. 2 oz.	Paul H. Flanagan	Lake Marlon	1949
South Dakota	8 lbs. 14 oz.	Irene Buxcel	Jackson C. Stk. Dam	1986
Tennessee	14 lbs. 8 oz.	Louge Barnett	Sugar Creek	1954
Texas	17 lbs. 10.72 oz.	Mark Stevenson	Lake Fork	1986
Utah	10 lbs. 2 oz.	Sam LaManna	Lake Powell	1974
Vermont	10 lbs. 4 oz.	Tony Gale	Lake Dunmore	1988
Virginia	16 lbs. 4 oz.	Richard Tate	Lake Conners	1985
Washington	11 lbs. 9 oz.	Carl Pruitt	Banks Lake	1977
West Virginia	10.8 lbs.	William Wilhelm	Sleepy Creek L.	1979
Wisconsin	11 lbs. 3 oz.	Robert Miklowski	Lake Ripley	1940
Wyoming	7 lbs. 2 oz.	John Teeters	Stove Lake	1942

*All Tackle World Record

SMALLMOUTH BASS

State	Weight	Angler	Water	Year
Alabama	10 lbs. 8 oz.	Owen F. Smith	Wheeler Dam	1950
Alaska	None			
Arizona	7.96 lbs.	Dennis K. Barnhill	Roosevelt Lake	1988
Arkansas	7 lbs. 5 oz.	Acie Dickerson	Lake Bull Shoals	1969
California	9 lbs. 1 oz.	Tim Brady	Clair Engle Lake	1976
Colorado	5 lbs. 8 oz.	Janie Novak	Pueblo Reservoir	1987
Connecticut	7 lbs. 12 oz.	Jos. Mankauskas Jr.	Shenipsit Lake	1980
Delaware	4 lbs. 7 oz.	Richard Williams	Quarry Pond	1983
Florida	None			
Georgia	7 lbs. 2 oz.	Jack Hall	Lake Chatuge	1973
Hawaii	3 lbs. 11 oz.	Willie Song	Lake WIlson	1982
Idaho	7 lbs. 5.6 oz.	Don B. Schiefelbein	Dworshak Reservoir	1982
Illinois	6 lbs. 7 oz.	Mark Samp	Strip Mine	1985
Indiana	6 lbs. 15 oz.	Ray Emerick	Sugar Creek	1985

Iowa	6 lbs. 8 oz.	Rick Pentland	Spirit Lake	1979
Kansas	5.56 lbs.	Rick O'Bannon	Wilson Reservoir	1988
*Kentucky	11 lbs. 15 oz.	David L. Hayes	Dale Hollow Res.	1955
Louisiana	None			
Maine	8 lbs. 0 oz.	George Dyer	Thompson Lake	1970
Maryland	8 lbs. 4 oz.	Gary Peters	Liberty Reservoir	1974
Massachusetts	7 lbs. 4 oz.	Michael Howe	Quaboag River	1984
Michigan	9 lbs. 4 oz.	W. F. Shoemaker	Long Lake	1906
Minnesota	8 lbs. 0 oz.	John A. Creighton	W. Battle Lake	1948
Mississippi	7 lbs. 15 oz.	Thomas Wilbanks	Pickwick Lake	1987
Missouri	7 lbs. 0 oz.	Richard J. Bullard	Stockton Lake	1988
Montana	5 lbs. 11 oz.	Marvin Loomis	Fort Peck	1987
Nebraska	6 lbs. 1½ oz.	Wally Allison	Merritt Reservoir	1978
Nevada	3 lbs. 8 oz.	Glen C. Deming	Dry Creek Reservoir	1989
New Hampshire	7 lbs. 14½ oz.	Francis H. Lord	Goose Pond	1970
New Jersey	6 lbs. 4 oz.	Earl H. Trumpore	Delaware River	1957
New Mexico	6 lbs. 8¾ oz.	Carl L. Kelly	Ute Lake	1972
New York	9 lbs. 0 oz.	George Tennyson	Friends Lake	1925
North Carolina	10 lbs. 2 oz.	Archie Lampkin	Hiwassee Reservoir	1953
North Dakota	5 lbs. 1 oz.	Denise Hoger	Lake Sakakawea	1987
Ohio	7 lbs. 8 oz.	James Bayless	Mad River	1941
Oklahoma	6 lbs. 14 oz.	Steve Bruton	Lake Texoma	1990
Oregon	6 lbs. 14 oz.	Reuben Klevgaard	Columbia River	1989
Pennsylvania	7 lbs. 10 oz.	Charles Pence	Lake Erie	1990
Rhode Island	5 lbs. 15 oz.	Butch Ferris	Wash Pond	1977
South Carolina	6 lbs. 12 oz.	Gerald B. Knight	Broad River	1988
South Dakota	5 lbs. 3⅓ oz.	Robert Kolden	Clear Lake	1988
*Tennessee	11 lbs. 15 oz.	David L. Hayes	Dale Hollow Res.	1955
Texas	7 lbs. 11½ oz.	Ronald O. Garner	Lake Whitney	1988
Utah	6 lbs. 12 oz.	Roger L. Tallerico	Lake Borham	1983
Vermont	7 lbs. 12 oz.	Jean Houle	Connecticut River	1988
Virginia	8 lbs. 0 oz.	C. A. Garay	Claytor Lake	1964
Washington	8 lbs. 12 oz.	Ray Wanacutt	Columbia River	1967
West Virginia	9.75 lbs.	David Lindsay	South Branch	1971
Wisconsin	9 lbs. 1 oz.	Leon Stefoneck	Indian Lake	1950
Wyoming	4 lbs. 12 oz.	D. Jon Nelson	Southeast Pit	1982

*All Tackle World Record (recognized as state record by 2 states)

SPOTTED (KENTUCKY) BASS

I.G.F.A.

This 9-lb. 4-oz. spotted bass is recognized as the world record by the International Game Fish Association.

State	Weight	Angler	Water	Year
Alabama	8 lbs. 15 oz.	Phillip C. Terry Jr.	Lewis Smith Lake	1978
Alaska	None			
Arizona	None			
Arkansas	7 lbs. 15 oz.	Mike J. Heilich	Lake Bull Shoals	1983
California	9 lbs. 1 oz.	Jeff Mathews	Lake Perris	1984
Colorado	None			
Connecticut	None			
Delaware	None			
Florida	3 lbs. 12 oz.	Dow Gilmore	Apalachicola River	1985
Georgia	8 lbs. 1/2 oz.	Patrick Bankston	Lake Lanier	1985
Hawaii	None			
Idaho	None			
Illinois	6 lbs. 12 oz.	James M. Kyle	Strip Pit	1982
Indiana	5 lbs. 1½ oz.	John William	Pio Lake	1975

Iowa	None			
Kansas	4 lbs. 7 oz.	Clarence E. McCarter	Marion County Lake	1977
Kentucky	7 lbs. 10 oz.	A. E. Sellers	Nelson Co. Water	1970
Louisiana	4 lbs. 14 oz.	Vern C. Johnson Jr.	Tickfaw River	1976
Maine	None			
Maryland	None			
Massachusetts	None			
Michigan	None			
Minnesota	None			
Mississippi	8 lbs. 2 oz.	S. Ross Grantham	Farm Pond	1975
Missouri	7 lbs. 8 oz.	Gene Arnaud	Table Rock	1966
Montana	None			
Nebraska	3 lbs. 11 oz.	Tom Pappas	Sandpit	1968
Nevada	None			
New Hampshire	None			
New Jersey	None			
New Mexico	4 lbs. 8 oz.	Sam Evola	Cochiti Lake	1988
New York	None			
North Carolina	4 lbs. 8 oz.	Ronnie McDonald	Lake Chatuge	1988
North Dakota	None			
Ohio	5 lbs. 4 oz.	Roger Trainer	Lake White	1976
Oklahoma	8 lbs. 2 oz.	O. J. Stone	Pittsburg Co. Pond	1958
Oregon	None			
Pennsylvania	None			
Rhode Island	None			
South Carolina	4 lbs. 7 oz.	Glen Pritchart	Lake Hartwell	1989
South Dakota	None			
Tennessee	5 lbs. 8 oz.	Gary Martin	Center Hill Lake	1989
Texas	5 lbs. 9 oz.	Keith Turner	Lake O' the Pines	1966
Utah	None			
Vermont	None			
Virginia	6 lbs. 10 oz.	Joe Jett Friend	Flannagan Res.	1976
Washington	None			
West Virginia	3.82 lbs.	Leonard Blankenship	R. D. Bailey Lake	1988
Wisconsin	None			
Wyoming	None			

REDEYE BASS

State	Weight	Angler	Water	Year
Alabama	2 lbs. 11 oz.	Winston Baker	Upper Tallapoosa R.	1989
*Georgia	2 lbs. 12 oz.	Tony Calloway	Tugalo River	1987
*South Carolina	2 lbs. 12 oz.	Tony Calloway	Lake Hartwell	1987
Tennessee	1 lbs. 1 oz.	Gene H. Burchfiel	Little River	1978

*All Tackle World Record (recognized as state record by 2 states)

GUADALUPE BASS

Allen Christenson's 3-lb. 11-oz. world record Guadalupe bass.

I.G.F.A.

State	Weight	Angler	Water	Year
*Texas	3 lbs. 11 oz.	Allen Christenson Jr.	Lake Travis	1983

*All Tackle World Record

SUWANNEE BASS

State	Weight	Angler	Water	Year
*Florida	3 lbs. 14¼ oz.	Ronnie Everett	Suwannee River	1985
Georgia	3 lbs. 9 oz.	Laverne Norton	Ochlockonee River	1984

*All Tackle World Record

SHOAL BASS

I.G.F.A.

David Hubbard's 8-lb. 3-oz. world record shoal bass.

State	Weight	Angler	Water	Year
Alabama	6 lbs. 8 oz.	Thomas L. Sharpe	Hallawakee Creek	1967
Florida	7 lbs. 13-1/4 oz.	William T. Johnston	Apalachicola River	1989
*Georgia	8 lbs. 3 oz.	David Hubbard	Flint River	1977

*All Tackle World Record

Records lists compliments of The National Fresh Water Fishing Hall of Fame, Hayward, Wisconsin.

EVERYONE'S FISH

And what about accessibility, perhaps the most attractive attribute of the largemouth bass? Bass have adapted to and have thrived in a variety of waters in almost every region of the country. Wherever you are, a bass isn't far away. In fact, few Americans live far from good bass fishing.

Largemouth bass adapt to many different types of water. They live in still water and rivers. They live in natural lakes and manmade reservoirs. They live in pocket-size farm ponds and huge bodies of water like Lake St. Clair. They live in freshwater, brackish coastal estuaries, mucky prairie lakes, and stone-walled mining pits. They thrive among alligators in tropical lakes and in water that's frozen over five months a year.

The geographic spread of bass is amazing. In the U.S., bass occur in the lower 48 states, plus Hawaii. It's easier to say where they don't occur. They're absent in Alaska, the Rocky Mountains, and certain arid regions of the Great Plains.

Much of the present bass range has been established by stocking. Originally, bass were present only in the eastern half of the continental United States, excluding the eastern seaboard states. With railroad construction booming and bass interest growing in the 19th century, bass were transported in milk cans via rail to new waters across the country.

Largemouth bass have adapted well in artificial lakes and ponds; this

REGIONAL BASS* POPULARITY

□ bass the most popular species group
□ bass among top-three preferred species groups
□ bass not among top-three preferred species groups
■ preference data on bass not available

Surveys conducted by state management agencies of angler preference for types of fish show bass are top-rated throughout the Southeast. But they're also most popular in parts of the Northeast and Midwest. Bass are among the most preferred fish from coast to coast.

In Canada, bass distribution is limited to the southern fringe of provinces. Within that region, they're eagerly sought by both resident and tourist anglers.

**Includes largemouth bass, smallmouth bass, spotted bass, shoal bass, Suwannee bass, redeye bass, Guadalupe bass.*

more than anything else has increased their range. In response to the water-starved "Dust Bowl" days, beginning in 1936, federal and state agencies encouraged farm pond construction. Over 300 million farm ponds were built and most were stocked with bass.

In Kansas, for example, 43 percent of bass habitat is in private ponds of 20 acres or less. Without ponds, Kansas bass anglers would lose almost half their bass fishing waters. Ponds are important in the Southeast and Midwest, too.

Nearly all American rivers have been impounded in the last 50 years. Reservoirs total about 10 million surface acres. Excluding the Great Lakes, reservoir construction has doubled the nation's total lake surface area.

And no gamefish has succeeded in reservoirs as well as the largemouth bass. Bass adapted to reservoirs as if they were the habitat they had evolved in.

No wonder bass are popular. They're sporty, interesting, challenging and available.

THE TOURNAMENT FISH

The popularity of largemouth bass is in part dependent on its status as a tournament fish. Tournaments have influenced bass fishing by:

- Popularizing bass fishing and making the bass a media star.
- Creating pro bass anglers—anglers, who in their multifaceted role of educators, professional athletes, and tackle promoters, have exerted a powerful influence on American fishing.
- Advancing the art of bass angling by bringing the most skillful bass anglers in the world to events where they can continue to learn from one another.
- Educating thousands of anglers in advanced bass fishing techniques.
- Promoting conservation, including catch and release and better management of bass stocks.

That's impact! Amazingly, it happened largely because of Ray Scott, the founder of Bass Anglers Sportsman Society (B.A.S.S.). Scott may be the most influential person in the history of bass fishing.

When a group becomes as large and influential as B.A.S.S., it's easy to think that "it was just a matter of time" before somebody would have assembled such an organization. But before Scott, other people had run bass fishing derbies. The events weren't popular, successful, or respected—the usual assumption was that they were won by "some jerk who had a freezer full of bass."

After the success of B.A.S.S., many groups tried to duplicate Scott's accomplishment. Today, several well-run tournaments and circuits aren't affiliated with B.A.S.S.

Scott organized B.A.S.S. in 1967. At the time, he was a young Alabama insurance salesman who loved bass fishing. Insurance taught Scott salesmanship, which enhanced his boldness and entrepreneurial flair that were to symbolize his organization. He saw the potential popularity of a circuit of bass tournaments that were above scandal.

Ray Scott emcees the 1968 Lake Eufaula National. B.A.S.S., Inc.

THE FIRST B.A.S.S. TOURNAMENT

Ray Scott's first tournament was held on Beaver Lake in northwestern Arkansas in 1967. Scott had not yet coined the acronym B.A.S.S., though this event is considered the first B.A.S.S. tournament.

With characteristic daring salesmanship, Scott called the Chamber of Commerce in Springdale, Arkansas. Identifying himself as the president and executive director of the "All-American Bass Tournaments," he congratulated them on being selected the site of the "next" invitational bass tournament.

The tournament was funded precariously on borrowed money and anticipated entry fees. To inspire more entrants, Scott contrived a rivalry between Tulsa and Memphis bass anglers.

This Beaver Lake tournament was remarkable for:

- *Attracting top bass fishing talent, including Bill Dance and Tom Mann.*
- *Succeeding financially, though just barely.*
- *Bill Dance outrunning the competition with his big motor—60 hp instead of the prevailing 30. Thus began the horsepower race.*
- *Being won by Tennessee law enforcement officer Stan Sloan, who seems to have been the first man to put an electric trolling motor on the front of his boat. When asked why, he replied, "Is it easier to push a chain or pull a chain?"*

Ray Scott awarding Al Lindner the first-place trophy for winning the Tennessee Invitational B.A.S.S tournament on Watts Bar Lake in 1974.

Al gave up tournament fishing several years later to devote full time to building the In-Fisherman Communications Network. Ray Scott went on to build the B.A.S.S. network.

He also saw the need to go beyond running tournaments to building a federation of bass clubs modeled after the U.S. Golf Association. In 1990, the B.A.S.S. Federation had grown to include 2,144 clubs ranging in size from half a dozen members to over a hundred. Clubs average an activity a month—tournaments, informational meetings, charity events, and conservation work. The net effect has produced a huge organized interest in bass. In addition, many clubs not affiliated with B.A.S.S. adopted similar programs.

WOMEN BASS FISHERMEN

Fishing isn't an all-male activity. Women spend 128 million dollars annually on fishing tackle, much of it for bass. And women have their own bass organizations. The largest and oldest is Bass'n Gal, a tournament circuit, club, and magazine for female bass anglers, organized in 1976 by Sugar Ferris. By 1990, the organization claimed over 26,000 members and 73 affiliated clubs. Bass'n Gal holds four national tournaments, plus a classic. The rules are similar to those in B.A.S.S. tournaments, though competitions are shorter. Bass'n Gal also sponsors youth education and conservation activities.

Women quickly proved how well they could fish. Bass'n Gal tournaments produce highly skilled anglers who get sponsorships and endorsement contracts from tackle companies and boat manufacturers. In a tournament in New York, Bass'n Gal competitors outfished all previous tournament anglers on those waters.

CATCH AND RELEASE

Although anglers in some European countries have been catching and releasing fish since the early 1900s, the North American trend toward voluntarily releasing gamefish seems to have originated with trout and salmon angler Lee Wulff.

Fishing pressure was hurting New England trout fishing in the 1930s. The response was to load streams with hatchery trout, which Wulff found inferior to native fish.

Wulff's answer was separating *catching* fish from *killing* fish. He wrote, "A good gamefish is too valuable to be caught only once." The idea slowly took hold in trout fishing circles, but ran against prevailing customs and management theories in other fisheries.

In 1971, while attending a trout fishing conference in Colorado, Ray Scott

saw the enthusiasm for releasing trout. He thought, "If it's that much fun to let a 10-inch trout go, think what a thrill it would be to release a 6-pound bass to test an angler another day."

Besides that, however, Scott's tournaments met resentment from local anglers who didn't like a group of hotshot anglers swooping in on their lakes and killing a lot of "their" fish. Why not give local anglers their fish back?

Scott began rewarding contestants for keeping fish healthy. Bass boat livewells had no aerators in 1972, and many were poorly designed. That quickly changed. At the same time, B.A.S.S. tournaments were scheduled to minimize the number of fish killed because of warm water temperatures.

The early move to catch and release in bass tournaments was motivated more by political shrewdness than management concern. Before long, though, evidence proved that modern anglers were capable of damaging bass populations, and that voluntary release could help sustain good fishing.

Many bass anglers were shocked, for example, when Georgia's new West Point reservoir, which opened to fishing in 1976 with a large population of virgin bass, just two years later showed evidence of serious stock depletion. Thoughtful anglers across North America began to see voluntary catch and release as an important way to sustain good bass fishing. And fishery managers began to see a need for mandating release through stricter regulations.

The most recent trend in voluntary fish conservation is toward the In-Fisherman concept of "selective harvest™."

Catch and release is important, but it should not be a knee-jerk reaction to every situation, for in some situations catch and release isn't necessary and can do more harm than good. The objective is to release the right fish to sustain good fishing, while keeping more numerous portions of fish populations to eat.

Briefly, selective harvest™ calls for maintaining a tradition of harvesting some fish; for they are nutritious, delicious, and when harvested wisely, renewable. But to sustain good fishing, less numerous species and size-classes must be released.

Fishermen must step away from traditions of the past. As tackle and technique become more sophisticated, and subsequently fishermen become more successful, stringer shots to prove fishing prowess must cease. Keeping trophy after trophy, no matter the species, must give way to releasing unique fish to thrill other anglers. This is keeping fish selectively—selective harvest™.

Fishermen who want to eat fish must focus on readily expendable species like panfish—bluegills, crappies, perch, or bullheads—remembering, however, the importance of releasing larger panfish. Or they must focus on smaller size-classes of larger predatory fish. Most 18-inch-plus bass, fish that are less numerous and have surmounted huge odds to grow so large, should be released in favor of keeping several small bass to eat. Only a few fish are needed as the focal point for a fine meal. This, too, is keeping fish selectively—selective harvest™.

THE BASS FISHERMAN

Who is the American bass angler? Many people. No doubt, the most efficient bass anglers on earth are anglers like Roland Martin, Rick Clunn, Larry Nixon, and Tommy Martin, pros who win tournaments on varied waters year after year. They put their reputations on the line each time they compete, and their results aren't lucky or phony.

Because the most successful bass pros are the media stars of today's bass world, thousands of enthusiastic anglers model themselves after those stars.

THE TROUTIN' MAN *THE BASSIN' MAN* *THE CATFISHIN' MAN*

These enthusiastic imitators fish in club or local contests. Others, though they never compete, own the same equipment and fish in the same ways. In some states, about 1 in 5 bass anglers competes. Research shows that club anglers are more knowledgeable and supportive of restrictive regulations than other anglers.

As noted, these anglers are dear to the hearts of tackle and boat manufacturers because they spend much of their discretionary income to catch bass. They own an assortment of graphite rods; their boats are metal-flake rockets, costing as much as a modest house; they use high-tech electronics; and their tackle boxes are filled with lures whose total value is a carefully kept secret.

But high-tech anglers aren't the only good bass fishermen. And they may not be typical, though conspicuous. Many bass fishermen resent or misunderstand those no-expense-spared fishermen wearing jackets covered with patches, who roar around lakes.

Doug Hannon, to use one example, is one of the world's most knowledgeable bass anglers, but an exception to the stereotype high-tech pro angler. Hannon often fishes from a small metal jonboat that looks more like a duck boat than a bass boat. Though his tackle is high

Don Wirth

A low-profile approach to bassing often produces larger bass than the faster methods typically used in tournament fishing. Doug Hannon (pictured) has caught hundreds of bass weighing 10 pounds or more.

quality, he doesn't carry many lures. His clothing is drab; he often wears an old campaign hat that looks like it came from the dumpster behind a Goodwill store. Yet Hannon is an acknowledged master of lunker bass. His low-profile approach to bass angling has as much to teach as the frenetic high-speed approach of the tournament pro. This has been the tradition of the In-Fisherman network: to give readers tournament wisdom as well as the finest theoretical thinking from North America's best bass researchers—members of the In-Fisherman staff, plus men like Doug Hannon, Rich Zaleski, Tom Seward, and Ralph Manns.

Fly-fishermen also pursue bass. They enjoy manipulating big bugs and the easy rhythm of the long rod. Some gave up fishing in the style of the modern bass pro because it was no longer fun. The best fly-fishermen catch a lot of bass and prefer fly-fishing. And in certain situations, fly-rods offer advantages over other tackle.

Betty Thurmond, one of the most accomplished anglers with live shiners, is another model of today's bass angler. Like Hannon, Thurmond doesn't look like a tournament pro. Her boat isn't flashy; she dresses in subdued colors and usually is barefoot. But her understanding of stillfishing with shiners has made her one of the most respected guides for large bass.

Indeed, bass anglers are varied—a college professor who fishes inner-city lakes from a canoe with an electric motor; a traveling salesman with a bit of tackle and a belly boat in the back of his station wagon; a prairie rancher who dug 32 stock dams across his property and lets polite strangers fish all but one of them; a kid who rushes home from school to make a few casts in the local lake before supper.

Bass anglers are men, kids, women, and seniors. Exceptional strength isn't necessary to catch bass. Bass fishing is easy to enjoy.

While there's no single right way to fish for bass, some fishing styles produce more tournament "weigh" bass than others. Some produce rare old trophy fish. The world of bass fishing is diverse. We'll explore that diversity as we continue.

Chapter 3

ABOUT BLACK BASS

Types of Bass, Size, and Range

Confusing. The fish we call "bass" aren't bass. And all those other fish called bass . . . well, they're not even slightly related to the largemouth bass, which is a sunfish.

The largemouth is the world's largest sunfish. The sunfish family, *Centrarchidae,* includes 33 species which live in warm to cool water. Their bodies are flattened and offer plenty of fin area for bursts of speed and for maneuvering in tight quarters.

Sunfish have spiny dorsal fins. The name "bass" is derived from the Old English word *baers,* meaning bristly like a wild boar. Spines give sunfish limited immunity to attacks by other predators because predators often take soft-rayed prey in preference to spiny sunfish.

Sunfish are shallow water nest-builders. The male protects eggs and young, with the single exception of the Sacramento perch, which is a sunfish, not a perch. The Sacramento perch is also the only sunfish to originally occur west of the Rocky Mountains. And as we noted in Chapter 1, the sunfish family originally existed only in North America.

Largemouth bass differ from their sunfish cousins in obvious ways. Most sunfish have small mouths designed for feeding on insects, zooplankton, and small crustaceans. The largemouth bass is much larger and heavier bodied with a huge maw.

Will Murphy's first encounter with a Largemouth Bass.

Those characteristics apparently are efficient for a predator since other fish unrelated to bass have evolved similar shapes. Peacock bass, sea basses, white, yellow, and striped bass are not related to the largemouth bass, but are called "bass" because of their similar body forms. The word bass, in fact, has been applied to many species with chunky bodies, spiny dorsal fins, and big mouths.

THE BLACK BASSES

The largest members of the sunfish family are called *black bass*, also a confusing name since they aren't black, though they're generally darker than other sunfish. In order of their extent of distribution, the black basses include the largemouth, smallmouth, spotted, redeye, shoal, Suwannee, and Guadalupe.

Taxonomists, scientists who study the naming and grouping of animals, have long been divided into "lumpers" who prefer large encompassing categories and "splitters" who are more preoccupied with differences in fish than in similarities.

Six or seven black bass exist, depending on whether you to talk to a lumper or a splitter. Older references include shoal bass as a branch of the redeye bass species. Until 1927, taxonomists recognized only two distinct bass species, the largemouth and smallmouth. Species and subspecies have continually been lumped and split since then. The current status of the black basses as of 1990:

SMALLMOUTH BASS

Joe Tomelleri

The northern smallmouth bass *(Micropterus dolomieui dolomieui)*.

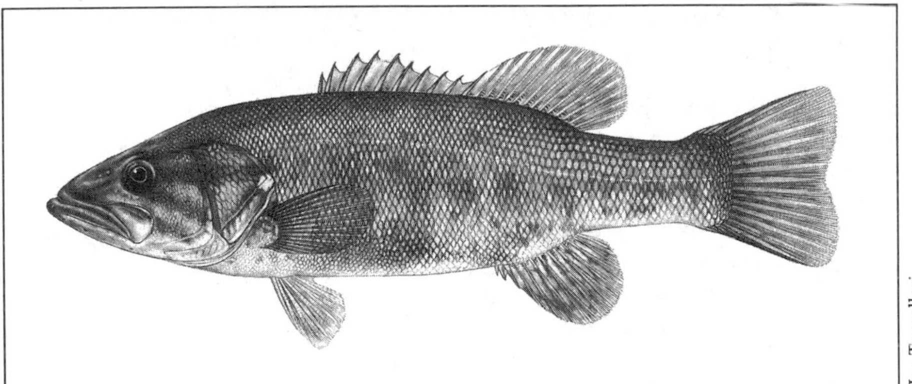

Joe Tomelleri

The Neosho smallmouth bass *(Micropterus dolomieui velox)*.

Smallmouth *(Micropterus dolomieui)* and largemouth bass *(Micropterus salmoides)* are the two most widespread, popular, and important of the black bass species. For a detailed discussion about smallmouths, refer to *Smallmouth Bass—An In-Fisherman Handbook of Strategies*.

Smallmouths and largemouths differ in many ways, the most obvious being their mouths, as their names imply. The jaw of a largemouth extends past the eye, whereas the jaw of a smallmouth ends before the eye.

Largemouth bass also usually have a dark horizontal stripe (thus their common name "linesides"), while smallmouths typically have dark vertical bars on their sides. And though both species change colors to blend into their surroundings, largemouths are often dark to light green, whereas smallmouths are typically golden bronze or brown.

Largemouths and smallmouths are omnivorous, opportunistic feeders, but

SMALLMOUTH BASS DISTRIBUTION

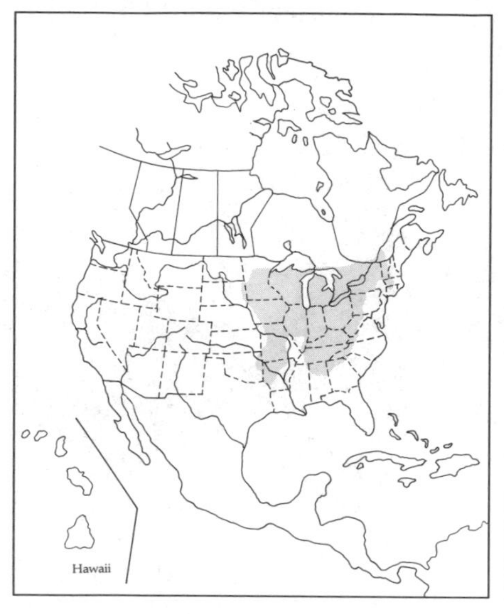

Native Smallmouth Bass Distribution

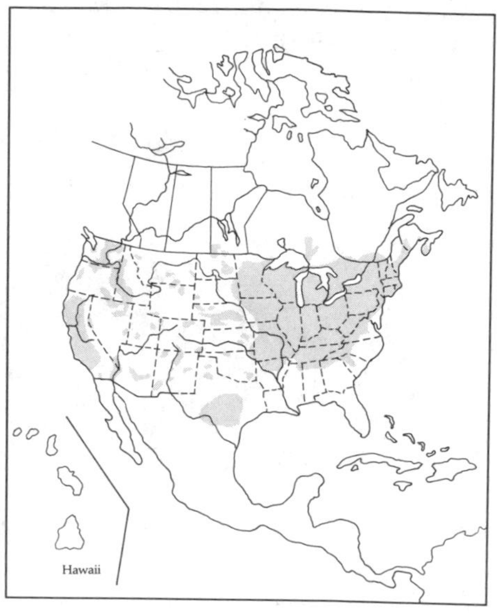

Present Smallmouth Bass Distribution

Maps adapted from *Atlas of North American Freshwater Fishes.* N. Carolina State Mus. Nat. Hist., Raleigh, NC.

smallmouths are better adapted to feeding on crayfish in rock crevices. The mouth of the smallmouth is narrower and more pointed; better for feeding down than the largemouth's mouth. Smallmouths also have streamlined bodies that allow efficient movement in river current.

Like the largemouth, smallmouth bass have been widely transplanted outside their native range. Significant introductions have occurred in the Canadian Shield lakes of northern Minnesota and northwestern Ontario, plus a variety of lake types in Canada, New England, and the mid-Atlantic states. Bodies of water that once held no smallmouths now offer world-class smallmouth angling. Introductions into rivers and reservoirs in the western United States have also produced excellent fisheries.

Although largemouths and smallmouths evolved in different habitats, in some areas, they can be found in the same bodies of water. Smallmouths, however, typically thrive in clear lakes and cool rivers with rock-gravel bottoms and moderate flows.

Imagine a long river. The headwaters are cold and clear—trout water. The middle section becomes slower and warmer as it runs through fertile watersheds. That stretch would hold smallmouths and walleyes. As more tributaries enter, the river slows, widens, and forms oxbows and backwaters. These areas hold largemouth bass.

Smallmouth and spotted bass thrive in highland reservoirs, while largemouth bass do best in hill-land, flatland, and lowland reservoirs. Some highland reservoirs provide habitat for smallmouths in the lower third, spotted bass in the deep midsection, and largemouth bass in shallow arms of the upper third.

SPOTTED BASS

Joe Tomelleri

Spotted bass *(Micropterus punctulatus)* are genetically close to smallmouth bass and may hybridize with them. Yet they look more like largemouths. Three subspecies are recognized: Alabama spotted bass, northern spotted bass, and Wichita spotted bass. The Wichita type is feared extinct. Consult dichotomous keys in reference books to identify specimens where several bass species coexist.

Also called "spots" and "Kentuckys," spotted bass often use deeper water than largemouths and are important gamefish in some regions. They're identified by a line of regular spots just below the lateral line.

Spotted bass originally occurred in waters from east Texas to western Georgia and as far north as Ohio. Spots have been stocked successfully in several states and African countries.

The spotted bass record is jointly held by two 9-pound 4-ounce fish taken from Lake Perris, California in 1987. The International Game Fish Association, generally the strictest record-keeping organization, lists those records. The state of California, however, lists a 9-pound 1-ounce Lake Perris specimen taken in 1984 as their record. And the National Fresh Water Fishing Hall of Fame lists an 8-pound 15-ounce fish from Lewis Smith Lake, Alabama, as the all-tackle standard.

SPOTTED BASS DISTRIBUTION

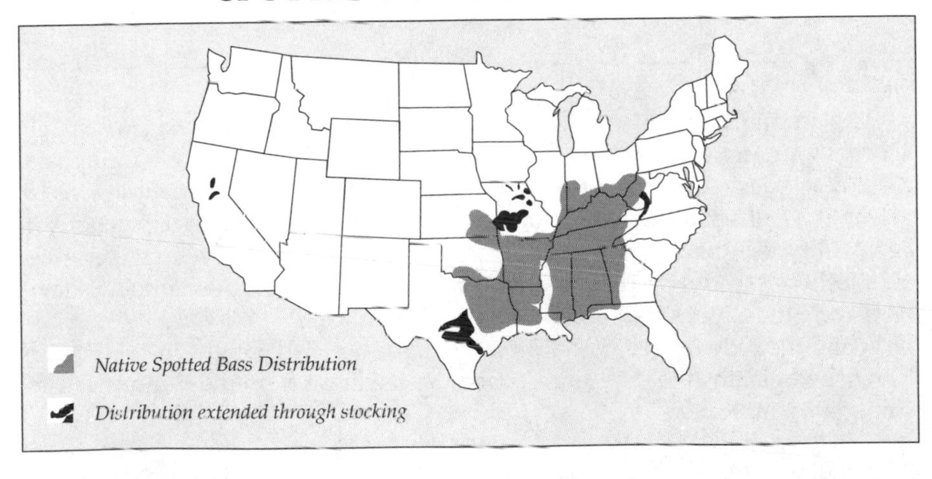

REDEYE BASS

Joe Tomelleri

Redeye bass *(Micropterus coosae)*, a fish of running waters, looks like the smallmouth. Also known as Coosa bass, redeyes have reddish fins and red eyes. The redeye originally occurred only in river systems of specific areas in Alabama, Georgia, and southeastern Tennessee. They have been introduced, though, into waters in California, Kentucky, North Carolina, and Arkansas. Some introductions, however, have not produced sustaining populations.

SHOAL BASS

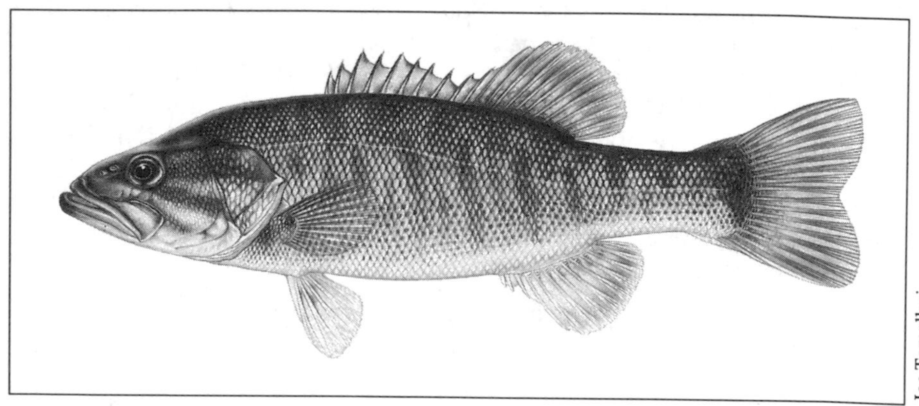

Joe Tomelleri

Anglers and biologists widely recognize the shoal bass *(Micropterus* sp. cf. *M. coosae)*, native to several rivers of Alabama, Florida, and Georgia, as a distinct species. Taxonomists are still cataloguing its characteristics prior to giving it a full scientific name. Because the status of this species has not yet been fully documented, confusion clouds record books as well as literature on southeastern river bass. And its common names include Chipola redeye bass and Flint River smallmouth, as well as shoal bass.

While the redeye record is a 2-pound 12-ounce fish caught in the Tugalo River, Georgia, in 1987, the largest shoal bass was an 8-pound 3-ouncer from Georgia's Flint River.

SUWANNEE BASS

Suwannee bass *(Micropterus notius)* is another species at home in small rivers. Suwannees inhabit low-gradient black-water streams of Florida and south Georgia. This bass is distinguished by a blue chin and throat and a chunky body shape. The all-tackle record, 3 pounds 14½ ounces, was taken in the Suwannee River, Florida, in 1985. Florida restricts harvest and lists the Suwannee bass as a species of special concern due to its limited habitat.

DISTRIBUTION OF REDEYE, SHOAL, AND SUWANNEE BASS

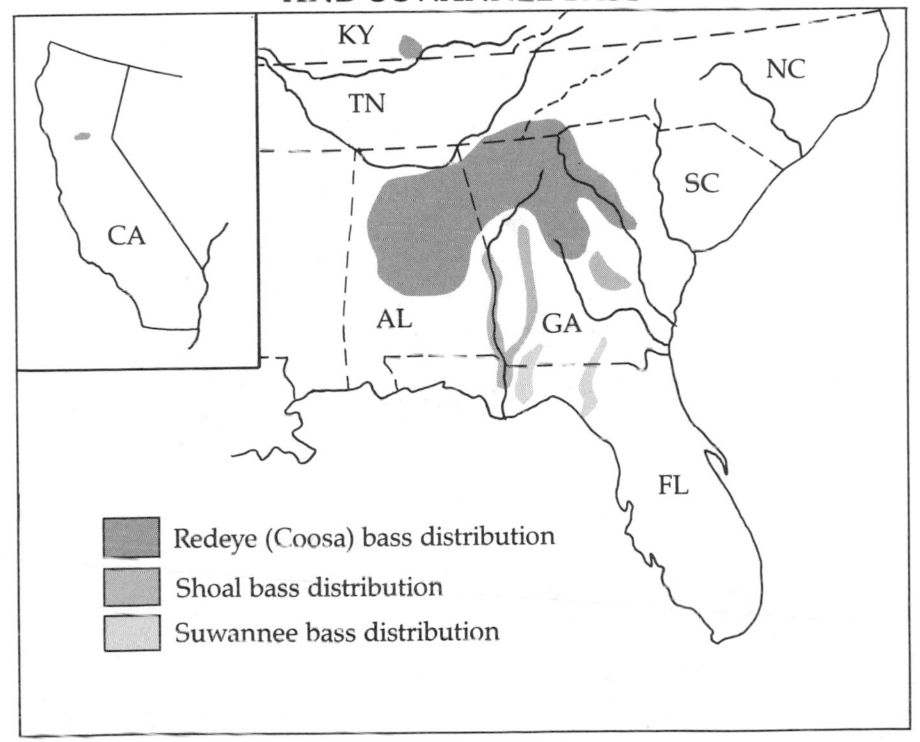

GUADALUPE BASS

Joe Tomelleri

Guadalupe bass *(Micropterus treculi)* is native to the Guadalupe River drainage in central Texas. A small fish, closely related to spotted bass, the Guadalupe has rows of spots above and below the lateral line. Populations of Guadalupe bass have recently been lost through hybridization with introduced smallmouths. The record is a 3-pound 11-ounce fish from Lake Travis, Texas, caught in 1983.

GUADALUPE BASS DISTRIBUTION

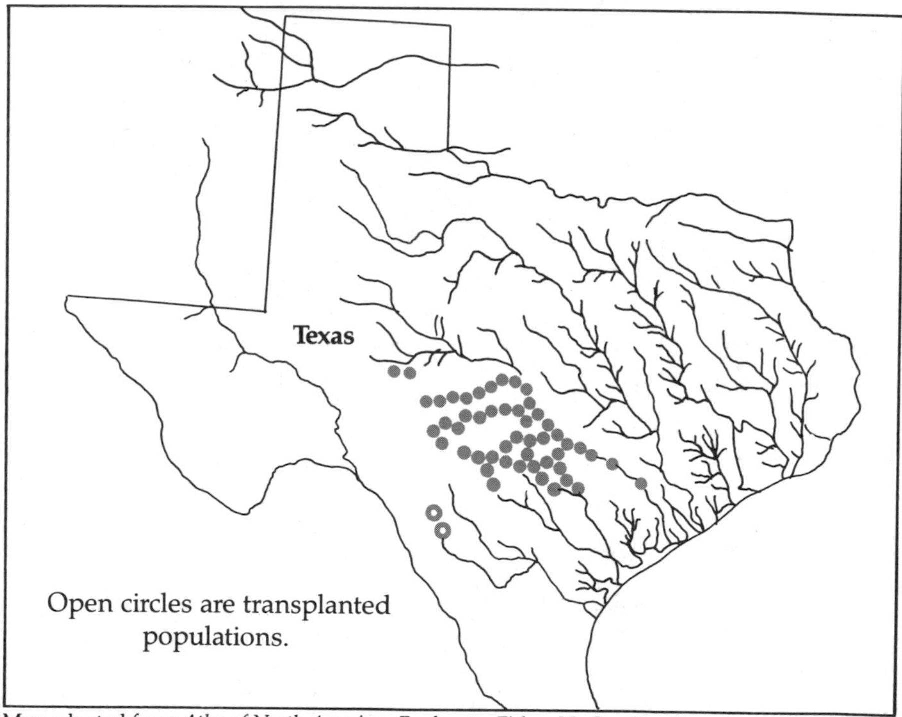

Map adapted from *Atlas of North American Freshwater Fishes.* N. Carolina State Mus. Nat. Hist., Raleigh, NC.

LARGEMOUTH RANGE EXTENSION IN THE U.S.

When largemouth bass finally gained popularity with American anglers, it was in a big way. In the years following the Civil War, a frenzy of bass stocking occurred. Between 1870 and 1894, largemouths were stocked in just about every state where they hadn't been native.

Several factors led to this stocking binge in the late 19th century. Railroad expansion allowed fish to be transported long distances in a relatively short time. In *Book Of The Black Bass*, Dr. Henshall cited an article in the June 1874 *Baltimore American* newspaper that illustrates the zeal of early bassers: "It was twenty years ago, that Alban G. Stabler and J. P. Dukehart, together with Forsythe and Shriver, brought a small lot of Black Bass in the tender of a locomotive from Wheeling Creek, West Virginia, and put them in the Potomac. From this small beginning, sprang the noble race of fish which now swarm in the river."

The earliest bass in Nebraska were fish that escaped into the Elkhorn River after a train wreck. The great stocking movement was also boosted by the establishment of federal and state hatcheries, or "cultural stations" as they were called.

Most attempts at establishing largemouth bass in new waters were made before managers knew about small, but critically important differences

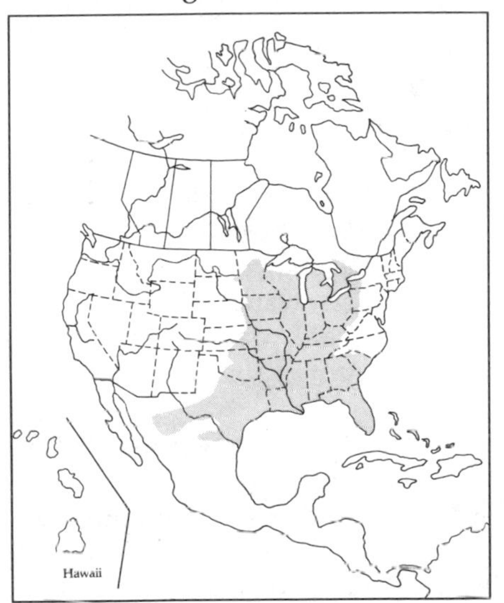

Native Largemouth Bass Distribution

Present Largemouth Bass Distribution

Maps reveal where largemouth bass were native and have been successfully introduced in North America. Major range extensions occurred in (1) New England and the mid-Atlantic states; (2) the Great Plains region from North Dakota to west Texas and westward into Colorado and Montana; (3) west of the Rocky Mountains, especially California, Oregon, and Washington; and (4) Mexico and Central America.

Maps adapted from *Atlas of North American Freshwater Fishes*. N. Carolina State Mus. Nat. Hist., Raleigh, NC.

between the genetics of bass from different regions. Early plants were made with bass from Mississippi flood plains. Many later stockings used bass from U.S. Fish Commission facilities in Illinois and Washington, D.C. Many failed plantings might have succeeded if bass from the right region had been used.

THE INTERNATIONAL LARGEMOUTH

The largemouth bass is a hardy, versatile, and adaptable fish that has survived and reproduced in many foreign waters. The greatest flurry of international stocking activity took place from the 1870s through the 1930s and involved individual fishermen and fishing clubs as well as government agencies. Most stocking took place during an age when fisheries managers were generally unaware of the pitfalls of introducing exotic species. They assumed that a fish desirable in one environment would be desirable elsewhere, and the more the better.

Several factors affected stocking success. Some plants failed because their new environment was too warm or too cold for bass. Other plants in turbid water failed because largemouths are primarily sight feeders that do better in clearer water. Bass stocked into waters without appropriate forage didn't grow well. And other stockings failed when largemouths had to compete with established predator species. Some plants in rivers were unsuccessful because bass need specific backwater habitat to survive.

Successful efforts to introduce largemouth bass around the world:

Canada—Largemouths were native only in parts of southern Ontario and Quebec. They now also occur in Manitoba, Saskatchewan, and British Columbia. Though stockings in some watersheds didn't work, largemouth fishing is superb in many natural lakes of southern Ontario.

Mexico—Anyone who watches television fishing shows knows about the excellent largemouth fishing on some central Mexican waters. Though early plantings were marginally successful, more recent plants have firmly established largemouth bass in Mexico. They grow rapidly in the mild Mexican climate.

Central and South America—Largemouth bass have been planted in 14 countries in Central and South America. They now provide self-sustaining fishing in Brazil, Cuba, Guatemala, and Honduras, plus the territory of Puerto Rico.

Cuba probably has the best bass fishing south of the border. When travel restrictions between the U.S. and Cuba were relaxed in the 1970s, anglers travelled to Cuba for a crack at a bass over 10 pounds. Many were successful. Bass over 11 pounds have been taken in Guatemala, over 16 pounds in Honduras.

Africa—Stockings in Africa have ranged from utter failures to phenomenal successes. Some introductions worked so well that bass are holding their own in the face of commercial fishing. Largemouth bass populations reportedly occur in at least 10 African countries. The best populations seem to be in Kenya, Morocco, Zimbabwe, South Africa, and Swaziland. Bass clubs hold tournaments on larger waters.

Asia and Oceania—Largemouth bass are established in most reservoirs on the islands of Kauai, Oahu, Maui, and Hawaii, where they do well in water stored for irrigating sugar cane and pineapples. Bass have also been successfully stocked in the Phillipines.

Japan—Largemouth bass were also introduced into Japanese lakes in the 1920s. Most Japanese bass lakes are located in agricultural regions and are small, though Lake Biwa is a huge impoundment. Japan reportedly has more than 5,000 bass anglers. Although many belong to the Japanese Bass Tournament Association, some also belong to America's Bass Anglers Sportsman Society.

THE GENETIC LARGEMOUTH

Joe Tomelleri rendition of Florida-strain largemouth bass.

Joe Tomelleri rendition of northern-strain largemouth bass.

There are two largemouth subspecies, *Micropterus salmoides salmoides* (northern largemouth) and *Micropterus salmoides floridanus* (Florida largemouth). The subspecies interbreed freely when they occupy the same water, producing "hybrid" largemouths. Further spawning among hybrids or between hybrids and parental types produces "blackcrosses" or "intergrades."

Florida bass, from semitropical peninsular Florida, aren't tolerant of cold

LARGEMOUTH BASS SUBSPECIES

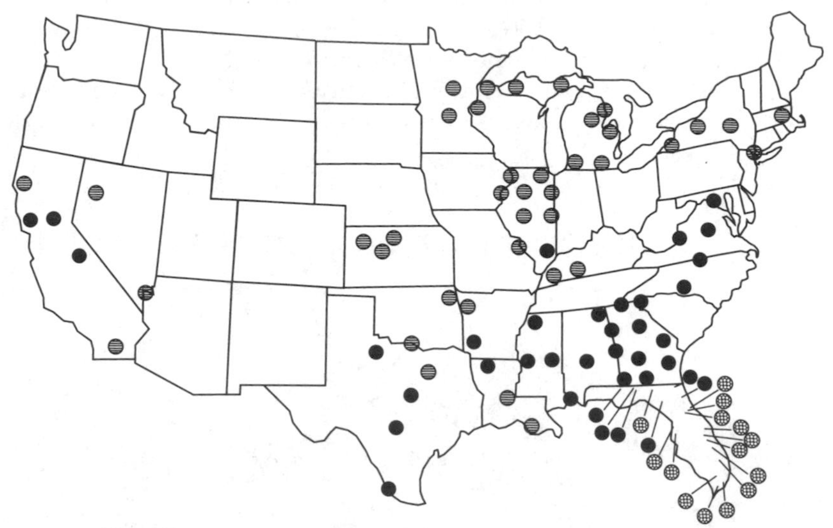

- northern subspecies
- Florida subspecies
- hybrid or intergrade populations

Dr. Dave Philipp, a fish geneticist at the Illinois Natural History Survey, checked the genetic makeup of largemouth bass from 90 populations across the United States. He and his colleagues determined bass identity with a process called electrophoresis, which chemically identifies proteins that are characteristic of genetic types. Florida and northern subspecies have slightly different physical characteristics, but they aren't always reliable indicators of a bass' identity. And bass that are hybrids of the subspecies or intergrades (offspring of spawning among hybrids or of hybrids and parent species) can't be identified without protein analysis.

Pure Florida bass were found only in peninsular Florida. Genetically mixed populations occurred throughout the Southeast. And bass samples from most other areas were pure northern subspecies.

A natural "intergrade zone" apparently extends from South Carolina through Mississippi, including north Florida. Bass in this region are adapted to environmental conditions intermediate between north temperate waters and semitropical peninsular Florida. Their genetic patterns show their intermediacy.

Genetic mixtures outside this zone were due to stocking bass with Florida genes outside their native range. Many fishery biologists and anglers were surprised at the extent of genetically mixed largemouth bass populations when Dr. Philipp published his results in the early 1980s. Further stocking of Florida bass has expanded the zone of genetic mixing.

Through information from record-keeping organizations, newspapers, state-issued news releases, and other sources, we've compiled a list of the 20 largest bass caught and officially weighed. Every few years, rumors of other giant bass surface, some of world-record proportions. Without substantiating evidence, they must be dismissed.

20 BIGGEST BASS ON RECORD

Weight	Water	State	Year
1. 22-4	Ocmulgee R. (Montgomery Lk.)	GA	1932
2. 21-3	Lk. Casitas	CA	1980
3. 21-0	Castaic Lk.	CA	1990
4. 20-15	Lk. Miramar	CA	1973
5. 20-4	Lk. Hodges	CA	1985
6. 20-2	Big Fish Lk.	FL	1923
7. 19-8	Lk. Miramar	CA	1988
8. 19-4	Lk. Miramar	CA	1977
9. 19-3	Lk. Morena	CA	1987
10. 19-3	Lk. Wolford	CA	1986
11. 19-1¼	Lk. Miramar	CA	1988
12. 19-1	Lk. Miramar	CA	1977
13. 19-0	Castaic Lk.	CA	1989
14. 19-0	Lower Otay Lk.	CA	1986
15. 19-0	Lk. Poway	CA	1981
16. 19-0	Lk. Tarpon	FL	1961
17. 18-13	St. Johns R.	FL	1987
18. 18-12	Lower Otay Lk.	CA	1980
19. 18-12	San Vicente Lk.	CA	1981
20. 18-11	Lk. Casitas	CA	1980

International Game Fish Association

The biggest bass ever photographed. Raymond Easley's 21-pound 3-ounce largemouth from Lake Casitas, California, in 1980.

water. A large "intergrade zone" from South Carolina through Mississippi, including northern Florida, contains largemouth bass intermediate between northern and Florida bass. Bass there are best suited to the environment of that region.

California was the first state to stock bass from Florida, intending to produce larger bass. In 1959, Florida bass were stocked in several small reservoirs near San Diego. The experiment was forgotten until anglers began catching huge bass. California's record went from 10 pounds to 15, then 17. In 1974, Dave Zimmerlee caught a 20-pound 15-ounce bass from Lake Miramar. Suddenly it seemed the new world record would come from California. Six years later, Ray Easley caught a 21-pound 3-ounce bass from Lake Casitas, not far from Los Angeles.

In response, anglers across the nation urged their fishery agencies to stock Florida bass in local waters. Stocking Floridas soon became one of the hottest topics in largemouth bass management.

Interest in stocking Florida bass peaked again in the mid-1980s when Texas lakes and reservoirs stocked with Florida bass began producing remarkable numbers of huge bass. The Texas state record went from 13½

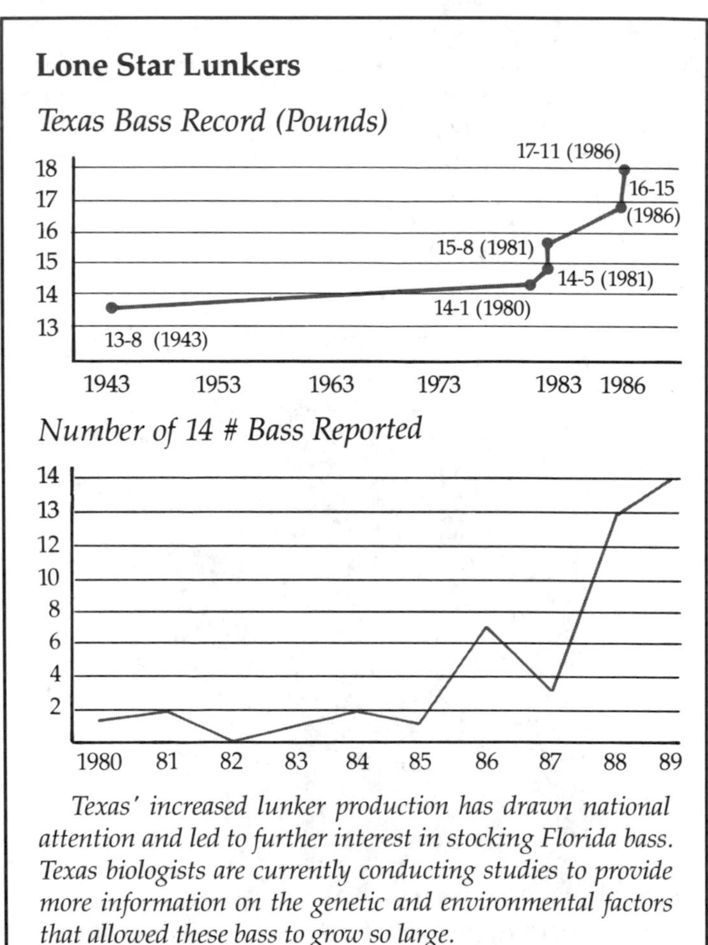

Texas' increased lunker production has drawn national attention and led to further interest in stocking Florida bass. Texas biologists are currently conducting studies to provide more information on the genetic and environmental factors that allowed these bass to grow so large.

pounds, where it had stood for 40 years, to almost 18 pounds in 1986. The Texas annual catch of 14-pound-plus bass has also climbed dramatically.

Pressure to stock Florida-strain largemouths was especially strong in Oklahoma. Giant bass were being taken from Lake Fork, less than 100 miles from the Texas-Oklahoma border. Anglers hoped Florida bass would reach sizes in Oklahoma comparable to the huge bass caught in Texas.

But the issue is complicated. Oklahoma has stocked Florida bass in 70 reservoirs, starting in 1972. And though larger bass have resulted and three state records were set in the late 1980s, results haven't been as impressive.

Climate is one reason. Though Oklahoma borders Texas, Oklahoma waters are cooler than Texas waters. Florida-strain bass are adapted to conditions in Florida that aren't duplicated elsewhere. Florida bass are "out of synch" with cooler environments. They may not spawn at appropriate times, feed and grow as well, or withstand frigid conditions.

Studies conducted by the Oklahoma Fisheries Research Lab also showed that, in time, the percentage of Florida genes in bass tended to decline. Apparently bass with Florida genes don't survive as well in some waters as bass with more northern subspecies genes.

It's possible that even when a Florida plant appears to be a great success, as in Texas, it might represent a short-term gain with undesirable long-term consequences. Unfortunately, it's easier to see the gains (big bass) than the costs (less well adapted bass that don't contribute to the fishery). It remains to be proven that Florida bass stocked in other waters will produce numbers of large bass over a period of many years or decades.

Results of some studies suggest that native bass perform better in their natural environment than bass from elsewhere. A Michigan bass not only survives and reproduces better in Michigan waters than a Florida bass, it probably will grow larger, too. The Florida bass is a great bass—in Florida. Expecting Floridas to thrive in New York waters is like releasing howler monkeys in New York's Central Park and expecting them to thrive.

Still, the mystique of big bass is so strong that anglers are willing to stock Floridas in local waters to see how they'll do. And why not? What's the harm?

Planting Florida bass in an Ozark reservoir or Ohio river is entirely different from stocking monkeys in Central Park. The monkeys wouldn't last long or find suitable mates, whereas introduced bass interbreed with local bass and mix the native genes with genes appropriate for a tropical climate. One careless stocking has the potential to interfere with the precious genetic heritage of many centuries of natural selection.

In a sense, the life of any species in a given region is a continuous genetic experiment. For every bass that survives long enough to reproduce, many thousands of its siblings and millions of its year-class (fish hatched in the same year) must die. The process of natural selection seems wasteful and "cruel," but it's an efficient process for producing fish with the best chance of surviving, growing, reproducing, and persevering through normal environmental fluctuations.

Managers now see the wisdom of *genetic conservation*, protecting a local gene pool from contamination from fish of the same species that have evolved in other waters. Managers are looking more carefully at the fish they stock, due to an awareness of potential problems and the process of electrophoresis, a genetic sampling technique for measuring genetic variations. This is one of the most promising and important new directions in sportfishery management.

Genetic processes are more complex than we've been able to show in this brief summary. Scientists don't understand all the ways genetics and environmental variables combine to produce bass with certain qualities. Genetic studies of subtypes of fish species have just begun. In the future, it may be possible to produce bass that anglers prefer through study of bass genetics and application of theory to fish culture and stocking.

Until then, many managers choose to be conservative. It isn't clear that a better bass can be stocked than the bass that evolved in certain waters. It is clear that careless stocking can do more harm than good. Until managers learn much more than they know now, the wisest policy is not to tamper with natural selection.

A MILLION DOLLAR RECORD

The largemouth bass record is the most coveted world record in fishing. Men have made the conquest of that record their sole pursuit in life. The angler who breaks the record will be an instant celebrity, and some observers believe breaking the record could be worth a million dollars if the new record fish is caught by a canny promoter.

Because of intense interest in this record, someone who breaks the record may want to release the fish. That person will be subjected to furious, exhaustive public scrutiny. Charges of fraud are probably inevitable.

Credible reports exist of sightings of fish large enough to break the record. Doug Hannon, the "Bass Professor," has friends who are sure they've seen world record bass. Hannon especially trusts the judgment of one friend who claims to have studied an estimated 25-pound bass from a distance of six feet.

San Diego reservoirs are still producing huge, but not quite record-size bass. In March 1988, Sandy DeFresco landed a bass that weighed 21 pounds 10 ounces from Lake Miramar. A taxidermist preparing the fish found a 2-pound 8 ¾-ounce scuba diving weight in the fish's stomach. Examination revealed that the weight had been inside the bass for some time, either ingested by the fish or previously inserted into its stomach. Imagine the controversy if the diver's weight had put DeFresco's bass over 22 ¼ pounds!

Few anglers have given as much thought to big largemouth bass as Doug Hannon. Hannon believes northern or central Florida will most likely produce the new record. Conditions seem right there to produce a huge bass—the gene pool is conducive to large size and the growing season is long. Yet water is not so warm that bass grow quickly and "burn out," dying before they attain 23 pounds. The bass, Hannon thinks, will come from dense cover that's hard to fish effectively.

Indeed, Hannon notes that huge bass almost always come from unexpected locations. Part of the thrill of bass fishing is that monster fish can come from relatively small lakes. A bass could surpass the magic 22 ¼-pound

GEORGE PERRY'S WORLD RECORD BASS

A graphite replica of George Perry's world record, compliments of Artistic Anglers of Nisswa, Minnesota. The lure is a Creek Chub Wiggle Fish.

The most famous largemouth ever caught was landed by George Perry, a man in search of a family meal. Perry's father had recently died, leaving the 20-year-old resident of McRae, Georgia, head of a family of seven. The year was 1932, early in the Depression.

Perry went bass fishing with Jake Page on June 2 in an old homemade skiff. They fished a swampy cypress oxbow known as Montgomery Lake on central Georgia's Ocmulgee River. The oxbow, a spooky bayou with towering cypress trees and Spanish moss, lay within the intergrade zone where largemouth bass are generally intermediate between Florida and northern subspecies.

Perry's ancient baitcasting reel and short, stiff rod was rigged with 20-pound dacron line. His bait was reportedly a Creek Chub Wiggle Fish, perch finish. The Wiggle Fish, recently back on the market, is a jointed plug with a lip, two treble hooks, and a fluted metal tail.

The only fish they caught that day struck a cast Perry made to a fallen log. We know nothing of the fight. Since Perry was curious about how much his fish weighed, he took it to nearby Helena, where he was told the fish might place in the national Field and Stream *fish contest. He had the application notarized. The bass weighed 22 pounds 4 ounces, was 32 inches long with a girth of 28½ inches.*

Perry didn't photograph his bass or send it to a taxidermist. His family served it with fried onions, tomatoes, and corn bread. Perry later learned he'd won $75 worth of merchandise for entering the biggest bass in the contest that year. In that era of casual attitudes toward records, the news that his bass was the largest largemouth ever caught didn't mean anything for years.

By the 1950s, Perry's fish was universally recognized as the record largemouth and Perry gained a bit of fame. When bass fishing popularity soared in the 1970s, Perry was frequently called for interviews. Shortly before his death in 1974, when asked his opinion of the California bass then making headlines, Perry said, "Sounds to me like they're pen-feeding bass. A record bass should be taken in its natural state."

Perry took another big bass weighing just under 16 pounds, but he never claimed to be an expert. He was glad to have won the $75, noting it was a lot of money at the time. A family friend remembers, "George was never impressed by his fish or interested in impressing anyone else."

mark in only a few acres of ideal habitat. Even in the face of modern fishing pressure, countless small waters that are inaccessible or hard to fish often go years without seeing an angler's lure.

As time passes, the likelihood of a new record bass declines. Increased fishing pressure means baits are presented in every corner of most bodies of water. Even the sagest old bass can only resist so much temptation, particularly during prespawn and spawning vulnerability. And even dedicated catch-and-release anglers are likely to keep a huge personal-best bass, although it's far smaller than record proportions, eliminating the possibility that it might reach the mark.

Bass are now more difficult to catch for several reasons: Fishing pressure reduces their willingness to bite lures, even if they're not hooked. Human presence and the repeated appearance of lures apparently "smartens" them. Individual bass also vary in their catchability or willingness to bite. Experiments show this trait is inherited (passed from parents to offspring). Decades of harvest have removed the most catchable bass, leaving generations of fish that are less aggressive, "smarter," or that inhabit areas where fishing is more difficult.

Bass growth rates are fastest in newly impounded waters or in waters where they're initially stocked; growth declines more than 50 percent in subsequent years. Far fewer reservoirs and ponds have been built in the last decade. Even fewer are projected for the future. Since near-record bass are usually fast growers, this factor also reduces the likelihood of George Perry's record being broken.

Genetic manipulation of fish is of biological interest and probably will be a boon to aquaculture. Tampering with gamefish such as bass, however, is of questionable management value. Largemouth bass with extra sets of chromosomes, or those treated with hormones or injected with growth genes are no longer largemouth bass. If a record-size bass is ever produced by these techniques, we feel that bass shouldn't qualify for record status.

Chapter 4

MEET THE LARGEMOUTH BASS

A Unique Package of Abilities

Every species has a unique "survival kit," a distinctive set of physical attributes and senses that let that animal function—survive, grow, and reproduce—in its environment. Animals can be grouped into two categories: specialists and generalists.

Specialists have survival kits that work well in specific stable environments, but they can't cope well with change. Environmental changes caused by man or abrupt natural fluctuations often mean disaster for specialists.

Generalists are flexible—adaptable. They lack specific approaches for feeding, but compensate by hustling and experimenting to find and eat a variety of prey. Generalists adjust when their environment changes. For generalists, nothing is easy, but much is possible.

The largemouth bass is a generalist, not bound to a narrow environmental niche or type of forage. He's a "street smart" hustler who can function in diverse situations. This flexibility lets him survive environmental change and thrive in varied settings—stark canyon reservoirs, brackish tidal rivers, and fertile farm ponds.

FEEDING STYLES: BASS VERSUS TROUT

Stream trout are adapted to life in current. Current brings them food, but also saps their energy. Indeed, continuous energy use requires a constant energy supply. But trout must resupply energy efficiently. They can't afford wide searches for food or make poor use of food that flows toward them. They seek feeding stations where current is partially blocked. There they conserve energy while often spending hours feeding.

Insects, especially large hatches of aquatic species, are the most reliable supply of food for average-size stream trout. But not all items floating downstream are edible, so trout need eyes capable of identifying food from nonfood. Trout visually "lock in" on the most abundant food type. They feed selectively and therefore, in most instances, efficiently.

Trout can, for example, lock on a single life-stage of a single insect, ignoring other food that drifts by. Trout often ignore frogs, but feed for hours on insects to gain the food value equal to one frog.

Largemouth bass are distinctly different. Their huge mouths and big bellies let them exploit varied prey types. Largemouths can seize and digest any food that will fit the width of their mouths. Mighty big! The supply of

food for bass is much more flexible than for stream trout. Snakes, ducklings, turtles, frogs, dragonflies, or mice are fair game.

Bass also are less finicky than trout about what they eat. Trout can't afford to feed experimentally, while bass can't afford not to (although they usually ignore carrion). Bass key on vibrations and patterns of movement that suggest prey vulnerable to attack—one reason bass lures come in a variety of shapes, colors, and actions.

As opportunists, bass switch locations and feeding strategies to make the best use of available food. This affects the ways we fish for them.

Presentation for average-size stream trout often must imitate the food they eat. Presentations for largemouth bass, on the other hand, often need only to appear alive and vulnerable to attack. To look alive, food must move. To look vulnerable, it must first be within striking range.

Unusual prey make up a small part of most bass diets. The most common and nutritious bass prey are dozens of species of small fish. Crayfish are also a predominant prey in some waters.

Experienced bass may feed selectively, ignoring animals they've learned are hard to catch. They may also have learned to avoid fish with spiny defenses in favor of soft-finned prey. Yet bass often continue to be ready to grab potential food items even though they don't look like anything they've eaten before. This quality is but one of the things that makes fishing for bass fun.

THE PHYSICAL BASS

Bass are chunky fish with a lot of fin area; so they're powerful fish that move well in confined areas. But again, it's the mouth of a largemouth bass that is its most prominent and important feature. Largemouths lack the sharp teeth of walleyes and pike, but their cavernous mouths easily engulf most prey.

When a bass attacks a school of minnows, the big mouth is a feeding advantage—like using a fly swatter rather than a yardstick to squash a bug. Along with that bucket mouth, the largemouth has an expandable belly that stretches to accommodate anything it swallows. Bass can catch and swallow a variety of prey types and sizes, but they're limited to food they can swallow whole.

The lower jaw of largemouth bass is large and underslung, a feature making them less adept at picking food off the bottom, especially prey in rocky crevices. The more tweezerlike jaws of smallmouth bass, on the other hand, let them more easily pick crawfish from the bottom. Studies suggest that largemouths are most effective when they feed upward, even though they also take prey on the bottom, at middepths, and near the surface.

Like other sunfish, bass are adapted to living in cover, usually weeds or wood. A pike's missile-shape body allows greater forward speed due to its hydrodynamic shape and rear location of the dorsal and anal fins. But pike can't maneuver well to catch prey moving erratically in cover. Largemouths, on the other hand, precisely and quickly maneuver in cover like weed stalks. Bass can quickly change direction while maintaining speed.

FISH SHAPE

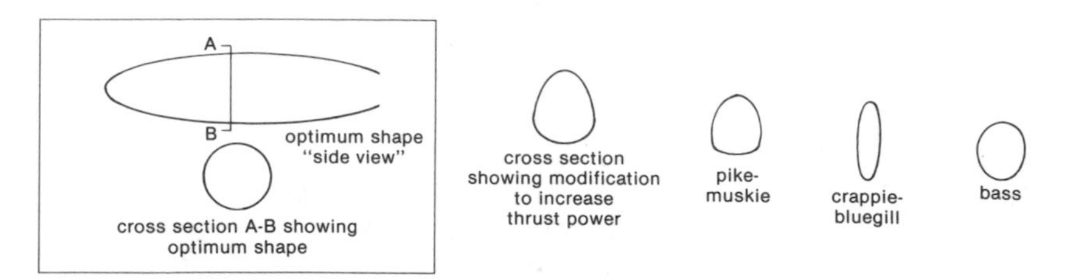

A multitude of body shapes exist among the more than 20,000 species of fish found worldwide. Different designs are adapted to the wide range of habitats and behavioral diversity that fish exhibit.

Because water density is much greater than air, fish face resistance to forward motion. Streamlined shape minimizes resistance. Some open-water species resemble cigars. But body shape is a compromise because forward propulsion is by lateral body thrusts supplemented by caudal, dorsal, and anal fins. Flattened forms provide good propulsion and also facilitate maneuvering in cover.

Pike and muskies approach optimum hydrodynamic shape; their large rearward dorsal and anal fins allow bursts of lightning speed, but they fall short in maneuverability. The flattened bodies of crappies and bluegills don't allow fast forward movement. These fish can, however, make sharp turns and easily pivot up and down. Their rounded shape and large fin area also facilitate swimming backward.

Largemouth bass and similar shaped fish have compromise shapes that allow them to operate in a broad range of habitats. They can function in open water and in dense cover.

Bass can swim about 2 mph for long periods. Their burst speed has been estimated at about 12 mph, five times faster than you can retrieve a crankbait.

Bass have scales that reduce their ability to sense the environment through their skin. In scaleless catfish, for example, the skin is an important sensory organ. Scales, however, protect bass from parasites and attacks from predators.

Bass blend into their habitat. Their back and sides are dark; their belly is light, a pattern called countershading. Since light enters the underwater world from above, the bass's light belly blends into the lighted surface when viewed from below. This camouflage means protection from predation on one hand, and the ability to remain undetected to prey, on the other hand.

Murky water transmits less light. In murky water, bass color fades, making them less conspicuous. Bass exposed to sunlight in shallow clear water have black backs and bright green sides, while bass from deep or turbid water are pale and silvery. Active bass are darker than inactive bass, and their green coloration camouflages them in weedy habitat and wherever plankton and algae are present.

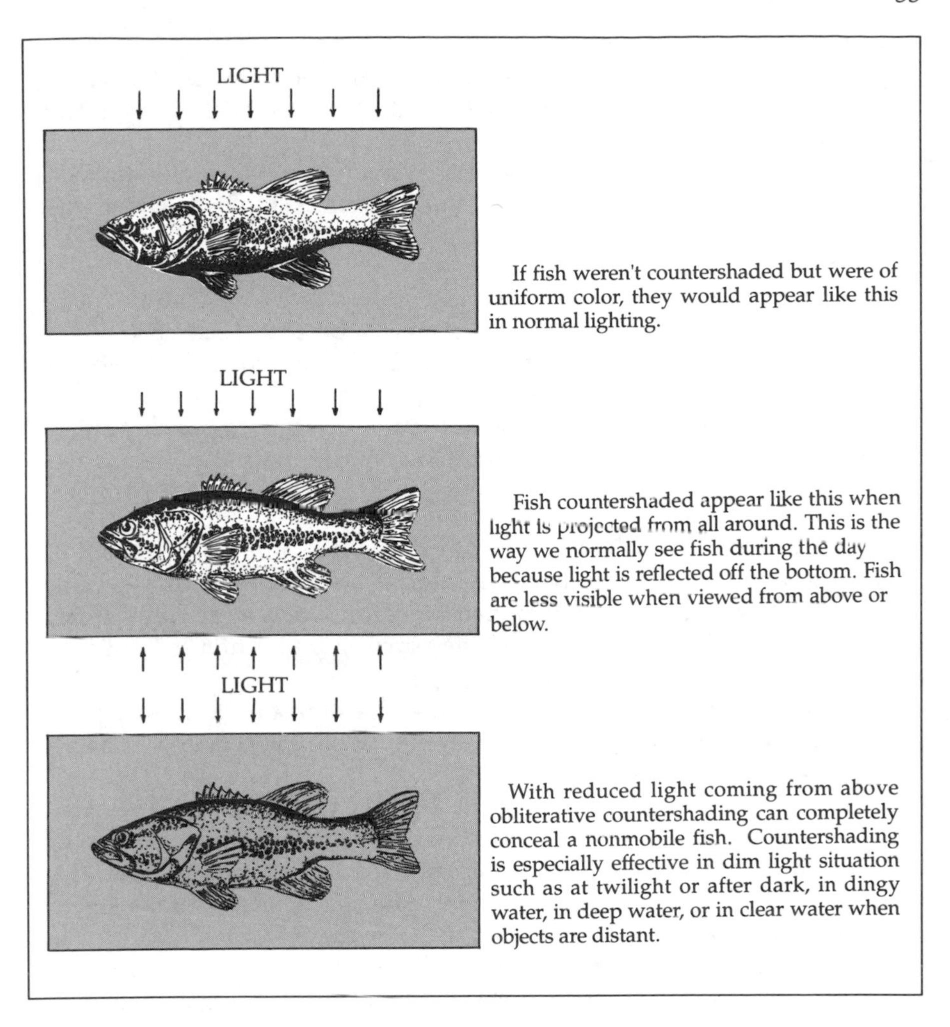

GROWTH

Most big bass are females because they live longer than males. In some areas, females also grow faster. Males are generally more compact and lean, females broader and heavier bellied. These differences are most distinct around spawning time.

Bass probably don't grow in water colder than 50°F and grow slowly in water between 50°F and 60°F. Northern bass have a shorter growing season than southern bass. Bass in some southern areas grow every month of the year. Bass in northern states, however, may live more than 15 years, while 10 years is old for southern bass. Though growth rates are extremely fast in Mexico and Cuba, bass there don't seem to live long enough to reach record size.

FOODS

When bass hatch, they're nourished by a yolk sac for several days while their mouth completes development. Then bass "fry" rely on zooplankton and tiny crustaceans. When they get a little bigger, they switch to insects and small fish, including each other.

While bass eat many things, they're generally piscivorous (fish eaters). They often select soft-rayed minnows, but will also eat sunfish, spiny channel catfish and bullheads, or smaller bass.

Shad are a major food source for bass in many reservoirs, although shad are an atypical food, since bass usually don't chase food in open water where shad often school. But shad are so nutritious and abundant that bass have adapted to feeding on them.

Crayfish are also an important food source in many waters. When crayfish are abundant, bass often feed primarily on them. Crayfish migrate to the shallows in spring, then move steadily deeper, but rarely below the thermocline.

Though frogs are strongly associated with largemouth bass, they aren't a major food item except in fall when frogs make their annual run from

PREY SIZE FOR LARGEMOUTH BASS

Bass may try to eat prey almost as large as themselves, or they have to settle for larger forms of tiny animal plankton when larger prey aren't available. Nevertheless, bass size sets practical upper and lower limits on prey size.

The lower limit is set by several factors. Prey must be large enough to be visible and worth chasing. Bass rarely waste more energy chasing food than they get from digesting it.

Prey also must be large enough to be held by the gill rakers—thin, forklike spines blocking the areas between the gills. Water flows out, while food items remain in the bass's throat. Prey smaller than the spaces between rakers usually escape. The space between rakers gets larger as bass grow, so the minimum size of food gets larger.

Upper limit of prey size is determined by the gape of the mouth and throat and the ability of bass to catch and hold strong and struggling prey. Crayfish may be too tough or painful to eat, even if they fit into a bass's mouth. Large gizzard shad may be strong and swift enough to escape unless they're taken headfirst. Catfish and bullheads erect spines and wriggle strongly to escape. Such preyfish may be low-percentage targets.

Maximum length of prey varies with the shape of the prey and other features like spiny fins. Bass take longer thin preyfish in longer sizes than thicker sunfish. Studies show that bass occasionally eat fish that are about 60 percent of their own length. Stomach samples show, however, that bass typically eat prey between 10 percent and 50 percent of their own length. Twenty percent to forty-five percent are the most typical sizes. Preyfish this size are the best balance between the energy used to capture and the energy gained from eating.

Each prey species has special abilities and tactics to avoid being eaten. The dash speed of fish increases with size. Bass need a proportional size advantage to run down prey. They usually attack only injured or sick larger prey.

shallow marshy areas and meadows to hibernate in deeper water. Bass sense the heightened frog activity and intercept them. Salamanders and large insects also are important prey in some waters.

THE SENSES OF BASS

In addition to the typical five senses—sight, hearing, touch, taste, and smell—bass have a sixth sense, lateral-line sensitivity. This sense lets them perceive low-frequency vibrations through sensors located on each side of their bodies.

These six senses convey environmental information that bass need. Reliance on a particular sense varies with the environment. In clear water, bass rely heavily on sight; in murky water, sight is important, but lateral-line perception and hearing gain importance.

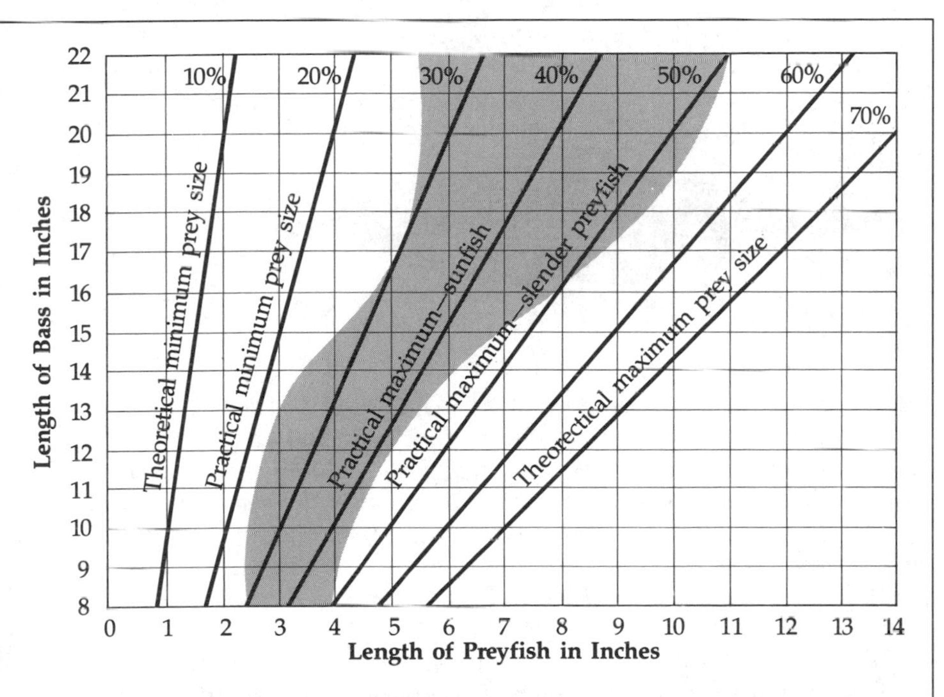

The shaded area shows the actual size of preyfish bass typically eat. Although bass may eat preyfish as small as about 10 percent of their own length, or as large as 60 to 70 percent, most preyfish fall between 20 and 50 percent.

Larger bass tend to eat larger prey. Most of the food of young adult bass falls between 20 percent and 40 percent of their own length, while older and larger bass tend to select preyfish in the 30 to 50 percent range, depending on prey shape.

(Chart based on Adams, S.M., R. B. McLean, and M. M. Huffman. 1982. Structuring of a predator population through temperature-mediated effects on prey availability. Can. J. Fish. Aquatic Sci. 39(8):1175-1184.)

SIGHT

Sight is the single most important sense for largemouths. Some sources overemphasize lateral-line perception and underplay vision. Bass can inhabit dingy water, but they don't feed as well when their vision is impaired.

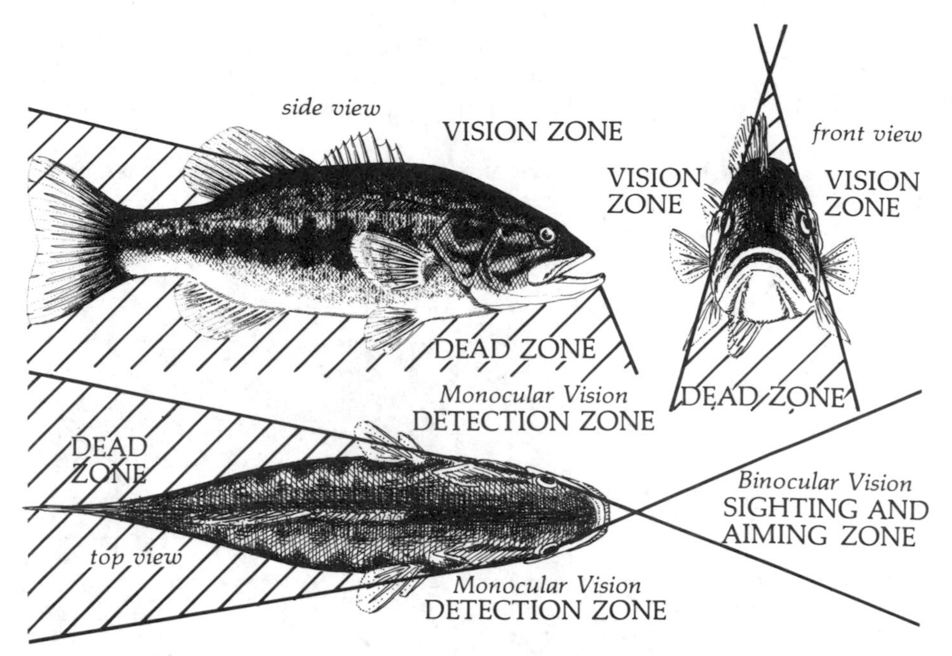

The eyes of bass are positioned for good vision to either side and binocular vision in a forward and slightly upward direction. Blind zones exist to the rear and underneath. Prey or lures in the binocular (sighting and aiming) zone are the most easily and accurately attacked. Prey and lures in other detection zones, however, may also be successfully attacked if the bass has time to turn and focus in the binocular zone. Items in dead zones may go undetected. Bass learn to fear attack from the rear, so inactive fish often back into cover to protect themselves.

Bass eyes are set on the sides of their head. With this placement, they can see food or danger from everywhere except directly behind and below their bodies.

Bass have 3-dimensional vision only in a small area in front of their noses, the only place where 3-dimension is needed because that's where they focus on food. Even clear water carries plankton, silt, and other particles that limit vision to short ranges. Water also impedes motion, so fish are concerned only with food or threats at short range. At rest, bass focus on objects about a foot away. But they can change focus to see objects as far as 30 or 40 feet away in clear water.

Bass can see above and below the water. An aggressively feeding bass may snatch a lure before it touches the surface. Bass in deeper water have a broader view of objects above water. Also, the higher an object is above the water line, the easier it is for bass to see. Bass anglers should keep a low

THROUGH THE FISH'S EYES

Have you ever wondered how much a fish sees above the water surface? In other words, can they see us and if they can, how clearly?

In calm water, a fish has a good view of surface objects. As water becomes choppy, vision above water worsens. Can fish see you? Yes, in most instances.

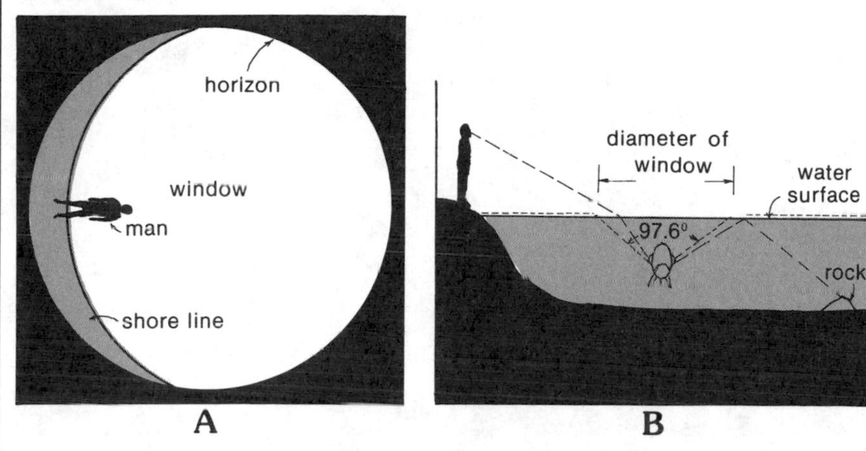

This illustration shows what a fish sees in an upward direction when the water surface is perfectly calm.

(a) Water surface and aerial window as seen from beneath.

(b) Explanation of window: rays striking the surface at an angle within the window are refracted (bent) to the eyes of the fish, but rays striking outside the window from beneath are totally reflected. Within an angle of 97.6°, the fish sees out into the air, but outside this angle, it sees objects on the bottom reflected in a silvery surface. (Redrawn from Walls in Frost and Brown, The Trout, *1967.)*

Source: *Mary Pratt,* Better Angling With Simple Science, *Fishing News Books Ltd., Surrey, England.*

profile when they're after big bass in clear shallow water.

Scuba observations show that bass make no effort to avoid sunlight, contrary to the myth that sunlight hurts bass eyes because they lack eyelids. Bass make internal adjustments in their eyes to reduce their sensitivity to intense light. Cover objects and particles in water also reduce light intensity.

Bass don't need to avoid bright areas, but they usually seek shade. They lurk in shade because they're safer from predators there. And bass in shade see prey better than prey can see them, an obvious feeding advantage.

Bass eyes have both rods and cones, as do those of most fish species. Rods are black-and-white sensors that excel in dim light. Cones are color receptors. Bass shift reliance on rods or cones as light levels change. They see colors when light is adequate, but only shades of black and white when light is dim. Bass see better in dim light than humans do, but not as well as fish like sauger that have eyes adapted for minimal light. Bass feed at night by silhouetting prey against light coming from the sky and by using a combination of hearing and lateral-line senses.

Shade:

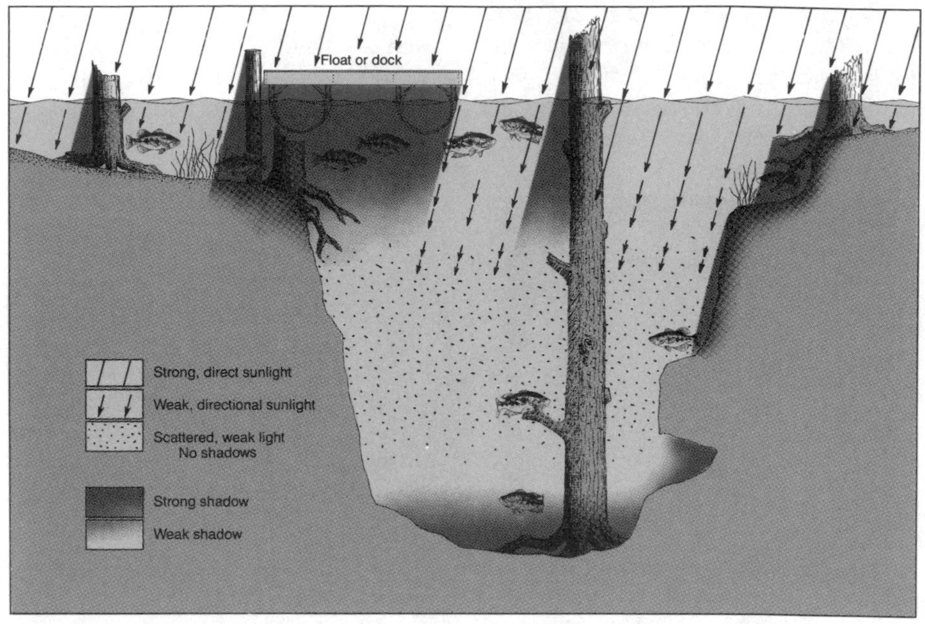

The absorption and scattering of light underwater reduces and eliminates shadows. Shadows usually disappear at about twice the depth an angler can see a large fluorescent or white lure.

Research on color vision in bass has provided sometimes contradictory data:

- Bass see colors, discriminate between them, and learn to avoid colors associated with negative consequences.
- One study found that bass saw black best, followed by yellow, white, green, and blue. Another report found they saw red best, but were attracted to yellow.
- Underwater observations show that bass can discriminate between strands of different color monofilament line.
- That study suggested bass are repelled by bright yellow fishing line, but are attracted to fluorescent blue-green line.
- In another study, bass in tanks chose minnows dyed red over natural minnows.
- Another study showed red and white lures particularly effective.

HEARING

Water transmits sound vibrations five times better than air. Struggling prey send distinct vibrations. Bass rely on these vibrations to detect, locate, and seize prey, as well as to avoid predators.

We separate "hearing" that comes through the ears and "lateral-line perception" that is felt. Yet both senses involve sound waves. A bass hears high-frequency sound waves (20 to 1,000 cycles per second). Its lateral-line sensors pick up low-frequency sound waves (4 to 200 cycles per second).

COLOR VISION

Accurate descriptions of the colors fish see are impossible until more is learned about how fish's eyes work. In the meantime, scientists make speculations based on the relative sensitivity and numbers of different types of color-sensitive cells (cones) in the eyes of each species studied. The eyes of only a few species have been examined, so scientists must assume that related and similar species have similar eyes.

Goldfish and some minnows have four sets of color-vision cells (cones) that have peak sensitivities to orange, yellow-green, blue, and ultraviolet (UV) light. The output of these sets seem to be evenly matched, so goldfish see blue and UV light as brightly as yellow and orange light. Apparently, goldfish, minnows, and similar species have adapted to clear water where UV and blue light are commonplace. Other fish species that have adapted to similar clear-water environments probably have similar color-vision abilities. Trout, for example, seem to see UV light well.

Walleye and sauger lack blue cones and apparently sense the entire spectrum using only orange and green cones. They're adapted to murky river water that absorbs most of the blue and green light and reflects and scatters mostly red, orange, and yellow light. The UV sensitivity of walleye hasn't been checked, but murky water also rapidly absorbs UV light. It's unlikely that walleyes see UV light.

About 90 percent of the walleye's cones sense the red-orange-yellow portion of the spectrum. The other set senses yellow-green, blue, and violet. As a result, scientists presume walleyes see red-orange, orange, and yellow-orange as bright colors. Green is an intermediate color, but blue and violet are weak and likely appear dark and nearly black.

Black bass and sunfish have cones that seem similar to those of walleyes, although they don't have the same reflective eyes and super-sensitive night-vision cells (rods). Tests of bass vision indicate that bass discriminate poorly between yellows and grays and show some preference for reddish colors. This suggests bass, like walleye, may have only two sets of cones. Bass, however, may not depend as heavily on the red end of the spectrum as walleye. Bass UV abilities haven't been described.

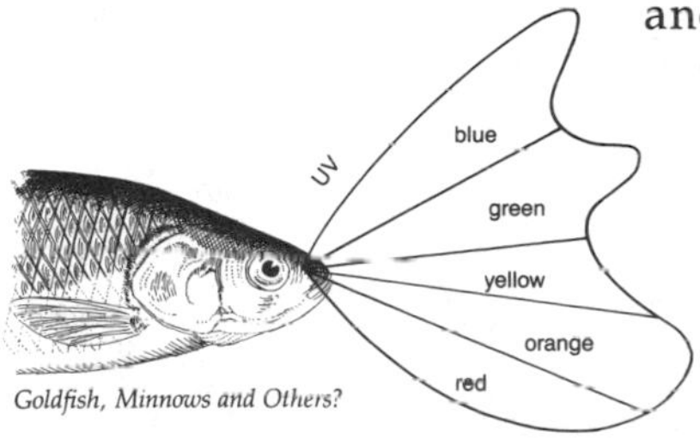

Goldfish, Minnows and Others?

Four different cones—orange, yellow-green, blue, UV—provide a comparatively balanced color range.

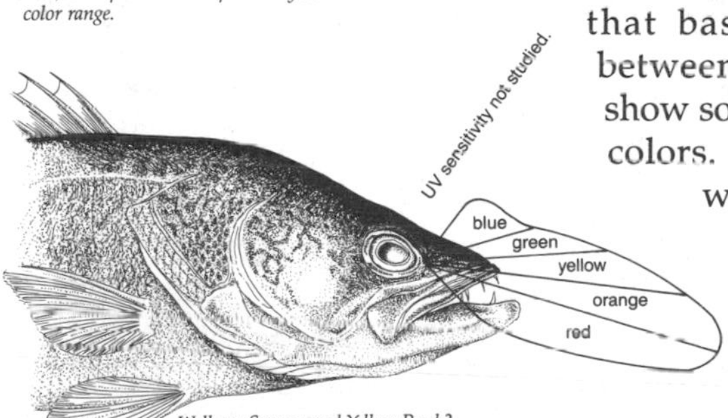

Walleye, Sauger, and Yellow Perch? Black Bass and Sunfish? Others?

Most cones peak at orange; a few sense green.

Hearing and Lateral Line in Fish

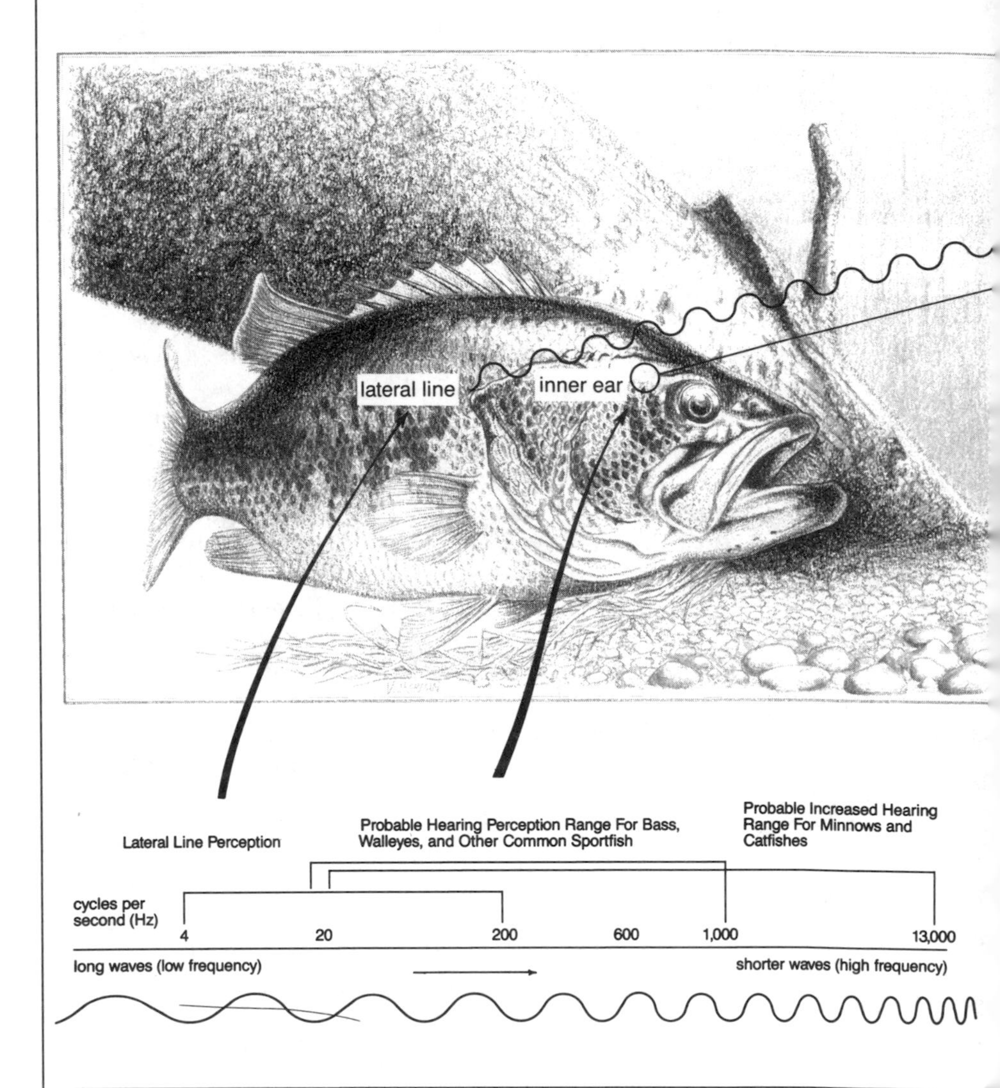

When Sound Becomes Feeling

Some vibrations can only be *felt* (lower pitches or frequencies within about the 1 to 200 cycle per second [Hz] range), while other vibrations can only be heard (higher pitches within about the 100-600 to 3,000-13,000 Hz range, depending on the fish species). There apparently is an area of overlap where a fish can hear and feel vibrations (about 20 to 200 Hz).

A bait moves toward a fish. At 50 feet, higher-frequency sound waves from the rattling shot and the hooks tinkling on the body of the bait reach the fish's inner ear, and low-frequency vibrations from the plug's wobble reach its lateral

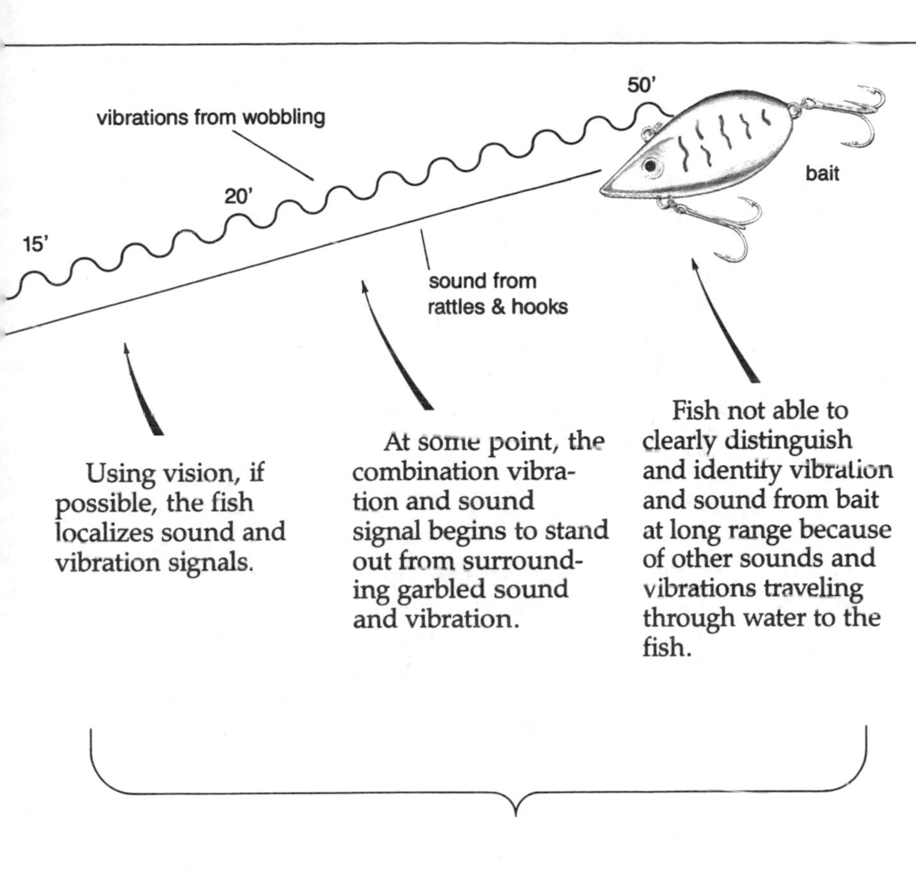

line. Something's out there, but it's probably insignificant, given myriad other vibrations and sounds reaching the fish.

As the lure comes closer, however, the vibration and sound from the bait begin to stand out from the drone around the fish.

Using vision in combination with hearing and feeling, the fish tries to localize where and what the thing (lure) is. The closer it comes, the more distinguishable it becomes.

Note the overlap.

The lateral-line sense perceives the swish of a minnow's tail or the gentle kick of a frog. Silent lures like jigs, plastic worms, and crankbaits produce vibrations that bass easily sense—hear and feel. A slowly worked soft bait may be extremely attractive to bass because it closely mimics sounds of distressed prey.

Yet as important as hearing and lateral-line senses are, they remain secondary to vision. In tank tests, blindfolded bass caught live minnows, but fed less accurately and efficiently. Bass feed most efficiently when they combine sensory input.

Much remains to be learned about sound patterns attractive to bass. Research hasn't identified a wave frequency that automatically attracts bass, but irregular sounds made by lures that stop and go or collide with cover may be more appealing. Attractive sound patterns may vary according to the prey bass are keying on. Scientific research on lure design based on sound could make big gains in the future.

Bass certainly associate certain sounds with danger. Most noises above water bounce off the surface; so ordinary conversation doesn't spook bass. But scuba divers report bass spooked when electric trolling motors are turned on and off. Divers also observed that standing to cast, which causes a boat to twist in the water, sends waves that spook bass.

While bass are extremely sensitive to noises like an oar banging or an object dropped in a boat, outboard motors running continuously are part of the usual noisy world for most bass. They're spooked by close, erratic, and unfamiliar sounds especially when they're in open areas. Bass in cover seem more secure.

SMELL

Although taste and smell are often lumped together, in fish they perform distinctly different roles. Fish nostrils (nares) bring water into contact with olfactory organs. Trout and catfish have highly developed olfactory organs with many folds. In bass, organs of smell are less developed.

Bass use smell as a social sense, giving cues to other bass and receiving cues from them. For example, spawning cues seem to be perceived through the sense of smell. Bass also seem to react to smells given off by wounded or distressed bass. And they may smell wounded baitfish. In the 1970s, the scent topic became controversial as scent attractants became popular. Little controlled research has occurred, almost none if you discount studies conducted by scent-attractant manufacturers.

Do scents attract bass? Probably only at short range; baits must pass close to bass. We believe scents may encourage bass to bite in some situations, particularly slow-moving baits for inactive bass in cold water.

TASTE

Taste is even more of a close-range sense than smell. Bass have taste receptors on their lips and in their mouths. But compared to species like

ANATOMY OF TASTE

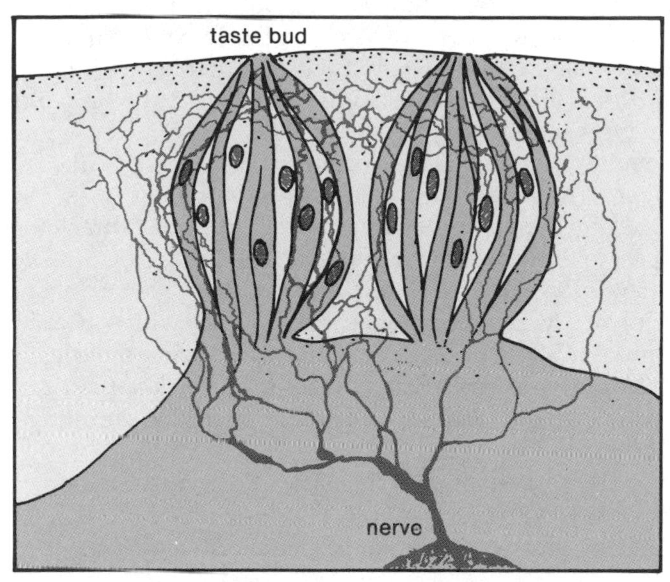

Fish taste chemical substances through receptor cells located in bundles called "taste buds." Unlike humans, however, whose taste buds are restricted to the tongue and palate, fish species may have widely scattered buds. Sharks have taste buds scattered mainly within their mouth and throat. Catfish, however, have thousands of taste buds scattered over their whiskers, inside their mouth and throat, over their head and body, and even on their fins. Each cell within a taste bud can be stimulated by a chemical substance dissolved in water. When stimulated, taste receptor cells fire impulses to taste centers in the brain, the taste sensation is interpreted as either a "food" or "nonfood" taste.

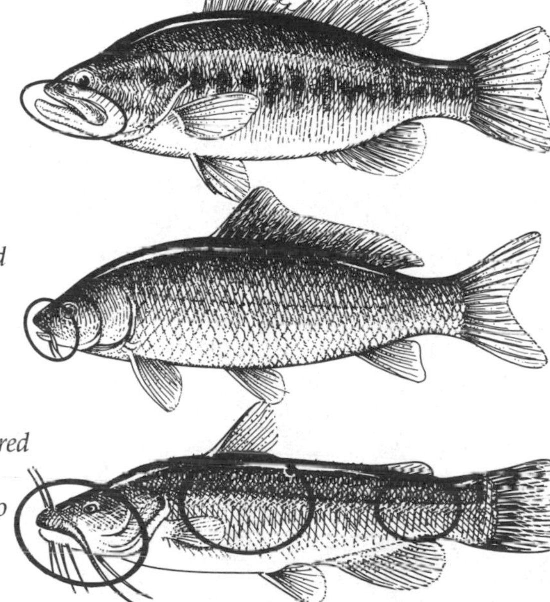

Bass, Walleye, Pike: Taste buds centered around mouth and lips.

Carp: Taste buds centered around mouth, lips, and especially barbels.

Catfish: Taste buds centered around mouth, lips, and especially barbels, but also distributed over body.

catfish, bullheads, carp, and sturgeon, bass have few taste receptor cells. The only time a bass tastes something is after grabbing it.

That doesn't make taste unimportant. After a bass hears, sees, and grabs a possible food item, taste often tells it whether that item is food.

Scuba divers have seen bass inhale plastic baits and blow them out without anglers sensing they've had a strike. Bass may even grab a crankbait without sending signals an angler can feel. If items taste like food, bass hold them longer. The longer and more firmly bass hold lures, the better your chances are of feeling and hooking those fish. Bass attractants, then, more likely appeal to the sense of taste, not smell.

What flavors appeal to bass and how can those flavors most effectively be added to a bait? Most work in this area has been with soft plastic baits since flavor compounds can be added to plastisol during molding. Plastic baits were first impregnated with salt, which toughened the plastic, made the bait less translucent, and added flavor that is supposed to encourage bass to hold worms longer.2

Recently, baits have been impregnated with some amino acids. Some of these baits are also biodegradable. Berkley and Blue Fox are producing edible soft baits, an area with potential for effective products.

FEEL

Bass determine that something is food based on how it looks and sounds. After grabbing it, they sample it for flavor and texture. They hold something soft and squashy longer and more firmly than something hard like a crankbait. Feel also helps bass move through rock or weed cover.

Bass senses work primarily at short range. It's the little sphere around the face, a sphere we call a strike zone, that fishermen need be concerned with.

Much writing in the 1970s and 1980s emphasized bass limitations. But bass aren't so much prisoners of their environment, reflexes, or abilities, as they are capable predators, superbly adapted to catching a variety of prey.

HOW BASS FEED

Bass grab food in several ways. The most common method is to rush toward the target and engulf it. They usually seize large or rapidly moving prey this way. It's also how they usually hit topwater baits, crankbaits, or spinnerbaits.

Bass inhale small slow-moving objects, especially if the object seems unable to escape. A bass approaches prey, flares its gills, and sucks it in. If the bass senses a problem, it reverses the action, blowing the object out. Inhaling and expelling is so rapid that the human eye has trouble following the action.

Bass have a reputation for feeding by reflex, snapping up food that appears at close range. Recent studies, however, indicate that bass aren't triggered into striking objects they don't want to hit. A Texas study suggests that quick-moving targets produced responses from bass because the bass didn't take time to decide. But they were still feeding by intention.

Apparently, we can't make bass hit by reflex.

To survive and grow, bass must balance energy expenditure and food intake. They can't afford to waste energy on fruitless strikes. Tank observations show that 60 to 80 percent of bass strikes within 18 inches of prey are successful. Longer strike distances and heavy cover lowers this success ratio.

FEEDING STRATEGY

Each fish species uses one or more of four basic feeding strategies: (1) running down food, (2) stalking, (3) habituation, and (4) ambush. Feeding tactics depend on the predator's body shape and the shape and behavior of its prey.

Running down food is a common tactic of streamlined open-water fish like salmon and tuna. They overwhelm prey with bursts of speed and can maintain pursuit for long distances.

Muskies and other predators with forward-oriented fields of vision generally stalk prey. They move close, then overtake prey with an explosion of speed, relying on the initial rush for capture. They don't usually follow missed prey.

Chunky fish use habituation, a sneak tactic. They hover near prey without giving off strike signals. When prey gets careless or shows signs of weakness, the predator swiftly strikes.

Ambush is passively lying still, waiting for prey to come close enough for a short strike. Ambush predators often are bulky, slow, and highly camouflaged.

Because bass spend so much time resting in shade in heavy cover, anglers sometimes assume they're primarily ambush predators. But for largemouths, feeding only by ambush would be a great waste of talent.

Largemouth bass are generalist feeders. They use all four tactics at various times, depending on their activity level and the size, availability, and type of prey.

Inactive bass retreat to cover and feed by ambush, if at all. More active bass may hold near cover and close to potential prey, using the habituation tactic. If a creature gets close enough or appears disabled, the bass strikes. This tactic, like ambush, is passive and usually won't provide a full day's ration, but it doesn't require much effort.

The most important feeding tactic of active bass is to stalk prey by swimming near cover in small groups, stopping periodically to check for vulnerable prey. They also cruise open water near cover to flush prey. By swimming aggressively near cover, bass startle prey into making mistakes. Bass then swiftly attack.

In reservoirs, bass use the run-down tactic to capture shad from below, pinning the school on the surface. This tactic is primarily used by 1- to 2-pound "school" bass. Although bass aren't built for sustained chases, the feeding frenzies of "schoolies" represent this tactic.

These feeding strategies apply to our fishing. Inactive bass aren't feeding, but might launch an attack from ambush or after habituation. Put a lure that looks easy to catch, like a jig or worm, in front of them.

Stalking bass actively seeking food above or near cover hit rapidly moving presentations. Schooling bass are more vulnerable to active shad imitations.

Anglers face inactive or neutral bass more often than active bass. When bass are actively feeding, fishing's great. Much of the time, though, precise presentations are necessary for bass in an inactive feeding mood.

PRESENTATION BASED ON BASS FEEDING STRATEGIES

When you approach an area, in this case, a timbered point, consider that bass may be "running bait down" or "stalking" if they're active, "hovering near cover" (habituating) if they're in a neutral mood, or "in cover" (ambushing) if they're inactive.

One approach would be to start by quickly running a crankbait through open-water areas near cover. Then move closer to cover, quickly fishing a shallow-running crankbait, spinnerbait, or swimming worm or shad bait over timber. Finally, fish the deep zone with a deep-running crankbait, or a jig and eel or jigworm.

The near-cover zones may be used by bass in two different feeding attitudes, using two different feeding tactics. If you fish quickly through the two near-cover zones, you're likely to contact active stalking fish, but perhaps not neutral hovering fish. You might slow down, thoroughly fishing the two near-cover zones again, this time using presentations more appropriate for neutral fish.

Finally, it's time to probe inside. Bass holding there likely are neutral or inactive. Baits must move slowly and be presented very close to fish. Short casts or flips with plastic worms, jig-and-eel combos, or even livebait are appropriate.

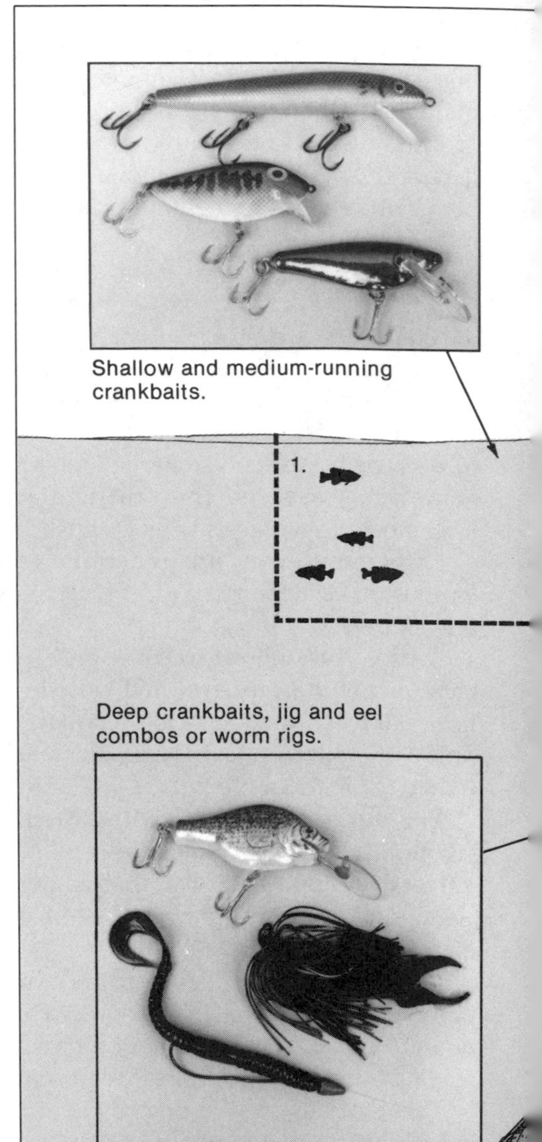

AGGREGATIONS

Bass were generally considered solitary until Buck Perry proclaimed them schooling fish. In tournaments, anglers often succeed or fail by how well they stay on a school that moves or changes feeding attitude.

Do bass school? Depends on how you define "school." Most often, school refers to a group of fish that live together and move in unison. Minnows live

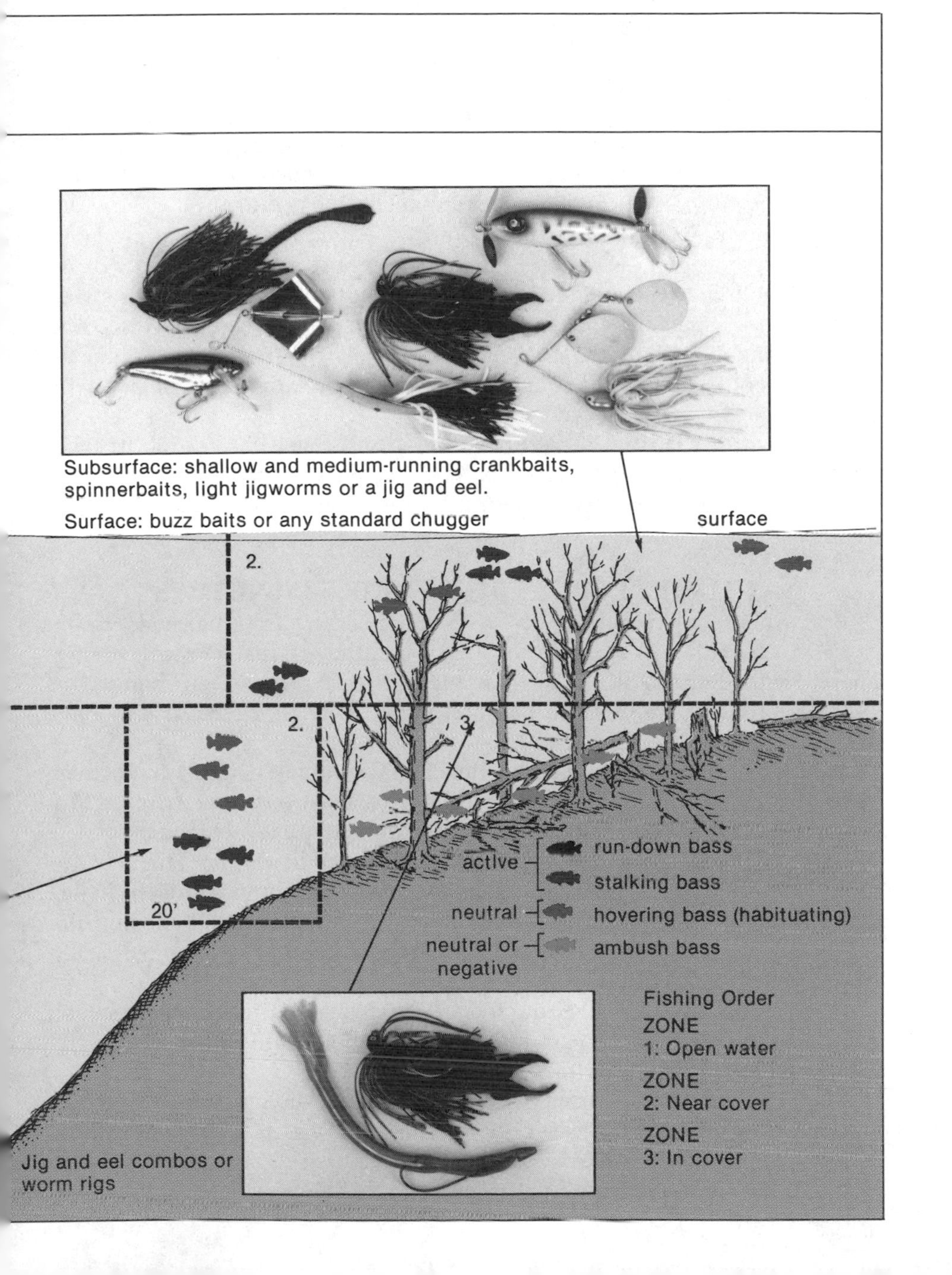

in schools. By huddling together in groups, they present a confusing target to predators. Predatory schooling fish may find or capture prey more efficiently than solitary species. Schooling also facilitates finding mates at spawning time.

Bass swim and feed together, but in groups more accurately called aggregations. They don't coordinate movements, but prowl an area at the same time. Their feeding efforts aren't coordinated, and they don't remain in the same group. Bass, therefore, don't exhibit true schooling behavior.

But actively feeding bass often group in certain areas because they're drawn by the same food source. Catch one bass and you'll often find other bass nearby.

Bass of similar size and ability also tend to be together. Small bass usually don't feed with 7-pounders, perhaps as a result of "pecking order." Small bass feed where they can; big bass command the most favorable feeding locations. Food preferences of large and small bass also differ.

When an angler finds bass on a point at 8 feet and a short time later catches fish at 18 feet, he's apt to think the "school" moved deeper. Recent studies cast doubt on that. Because bass must inflate and deflate their swim bladders to substantially change depth, a gradual process, they usually don't do so during short time periods. It's more likely that two aggregations at different depths shifted horizontally. The angler probably lost contact with one group and another moved into range.

Open-water feeding behavior seems the closest bass come to true schooling. Individual fish, however, don't coordinate movements. These "schools" are really bass aggregations feeding on the surface.

ACTIVITY LEVELS AND STRIKE WINDOWS

Bass exhibit varying activity levels. No animal can afford the energy drain of being constantly alert; so most of the time they're inactive, conserving energy by holding in cover. They become active only when their chances for successful feeding are highest. Bass feeding actively are aggressive, mobile, and very aware.

We refer to bass activity levels as inactive (negative), neutral, and active. Active bass are very catchable, while inactive bass are very unresponsive. To be successful, your presentation must match the activity level of the fish.

The activity level of a bass determines the size of his "strike window" or strike zone—the distance a bass will move to take food. A lure must be in the strike window to draw a strike. Compare a strike window to a balloon, with the bass's snout tucked in one end. The size of the balloon changes with changing activity levels.

Inactive fish often are digesting food. Cold fronts or other environmental conditions may also make bass inactive. They hold tight to cover, scarcely move, and are unresponsive even to nearby prey.

The strike window of an inactive bass is small. A lure might have to move slowly within a foot of the bass's nose to draw a strike. Heavy cover further reduces the size of the strike window of inactive bass because vision may be blocked. The less active a bass is, the closer and slower you must present a lure to draw a strike.

For inactive bass, use jigs, grubs, worms, or other plastics. Stick to smaller lures in neutral colors (black, brown, or smoke). Fish the lure slowly in cover, quickly bringing it back to the boat when it reaches the edge of cover.

STRIKE WINDOWS

Strike Window Size for Active Bass

The strike windows of active bass change shape and dimension as bass swim faster. With greater speed, bass gain forward range, but lose ability to turn to either side. A bass at cruising speed extends its forward range to about 6 feet. One dashing after prey may be able to capture prey or lures that come within its window at ranges of more than 10 feet.

These windows are, however, less accurate predicators of the ability of bass to catch prey than windows of stationary bass. As the speed of the bass increases, the importance of the relative speed and direction of the preyfish increases.

The windows are relatively realistic for prey moving in the same general direction as bass, but prey moving away from the track of bass,

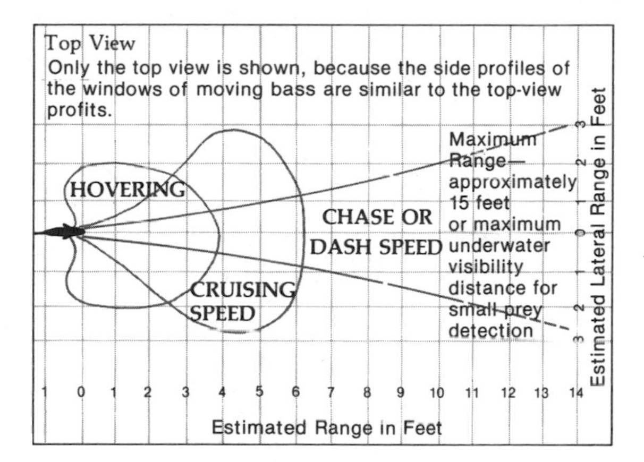

particularly those moving away and toward the rear of bass, may not be vulnerable even though they're briefly in the window. If a preyfish (or lure) moves out of the window before a moving bass reaches it, it is uncatchable and ignored.

As a result, bass typically move at chase speed only when they're able to position behind a fleeing prey. When behind such a baitfish (or lure), a bass is likely to catch it. Lures crossing the window of rapidly moving bass are likely to be ignored unless they move into the narrow stem of the window within about 3 feet of the bass. The most effective lure presentation to chasing bass is to move the lure in the same direction, parallel to the course of the bass, and into the window. This gives bass a vulnerable target.

Strike Window Size for Hovering Bass

In front and around the snout of each bass is a space called a strike window. A bass can be reasonably sure of a successful attack on preyfish (or lures) that move into this window.

The size of the window varies with how active bass are. Inactive bass have a tiny window, neutral bass have a larger window, and active bass have an even greater range. To catch a bass, present a lure within a window, or tempt a bass to move so the lure is in the window.

While no one has measured the striking limits of wild bass, the windows are estimates of the average ability of hovering bass to catch average preyfish. Obviously, window shapes vary, based on the willingness and ability of individual bass to turn to prey, accelerate, and chase it.

Bass of different sizes also have different abilities to turn and to accelerate. Plus, they also have different learning experiences with various prey species that tend to modify their maximum ranges and vulnerability estimates for each prey. Moreover, the direction of movement of prey toward or away from a bass can modify the range bass can attack at successfully.

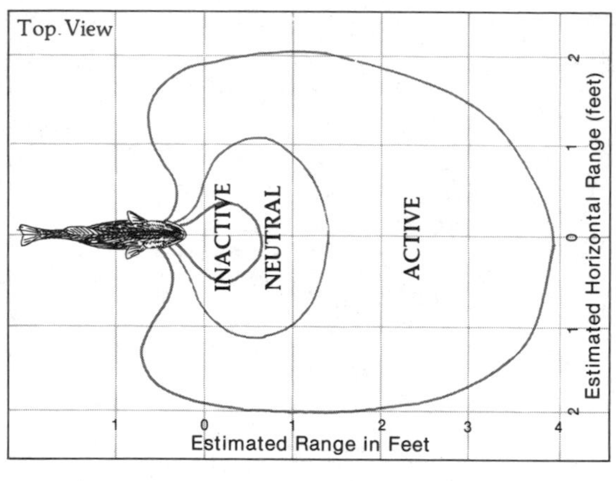

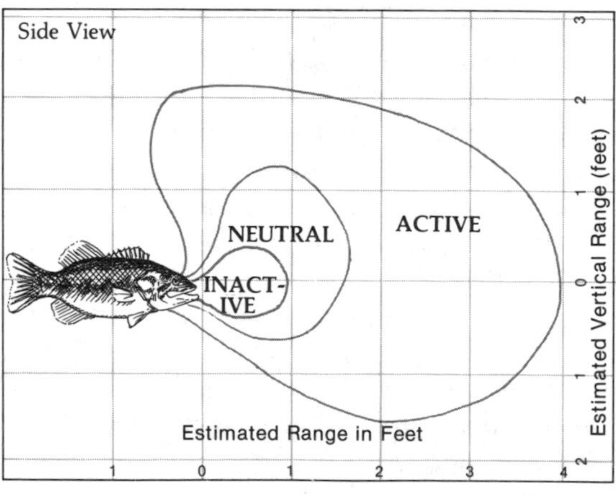

Flipping is an ideal presentation for accurately dropping lures in cover where inactive bass often hold. Expect light strikes. Live bait may also be effective on inactive bass. But again, the emphasis must be on placing the bait within the strike windows.

Bass are neutral most of the time. Their strike windows are larger than strike windows of inactive bass. They're not hunting, but will strike vulnerable looking prey nearby. They may also move a short distance to investigate a possible food item. The attack of a neutral bass is usually short and slow, though they may slowly swim off with soft baits.

'Bout as cold as it gets. And they still bite!

Neutral bass strike a variety of bass lures, but lures that work well on a slow retrieve are most effective. Present these lures so they look disabled or weak. Neutral or natural colors are a good bet in clear water; brighter colors in dirty water.

Try spinnerbaits and crankbaits fished slowly or with erratic pauses on neutral bass. Fish worms and jigs with a lift-drop technique for bass holding just off bottom. In high-percentage areas, dead sticking—letting lures lie on the bottom—or retrieving with long pauses often produce bites from neutral bass.

Bass feed actively only for short periods. They cruise in small groups just outside cover, stopping periodically to look for vulnerable prey. A splash doesn't spook them; indeed, they may move to check it out. Active bass compete with each other to attack your lure, sometimes leading to the two-bass-on-one-lure phenomenon.

Active bass have the largest strike windows. They may dash 12 feet to grab prey or stalk close for a short-range attack. They're usually most active at dawn and dusk, but also feed at other times, particularly when they're in deeper water.

For active bass try buzzbaits, fast-moving topwaters, or quickly retrieved spinnerbaits and crankbaits. Move quickly and retrieve quickly to show your bait to as many fish as possible.

Several environmental factors affect the size of the strike window:

- Water clarity. Clear water generally enlarges strike windows because bass can see farther.
- Shade, at least in shallow water, tends to enlarge strike windows. Bright sunlight shrinks them.

• Cold water generally shrinks strike windows.

• Warm, stable weather expands strike windows. Just before a weather front hits, strike windows are often large. A cold front shrinks strike windows.

• Fishing pressure shrinks strike windows, making bass more difficult to catch.

Levels of activity and the resulting size of strike windows determine how close you must present a lure to bass and how lifelike the lure must appear. Large strike zones call for rapid horizontal-moving presentations. Small strike zones demand slower, more vertical-moving presentations.

The largemouth bass is a unique package of abilities. And it's understanding those abilities in relation to the variety of fishing approaches at your disposal that lets you pick the right spot at the right time to fish the right bait just right—success!

Chapter 5

THE WORLD OF LARGEMOUTH BASS

Mr. Adaptable—At Home in Many Environments

Largemouth bass live in pits, ponds, impoundments, rivers, estuaries, and natural lakes. They do best when these environments offer moderately clear, moderately warm water with plenty of oxygen.

The northern edge of largemouth bass distribution is limited by their need for warm water in summer and about a four-month growing season. The southern limit of their distribution seems determined mainly by geographic barriers. They have, of course, been stocked into suitable waters in Europe and Asia. Wherever bass live, however, cover such as weeds and wood enhances the success of their populations.

Bass require good-quality water. Salty, very dingy, acidic, or stagnant water limits spawning success and kills fish. Yet largemouth bass are surprisingly resilient.

Bass are, for example, moderately tolerant of saltwater, as some other sunfish species are. They live in salt concentrations up to 10 parts per thousand, one-third the strength of seawater. Particularly in fall, brackish estuaries along the Gulf and Atlantic coasts offer some of the nation's best bass fishing. Spring runoff brings fresh water, making lower sections of estuaries hospitable to bass. Later they retreat upstream as spring runoff subsides, bringing saltwater into estuaries.

Bass do best in moderately clear water because they are sight feeders. Reproduction suffers in very dingy water, probably because silt smothers eggs. Yet lakes with extremely clear water rarely are fertile enough to support many bass. They need an environment full of life: floating aquatic plants (phytoplankton); emergent and submergent weeds; tiny animals called zooplankton; myriad minnows and small fish that feed on them; and finally, a thriving succession of progressively larger fish, both predators and prey.

Largemouth bass also tolerate acidic water better than many other species. Although normal pH ranges from 6.5 to 8, bass in some black-water streams in the Southeast have adapted to pH levels from 5.5 to 6.5. High acidity (low pH) or high alkalinity (high pH) can damage gills and other sensitive membranes. Water with pH under 4 or over 10 is toxic.

Most fish, including bass, require plenty of dissolved oxygen. Oxygen content from 5 parts per million (ppm) to 10 ppm is ideal for largemouths. While they can survive briefly in water with oxygen levels of 2 ppm or 3 ppm, growth is substantially inhibited. Larger bass typically require higher oxygen levels than juveniles.

The oxygen content of a body of water fluctuates daily and seasonally. Levels often drop at night and rise throughout the day, particularly where aquatic plants, algae, and phytoplankton (tiny floating plants) abound. Shallow ponds in the South often suffer fish kills at night when oxygen levels drop too low. Shallow lakes and ponds in the North "freeze out" in winter when oxygen levels drop too low. In lakes and reservoirs that stratify thermally and chemically, the hypolimnion (deep, cool section below the thermocline) typically holds insufficient oxygen for bass to survive.

Finally, pesticides and other pollutants can kill bass or inhibit feeding, spawning, and other activities, in addition to making the fish unsafe to eat. Chemicals like hydrogen sulfate and ammonia, which sometimes occur naturally, can also impair growth and cause mortality. Not surprisingly, young fish are more sensitive than adults to toxic chemicals. Sensitivity to chemicals also depends on water quality—temperature, oxygen, pH, and carbon dioxide.

LAKE CLASSIFICATION

The In-Fisherman "lake classification system" ranks bodies of water according to one indication of their trophic or productive state—how old

Largemouth Bass Water Quality Needs

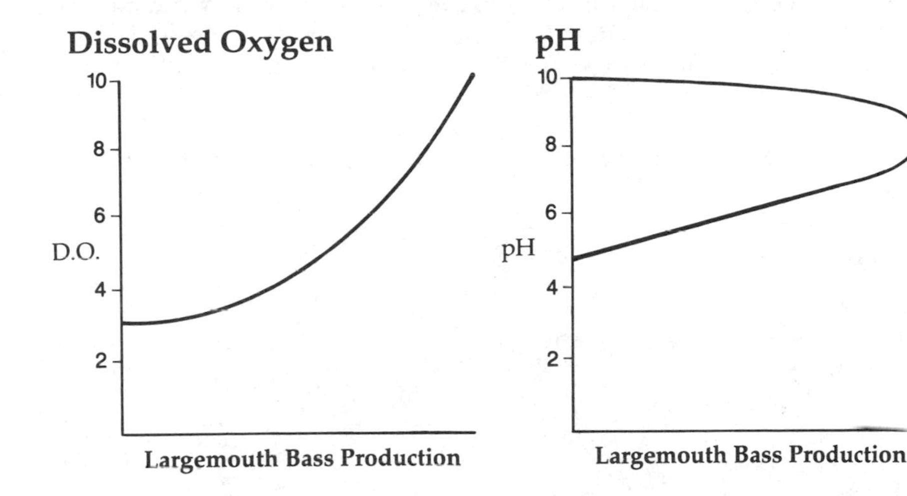

Dissolved oxygen probably is almost as widely studied an environmental parameter as temperature. Bass do best when dissolved oxygen concentrations are over 6 parts per million (mg/l). When dissolved oxygen drops to 3 mg/l, bass are stressed, growth slows, and they more likely contract diseases. Below 2 mg/l, bass and other species often rise to the surface to breathe air. In lab studies, though, bass have survived dissolved oxygen levels slightly below 1 mg/l for short periods of time.

The measure of hydrogen ion concentration, termed pH, is critical for maintaining chemical balance within a bass' body. Negative effects on fish populations of low pH (acidic water) from acid rain and other causes have been documented. High altitude northern ponds and rocky streams that aren't customary bass habitat are most susceptible to acidification. Ranges of 6.5 pH to 8.5 pH seem best for bass. Populations suffer as alkalinity increases above 9.5 pH or acidity increases (drops) below 5.5 pH.

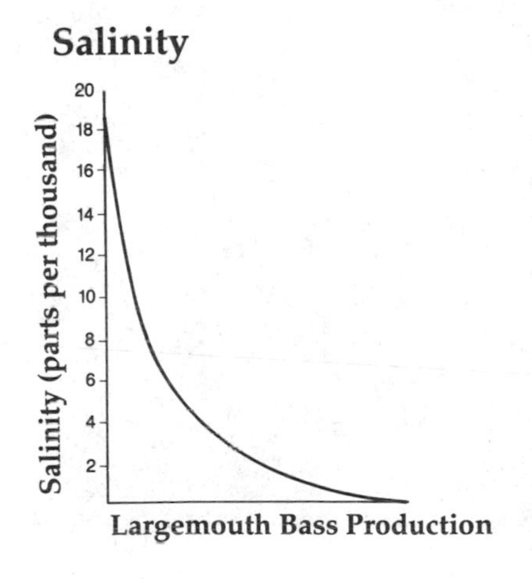

Largemouth bass are typically freshwater fish. In eastern rivers like the Connecticut, James, and Hudson, bass populations dwindle as water downstream becomes increasingly brackish. Yet in Louisiana bayous and other estuaries, largemouth bass have been collected in salinities over 10 parts per thousand, one-third the strength of seawater. Bass spawning ceases at salinities greater than 4 parts per thousand, and in these situations, growth is slow.

they are. We classify waters from young to old based on recognizable physical features, not on chemical measurements.

The youngest lakes (oligotrophic) are extremely clear, rock bound, and weedless—infertile. The oldest (eutrophic) have silty bottoms and heavy microscopic plantgrowth—very fertile. Mesotrophic waters fall between

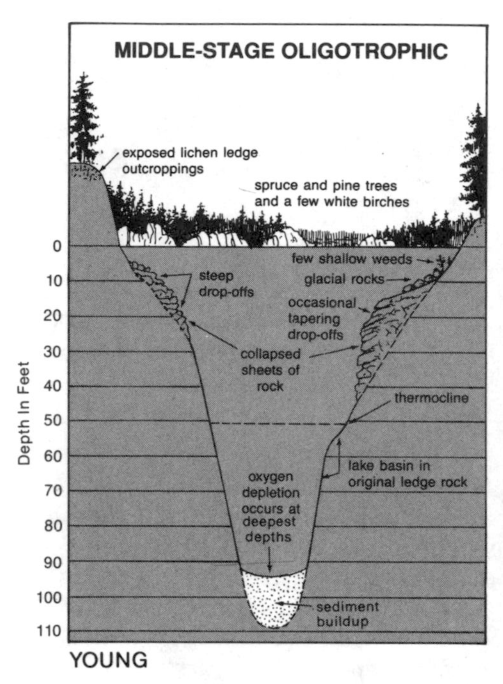

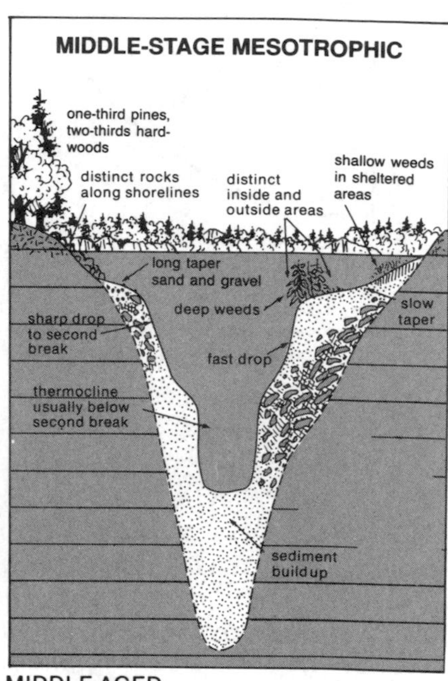

MIDDLE-STAGE EUTROPHIC

sparse hardwoods, open farmlands

shorelines have gradual slopes

very heavy weeds all through shallows no major structures

medium reeds and lily pads

weeds to 12 ft.

sand and muck

hard bottom

no thermocline

muck

sediment buildup

Depth In Feet

0 10 20 30 40 50 60 70 80 90 100 110

OLD

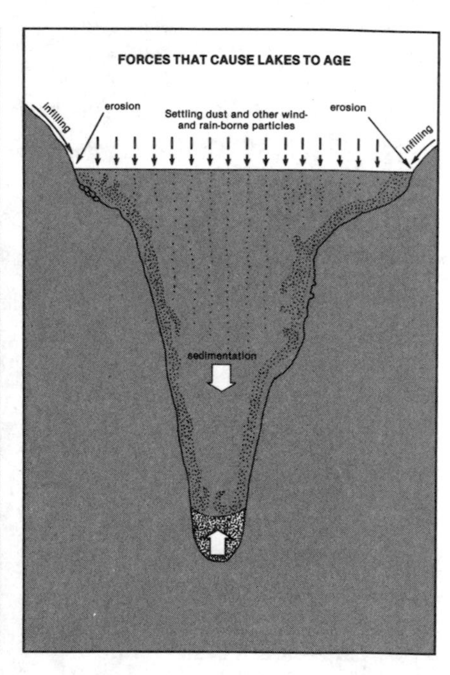

oligotrophic and eutrophic and are moderately clear, moderately fertile, and contain submergent and often emergent weeds.

Lakes age naturally over eons. Initial stages of lake aging and physical changes that result may take place over thousands of years. Later, aging processes accelerate, and the natural aging process is further accelerated by human activity, a process called "cultural eutrophication."

Lake structure, depth, water color, weedgrowth, and fish species change dramatically as a lake ages. Geologically young lakes (oligotrophic) are typically deep with well-oxygenated water in their hypolimnion (the deep, cold zone below the thermocline) during summer. Increased living and dead organic matter in mesotrophic lakes depletes oxygen as the matter decays, resulting in oxygen-poor hypolimnions.

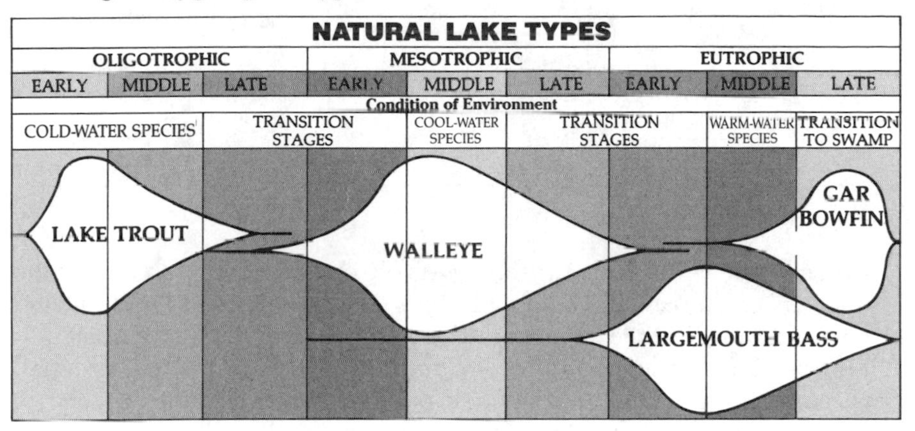

Bass thrive in early stage eutrophic lakes, but can survive and reproduce in early stage mesotrophic lakes with weedy bays (the primary focus of bass activity), as well as at the opposite extreme, middle-stage eutrophic lakes. An ideal bass lake is more fertile and weedy than classic walleye water, but not as shallow, swampy, and turbid as a fertile bullhead pond. Some large mesotrophic or oligotrophic lakes contain eutrophic bays—sections where largemouths are abundant.

RESERVOIR CLASSIFICATION

The In-Fisherman reservoir (impoundment) classification system is based on the topography of the impounded basin. Impoundments are set in geological landforms that determine the aquatic environment. Impoundments fall into 6 broad categories: (1) canyon; (2) highland; (3) plateau; (4) hill-land; (5) flatland; and (6) lowland (wetland). Largemouth bass exist in each reservoir type.

The reason for building a reservoir determines its form and function. Its purpose—flood control, electrical generation, water supply, pumped storage, or recreational use—determines a reservoir's size, shape, geographical and geological location, flow rates, and other important characteristics. Physical features then limit type and abundance of fish that can live in it.

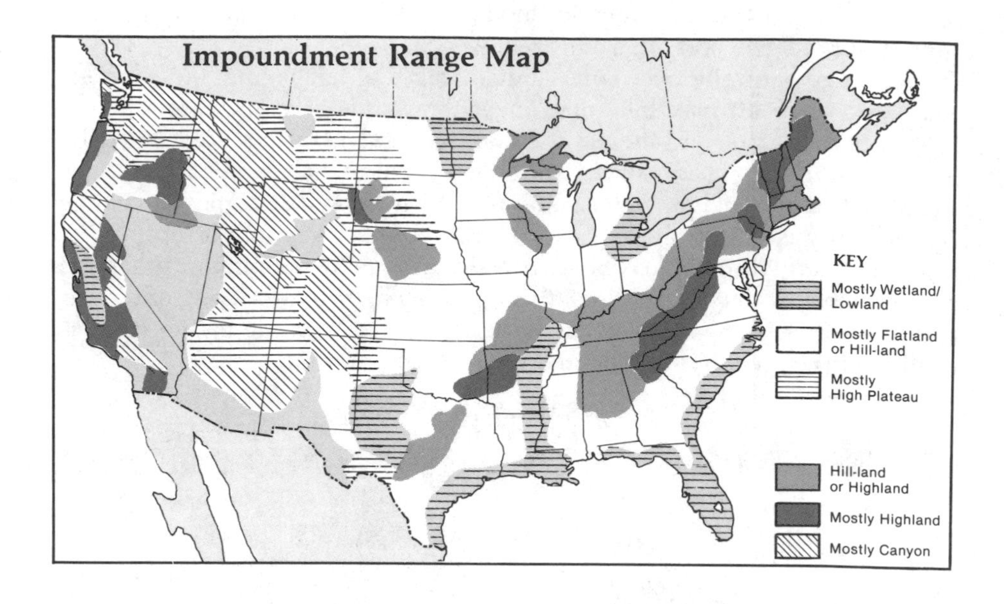

While shape is the basis for this reservoir classification system, fertility also affects the success of largemouth bass. Flooded lowland and flatland rivers usually have fertile floodplains that add to a reservoir's productivity.

Nutrients foster growth of phytoplankton that are grazed by small crustaceans (zooplankton) that swim through the water column. Young fish and adults of some species that are important food for largemouth bass (sunfish and shad) prey on zooplankton. This prey base determines predator abundance and size.

Farms in the watershed—the runoff area around the reservoir—add nutrients from fertilizers. Upstream reservoirs, lawn cultivation, sewage treatment facilities, and other types of urban runoff affect productivity and often add pollutants that limit fish production or make fish unsafe to eat.

Water color in reservoirs varies from clear to chocolate pudding. Rainwater flowing over loose soil adds turbidity that temporarily creates murky water; abundant phytoplankton adds a green tint. Water clarity as well as available nutrients and bottom content determine extent of weedgrowth, a critical location factor for largemouth bass.

Even though canyon and highland reservoirs are infertile and often lack adequate cover, largemouth bass survive in them. They're most at home, however, in fertile lowland, hill-land, and flatland reservoirs that contain abundant and diverse cover.

The success of largemouths in reservoirs presents a confusing impression of their habitat preferences. In newly flooded impoundments, bass use timber and brush, the best available cover. Many fishermen assume, therefore, that bass prefer such cover. Yet as the reservoirs created in the 1950s and 1960s aged and extensive weedbeds appeared, largemouths generally abandoned deteriorating brush and timber for these weeds, a more natural habitat.

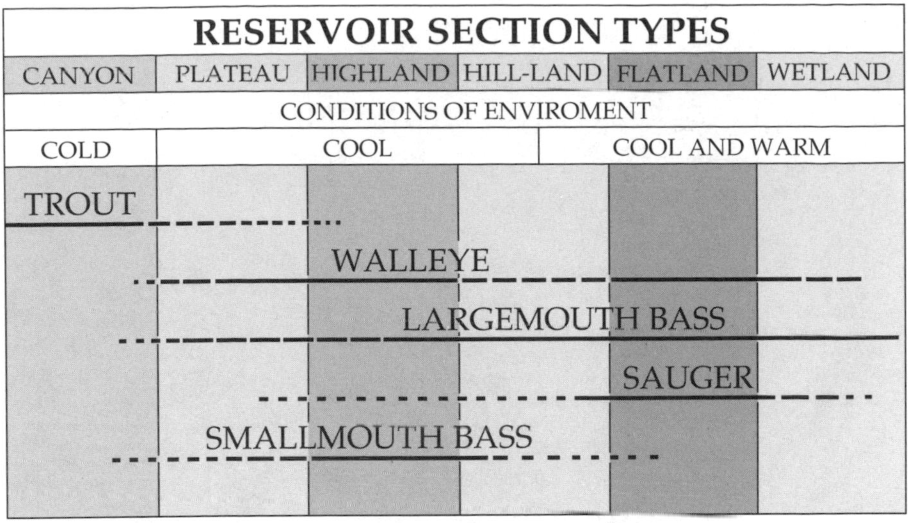

RESERVOIR SECTION TYPES					
CANYON	PLATEAU	HIGHLAND	HILL-LAND	FLATLAND	WETLAND
CONDITIONS OF ENVIROMENT					
COLD	COOL			COOL AND WARM	

TROUT

WALLEYE

LARGEMOUTH BASS

SAUGER

SMALLMOUTH BASS

Due to the wide geographic distribution of the various reservoir types, it's difficult to generalize which fish species may be present. For example, a shallow wetland impoundment located in the North may contain walleyes and only a few largemouth bass. A wetland reservoir located in the deep South, in contrast, won't contain walleyes, but could have lots of big bass.

The geographic area of a reservoir has a direct bearing on the fishery. In general, reservoirs in the North provide a cooler environment than those in the South.

Largemouth bass adaptability is demonstrated by their presence and abundance in all reservoir types.

RIVER CLASSIFICATION

In-Fisherman classifies rivers as "young," "middle-aged," and "old." These terms describe the condition of the landscape through which the river passes more than the precise age of the river.

Young rivers race down rocky hills. As they mature, their flow rate declines and they meander as they pass through softer soil. Old rivers widen across broad floodplains and may finally meet the ocean in a wide, shallow delta.

Erosion or siltation is a major factor in river aging. In general, the farther a river flows, the more sediment is added. Watershed type and the aging process vary along sections of the same river. In navigable rivers like the Mississippi, pools provide a convenient delineation of river stretches.

Largemouths in rivers usually live in sloughs, oxbows, and backwaters with little or no discernible current. These habitats typically occur in middle-age and older river sections. During winter and at spawning time, they seek water without current. In summer, they often hold near objects like boulders or logs adjacent to current. This cover near current provides shelter from current, yet the bass are close to food the current delivers.

CANYON IMPOUNDMENT

Examples: Lake Powell, AZ/UT; Lake Havasu, AZ/CA; Lake Mead, NV/AZ; Flaming Gorge, WY/UT.

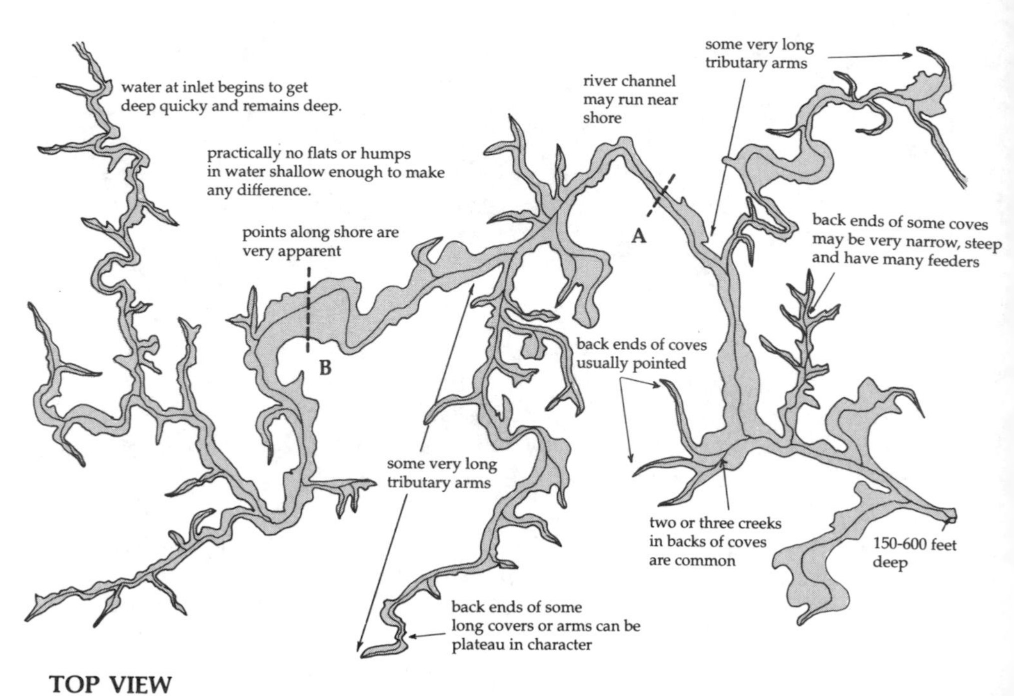

TOP VIEW

CROSS-SECTIONS

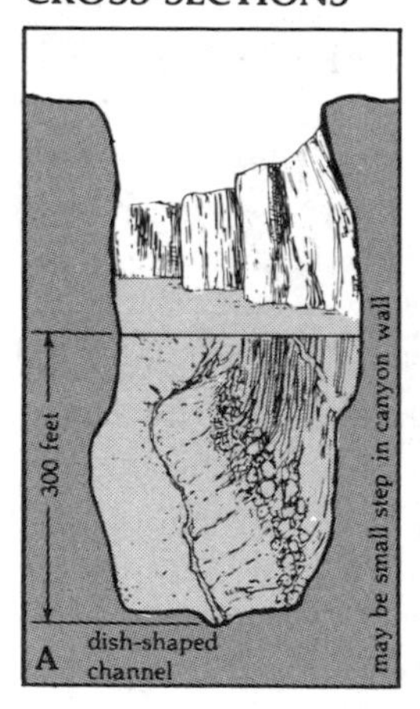

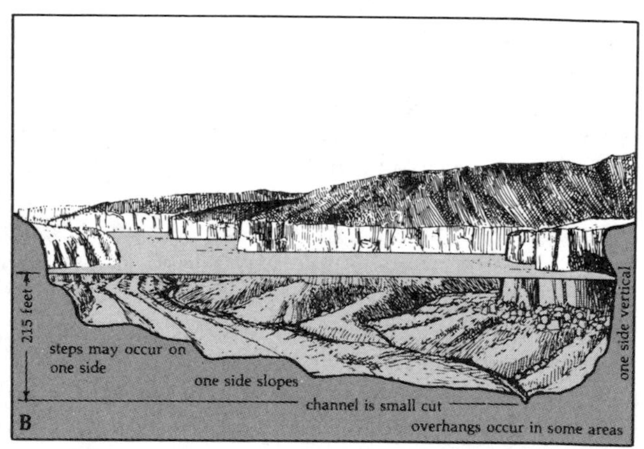

PLATEAU IMPOUNDMENT

Examples: Lake Meredith, TX; Roosevelt, AZ; Clear, CA; Ft. Peck, MT; Garrison, ND; Banks, WA.

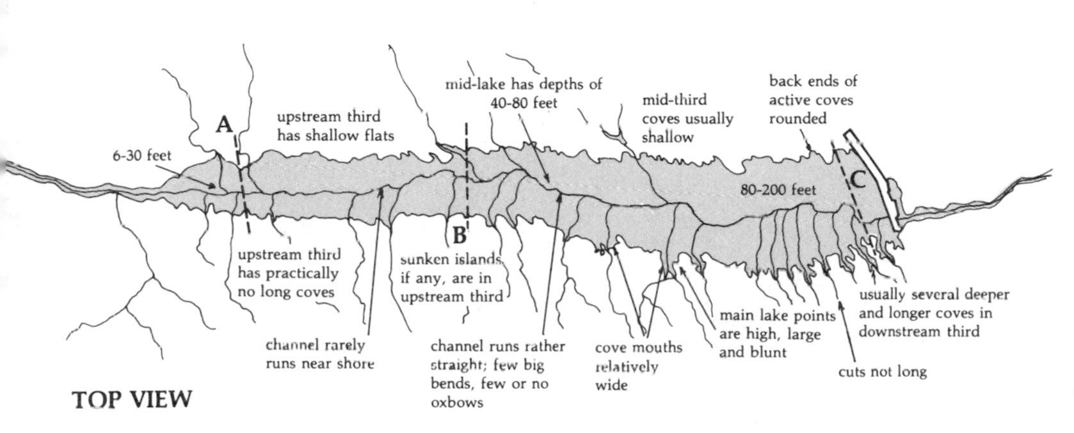

CROSS-SECTIONS

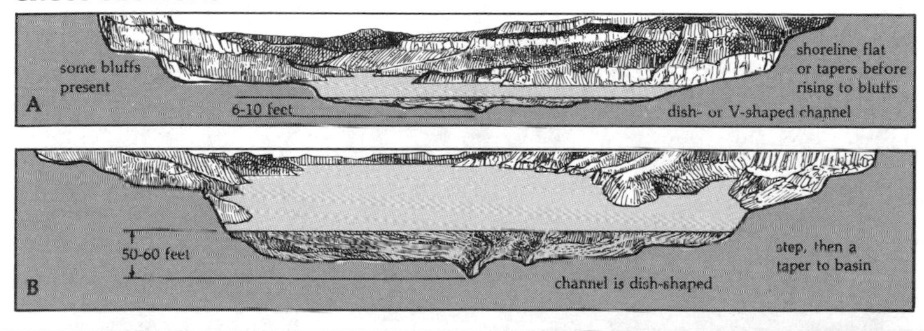

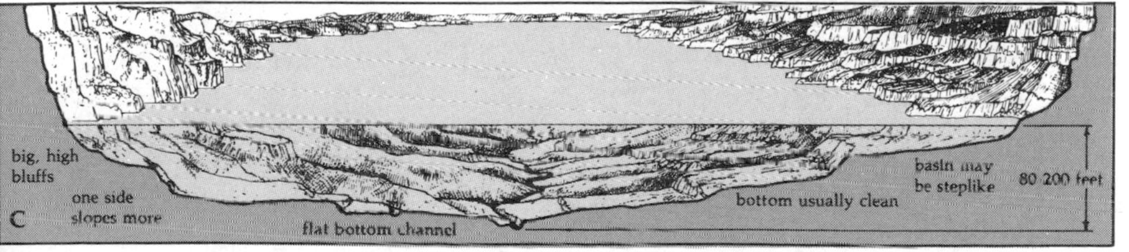

HIGHLAND IMPOUNDMENT

Examples: Bull Shoals, AR/MO; Dale Hollow, TN; Broken Bow, OK; Sidney Lanier, GA; Don Pedro, CA; Hopatcong, NJ; Amistad, TX.

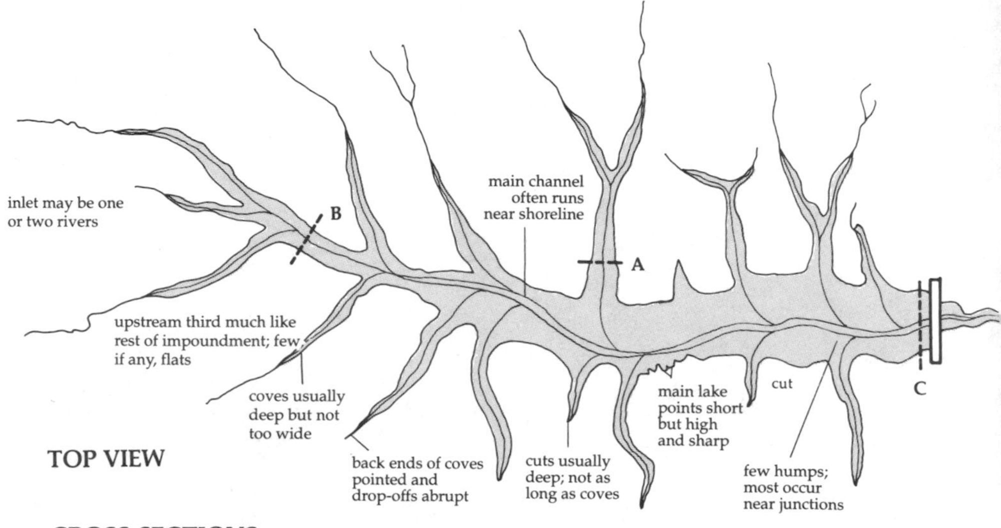

TOP VIEW

CROSS-SECTIONS

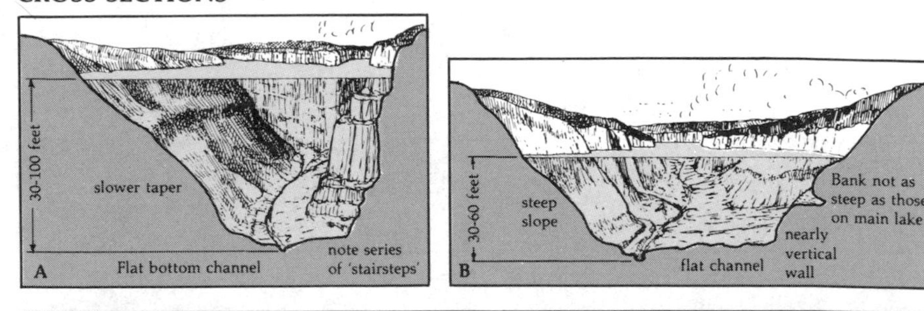

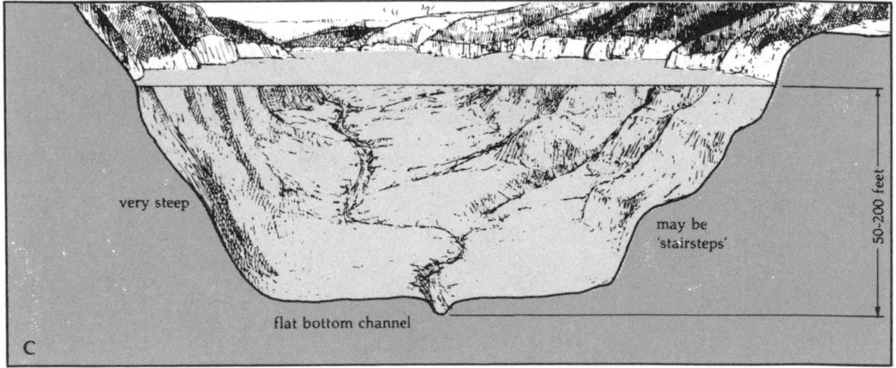

HILL-LAND IMPOUNDMENT

Examples: Lake Shelbyville, IL; Toledo Bend, LA/TX; Percy Priest, TN; D'Arbonne, LA; Kinzua Reservoir, PA; Council Grove Reservoir, KS.

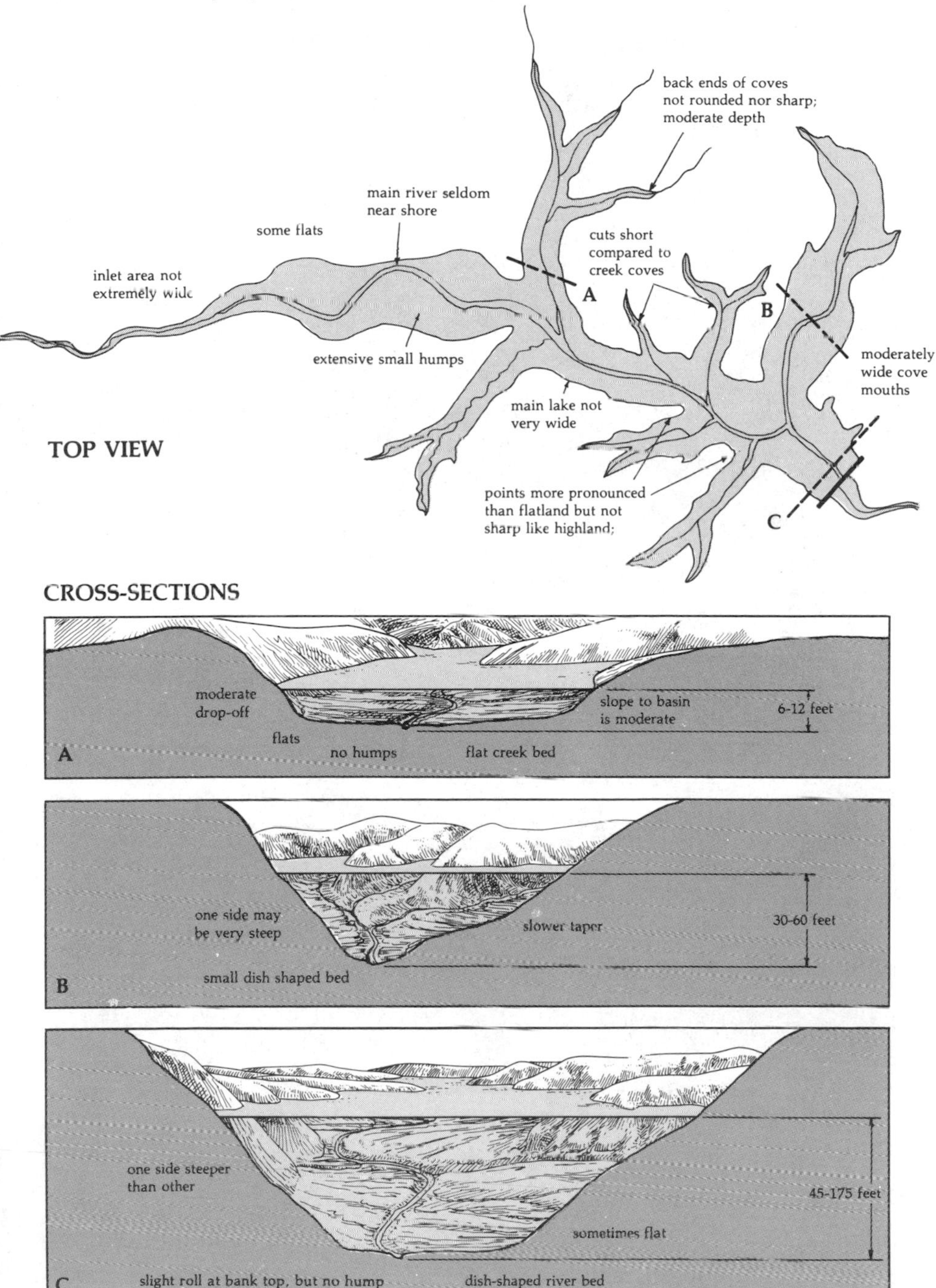

FLATLAND IMPOUNDMENT

Examples: Kentucky Lake, KY/TN; Santee Cooper, SC; Ross Barnett, MS; Greenwood, NJ/NY; Carlyle, IL; Lake Seminole, FL/GA; Castle Rock, WI.

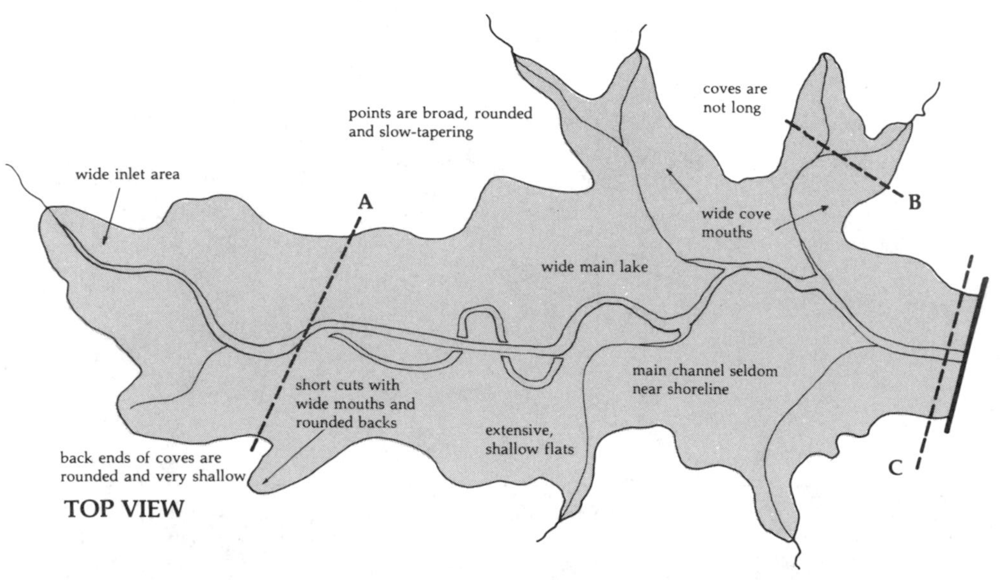

CROSS-SECTIONS

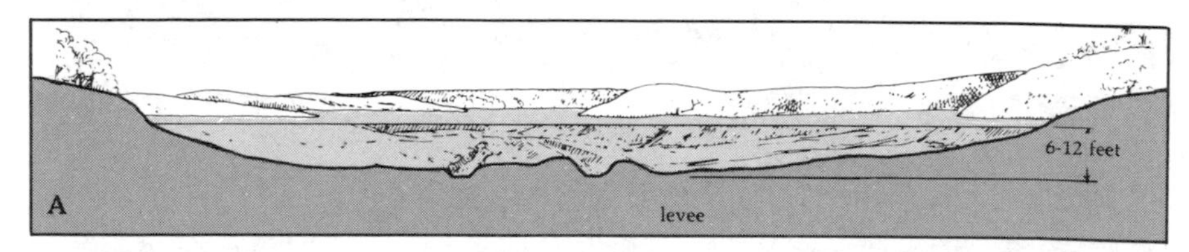

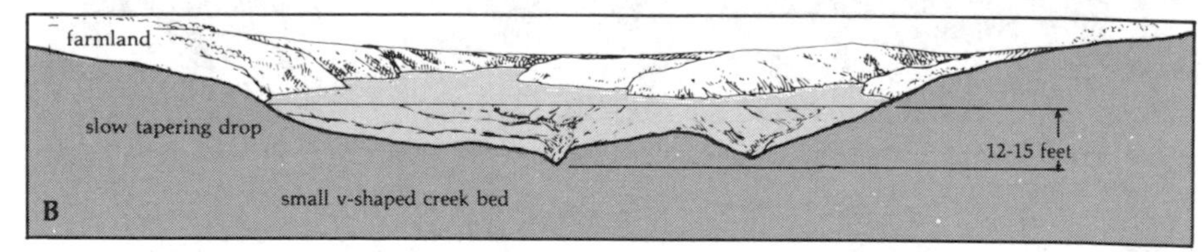

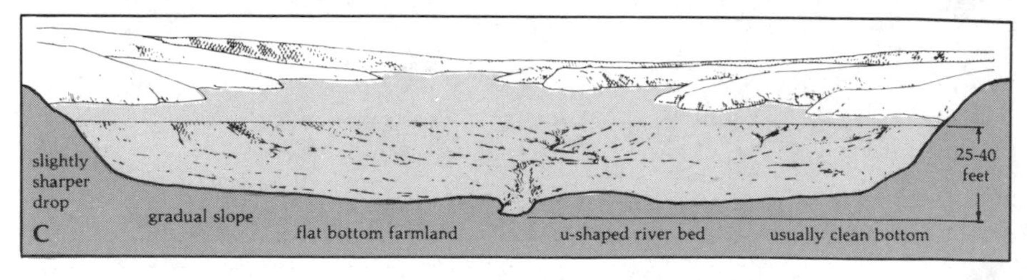

LOWLAND/WETLAND IMPOUNDMENT

Examples: Chippewa Flowage, WI; Bond Falls, MI; Black Bayou, LA; Taylor Creek, FL.

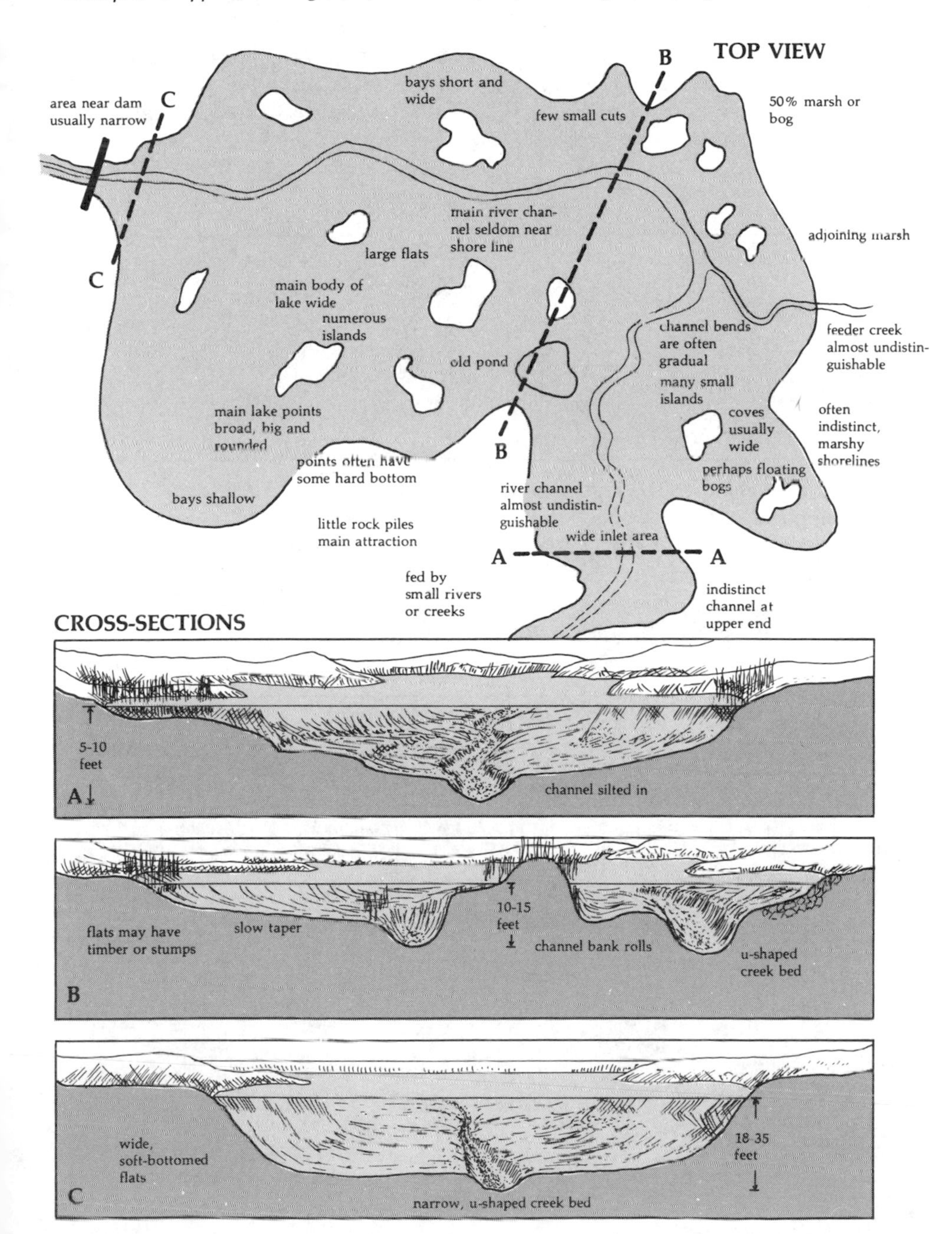

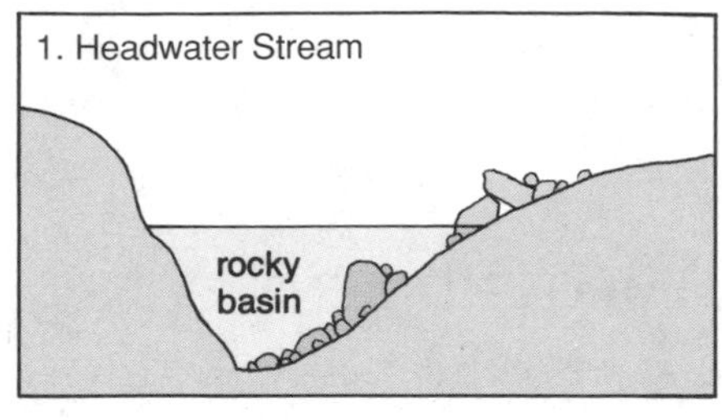

Bottom rocky; cool and clear water; shallow depth; narrow width; steep gradient; fast current; no aquatic vegetation. No largemouth bass habitat; smallmouths in lower reaches.

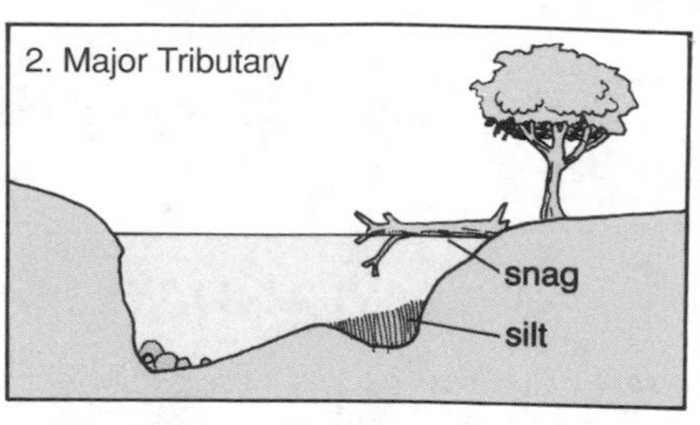

Bottom variable; deeper pools common; warmer and more turbid water, especially after rain; gradient and flow rate reduced; typical riffle-pool-run sequence. Fair largemouth habitat.

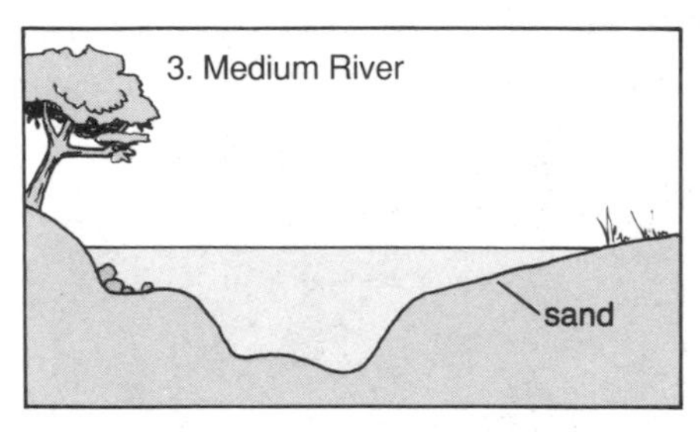

Bottom variable; riffle-pool-run sequence, but not well defined; water usually murky and warm; aquatic vegetation may be present on shallow banks; tributaries common. Good smallmouth habitat; fair for largemouths.

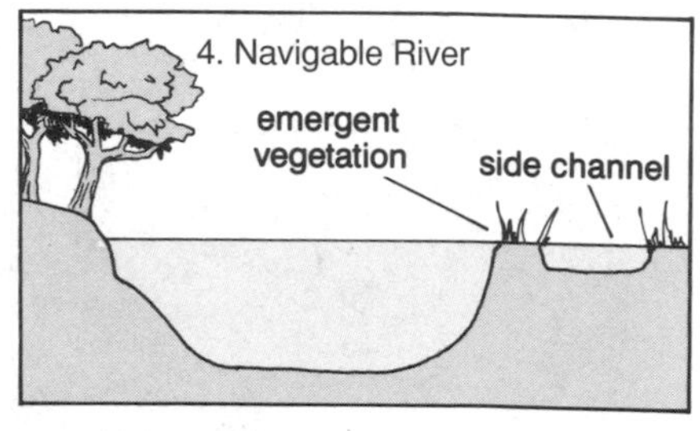

Moderate current; channel complex possibly dredged; aquatic vegetation locally abundant; soft bottom; murky, warm water. Largemouth bass abundant in backwaters.

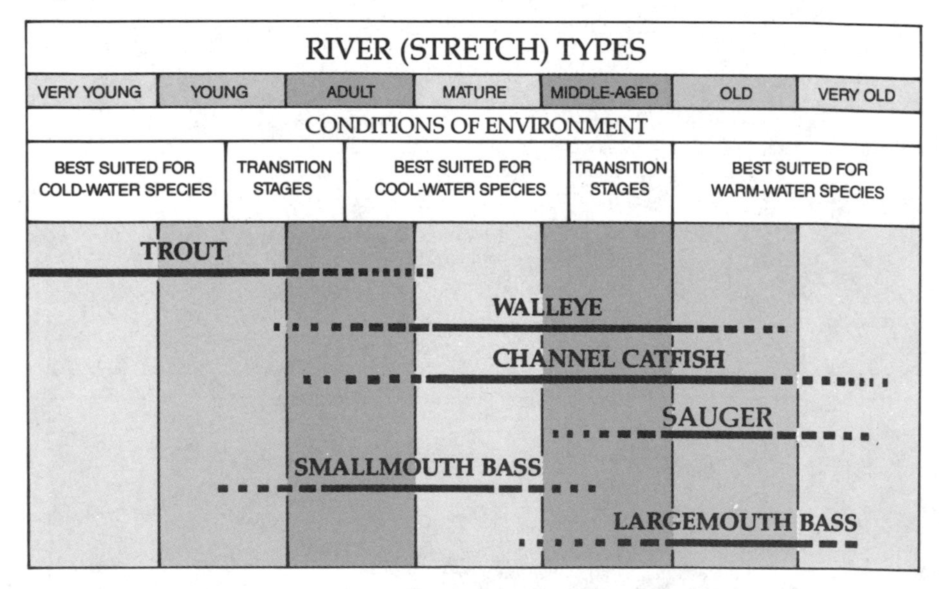

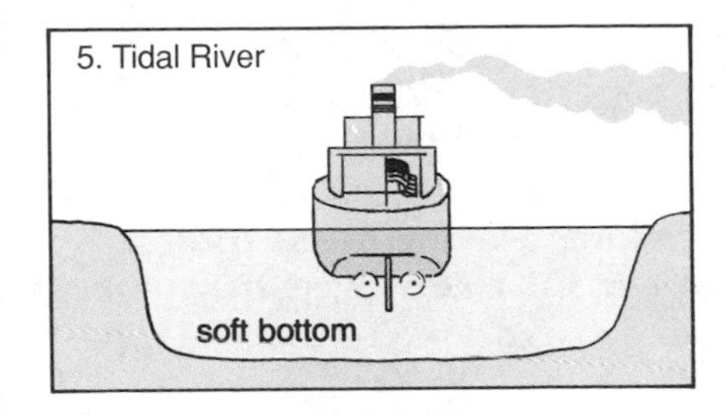

Water subject to tidal influence; salinity varies with location, tide, and rainfall. Largemouths inhabit backwater ponds, feeder creeks, and river structure, but move seasonally in response to flow and salinity.

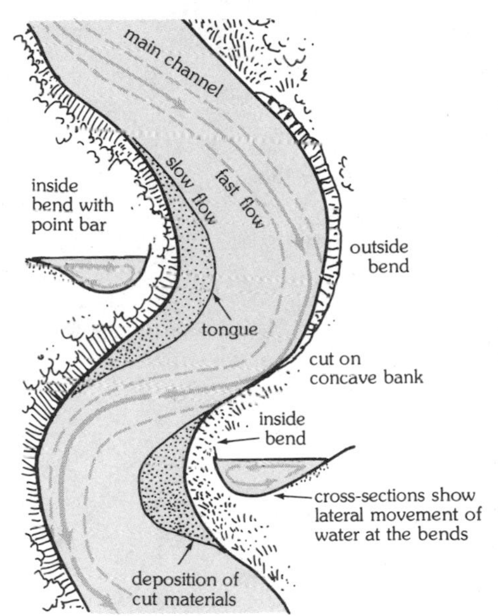

The force of water constantly changes a river. River courses change, forming adjacent flood plains. A river stretch without an extensive adjoining flood plain is stable or geologically very young. Water in time will chew away granite, dissolve iron, and move mountains!

In streams with heavy current, water action wears away the outside bend and deposits materials on the inside bend where current is less heavy. Notice how current has created a tongue-like structure. The deepest part of any river stretch is always the outide bend.

SMALL WATERS

A variety of small waters provide a large proportion of total bass habitat and fishing opportunities in the United States. Bass are commonly stocked in farm ponds ranging in size from one to 100 acres. Bass in ponds do double service: They're a sportfish and a predator that controls populations of bluegills or other sunfish to prevent stunting.

Largemouth bass spawn well in ponds, so only an introductory stocking is usually necessary. Cover options in ponds are generally limited, making bass easy to locate. Where fishing pressure is light, pond bass are often aggressive and amazingly easy to catch.

Proper pond management requires that harvest be limited so bass can fulfill their predatory role—prevent panfish overpopulation. Ponds are fascinating, but require a lot of work to maintain good fishing.

In mining areas, pits often fill with rainwater or spring water when mining operations cease. Where water chemistry is suitable, bass and many other species thrive. Pits are typically deep and clear, so their productivity

TYPES OF BASS PONDS

Pond structure and function (morphometry) are important in determining fish population characteristics and behavior. The size and type of watershed (the area around a pond that brings runoff to it) determine water level and clarity, productivity, flow-through, and water-quality characteristics like pH and dissolved oxygen.

Pond management—fertilization, stocking, feeding, weed control, drawdowns—affects the number and size of fish and the way they use structural elements. Most ponds are one of 3 basic types:

DUG POND

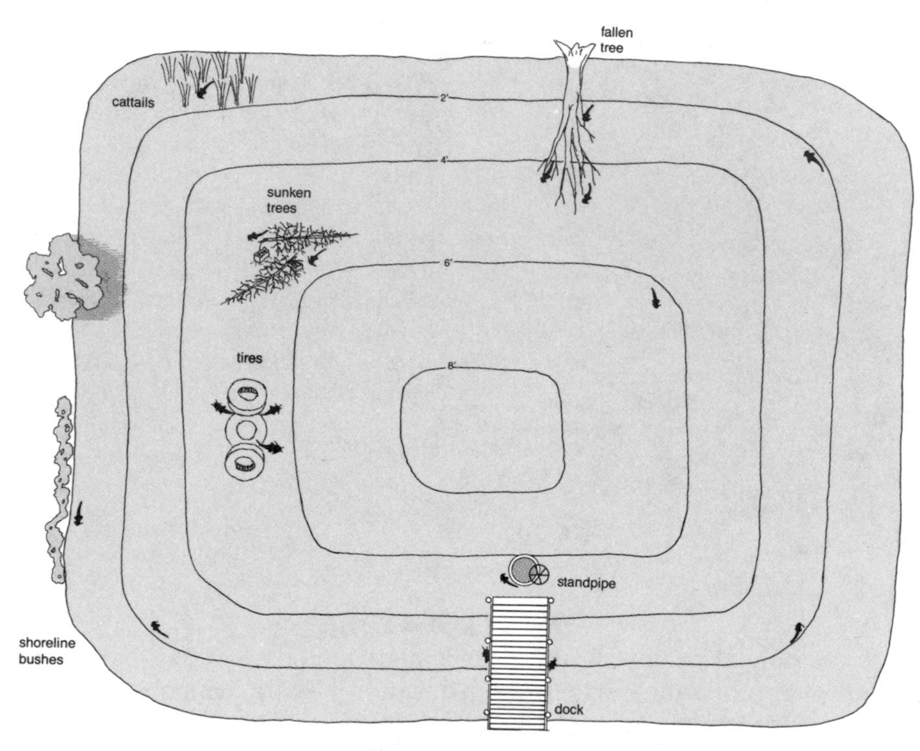

Farm ponds with shallow, featureless basins are often dug with earth-moving equipment. Runoff usually keeps them full, but supplemental pumping may be necessary during dry periods.

Dug ponds are generally less than 5 acres, but good management can make them productive for bluegills, largemouth bass, and channel catfish. Active bass roam shallow banks. They hold near cover like fallen trees, docks, and weedbeds, or in shoreline shade.

Corners and depth breaks attract bass when better cover is scarce. During summer, the deepest areas lack oxygen, so fish avoid them despite the cooler water. When water is pumped into a pond, preyfish and bass often are attracted to the flow.

BUILT POND

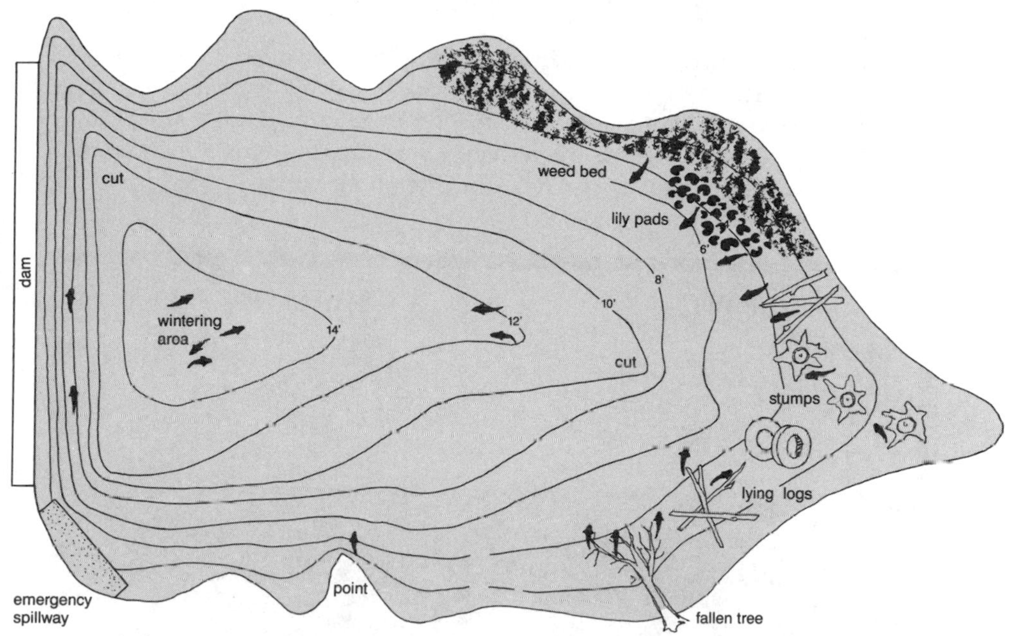

A dam across a low area often creates a pond as the dam backs up runoff. Ponds of up to 100 acres can form.

The area near the dam is deepest. Bass winter there and move toward shallow areas in spring. Cuts, points, and flats with wood hold spring bass. As the spawn approaches, bass move to wind-protected bays where males sweep circular nests on harder bottoms.

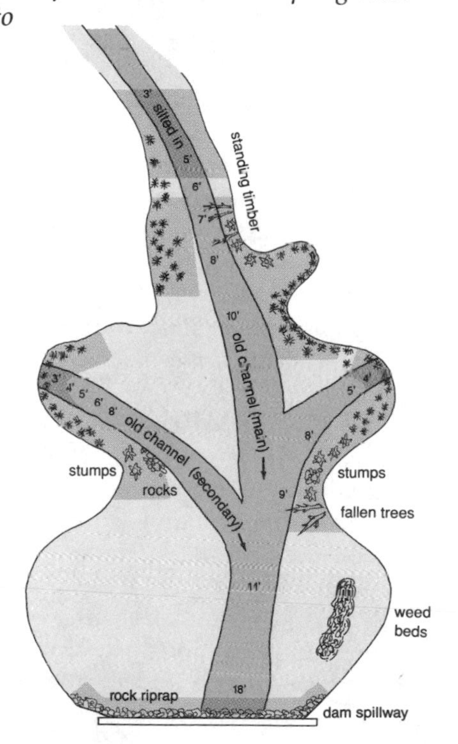

DAMMED CREEK

Creeks are dammed for irrigation and fishing. The creek channel is a focal point for bass during all seasons. Standing or submerged timber along channels are good spots.

Current in creeks often keeps ponds from stratifying, so some bass move deep in summer. Species diversity is usually high, and structural elements and cover are diverse.

Low fishing pressure can mean superb bass fishing.

varies with shape, fertility, forage fish, and fishing pressure. Some Florida phosphate pits are fertile and produce extraordinary bass fishing where harvest is controlled.

Highway construction often requires extensive excavation. Thousands of cubic feet of earth are moved, leaving broad and shallow holes that make good bass habitat where winter kill isn't a problem. And while they're always easily accessed, they're often overlooked. In southern climates, small waters like canals and golf course hazards often hold big bass.

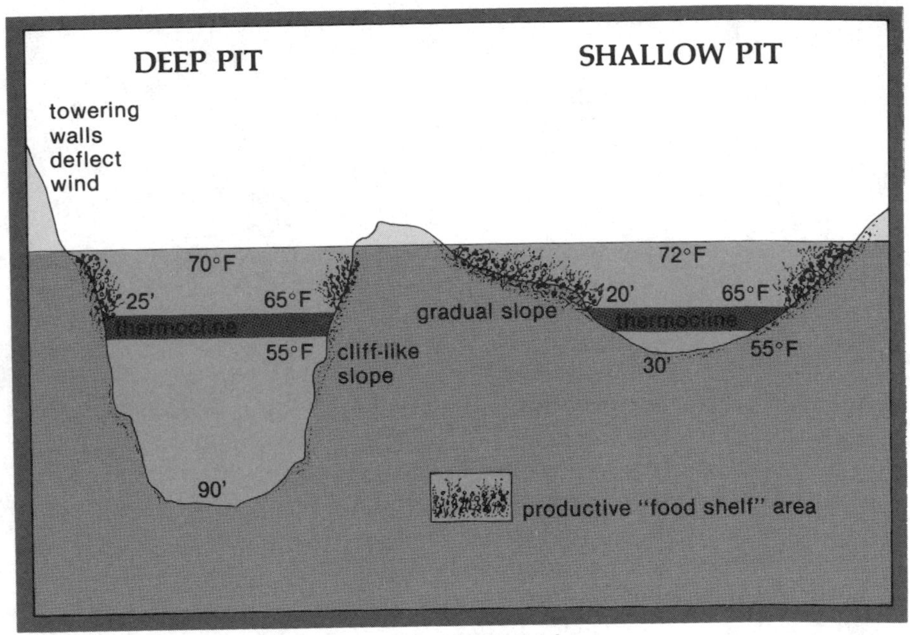

Facts of Pit Life

The clifflike walls of most deep pits provide little productive shelf. They're infertile compared to most shallow pits.

Towering walls surrounding many deep pits deflect wind. You can comfortably fish them even on windy days; but without wind, the depths don't reoxygenate to support much aquatic life below the thermocline. These pits may look like deep Canadian trout lakes. But despite their wilderness appearance, they're often infertile with limited ability to produce fish.

TEMPERATURE MYTHS AND FACTS

Largemouth bass tolerate one of the widest temperature ranges known to science, from just above freezing to over 95°F. Largemouth bass are cold-blooded, however, and water temperature affects their behavior and metabolism. Bass in cold water generally react more lethargically than bass in warmer water. Water above 90°F also tends to inhibit activity.

Also, bass from different geographical locations have adapted to temperature variations. Ichthyologists recognize two largemouth bass subspecies—Florida and northern. Northern bass are adapted to cooler temperatures than Florida bass. Northern bass also live in regions with wider temperature fluctuations, so they tolerate more temperature variation than Florida bass. Yet particularly within the northern subspecies, differences in temperature effects occur among populations. So northern bass from Minnesota probably are more tolerant of cold water than northern bass from Missouri.

Temperature preference is also dependent on bass size. Large bass tend to rest in cool water and visit warmer water to feed. Small bass inhabit warm shallow water where they feed most effectively and can escape predation.

Largemouth bass have no single preferred temperature or temperature range, but they generally function well in water from 65°F to 90°F. Given the option in lab experiments, they usually occupy water from 78°F to 86°F, the range at which their digestive systems operate most efficiently. So 78°F to 86°F might be considered a rough optimum for bass, though water that warm usually isn't available to bass in northern waters.

Bass could not thrive at a constant temperature, even temperatures within

TRUTH ABOUT TEMPERATURE

Fish are cold-blooded (poikilotherms), unable to regulate body temperature. Their body temperature is determined by the water temperature in their environment.

Laboratories allow controlled testing of temperatures that fish prefer. Observing bass in natural habitats, however, can verify or dispute the validity of experimental results on wild fish.

Studies have suggested largemouth bass prefer temperatures from 78°F to 90°F. Differences in test procedures may explain some variation. Size, age, genetic background, physiological condition, and season can also affect results.

Acclimation temperature—the temperature at which fish have been kept prior to the experiment—has a substantial effect. Bass held in warmer water generally select higher temperatures than fish kept cooler. They also survive higher maximum temperatures, up to about 102°F. Recently hatched bass are less tolerant, however.

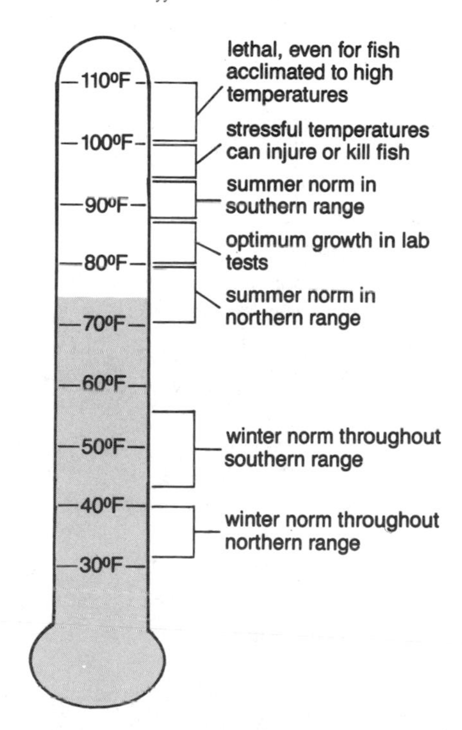

Bass that occupy abnormally warm waters, such as power plant cooling reservoirs, tend to be thin. They apparently can't eat enough to maintain their high metabolism. They also suffer a higher incidence of parasite invasion.

In North America where largemouth bass are found from southern Canada to south Florida (1,900 miles), wide differences in temperature tolerances, growing seasons, and other temperature characteristics illustrate largemouth bass adaptability. Yet countless individual populations, suited to the environment they inhabit, may not thrive if stocked elsewhere.

the 65°F to 90°F range. Spawning depends on an increase from the 50°F range into the mid-60°F range. Between 40°F and 50°F, bass don't move much. Below 40°F, activity is minimal, although bass continue to feed during winter. Energy requirements are slight due to reduced metabolism, so feeding is infrequent. A meal a week may suffice. This, however, doesn't mean they are uncatchable. Indeed, ice anglers often make good catches, including lunkers, particularly at early-ice and late-ice.

Bass prefer stable temperatures. They react most adversely to sudden drops in water temperature brought on by harsh cold fronts. This preference for stability is evident as bass gradually approach warmer water in spring. A steady spring warming trend promises temperature stability and leads to a major prespawn movement to protected shallow areas. A cold front that drops water temperature by even a few degrees stops the movement and may send bass back toward deeper water and more stable temperatures.

During fall, bass also seek temperature stability. Even during the day when water in the shallows warms into ranges bass prefer, they often hold in moderate depths where temperatures are more stable. Areas of stable temperature also draw preyfish. Bass frequently ignore ideal temperatures in favor of water with food and cover.

TRACKING STUDIES

Telemetry (tracking) studies with radio and ultrasonic transmitters provide insight into movements of bass and their behavior. Because of the diverse habitats bass occupy, results of one study don't always apply directly to other waters. We can, however, make noteworthy generalizations:

- Some bass rarely leave the shallows, while others occupy middepths or deep water. Neither bright sunlight nor heavy wave action usually cause bass to leave shallow water. Bass may, however, switch preferred locations for unknown reasons.
- Several studies indicate the presence of at least two distinct groups of bass. One group occupies a definite home area they rarely leave, while the other group constantly changes locales.
- Bass become active and hunt prey at a wide range of temperatures.
- Bass rest most of the time, becoming active and seeking food at regular intervals, often around dusk and dawn. Bass in shallow water feed primarily during low-light periods. Bass at greater depths are active later in the day.
- Bass sometimes are active at night, although they don't continually move and feed then.
- Resting bass aren't always in cover, but usually spend time near small openings in cover or where two cover types meet. Active bass often cruise the outer edge of cover and sometimes cruise along drop-off breaklines. Bass may also suspend at middepths and may feed on the surface in open water.
- Most bass movements are parallel to cover, involving minor depth changes. When bass move over deep water, they typically hold at a constant depth rather than following a bottom contour.
- Some bass seem to know their way around a large body of water. Other bass become disoriented and can't find their way back when they're removed from their home area. Bass in rivers or chains of lakes seem most

SEASONAL MOVEMENT IDENTIFIED BY TRACKING

Physiological needs change seasonally and determine location patterns for largemouth bass. Bass choose specific areas that are suitable to their specific needs.

Radio telemetry studies show that bass may move miles through murky water to a specific spot like a rooty stump in a timbered slough. One of many examples is demonstrated by the following:

John Pitlo Jr., a fishery biologist with the Iowa Department of Natural Resources, conducted an extensive radio telemetry study of largemouth bass in Mississippi River pools 12 and 13, between Iowa and Illinois. He studied nearly 100 bass. His results showed that bass make long-distance seasonal movements, perhaps because prime habitats for spawning and overwintering weren't abundant.

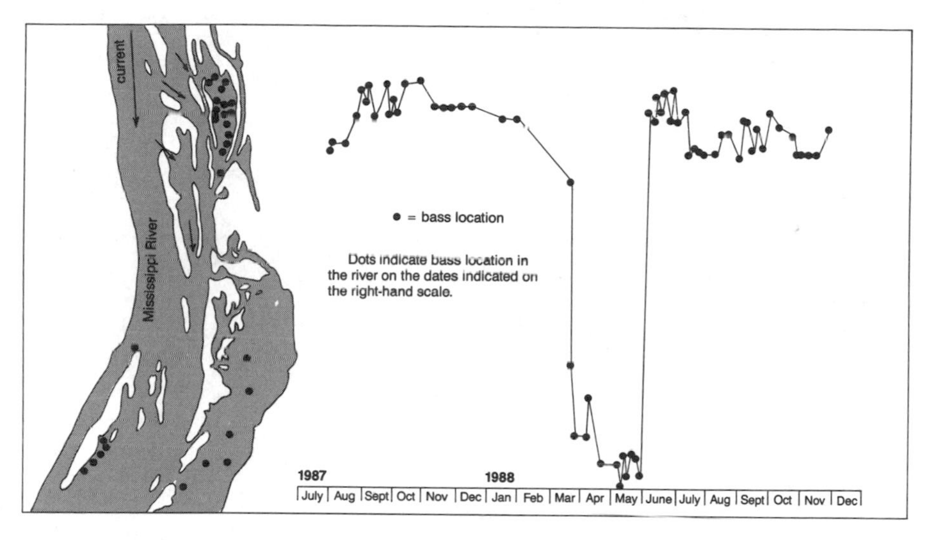

Locations of bass #1416 in pool 12 of the Upper Mississippi River determined by John Pitlo's radio telemetry studies during 1987 and 1988.

accustomed to long travel and often return home if displaced.

• Bass usually utilize shallow water and heavy cover. Several studies show they rarely went deeper than 15 feet. Yet where oxygen and baitfish are present, bass use depths to 80 feet or more.

• Bass react to changing water quality involving oxygen, temperature, and salinity by moving.

• As spawning approaches, largemouths move to traditional bedding sites—shallow protected bays and canals, preferably with wood or weed cover. Cues causing this movement include changing amount of daylight and water temperature.

• Bass often act as individuals, exhibiting varying activity cycles, cover preferences, and feeding habits. Some bass avoid boats and human activity. Others flock to busy marinas and may become "pets."

• Trophy-size bass may behave differently than smaller bass, often occupying middepth habitat or suspending.

Disproving Angling Theory

Results of 15 Electronic Black Bass Tracking Studies

Researcher (Publication year)	Bass Species	Number of Bass	Major Daily Depth Changes	Rapid Vertical Feeding	Offshore Suspension	Movement Parallel to Contours/ Breaklines	Feeding Move-ments to and from Deep Water	Location/State
Chappel (1974)	LMB	12		yes		yes	no	Keowee, SC
Clugston (1973)	LMB	12		yes	inf	yes	no	Par P., SC
Coutant (1975)	LMB	3	no	yes			no	Lambert Quarry, TN
Dupont (1976)	LMB	20			yes	yes	no	Par P., SC
Dufford (Guerri, 1979)	LMB	35	no		no	yes	no	Shelbyville, MO
Doerzbacker (1980)	LMB	15	no			yes	no	Atchafalaya R., LA
Hubert & Lackey (1980)	SMB	34				yes	no	Pickwick, TN
Knopf (1981) Knopf & Lenon (1981)	LMB	8	yes			yes	yes	Isabella L., MI
Lembeck (Circle, 1976) (Williams, 1979)	LMB	203	no	yes	yes	yes	no	4 San Diego lakes, CA
Manns (1981)	GB	14	no	yes	yes	yes	no	Travis, TX
Peterson (1975)	LMB	14			yes	yes	no	Center Hill, TN
	SMB	11			yes	yes	no	
	SB	4			yes	yes	no	
Prince and Maughan (1979)	LMB	13				inf	no	Smith Mnt., VA
Smith (1974)	LMB	9				yes	no	Keowee, SC
Warden & Lorio (1975)	LMB	16	?			yes	?	Loakfoma, MS
Winter (1977)	LMB	4	no	no	no	inf	no	Mary L., MN

Legend LMB = Largemouth bass SMB = Smallmouth bass SB = Spotted Bass
GB = Guadalupe bass
yes = The described activity was frequently observed
no = The activity was not observed
inf = The activity was not specifically observed, but may be inferred from the data
? = The author described movement to and from "deep" water, but the maximum depth was 14'
(blank) = The equipment used was not suitable to obtain these observations, or they were not reported

For years, many good bass anglers, perhaps most, believed the home of black bass was in deep water and that they made feeding migrations to shallow water. In 1984, In-Fisherman researcher Ralph Manns compiled this chart of the results of electronic tracking studies completed by 1981. In In-Fisherman *magazine Book #43, he concluded:*

"The deep-to-shallow-water migration (the home of the fish is deep water) theory doesn't stand up to scientific observation. While bass may make rapid vertical feeding movements in order to catch passing prey, bass movement is usually parallel to contours."

GUIDELINES FOR PICKING IDEAL NATURAL BASS WATERS

What makes a body of water good bass water? These tips can direct you to productive bass water; and in a large body of water, they'll direct you to productive bays:

- Half the lake (or bay or cove) should have an abundance of cover and be shallower than the first drop-off. Lakes can have too little or too much shallow cover. Fifty-fifty is about ideal.
- Bass function best in moderately shallow lakes or sections of lakes less than 40 feet deep.

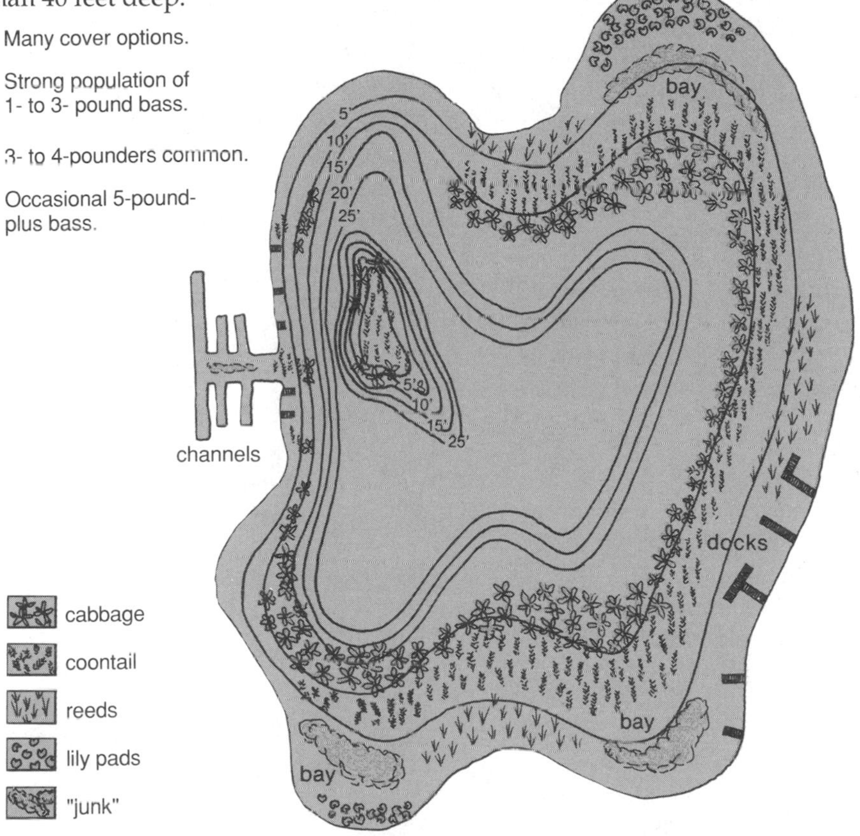

Many cover options.

Strong population of 1- to 3- pound bass.

3- to 4-pounders common.

Occasional 5-pound-plus bass.

bay
5'
10'
15'
20'
25'
channels
docks
bay
bay

cabbage
coontail
reeds
lily pads
"junk"

This map illustrates an ideal bass lake. If fishing pressure or environmental problems haven't diminished the population, expect to find lots of bass of all sizes, including a few trophy-size fish.

The lake also offers angling options that promise success during all seasons and weather conditions—good spawning locations and plenty of shallow weedy habitat to feed and shelter young and adult bass. Yet depth contours and the mix of weed species mean the lake won't be so weed-choked that effective fishing becomes impossible.

The lake has many edge areas—transitions from lily pads to coontail, coontail to cabbage, or cabbage to open water. A sunken island and docks provide further structure and cover options. Cover variety at different depths means you'll find catchable bass if you correctly identify location and presentation patterns.

• The lake (or bay or cove) must have adequate spawning and rearing areas—wind-protected bays and channels, mixed sand-muck bottom, and plenty of cover like weeds or stumps.

• Look for abundant shallow cover on the flat adjacent to (shallower than) the first drop-off. Some lakes have cover shallow and deep, but lack continuous cover from the shallows to the depths. An ideal lake should have weed cover at each of those depths; but weeds shouldn't cover more than 50 percent of the total surface area.

• The deep weedline should be 8 to 15 feet deep. A deep weedline at about 10 feet is typical of lakes that are moderately fertile—somewhat stained, but not dingy.

• Water quality should be good for bass and their prey—moderately fertile to fertile, but not soupy and eutrophic. Water temperatures, pH, and oxygen must fall within acceptable levels. A lake with a forage base of ciscoes and perch isn't fertile enough. Great bass waters have an abundance of minnows, sunfish, crayfish, perhaps shad or alewives, and aquatic invertebrates. Nutrient levels must be sufficient to support a high concentration of fish.

• Ideal bass waters can contain other top-line predators, but not excessive numbers. Lakes with large populations of pike, walleyes, muskies, smallmouths, or striped bass usually don't provide excellent largemouth bass fishing.

• The lake or lake area should receive minimal fishing pressure. Look for lakes with boat ramps too small to accept big boats, lakes with limited public access, or remote parts of big waters. Where fishing pressure is moderate, high rates of voluntary release or mandatory release through restrictive limits maintains bass abundance, particularly large fish.

• Finally, the ideal lake offers habitat options—timber, emergent weeds, docks, and submerged weedbeds.

Look for a small (400- to 500-acre) lake or a bay the size that meets these requirements. If you find one, practice catch and release and keep quiet.

Chapter 6

THE YEAR OF THE LARGEMOUTH BASS

Calendar Periods Key Understanding Bass Behavior

We divide the fishing year into 10 Calendar Periods of fish response, in order to help fishermen categorize seasonal fish activity. Once you categorize fish behavior by season, you can move from one body of water to another, even bodies of water in other regions, and have a general idea what bass will be doing on that body of water. Understanding Calendar Periods is one basis for consistent fishing success on a variety of lakes, rivers, reservoirs, pits and ponds.

During the Prespawn Period, for example, bass display characteristic behavior that includes movement from deeper water to shallow areas where the water temperature is steadily increasing. Shallow bass often are aggressive and bite surface baits, shallow-running crankbaits, or spinnerbaits.

When weather conditions destabilize due to a passing cold front, some bass move back toward deeper water. Others become inactive, remaining in the shallows. Now it may require slower-moving, more-subtle presentations such as a Gitzit-type grub or a 1/16-ounce head to get bass to bite.

This general characteristic of bass behavior during the Prespawn Period applies whether you're fishing in Florida in February or Maine in late May. Identification of the Calendar Period bass are in is a first step toward systematic comparisons that help you plan fishing strategy.

While the 10 periods occur in the same order in each region, the length of the periods may vary based on local weather conditions. The Prespawn Period, for example, may be compressed into weeks in Michigan, while it may occur over months in Georgia.

VEST POCKET GUIDE TO CALENDAR PERIODS

Winter: Coldest water of the year. Northern lakes are iced over; southern waters are as cold as they get. Bass are inactive.

Cold Water: Transition time. During spring, bass move from winter holding areas toward prespawn staging and spawning areas. They're grouped and generally inactive. Locational shifts may be dramatic.

Prespawn: Bass move shallow to check spawning areas and feed prior to

1	2	3	4	5	6	7	8	9	10
Prespawn	*Spawn*	*Postspawn*	*Presummer*	*Summer Peak*	*Summer*	*Postsummer*	*Turnover*	*Cold Water*	*Winter*

spawning. Prey and cover are scarce. Fishing success is largely dependent on stable weather and gradually warming water.

Spawn: This period of reproductive activities begins with males preparing nests and ends when free-swimming fry disperse. Weather affects the beginning and duration of the spawn as well as its success. During the spawn, bass don't feed much, but are vulnerable because of their defensive attitude and visibility in shallow nesting areas.

Postspawn: A brief transition period during which bass recover from spawning and move toward areas they'll occupy throughout summer. Fishing often is inconsistent because bass location and attitude as well as lake conditions and weather are in transition.

Presummer: A continuing transition period, but one with greater fishing potential than postspawn. Some bass have already settled in summer locations. Developing weedbeds key good fishing in many waters. Surface waters are warming rapidly, and bass are more likely to feed actively.

Summer Peak: Bass establish feeding patterns in a habitat that will sustain them during at least a portion of summer. Weeds near peak growth and newly hatched fish of many species are plentiful. Lakes that stratify do so during this period. Bass are very active and grouped enough to have to compete for food. Often this short hard-to-define period offers some of the best fishing of the year.

Summer: A long period when bass remain in areas that provide food and cover. Activity and location are predictable, although bass may be in many different locations from very shallow to deep water. Prey often is abundant, so feeding periods and movements become shorter as summer progresses.

Postsummer: A period that begins with falling surface temperature and ends at turnover; or in waters that don't stratify, when water temperatures fall into the 60°F range. Bass remain in predictable summer locations until changing weather conditions begin to move them.

Fall Turnover: A very short period during which mixing occurs from the surface to the bottom in stratified waters. Temperatures and oxygen levels become uniform at all depths. Fishing often is poor.

LARGEMOUTH BASS CALENDAR

Gregorian Calendar	Jan	Feb	Mar	Apr	May	June	July	Aug	Sept	Oct	Nov	Dec
Northern Range		10		9	1	2,3,4,5		6	7	8	9	10
Mid Range		10	9	1	2,3,4,5			6		7, 8	9	10
Southern Range	10	9	1	2	3,4,5			6		7	8	9, 10

1. Prespawn
2. Spawn
3. Postspawn
4. Presummer
5. Summer Peak
6. Summer
7. Postsummer
8. Fall Turnover
9. Cold Water
10. Winter*

*Coldest water of the year.

The 10 Calendar Periods of fish response can vary in length as much as 4 weeks from one year to the next. The periods aren't based on the Gregorian calendar, so they do not occur on specific dates each year. Instead, the Calendar Periods are based on nature's clock.

In addition, the Calendar Periods vary by regions of the country. Southern waters have an extended Summer Period and a brief Winter Period. In contrast, lakes along the U.S.-Canadian border have extended Cold Water and Winter Periods. Bass in Florida or Texas could be in the Spawning Period while those in Minnesota are still in the Winter Period.

CALENDAR PERIOD REGIONAL TIMETABLE

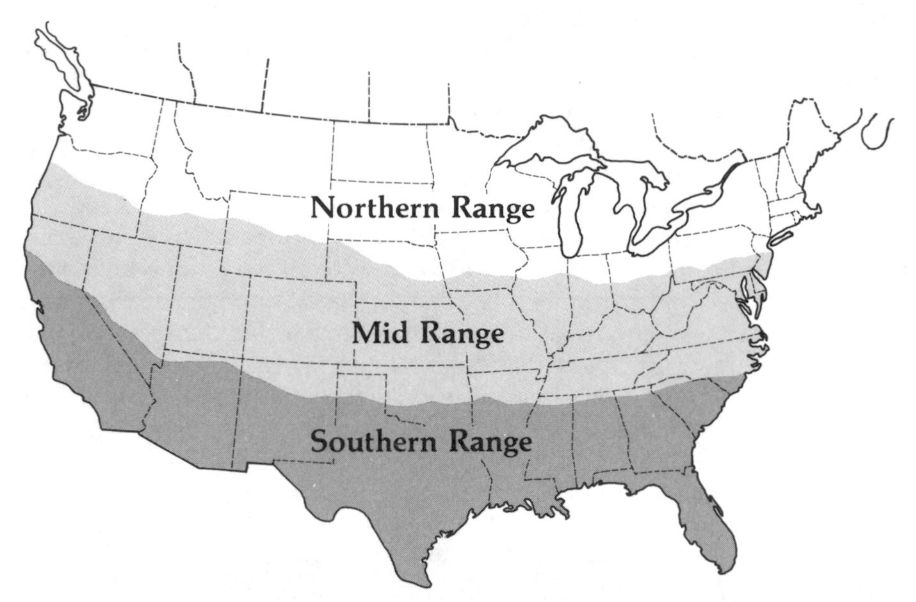

Cold Water: During fall, cooling continues toward winter lows. Bass aggregate in and around available cover, particularly remaining weeds. Fish feed sporadically, but large aggregations can provide good fishing.

Calendar Periods result from an interaction between fish instincts, weather, the physical properties of a body of water, and the changing seasons. Some Calendar Periods are brief, perhaps a few days, while others last months. Dates for period transitions and their duration may vary annually, even in the same body of water. But the succession of events doesn't vary.

The impact of the Calendar Periods is stronger in northern regions, where climate produces much wider temperature swings. So shifts from one period to the next are also more abrupt in the northern range. For example, the spring Cold Water Period is a brief transition after ice-out in the North, but is gradual and more significant in mid-continent climates.

Water temperature is an important impetus for seasonal shifts. But it doesn't work like a switch.

- No magic temperature pulls bass into the shallows for a prespawn feeding spree.
- No specific temperature triggers bass to spawn.
- Bass respond to temperature *trends* more than to degrees on a thermometer.
- Temperatures in one part of a lake or reservoir can vary substantially from temperatures prevailing elsewhere in that body of water. Bass activities in each location vary accordingly.
- Individual bass respond differently to temperature. Behavior depends on fish size as well as individual differences among fish.

Some Calendar Periods are triggered by events other than temperature.

Presummer is tied more to development of weedy cover than to temperature. Summer Peak is dependent on bass congregating for the first time since Prespawn and beginning to feed competitively in predictable locations.

WINTER

Water Temperature: At Its Coldest for an Extended Period
General Fish Mood: Inactive

Winter is a long period that can't be defined by precise environmental markers since bass live in a variety of geographical areas. This period is, however, characterized by the coldest temperatures of the year. Exact conditions depend on geographic location and winter's severity. In northern Minnesota, water on lakes and even parts of rivers is under 3 feet of ice. Water temperatures range from about 32°F directly under the ice to 39°F on the bottom. In southern states, water temperatures usually run in the 40°F range—upper 50°F range in Florida.

Bass bite when the snow flies and the water freezes, for those who know how, where, and when.

Largemouth bass generally hold in the deepest water they use all year. Just how deep depends on many circumstances; 20 to 30 feet is common in natural lakes; 50 feet in deeper reservoirs. In shallow reservoirs or ponds, bass will be in or near the deepest available water. River bass seek backwaters with adequate oxygen away from current during months of ice cover.

Bass move deep to water that's slightly warmer and more stable than water near the surface. Temperatures of 37°F to 39°F are common on the bottom, while water near the surface will be 33°F. Preyfish generally also are concentrated on middepth flats in or near the lake basin.

Huge winter aggregations of bass often exist. In reservoirs, these aggregations often suspend in timber near deep creek channels. Even though bass are inactive, aggregations are so large that a few fish are usually active enough to hit lures.

Cold water reduces bass metabolism. They feed infrequently, becoming active only periodically, especially early and late in the Cold Water Period. Ice fishermen, who usually seek other species, commonly catch bass through the ice. Lunkers are common just prior to ice-out.

Bass in shallow eutrophic waters are subject to lowering oxygen levels in winter due to oxygen use by all organisms and no replenishment from the air or by photosynthesis. In some lakes, oxygen deprivation in deep water forces bass to move shallower. In the most serious cases, winterkill occurs.

COLD WATER

Water Temperature: Cold but Rising
General Fish Mood: Inactive to Neutral

This period occurs as early as late January in the South and as late as late April in the most northern regions of the largemouth range. Water temperatures in the 40°F range early in this period rise into the 50°F range.

Bass move from their deepest wintering sites toward the shallows where they'll spawn. Reservoir bass typically move along creek channels or over deep flats. They sometimes hold in large aggregations where cover and baitfish are present. Ten to 20 feet is the average depth during early spring

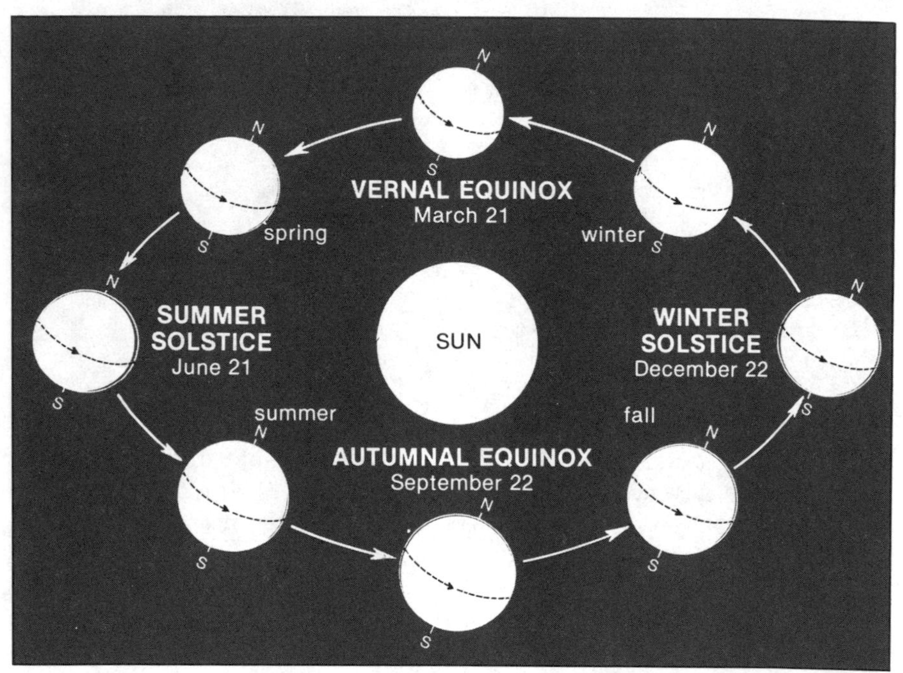

Spring, summer, fall, winter. The pendulum swings between seasons, bringing obvious changes on land, but more difficult-to-define changes underwater. Length of daylight influences the tempo of the environment, from microorganisms to top-line predators. The intensity and duration of light in a yearly cycle influences bass migrations, spawning, and feeding.

for bass in cold-water reservoirs. Lake fish move shallower more quickly because there's less deep cover. The Cold Water Period is short in northern lakes where water warms rapidly after ice leaves.

In the South, where the locational shift takes longer, fishing can be good, especially for big fish. Observant anglers can find holding areas that bass visit each year for a week or two. Typical locations are timbered holes in submerged creek channels near expansive flats or sloughs. As water warms, bass scatter toward shallower spawning and feeding sites.

In far-north waters shortly after ice-out, bass may move shallow into black-bottom bays or canals. They're spooky, but can be caught on slowly worked subtle presentations like tube jigs or unweighted plastic worms.

In many northern states, bass season is closed at this time. In northern areas where bass season is open, fishing is often difficult because of inconsistent weather.

PRESPAWN

Water Temperature: Cool but Rising
General Fish Mood: Positive

As the water warms, bass move shallower. Dark-bottom bays on northwest shores are first to warm, drawing panfish, minnows, and predator species. Insect activity is also greater here than in the main lake. Fish gather around limited available cover including weed and lily pad stalks, stumps and fallen trees.

In reservoirs, as coves and shallow creek arms warm, they draw prey species. Runoff from late winter rains often reduces water clarity. Clear water that's warmer attracts bass, so dead-end creeks and sloughs provide better fishing than active creeks. Because bass see and therefore bite better in clear water, upper reservoir reaches often don't produce well. Less dingy shallow coves in the lower third of the reservoir are often better.

Bass movement toward the shallows is sometimes tentative. They move into warming shallow bays, but retreat during wind or cold fronts to the first drop-off with available cover. They more likely retreat from shallows where weed cover hasn't developed.

Water temperatures must reach the low 60°F range before spawning activity begins. Bass in the South typically remain in prespawn at higher temperatures than northern bass who spawn at lower temperatures.

Most preyfish species are shallow during the Prespawn Period. Hungry bass must feed heartily to complete egg and sperm maturation. Water levels are usually higher in natural lakes, reservoirs, and rivers than at any other time of year. You usually find active bass in shoreline cover and flooded brush and trees.

During late prespawn, bass are aggressive and catchable. Cold blustery weather can turn off bass early in the Prespawn Period, but as the spawn approaches, they're almost always active, especially in northern waters. Warm, stable weather for several days may produce fantastic fishing.

Often the best fishing is toward evening on sunny days. Switch lake areas or lakes to get the longest possible prespawn fishing. By moving around,

Prespawn. Initially, bass move shallow, seeking warming water that draws prey. Shallow cover in bays, cuts, creek arms, and canals are some of the first places to draw bass. Bass often concentrate in these areas on individual cover spots such as weed points or cuts, or cover objects such as beaver lodges or fallen trees. Eventually, bass become preoccupied with spawning. Prespawn ends as bass bed and spawning begins.

you can stretch prespawn fishing more than a month in northern waters, two months in the South.

SPAWN

Water Temperature: Moderately Warm and Rising
General Fish Mood: Neutral, but Aggressively Defensive

Several factors trigger the spawn, the most important being day length and water temperature. Water temperature rising into the low 60°F range shifts male bass from prespawn feeding to nest preparation. But bass in a body of water don't all spawn at the same time. Indeed, they've been found to spawn in water temperatures from the high 50s to the low 80s. Water temperature also may vary among sections of a body of water. This scattered spawning protects bass from adverse weather destroying an entire year-class.

Bass usually spawn earliest in the upper reaches of reservoirs, latest in the lower portion, because warm shallow bays often are located in the upper reaches. Spawning can continue for four to six weeks in a reservoir.

Larger bass tend to spawn earlier than small bass; so a spawning area filled with small fish may indicate the spawn is almost completed.

Largemouth bass have spawned successfully in water from 6 inches to 15 feet deep, but typically nest in water 1 to 4 feet deep. The murkier the water, the shallower they spawn. Spawning versatility is yet another aspect of bass adaptability.

Because silt can smother and destroy the eggs, and because predators seek the eggs for their high-protein content, males must choose nest sites carefully. They often choose spawning sites in channels, coves, bays, and wind-protected shores. In rivers, bass seek quiet backwaters with medium to hard bottoms.

TYPICAL SPAWNING MONTHS

AREA	MONTHS
Florida	February and March
Mississippi	March through early April
Missouri	April
Pennsylvania	May
Minnesota/Ontario	mid-May to late-June

The timing of the largemouth bass Spawn Period illustrates the region-by-region progression of Calendar Periods. Region (latitude), water temperature, weather trends, length of daylight, interspecies and intraspecies competition for habitat, and an internal clock are some of the factors influencing the exact timing of the spawn. Not all bass spawn at the same time, even in the same body of water. While most adult bass in a lake may spawn during a couple weeks of ideal conditions, some will spawn earlier and some later.

Regionally, the onset of largemouth bass spawning may begin in February in the South or as late as mid-June in southern Canada.

Males sweep away fine debris to form a silt-free rounded nest site on firm bottom. In late-stage eutrophic lakes with softer bottoms, bass may bed on roots of aquatic plants. They often sweep out nests next to a rock, log, or weed stalks to reduce the area they must guard against egg stealers like sunfish, perch, and shiners.

After sweeping a nest, a male courts a larger female with nips, bumps, and short chases until they both position over the nest and spawn. A female deposits 2,000 to 7,000 eggs while the male simultaneously fertilizes them. Female bass may deposit additional batches of eggs hours or days later, often fertilized by a different male.

Males defend the eggs and fan the nest to provide oxygen, remove waste products, and prevent siltation. Females remain in spawning bays only until they've expelled their eggs. During this time they'll strike various baits. Many trophy bass are caught in states that allow fishing during the spawn.

Males remain on nests to defend eggs and often strike lures presented in or over the nest. The aggressiveness of their defense depends on weather conditions, fishing pressure, and the stage of egg development.

Males fan and guard their eggs for two to five days until they hatch. Hatchlings, sustained by their yolk sac, remain in the nest for up to another week. As fry emerge, they swim in a dark ball that the male continues to guard until the fry swim off.

Because of changeable spring weather, the success of a spawn varies. Even under the most favorable circumstances, only a fraction of one percent of fry reach catchable size.

During the spawn, fishing varies from poor to too easy. Males are particularly vulnerable while they're guarding nests. Females also are vulnerable during the time they reside in shallow areas where lure presentation is easy for fishermen.

In many northern states where the spawn is most synchronized and bass are most vulnerable, regulations prohibit bass fishing during the spawn to prevent overharvest.

POSTSPAWN

Water Temperature: Warming through the 70°F Range
General Fish Mood: Inactive to Neutral

Postspawn is a short transition period between completion of reproductive activities and the beginning of summer patterns. Bass leave shallow bedding areas and move toward areas they'll use all summer, lingering at times in emerging lily pads and submerged weedbeds that grow outside spawning banks.

During tournaments at this time, survival in livewells is difficult because livewell confinement increases stress on already tired fish. Providing cool water, continually aerating, adding chemicals to livewells, and not transporting fish over rough waters increase survival.

During postspawn, bass scatter, but not usually as a group. They're also not aggressive, due apparently to the physical demands of spawning. Fishing typically is difficult.

Until water warms and weeds reach the surface, bass tend to remain near bottom. Surface lures and spinnerbaits aren't as effective as they were when bass were massed in the shallows or as effective as they'll be when fish are feeding more aggressively. In a given body of water, however, individual bass may simultaneously be in Prespawn, Spawn, Postspawn, and Presummer Periods.

PRESUMMER

Water Temperature: Fairly Warm and Rising
General Fish Mood: Positive

As the water warms and weeds develop, bass move to depths with the best available cover. In natural lakes, that will often be major flats. At first, they cluster among weed clumps on flats. Later, they move deeper as weeds sprout in deeper water. Active bass feed on the outside or inside edges of weedlines, or over the weeds.

In reservoirs, bass move toward the mouths of small sloughs and shoreline points, especially those with a deeper nearby channel with stumps or timber. They often begin preying on shad over mainlake flats. Bass typically are aggressive, feeding to recover from spawning. They're catchable on a variety of presentations.

SUMMER PEAK

Water Temperature: Warm and Rising
General Fish Mood: Positive

Summer Peak is a short period when bass first occupy typical summer

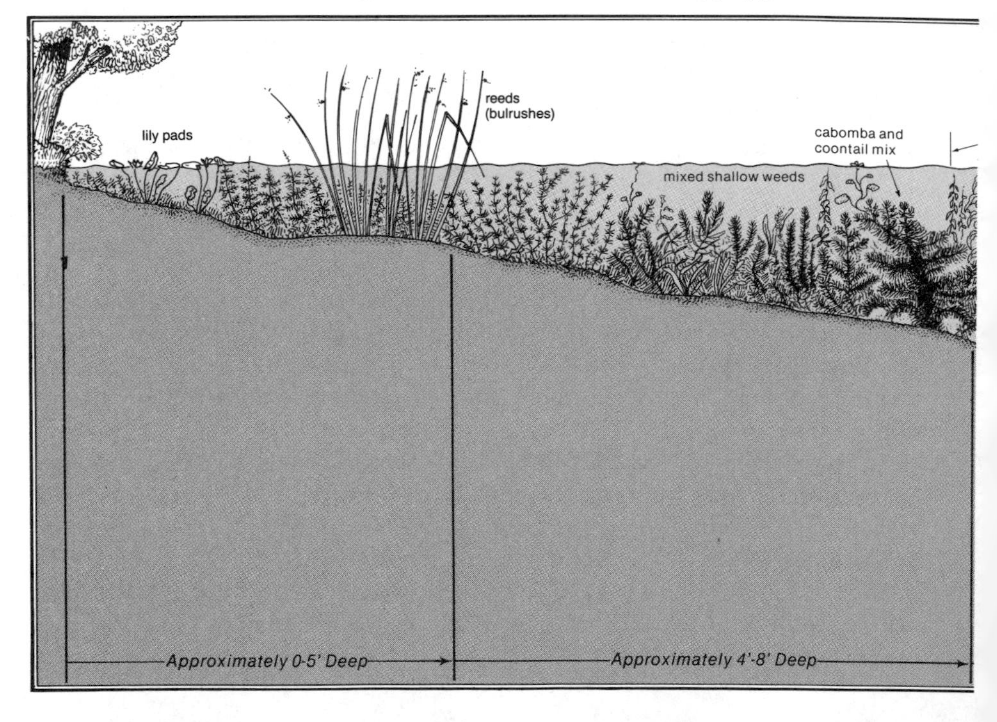

locations. Lily pads have formed, but aren't covered with algae. Most weed species have fully developed, producing well-defined inside and outside weededges. Oxygen levels are ideal and the water's clear. Lakes that stratify are in the process of doing so, or have already stratified.

Food is plentiful, as newly hatched baitfish grow large enough to be worth chasing. Adult preyfish have completed spawning, increasing their vulnerability to big predators. Bass feed aggressively unless early summer cold fronts are too severe. In reservoirs with strong shad populations, some bass begin to shadow shad schools offshore, particularly at dawn and dusk.

Bass location varies. Some bass are in heavy cover in shallow water while others prowl deep weedlines, timber, and stumpfields. Catch rates are typically high, but large bass are scattered.

During Summer Peak, bass may hold in deeper water if forage fish are available. Moderate water temperatures and high oxygen levels mean bass aren't restricted to a particular depth. Deeper bass are harder to locate, but are reliable biters because they don't change activity levels with minor weather changes. Aggregations are common on prime structural elements. Fishing doesn't get any better once you find fish.

SUMMER

Water Temperature: Maximum for Body of Water
General Fish Mood: Variable

During the Summer Period, water temperatures reach their maximum. Waters that stratify are divided into three zones: a warm surface layer (epilimnion); a layer of rapidly declining temperature (thermocline or metalimnion); and a deep cool layer (hypolimnion) with insufficient oxygen

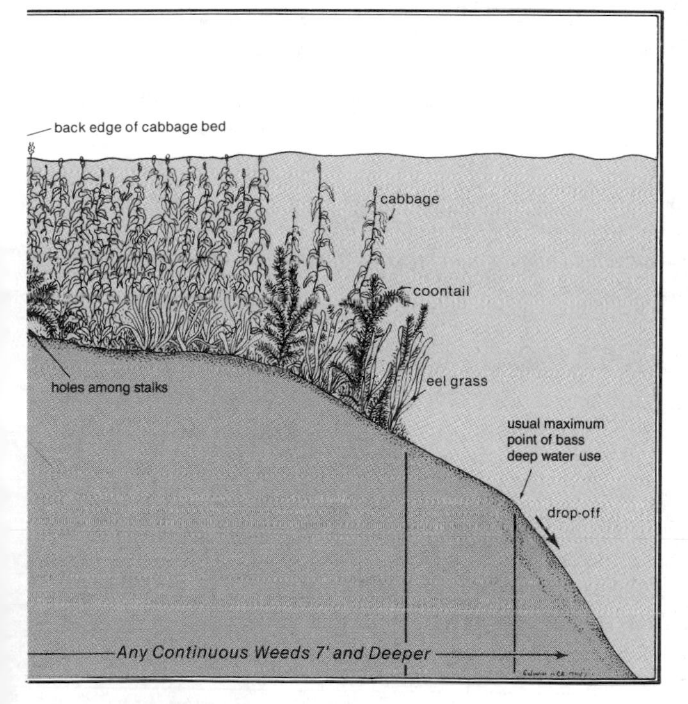

Summer Habitat

By Summer Peak, bass have settled into habitat areas they use throughout the summer. In lakes and increasing numbers of reservoirs, weedbeds become the focus of bass activity. They often reside in one of three general areas: heavy shallow weeds (slop); moderate depth weeds on the flat; and weeds along the deep weededge.

in most bass waters.

Minnows, shad, sunfish and other prey are plentiful in shallow areas. Bass feed heavily, but often briefly, for abundance of prey reduces competition for food. Fishing may get tough as bass become finicky and concentrate on specific prey during specific times. In fertile waters, lure or bait presentation can become difficult because of dense weedgrowth. Low oxygen levels at dawn in very fertile waters may hinder early morning fishing.

Groups of bass usually hold in many different habitats. Fishing at dusk or

Doug Hannon, the "Bass Professor," has offered many trend-setting observations about largemouth bass in the pages of In-Fisherman *magazine during the past decade. While many fishermen consider Prespawn the peak period for giant bass, Hannon has focused on the Summer Period for most of his hundreds of bass over 10 pounds. According to Hannon, summer brings stable weather, stable water conditions, and stable fish reaction. Subsequently, fishermen can key on peak daily and monthly periods of lunar influence.*

at night may provide the best action, because large bass leave heavy cover and prowl flats.

Summer is one of the most stable and predictable periods. It's also the longest period in southern climates—up to six months in Florida.

POSTSUMMER

Water Temperatures: Warm but Cooling

General Fish Mood: Variable

The declining length of daylight and cooling water gradually breaks up summer patterns. Some weed species die off and decay. Shallow vegetation declines first; deep weeds disappear as water becomes murkier due to wind action and plankton blooms. Shallow bass, gradually at first, and quickly later, move to prime remaining weeds in deeper water.

Reservoir bass may move to shallower cover as water temperatures moderate and shad move inshore. But fishing pressure has eliminated many bass and remaining fish often are easily spooked. Eventually, dropping water temperatures also reduce bass metabolism and feeding requirements.

Postsummer is transition time. Fishing can be good or poor, depending on the effect of climate conditions on the variables that give each body of water its unique character.

TURNOVER

Water Temperature: Uniformly Cool
General Fish Mood: Inactive

Fall weather cools surface water, making it heavy enough to mix with cooler water in the thermocline. Wind furthers the mixing as the thermocline narrows and finally disintegrates. As water mixes from surface to bottom, it may look dirty due to rising bottom sediments. Hydrogen sulfide and other gases trapped on the bottom may produce a musky or sulphur smell. The rapid change affects bass, as fishing invariably becomes difficult. A condition leading to turnover may extend over several weeks and cause poor fishing. The serious effects of the actual turnover, however, rarely last more than a week before conditions begin to stablize and the body of water enters the fall Cold Water Period.

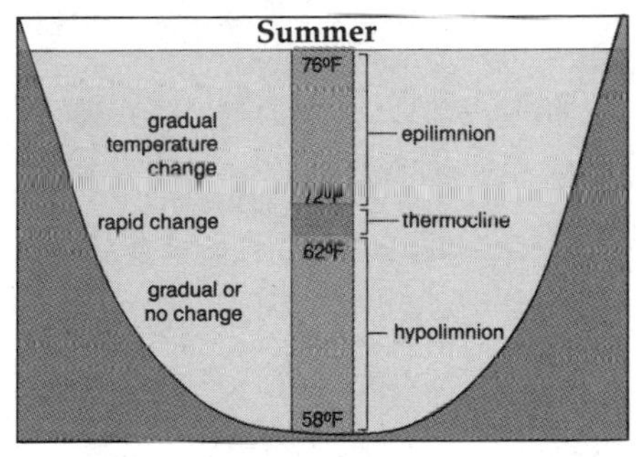

The upper layer (warm water) may be from 12 to 40 feet thick, while the thermocline may be 2 to 15 feet thick. The lower level (cold water) usually is lower in dissolved oxygen than upper layers.

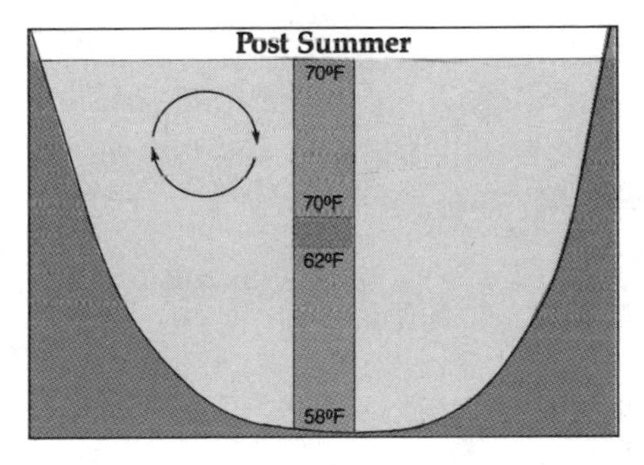

The water surface radiates heat to the atmosphere at night, as water above the thermocline gradually cools. The thermocline remains intact, but is close to the temperature of the layer above. Oxygen-poor water remains trapped below.

FALL COLD WATER

Water Temperature: Cool, Declining to Cold
General Fish Mood: Variable

Following turnover, water will usually be in the 50°F range. Cold temperatures and the breakup of summer fishing patterns end the season for most anglers. But during this period, many of the biggest bass of the season are caught. The average size of bass also increases.

Cooling water causes bass to aggregate around remaining cover. In some waters, they move to steep sloping structure where they can change depths without moving far horizontally. These areas become winter sanctuaries for large numbers of bass.

Bass that have been buried in shallow weeds all summer move first to cover on flats and finally to cover on or near drop-offs. They are readily accessible to anglers, often for the first time since spring.

In reservoirs, bass aggregate in creek channels and along outside edges of weedy flats. Where shad school offshore, bass in deep reservoirs remain deep.

While water temperatures remain in the 50s, bass may feed aggressively, often chasing lures. Slower presentations tend to maximize the catch, particularly after the more aggressive bass have been caught. Note, too, that slower presentations tend to work best for lunker bass.

Green weed patches, usually on drop-offs, key location for bass in natural lakes. Not all weeds die off at the same time. Coontail, for example, thrives in cool water, and both lily pads and milfoil hold up late into the season. As some weeds decline, those that remain concentrate bass.

Fish larger baits with full profiles slowly. When action slows, try smaller, more subtle baits like grubs and thin, short worms.

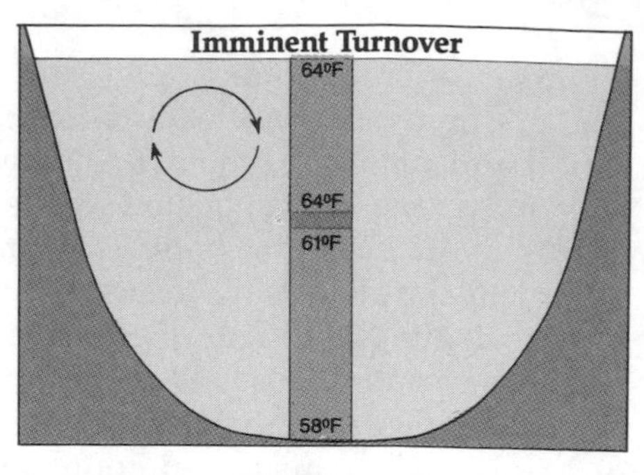

The thermocline shrinks as it approaches the same temperature as the uniform mass of water above.

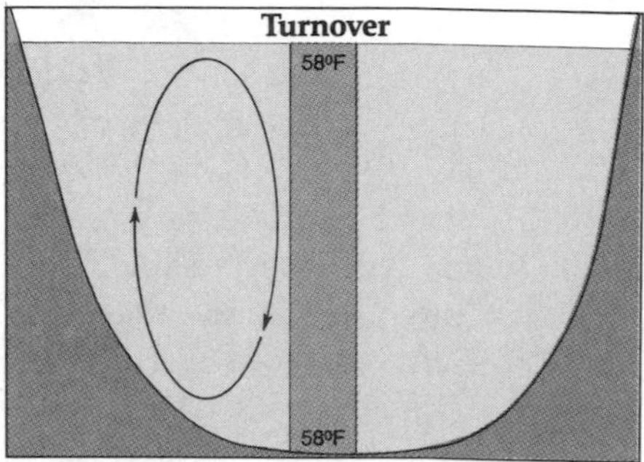

The thermocline disintegrates and water mixes from surface to bottom. The volume of water continues to cool as the water continues to circulate, aided by wind. Oxygen level of lake drops for a short time as oxygen-depleted hypolimnion mixes.

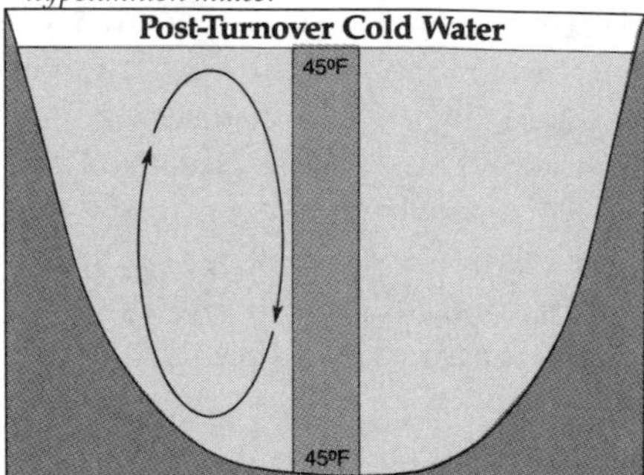

Temperature uniform. Wind action circulates and oxygenates water. The water is a uniform temperature.

Chapter 7

LOCATING BASS IN NATURAL LAKES

Where, When, Why—Terminology, Strategies, Tactics

Until perhaps 70 years ago, most largemouth bass lived in weedy natural lakes in the eastern United States, from the tip of Florida to southern Ontario. In southern states except Florida, where natural lakes are rare, fisheries also existed in flatland warm-water rivers or in calmer sections of rivers with significant flow.

Largemouth bass, of course, established their niche in the aquatic world long before the first Europeans set foot on the continent. As America developed, bass (and other species) were transplanted into a variety of waters they weren't native to. Little by little, bass spread and adapted to new habitat. Yet few innovations in bass fishing tackle or technique occurred.

Their reputation as gamefish lagged behind that of the more glorified stream trout until a major change propelled largemouths to the forefront of the angling world.

The construction of the vast American reservoir system doubled the amount of fishable water in the United States. Coast to coast and border to border, new angling vistas opened at a whirlwind pace. Manmade impoundments, ranging from 2-acre ponds to giants over 100,000 acres were poised to become new frontiers of American angling. But they needed a species to meet the challenge. The fish choice was the adaptable largemouth bass.

The bass's ability to expand and prosper in newly flooded waters made it a huge success. Bass populations quickly expanded in cover-laden shallows of new impoundments. In bass fishing circles, talk turned to fishing timber—trees, stumps, and logs. To riprap, bridges, and dams. To channel edges, bluffs, and creek arms. To fishing *structure.* The bass boom was on, spurring a whirlwind of new terminology, technology, and techniques.

Classic bass behavior in natural environments became less important than their behavior in their new environments. Yet this behavior was but an adaptation to new environments. Proof of this is visible today as reservoirs mature and flooded wood cover erodes and is replaced by weedgrowth. Largemouths shift back to natural behavior patterns—their patterns in weedy natural lakes.

The new structure fishing—fishing edges, drop-offs, and points—changed the face of modern angling. Most anglers applied the concepts strictly to changes in the bottom. A few innovative anglers fishing natural lakes, however, began applying the concepts to changes within the weeds. This thinking unlocked the mysteries of bass behavior in natural lakes—classic habitat—resulting in today's better understanding of bass in all environments.

No matter where you fish—lake, river, reservoir, pit, or pond—understanding bass behavior in natural lakes provides the foundation for catching them consistently.

SHALLOW FLATS

In most natural lakes, largemouth bass are creatures of shallow flats. Exceptions occur, but in most cases, bass inhabit shallow food-rich zones less than 20 feet deep.

The largemouth prefers warm water and its compact body shape is ideally suited for maneuvering in cover. It can also function in deep, open water if large numbers of more efficient open-water predators like pike, walleyes, or muskies aren't present.

When largemouths face heavy competition from other species, the typical condition in midwestern natural lakes, they're generally restricted to shallow weed zones. Smallmouths, by comparison, are more suited to deep water, so are commonly found on deep weedless structure. When both species inhabit the same waters, smallmouths are usually deeper.

The lack of large competing predators, abundance of suspended forage

TERMINOLOGY

Structure—the main features of a lake basin—the shape of the bottom. Major structural elements are points, bays, drop-offs, islands, humps, holes, and saddles. Good natural lake bass structure lies at a favorable depth and has a bottom content conducive to growing weeds. Areas with little or no depth or shape may grow the best weeds and host the most bass along distinct physical edges. Finding structure isn't the only key to locating bass.

Cover—any object on structure. Cover doesn't necessarily mean something a bass can hide in, under, or near; but many cover objects are things that bass can hide in. Cover refers to weeds, boulders, logs, docks, stumps, boulders, or anything else that breaks uniformity. Most cover provides shade for bass to rest in and gives them a visual advantage when they attack prey in bright sunlight.

Cover break—an abrupt change in cover. Sharp changes in depth or bottom content form obvious cover breaks. Changes from one weed type to another can be more subtle, yet something ends and something else begins. Cover breaks often concentrate bass.

Weededges are the main type of cover break bass use in natural lakes, primarily because bass feed most efficiently along weededges. Dense, continuous weeds make it hard for bass to launch successful strikes on prey. Though bass can feed in and around weeds, they're more efficient when they can catch their prey in the open water along a weededge. A feeding bass is almost always positioned near an edge, usually a weededge. Aggressive fish often patrol these edges in search of a meal.

Throughout the main part of the fishing season, most catchable bass in natural lakes are near cover breaks in weeds. They don't usually move far on a daily basis or change depth by more than a few feet. Identifying key features in weeds is the key to finding bass during most of the season.

This bass is holding along the outside (deep-water) edge of a weedbed along a bar. The bar is structure. The weeds are cover. The outside edge is a cover break. This is also a point in the weededge, a more distinct kind of cover break.

like shad, relatively high bass biomass, and lack of vegetation contribute to largemouth's use of deep open water in many impoundments. Bass colonize available habitat. These factors also explain why you can catch bass in 35 feet of water in some New England natural lakes where largemouths were introduced by stocking. These lakes host few if any pike and only a handful of small pickerel to compete with either bass species. Largemouths often inhabit deep water, unless smallmouths are numerous enough to outcompete them for prime deep spots.

In large, deep natural lakes with sparse weedgrowth on the flats, localized largemouth bass populations are often restricted to shallower bays or sections of the lake best suited to their basic nature. Deep, open sections are usually more suited to other species. Medium-size lakes usually have more weeds on the flats, and bass may be more common in mainlake areas, though pike or walleyes sometimes dominate deep weededges. Smaller natural lakes usually have fewer large pike or walleyes, so bass may be present throughout most weed areas.

If you know little about a lake, fish it, evaluate the balance of predators, and determine the lake's "personality." Fish populations increase and decrease, and other physical and biological conditions change. Principles provide starting points. The rest is up to you, which is what makes bass fishing so challenging and so much fun.

In most natural lakes, therefore, largemouths are predominantly a fish of the weeds. Deep weeds or shallow weeds are potential areas for largemouth use.

The key to locating bass is evaluating available weedgrowth options and then predicting how bass relate to them. It might be argued that the location of food is more important. Baitfish that bass feed on, however, also relate to weeds. The players are interwoven in the complex web of life.

When spring arrives, there aren't many weed options. Winter ice cover or extended cold water have decimated all but the most resilient, deepest weeds. As the lake warms and the environment shifts into high gear, however, shallow weeds sprout. Deeper weed zones also thicken as spring progresses.

Summer is often heralded by lush weedgrowth from the extreme shallows to the drop-off. Bass inhabit a variety of shallow zones, taking advantage of the abundant habitat.

Fall reverses the spring process. As days become shorter and water cools, weeds begin to die in extreme shallows that are most exposed to temperature fluctuations at night. The shallowest habitat becomes progressively less suitable for bass. By late fall, largemouths have retreated to the last stands of healthy green weeds bordering the deep basin of the lake—the last bastion of cover adjacent to the lake's relatively stable deep-water zone.

Throughout the year, bass continually shift location, following expanding or diminishing habitat. Small groups—not schools—of bass may simultaneously inhabit various areas. Seldom do all bass do the same thing at the same time. At the peak of summer, groups of bass are spread from the shallowest, thickest tangles to the deepest, greenest clumps.

We can't say one type of weed attracts bass more than another, but some common favorites are lily pads growing on shallow soft bottom; stands of reeds, maidencane, or other emergent plants on shallow sandy bottom; coontail or cabomba on middepth or deep flats; and cabbage (pondweed) bordering deep drop-offs.

Each lake has different combinations of options, and the attractiveness of each weed type varies during the course of the year. Bass react to the changing environment by moving to the most attractive zones. Successful anglers evaluate local conditions and determine options available to bass.

MORE THAN MEETS THE EYE

In each of these examples, the shape—structure—of the natural lake is the same. Note, however, that differences in weedgrowth, water color, and balance of predators creates subtle differences in bass location.

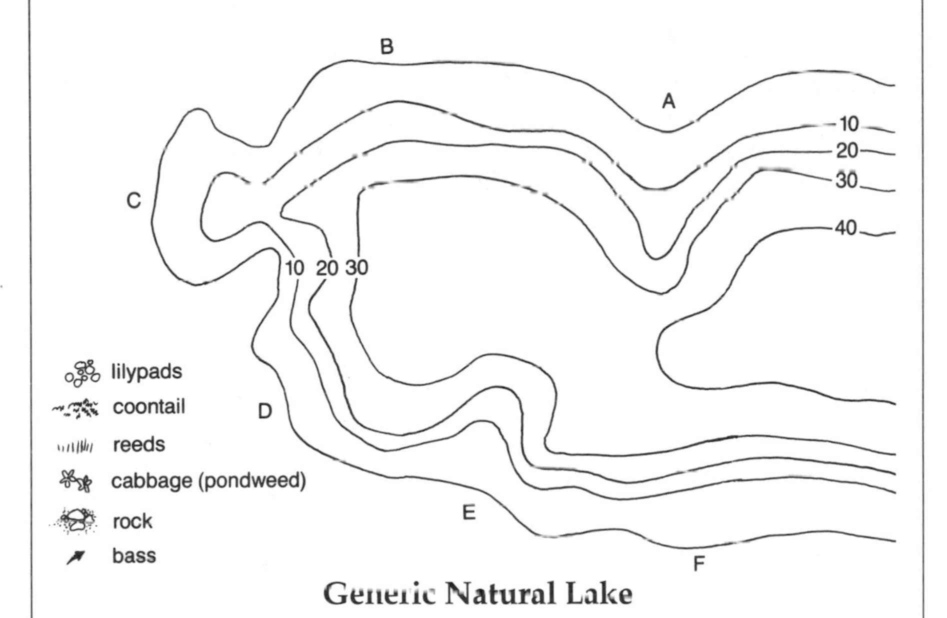

Generic Natural Lake

Many anglers automatically assume that **Areas A** and **E** are the best spots because they are obvious structure. Not necessarily. Weedgrowth plays an important role. In each example, bland-looking **Area B** is a potential spot even without distinct points or turns. The wide, shallow flat at **B** develops some of the best weedgrowth and bass habitat in the lake. Subtle changes in the weeds could hold many bass.

Changes by themselves don't attract fish. Changes in habitat do. First find prime habitat. Then look for edges and variations that concentrate active fish.

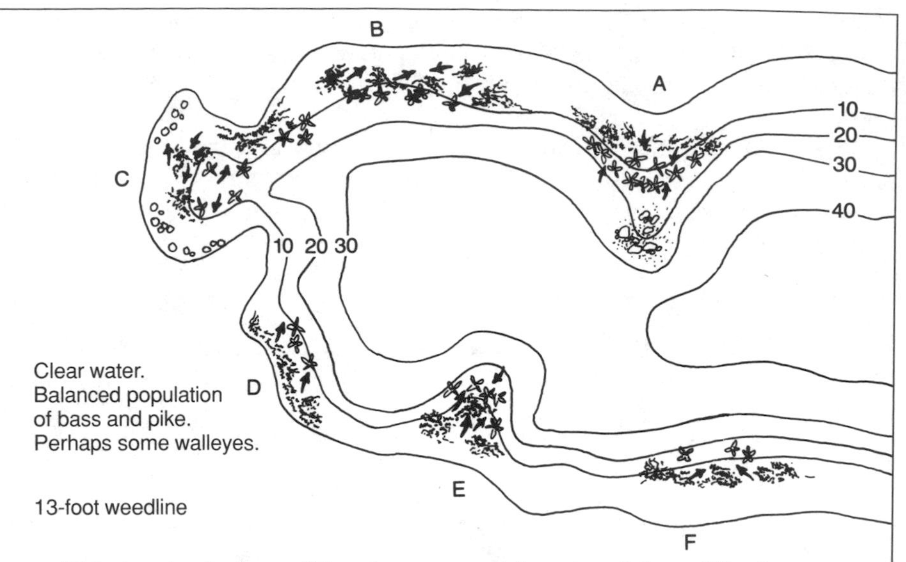

This is a typical condition in many midwestern lakes. Weedgrowth is abundant down to 12 to 15 feet, although significant numbers of shallow open areas with few weeds exist too. Largemouth bass are free to spread throughout the weed zones, although they must share the deep weededge with pike. Pike can drive them shallower than the deep edge at times, but some portion of the bass population will use the deep weededge during summer and fall.

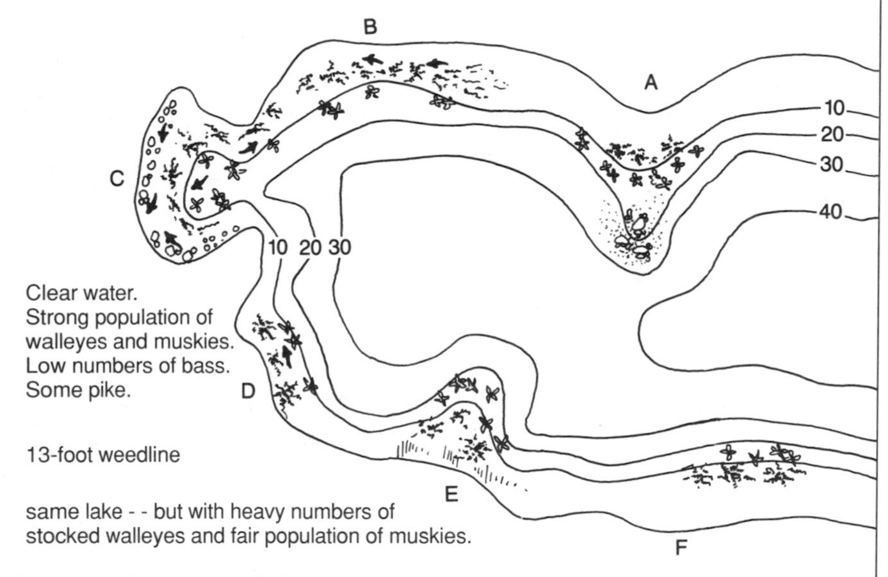

Most largemouth bass will be restricted to the shallow zones, particularly the bays. The bass population is lower than in the previous example.

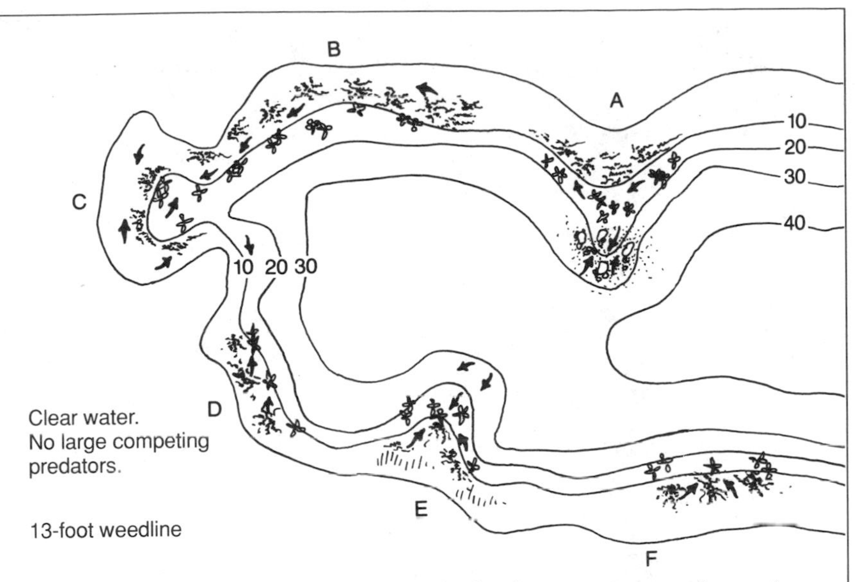

Same lake—in New England. The lack of competing predators lets bass expand throughout the lake and into the deep-water zones. The presence of small trout or alewives as open-water food sources may promote big bass use of deep structure. Bass are the dominant critters in the lake and can go wherever food and suitable habitat exist. Similar behavior occurs in Florida natural lakes, although the waters aren't as deep. Many pits and ponds fall into the same category.

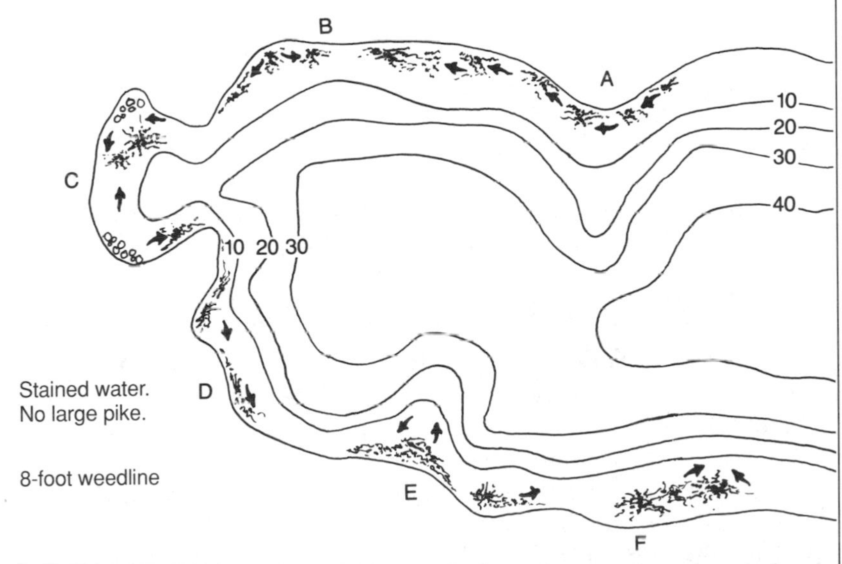

This lake has shallower weedgrowth than the previous examples due to its stained water color. Weeds are thick, clumpy, and extensive, however, with few open areas on the flats. Bass are spread throughout the lake, including along the deep weededge. Note that weeds don't grow all the way to the drop-off, creating ragged weededges rather than distinct outside weedlines.

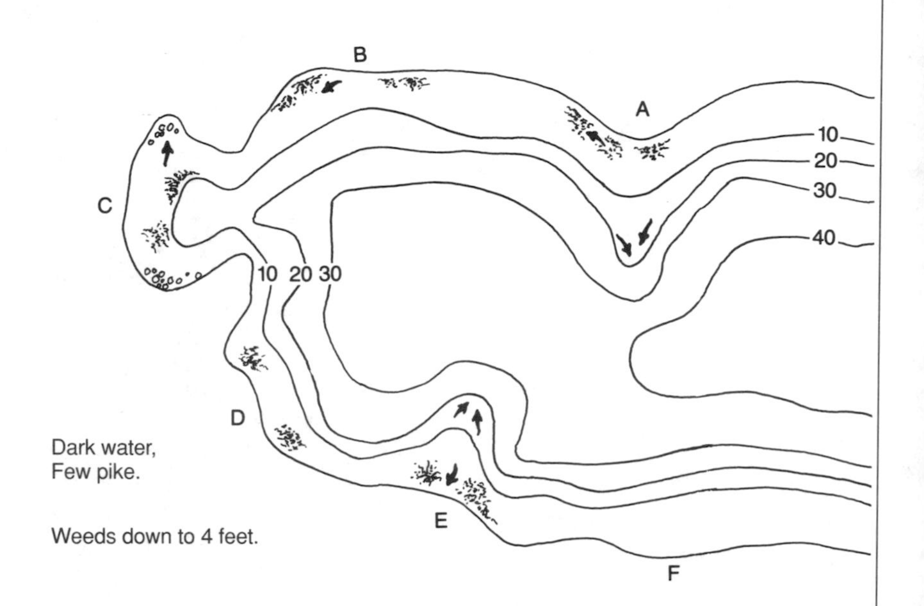

Dark water limits weedgrowth. Bass relate to the few weeds they can find. Yet with few other predators present, bass could use the clean points where weeds don't extend all the way to the drop-off. In dark fertile water, bass could grow quite large, but probably won't be abundant. If the lake is infertile, bass numbers and size may be small.

Natural lake environments can be more complex than they appear. Subtle interactions between fish species and available habitat affect bass behavior. In most cases, however, weeds are the key.

SPECIFIC LOCATIONS

Just before ice-out or at the end of winter in lakes that don't freeze, largemouths in natural lakes usually inhabit the deepest weed zones and are generally inactive. But conditions rapidly change after a few days of open water or a spring warming trend.

Shallow prespawn areas may begin attracting bass almost as soon as ice leaves the lake. This isn't a spawning movement even though bass may spawn in the same areas later. Instead, bass gravitate to these areas because the shallows offer food and warmth.

Wind-protected shallow areas are the first to warm, kicking off the food chain. Plankton attracts minnows, which in turn attract panfish and bass. While during winter, bass feed only often enough to maintain themselves, prespawn bass feed to build energy to draw upon during the spawn—when they expend energy and rarely feed.

Their move to the shallows and the intense feeding that follows are more pronounced in northern climates. Lakes that freeze limit bass activity for a long time, so during the rest of the year the Calendar Periods are more compressed. Bass change locations and feeding attitudes more dramatically than in areas where favorable water temperatures exist for more of the year.

Because prespawn bass are so concentrated and vulnerable in northern waters, many states protect bass with a closed fishing season at this time. Most of the middle and southern states don't close the season because in those regions the Prespawn Period is more drawn out and doesn't concentrate bass as much.

Prespawn bass move to areas that warm fastest. Such areas typically are shallow, have dark bottoms, and are protected from wind and current. The sun, still low in the southern sky, shines most powerfully on the northern portions of a lake. So northern bays warm up a week or so before southern bays.

Bays on the north and northwest shores receive maximum protection from predominant cold winds, another reason lakes "come to life" earlier on those

Just after ice-out, bass are drawn to shallow areas like bays and canals (Photo 1) that warm faster than the main body of water. Later during prespawn, shallow mainlake areas also draw bass (Photo 2). Shallow bass may roam, but often are concentrated by a cover break (Photo 3).

sides. The classic prespawn location is a shallow dark-bottomed bay on the north side of a lake. Channels between bays or lakes and dredged-out boat canals also warm quickly.

Water warms in two ways: (1) The heat of the sun and air warms the surface. (2) Dark-bottomed shallows and particles suspended in water collect heat like solar panels and release it into the water. The main body of a lake warms slowly from the top down. Dark-bottomed shallow areas warm from the top and the bottom, but especially from the bottom. Stumps, exposed boulders, and drowned timber also collect heat.

Weed cover is sparse in early spring, so bass make the best use of available cover. Bass hold by stumps or tuck under shoreline brush, drowned bushes, fallen trees, boulders, or remnants of old weeds.

Two fishing aids are important for finding bass during early spring. A surface water temperature gauge helps locate warm water. Although two bays might appear equal, the temperature gauge might show one warming quicker.

Polarized sunglasses may be even more useful. If you don't see fish in the shallows, they aren't there. If you don't see sunfish, minnows, and insects, bass aren't there either. Small fish move into the shallows quicker than bass. If you see sunfish, but don't catch bass, you might be an hour or two early.

Early in prespawn, bass won't hold in shallows overnight during cool and unstable weather. Instead, they retreat to slightly deeper water and don't immediately move to the shallows in the morning. They often hold a bit deeper until late afternoon when water temperature has peaked. Cold fronts, which are common at this time of year, also send bass retreating to the nearest deeper water—perhaps a depression or hole in a dark-bottom bay. When the front is severe and the water cold, bass might pull back to the first drop-off in front of the bay. They'll be inactive after a front, though you may catch some simply because so many are concentrated in an area.

Bass activity levels change as water warms during prespawn. Early, they are generally inactive. Fish slowly and close to cover with a subsurface lure like a lightly weighted plastic worm, tube jig, or small spinnerbait. When the water temperature rises into the 50°F range, bass become more aggressive. They start chasing and striking surface lures or large spinnerbaits. They're hungry and aggressive. When weed cover begins to sprout, fish more likely hold in shallow cover even if bad weather occurs.

During late prespawn, bass occupy typical spawning sites. These may be in or near the early feeding areas if suitable bottom content and cover are available. Otherwise, they move to more appropriate sites. Dark-bottom bays that drew bass after ice-out may be too silty for successful spawning. They move to spawn in bays with lily pads, reedbeds, or along protected shoreline areas in the main lake. If shallow cover isn't available, bass may spawn on sand or sandgrass bottoms along the inside edges of tall weeds like cabbage or coontail.

As we described in Chapter 6, male bass seek firm-bottom areas to build nests. The bottom must be solid enough so they can sweep away silt and debris and place the eggs on a clean bottom. Lily pad and bulrush areas are heavily used by spawning bass. Lily pad bays make good nest sites if the

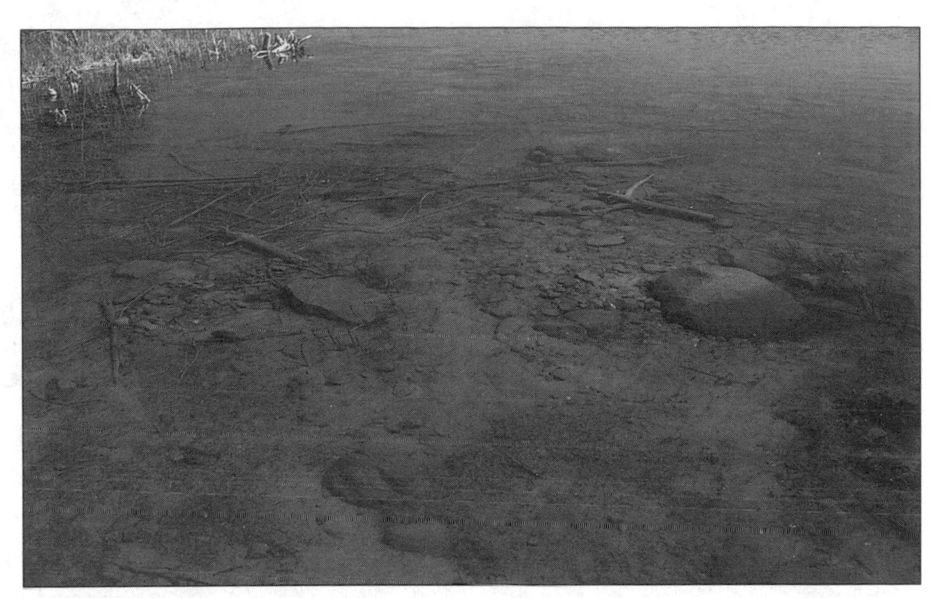

Nests are built on firm bottom.

bottom isn't too soft, and bass will even drop their eggs on the rootlike rhizomes of the lily pads. Many bass build nests in small openings in old bulrush beds. The nest will usually be in 1 to 4 feet of water, depending on water clarity. In very clear water, bass spawn deeper than 10 feet.

Year after year, bass build nests in the same areas, often in exactly the same site, to the inch. Perhaps bass use the same areas because a lake has a limited number of places that meet spawning requirements. When you know where bass have spawned before, you'll know exactly where they'll spawn again.

By the time the surface temperature in spawning areas reaches the low 60°F range, bass are usually ready to spawn. Water temperature is an indicator, however, not an absolute guarantee. Temperature fluctuates in the shallows according to weather, and trends are probably more important than actual thermometer readings.

During late prespawn, male bass sweep out nests. Females lurk somewhere nearby—usually a bit deeper. Nests are generally located near cover like weeds or wood and are easily visible in clear lakes. They're usually 1 ½ to 3 feet in diameter and look like bright sandy disks surrounded by a dark lake bottom. You can often see the male, his dark back contrasted against the light nest.

Both males and females become finicky at this time. As a protective reflex, males strike lures that approach the vicinity of the nest. Neither sex demonstrates the wild abandon they did earlier, so fish slower and more precisely—twitching a Rapala on the surface, for example, rather than using a fast-running spinnerbait.

FLATS

Rather than swimming directly to the deep drop-off, postspawn female largemouths typically disperse from the spawning area to the first adjacent cover on the flats. Developing weed clumps in the 4- to 8-foot range hold small clusters of fish. Females are seldom aggressive at this time, so fish slowly and carefully. After a week or two of recuperation, however, they resume normal feeding activity as they begin displaying typical summer aggressiveness. Once the fry hatch and disperse, males leave the nesting sites and join the females on the flats.

Weeds begin to bloom and thicken from shorelines to deep contour breaks. Bass continually shift and move, relating to the best available habitat as it forms. It's common to catch bass in one spot and find none there on the next trip. Fish are in transition, spreading throughout the expanding habitat.

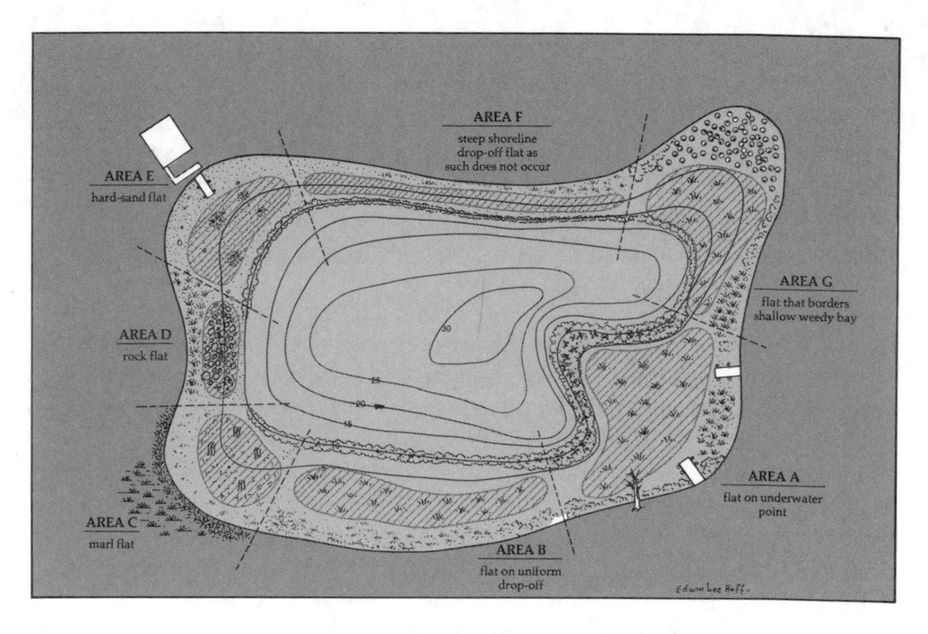

GOOD FLATS VERSUS BAD FLATS

Area A *is a large flat formed by an underwater point. It has thick clumps of coontail in the 5- to 8-foot range and a dense band of cabbage along the outer edge. The shoreline has a dense reed bank for spawning and summer use. The area provides a wealth of habitat and would host a large percentage of the lake's bass.*

Area B *has a thin band of cabbage along the drop-off and a fair coontail bed on the flat. Few distinct points or corners concentrate bass. The deep weedbed is narrow. The area is only fair.*

Area C *has a bottom content conducive to growing only a few sparse, stringy weeds. A waste of time.*

Area D *is a rocky flat with a few shallow reeds. It provides little largemouth habitat in mixed-species lakes, though it could attract smallmouths.*

Area E *is a sand flat with few weeds and even fewer bass.*

Area F *is a steep shoreline with thin bands of cabbage and coontail. Habitat is limited, with no visible irregularities to concentrate bass.*

Area G *offers a variety of bass habitat. The lily pad bay would attract a large percentage of the bass population in spring and support a group in summer. The coontail flat would host most of the bass in summer, since the cabbage rim is thin. A good spot.*

Flats are the key unless better options exist.

What is a flat? Lacking a technical definition, a flat is a region of relatively slight depth change located anywhere in the littoral zone of a lake. It's the food-producing area of a natural lake, starting at shore and extending to the deep weedline.

A good flat provides an extended area of favorable habitat at a depth conducive to supporting weeds. Sunlight penetration must reach bottom for weeds to grow. If the bottom is too hard or too deep, weeds won't develop.

All weedy areas are not flats. A steeply dropping shoreline may contain a band of weeds that offers food and shelter, but not much of either. It isn't a flat and has limited ability to hold fish.

Major flats offer a larger food and shelter zone—bass have more options. A flat can be a point, a weedy bay, a big sunken island, a slowly tapering straight shoreline, a bar, a reef, or almost any shape. It doesn't have to be a distinct structure to provide a broad area at the prime weed-producing depth.

Good weeds make a flat productive. Some flats have sparse weedbeds, and therefore aren't usually attractive to bass. Others have such thick weedgrowth that it's hard for bass to feed there. The best flats combine thick weeds with many edges.

WEEDS

The word "weed" refers to a variety of aquatic vegetation, each with its own profile, texture, height, stiffness, density, and other characteristics. Several things determine which weed species grow in certain areas. Most important are water depth and bottom type. Different varieties of weeds compete with each other for sunlight and growing room. The best flats often contain a variety of weed species, each with different profiles and characteristics.

Lily pads grow in the shallows on soft or semisoft bottoms. A layer of sand several inches beneath the overlying muck will allow bass to construct nests there. Fertile lakes, however, may have several feet of soft muck in lily pad bays, making them unsuitable spawning sites. Developing pads attract substantial numbers of bass during early- to mid-prespawn and host a resident population during the summer. Bass desert them in early fall when shallow weeds begin to die. Pockets, alleys, and outer edges concentrate active bass. Inactive bass bury underneath.

Reeds or bulrushes are a category of hard-stemmed, emergent plants growing in shallow water. They often provide good spawning conditions and also attract bass throughout summer. Thick reeds may hold a resident population of bass. Sparse or clumpy reeds more likely attract active bass from a nearby weed flat.

Thick clumps provide the best cover. In many cases, the shallow back edge of a reedbed attracts the most bass, but again, that depends on what's available. Pockets, alleys, and edges bordering heavy cover concentrate fish.

Maidencane refers to several species of tall branched emergent shoreline plants that grow in firmer soil than bulrushes grow in. Pockets and holes in

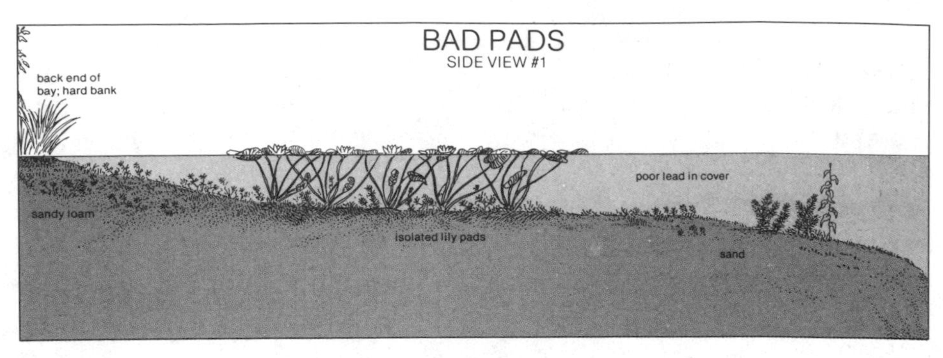

EVALUATING PADS

Sparse, isolated lily pads with poor surrounding cover are less likely to hold bass than areas with dense cover. Adjacent coontail or cabbage and a mixture of weeds within the pads attracts bass. The area must, however, have enough passages beneath the pads to permit bass movement, though you seldom find areas that are too thick.

Points, turns, pockets, depressions and variations in pads concentrate active bass. Inactive bass may be only a few feet away, buried beneath the canopy and difficult to trigger.

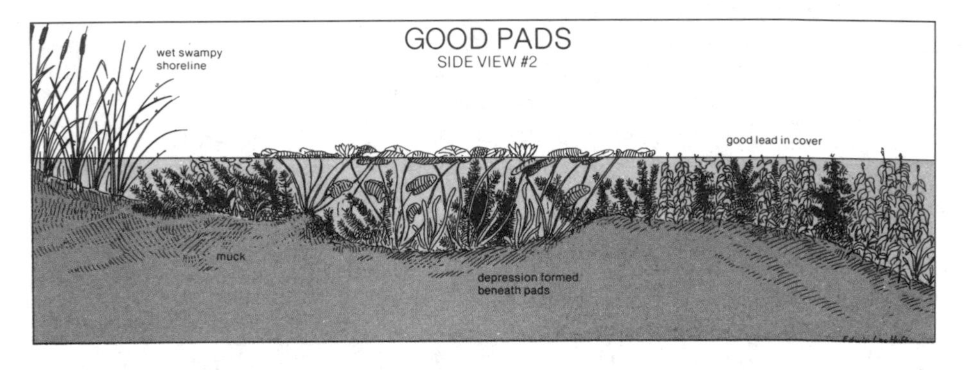

'cane are potential summer bass attractors if the water is 2 feet deep or more.

Middepth flats usually offer a variety of weedgrowth. Sandgrass, an algae that grows 6 inches to 2 feet off the bottom on sandy soil, offers little cover to bass.

Numerous shallow plants grow in thick stands that bass are unable to effectively use. Coontail is an example of middepth growth that's an excellent bass attractor. It rises to the surface and lays over, forming umbrella-shape overhead cover. Dense coontail is difficult to fish, but coontail usually has pockets, holes, and edges; or it grows in clumps with open water surrounding it. It may or may not extend to the deep weededge.

Various species of cabbage (pondweed) often form the deep weededge. These tall, standing, leafy plants are prime bass habitat. They're also easier to fish than coontail. Sparse cabbage has casting lanes between the individual stalks. Even thick cabbage is fishable, since a wrist snap cleanly breaks the leaves or stalk, freeing the lure. Try that with exposed hooks in coontail, however, and you'll foul the lure most of the time.

Some weed types are easier to fish than others, making them favorite

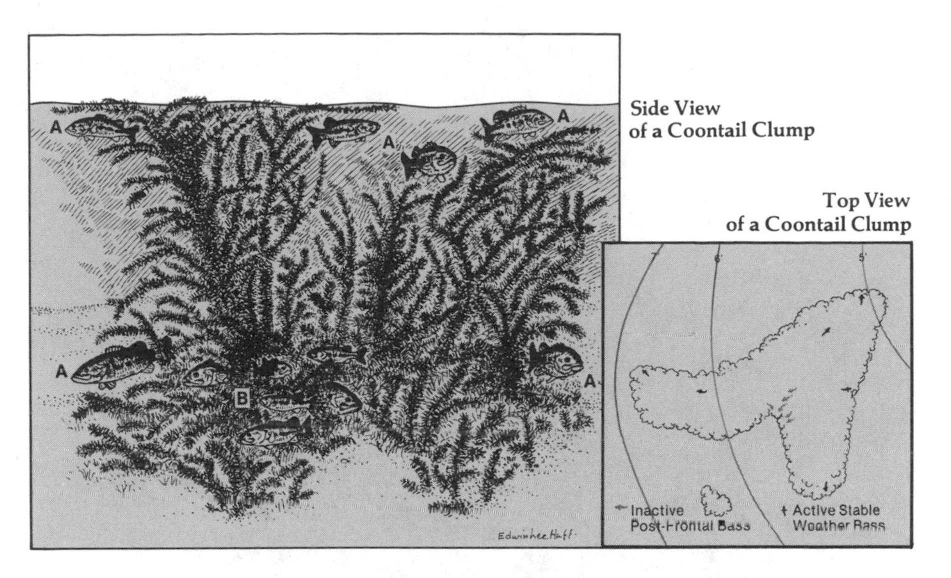

COONTAIL CLUMP

Active bass (A) favor points and tend to ride high. Inactive bass (B) tend to move to corners or penetrate the weeds and be tighter to bottom.

angling spots. Your individual lure preferences may favor certain types over others because you like to fish certain weeds and find others exasperating or simply less pleasurable to fish. Your favorite lures may frequently hang up, or you may have to use heavier tackle than you prefer.

The point, however, is that bass use the best available habitat, which doesn't always conform to angler's notions. To be consistently successful, you can't just fish lily pads or the deep outside edges of cabbage. Be versatile in your thinking and techniques, and approach each lake in a systematic fashion. Be prepared to effectively fish all weed zones until you identify the most productive patterns. Patterns change seasonally and also during the course of a day.

THE WEEDLINE—DEEP AND SHALLOW

Clarity determines how deep sunlight can penetrate the water in enough strength for rooted vegetation to grow. The deep weedline of good bass lakes often lies between 10 and 15 feet deep. In lakes with dark water, deepest weeds often end as shallow as 6 feet. In clear lakes, the deep weedline can be as deep as 20 feet. Unusual weather or algae blooms may cause the depth of the deep weedline to vary a foot or two from year to year, or the weeds may be sparser or thicker than the previous year.

Though the deep weedline generally stops at a certain depth, it isn't an exact line unless it's formed by a distinct drop-off. A deep weedline that typically ends at 12 feet might actually range from 10 to 14 feet, depending on bottom type and slope.

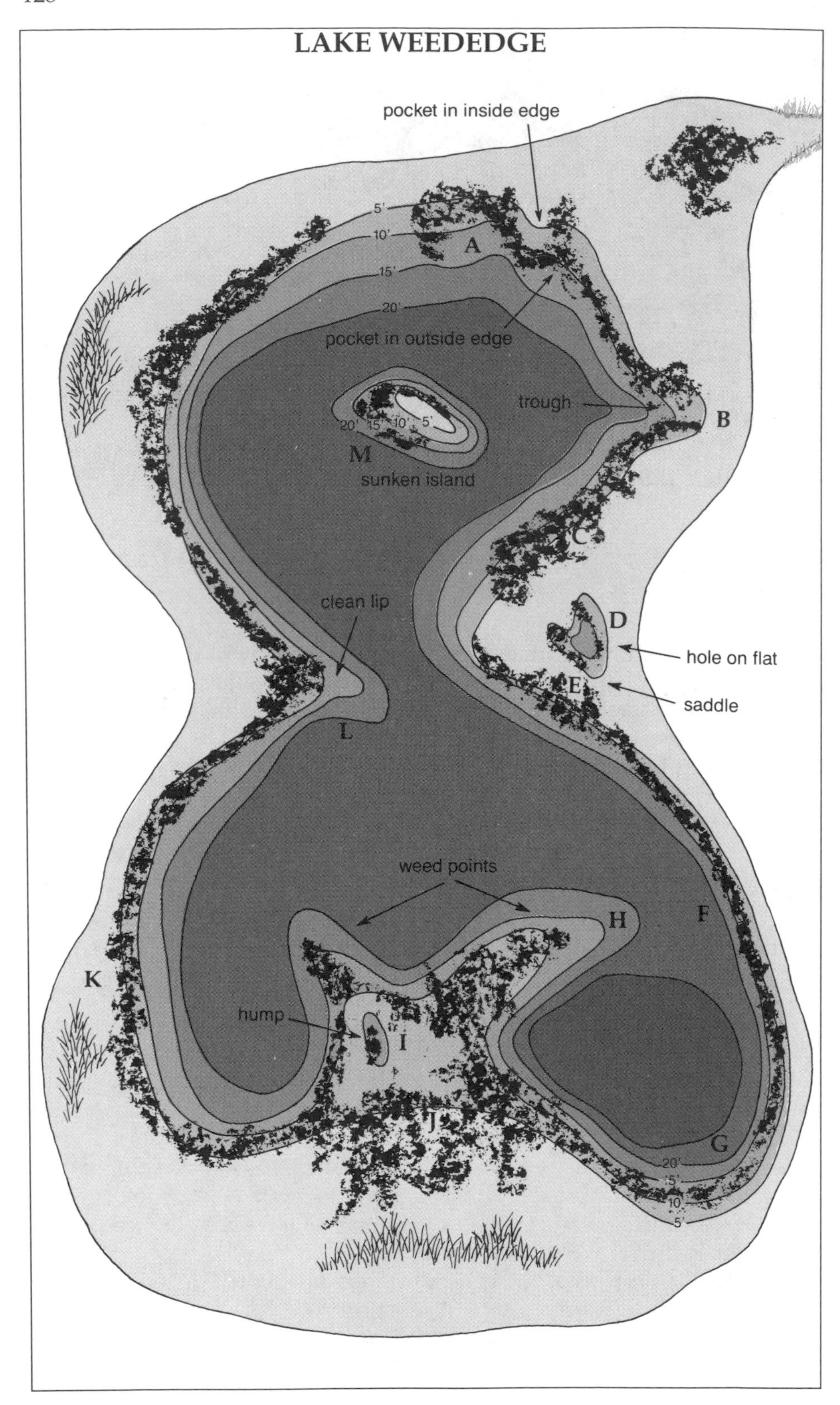
LAKE WEEDEDGE
pocket in inside edge
5'
10'
A
15'
20'
pocket in outside edge
trough
B
20' 15' 10' 5'
M
sunken island
C
clean lip
D
hole on flat
E
saddle
L
weed points
H
F
K
hump
I
J
G
20'
15'
10
5'

LAKE WEEDEDGE

A—Widely spaced, uneven contour lines foster a jagged weededge; look for points, pockets, lots of bass-holding cover.

B—Troughs are prime feeding areas and migration routes for bass.

C—Check inside edges on large flats. An inside edge can hold more bass than an outside edge.

D—A 10-foot-deep hole on a flat—bass magnet.

E—Hole near the drop-off creates a saddle, always attractive to fish.

F—Close, straight contour lines usually mean weed walls. Fish quickly by cranking parallel to the wall. Inside edges aren't as likely to hold fish.

G—A tight inside bend, a likely area for a curved weed wall. Search for active bass.

H—Weedy points near a deep hole; must be checked for weed clumps just off the main weedlines.

I—Hump on a flat, an excellent shallow bass attractor.

J—A large flat usually offers a variety of structural elements that attract and hold bass.

K—A small flat, not likely to hold many bass, in contrast to J.

L—A clean lip where weeds end abruptly and the point slopes gradually toward the drop-off.

M—A big offshore hump (sunken island) offering these fine weededge possibilities: sloping point; small clean lip; sharp drop for weed wall; wider contours for a jagged weededge; possibility of thick clumps on sloping, mainlake side; and a bald spot on top.

Slowly tapering bottoms most often have wandering weedlines with ragged, clumpy edges. Some patches extend farther on the taper than others. You can't simply position at a certain depth with a guarantee of staying on the edge. Watch your depthfinder for the presence of weeds, look into the water with polarized sunglasses, and feel for weeds with your lures. Following ragged weededges requires careful attention to detail, but it's worth the effort.

Throughout summer, the deep weedline is a great spot to contact feeding bass. Minnows and crayfish concentrate there, and feeding bass patrol above and along the weededge looking for food. It's also easy to fish because it's so accessible. Position the boat in deeper water and fish to the weedline, without the control problems you experience moving a boat in thick weeds. Bass along the deep weedline also tend to be more stable—less likely knocked off their feed by a passing cold front.

Since a deep weedline exists, logically a shallow weedline must also exist. The shallow weedline is the shallowest area where rooted vegetation grows. It's rarely as distinct as the deep weedline, often just a patch here and there. Yet it sometimes forms a distinct edge in portions of the lake.

Don't neglect inside edges. They don't get as much fishing pressure as deep edges, yet can be loaded with bass. Shallow weedlines are particularly

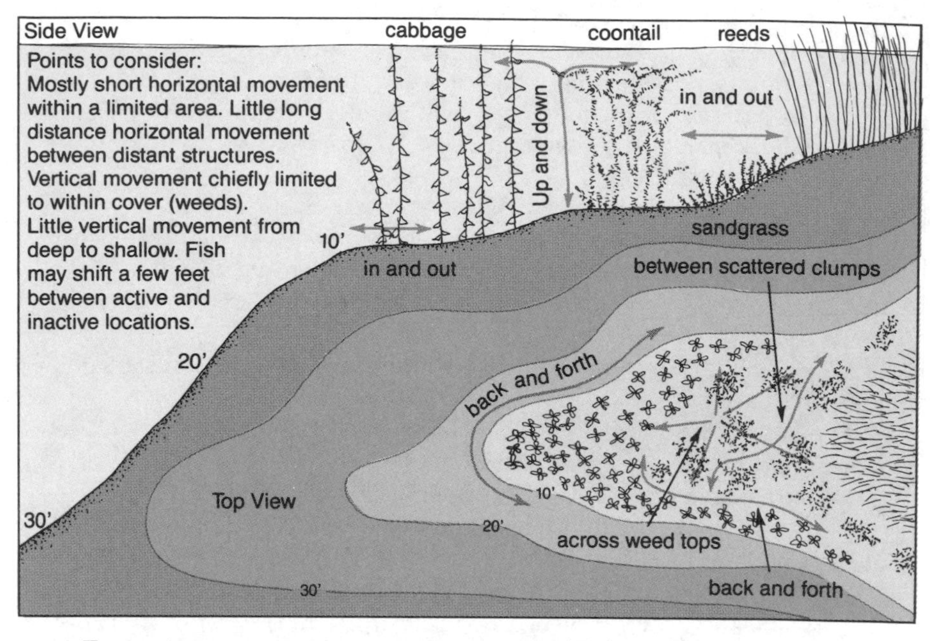

Exceptions are most common in natural lakes without significant numbers of competing predators, or if a group of several large bass (5 or 6 pounds plus) aren't shifted by predator species. Examples: Natural lakes in Florida or New England, or lakes that have exceptional bass populations due to high fertility or a lack of catch-and-kill fishing pressure. Otherwise, such bass are generally scarce and are often caught by accident while fishing for other species. In effect, the mythical school of natural lake deep-water largemouths is usually just that.

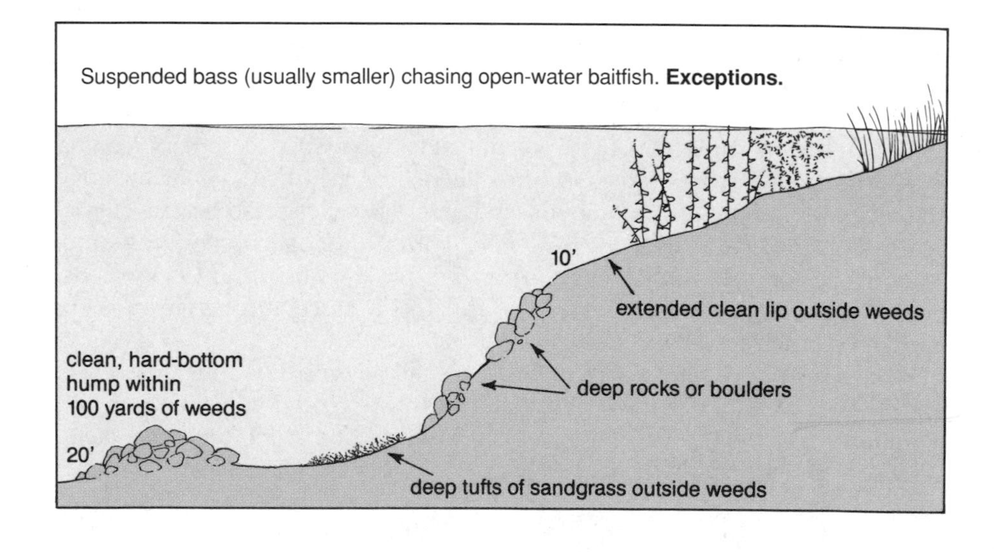

productive in early spring or early summer, especially during the morning or evening.

Weedy flats often have a top weedline—a space between the surface and the tops of most weeds. When there's enough room to run a spinnerbait, a spoon, or a shallow-running crankbait over the weeds, the top edge can be great. The top surface is often ragged, with clumps and small pockets to flutter lures into. Make accurate casts and steer your bait to key spots with your rod tip. When weeds extend to the surface, however, presentation options narrow.

Openings in the weeds form another important type of weededge typically formed by a change in bottom composition or depth. They're hard to find unless you can spot them visually, but they can be good spots because they attract fish and few anglers fish them.

POINTS AND INSIDE TURNS

Weededges can be straight and unbroken, or they can have points, breaks, and inside turns that commonly concentrate bass and other species.

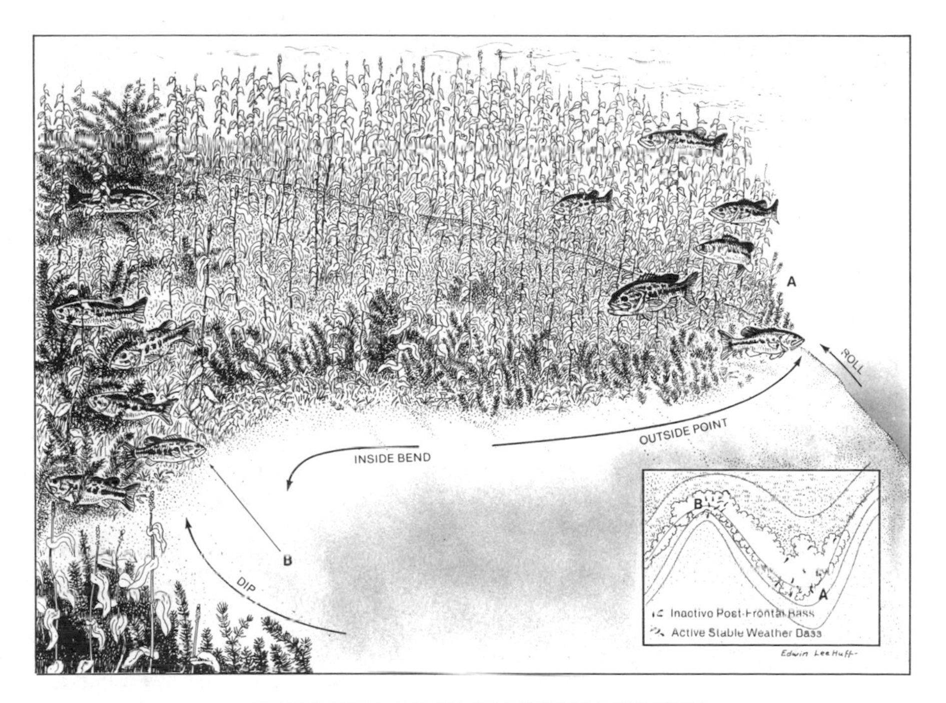

POINTS AND INSIDE TURNS

Point (A) and inside turn (B) in the weedline are distinct concentration spots. They are high-percentage areas for weedline bass unless weedgrowth is healthier elsewhere.

During stable weather, active bass tend to ride high along the deep face of weedbeds and spread along and above points. Neutral or inactive bass more likely tuck into inside corners and hold closer to the bottom. After a cold front, inactive bass may penetrate farther into the weeds and rest near bottom.

Aggressive bass often concentrate around or over the tops of points. They move as far toward edge-oriented food as possible without leaving weedy cover. Inside turns, meanwhile, concentrate bass that are more neutral, though still willing to feed. A bass tucked back in an inside turn is as deep in weeds as it can get and still be by a weededge to grab a meal.

Catchable bass along weededges tend to be along points or in inside turns. This concept applies as much to shallow cover or edges between weed types as it does to the outside edge. (The inside edge of the cabbage may coincide with the outside edge of the coontail, for example.) Figuring which kind of cover feature active bass are using is a major step in defining the most productive pattern.

The deep weededge is prime bass location in fall. As the water cools, shallow weeds begin to die, beginning with the extreme shallows and proceeding to the flats. Largemouths leave these areas, moving to healthy stands of deeper weeds. They concentrate in larger and larger groups as habitat diminishes.

By the time the water temperature dips into the 50°F range, most largemouth bass have gathered along the deep weededge. Even here the

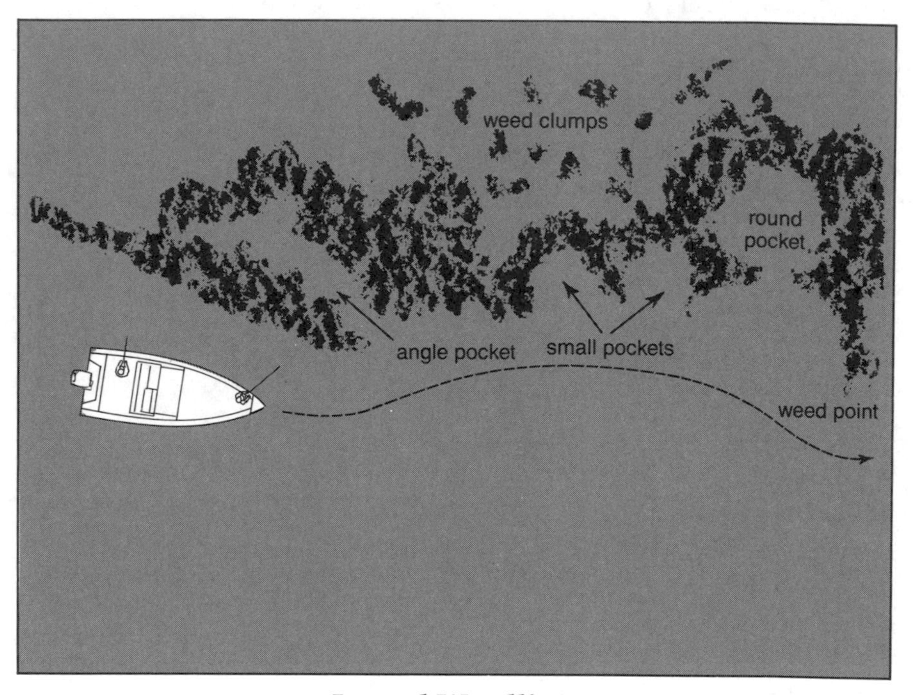

Jagged Weedline

Jagged weedlines offer abundant bass-holding cover. Anglers moving along the weedlines from left to right must watch closely to spot the angle pocket obvious to anglers moving from the opposite side. Bass may hold at the mouth, on edges, or in the center.

Smaller pockets are worth a few casts. Run a buzzer over clumps. Round pockets with interior weededges are good, too; bass may strike a spinnerbait the second it lands. Active bass use weed points.

weeds will have diminished. The healthiest stands of green weeds typically occur along sharp inside turns in the drop-off. Bass of all sizes stack into these areas as fish from the shallows, flats, and deep edges gather to form some of the largest concentrations of the year. This is trophy time.

Bass remain in these areas or areas adjacent to them throughout late fall and winter. They bite well on jig-n-pig combos, plastic worms or craws, and live bait until the water reaches the upper 40°F range. You can catch bass till ice-up with slow, precise presentations. Bass are concentrated, but not active. They're caught at early ice and throughout winter, but for most fishermen it's a long winter of hook sharpening and tackle organizing.

Different natural lakes have different combinations of weedgrowth. Each new lake is an adventure in interpreting new conditions. Each is a little different, but some general rules apply:

- Good flats have abundant weedgrowth with numerous edges. Dense unbroken weeds or weedlines with few changes provide few feeding zones for bass.
- The bigger the flat, the better. More habitat equals more fish.
- Proximity to deep water is important because it offers another option—a deep weedline—that can be a key summer spot and particularly good in fall. But deep water is not a prerequisite during most of the year, as the next two bass locations reveal.

SLOP BAYS

The slop bay is a distinctive type of summer flat. Most slop bays are relatively shallow with dense weedgrowth. They're often the product of nutrient overload, such as badly maintained septic systems, fertilized lawns, or incoming creeks flowing through fertile farmlands. Rooted vegetation often reaches its maximum growth early in the year. Coontail, cabbage, duckweed, and lily pads—especially lily pads—are typical weeds found in slop bays. In fact, lily pads are often referred to as "slop," although the term encompasses more than pads.

When rooted weeds are fully developed, at about the Summer Peak Period, many nutrients become available for filamentous algae to make slop bays sloppy. Filamentous algae lies on the surface like an "angel hair" Christmas tree decoration. It mats, glops together with the rooted vegetation, and forms a floating canopy of clingy gunk.

The floating canopy of slop provides bass from yearlings to trophies with overhead cover and shade. Water temperatures are about as warm under the slop as in sunlit areas, but bass tolerate the warmest temperatures that occur in northern lakes. In southern lakes, temperatures over 95°F can push bass out of slop.

Bass may remain in slop bays if conditions are adequate and prey abundant. Wild rice patches, common in the northern United States and Canada, function much like slop bays; they also hold subpopulations of largemouths all summer. Rice is even more difficult to fish than slop, and presentation options are limited to a handful of weedless spoons, rats or worms. Wild rice and slop are worth the effort, though. The thickest,

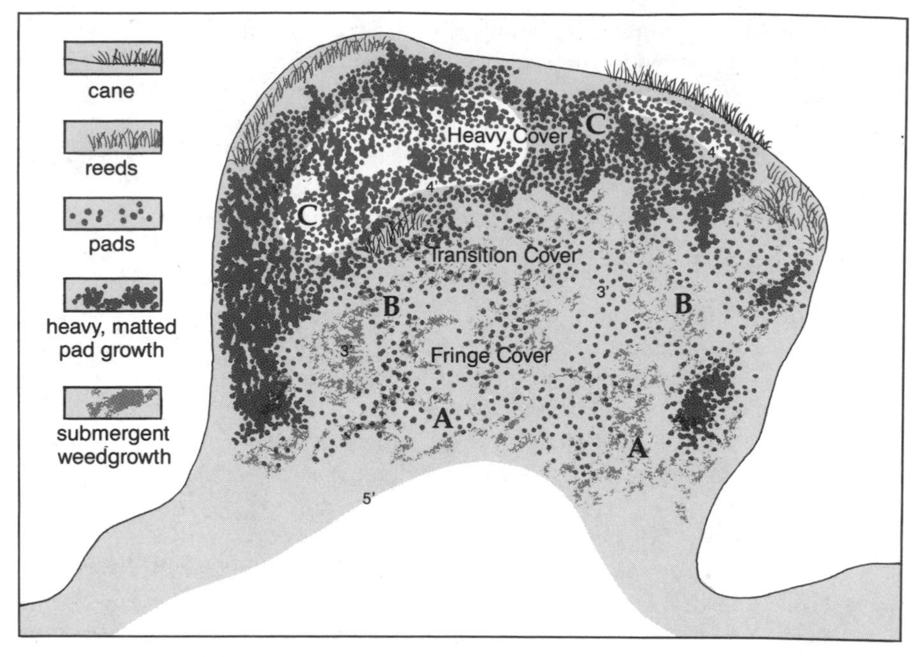

SLOP PATTERNS

Slop Bay

The bigger the bay and the more extensive and varied the weedgrowth conditions, the more bass the bay will hold. Good slop bays, however, must offer heavy surface cover.

*The thin cover in **AREA A** will attract bass sporadically during low-light periods. Heavier cover such as **AREA B** and especially **AREA C** offer enough overhead cover for shelter during the day. Deeper water under the heavy pad cover will draw most of the bigger bass.*

*Thin fringe cover (**AREA A**) should be fished quickly with a spinnerbait, buzzbait, or Johnson Silver Minnow. Heavier transition cover (**AREA B**) calls for a Silver Minnow or Timber King. Heavy matted cover (**AREA C**) calls for a Moss Boss, unless you're picking at individual pockets in the heavy growth. In that case, reach for a pork frog rigged weedless or a jig-n-pig combo.*

heaviest tangles of shallow cover often host the biggest largemouths during summer. Few anglers accept the challenge of tackling them, beyond making token casts to the outer edges of rice or pads.

Bass in slop and rice are extreme examples of homebodies. They remain in their hole or snag, though from time to time they may leave to roam the adjacent flats to hunt food. They frequent slightly deeper holes, fallen trees, exposed roots of stumps, and similar spots in dense vegetation. Incoming springs can also attract slop bass.

Some slop bass specialists prowl bays in early spring to locate stumps, holes, and other spots that hold bass when slop develops. During spring they can fish the bay efficiently, moving from one high-percentage spot to another without making a lot of noise and wasting time hunting for spots no longer visible under the canopy.

Slop bass become almost exclusively ambush predators. They don't see potential prey for long, and in such thick cover they can't easily run down prey. Slop bass are attuned to surface activity, using a combination of vision, hearing, and lateral line perception to pick up moving objects that might be food. When a possible food approaches, BAM!

Fishing for slop bass presents three difficulties. First, it's hard to identify key holding areas when you can't see through the slop. You must fish every inch of them the first time. Once you know key holding areas, though, concentrate on them on subsequent trips.

Second, it's not easy to move a boat in slop—stumps, drowned timber, weeds, and gloppy algae. Outboard motors make too much noise, and water pumps quickly clog and overheat. Even the best weed-chewing electrics bog down when wrapped in filamentous algae.

The best way to move a boat is with a long push pole with a "duckbill" end for getting a good bite in the bottom without sticking there. Reconcile yourself to fishing slower and more methodically.

Finally, it's difficult to land a bass. You need stout line and heavy, long rods to get a bass on top immediately without giving him a chance to get his head down and run for cover. Once a bass is skidding toward you, even a big fish can be controlled. But if a bass gets his head down and turns sideways, it's over.

Use your eyes. Spot bass by hearing or seeing their feeding swirls. A bass patrolling the shallow water of a slop bay will bump weeds or make a wake that tips you to its location.

To fish slop bays, work a lure over the slop and then bring it into small openings where bass can bust it. Spinnerbaits and buzzbaits, two good shallow-cover baits, may not work well if the turning blades get mired in algae. The best baits are weed-less spoons, weightless plastic worms, and

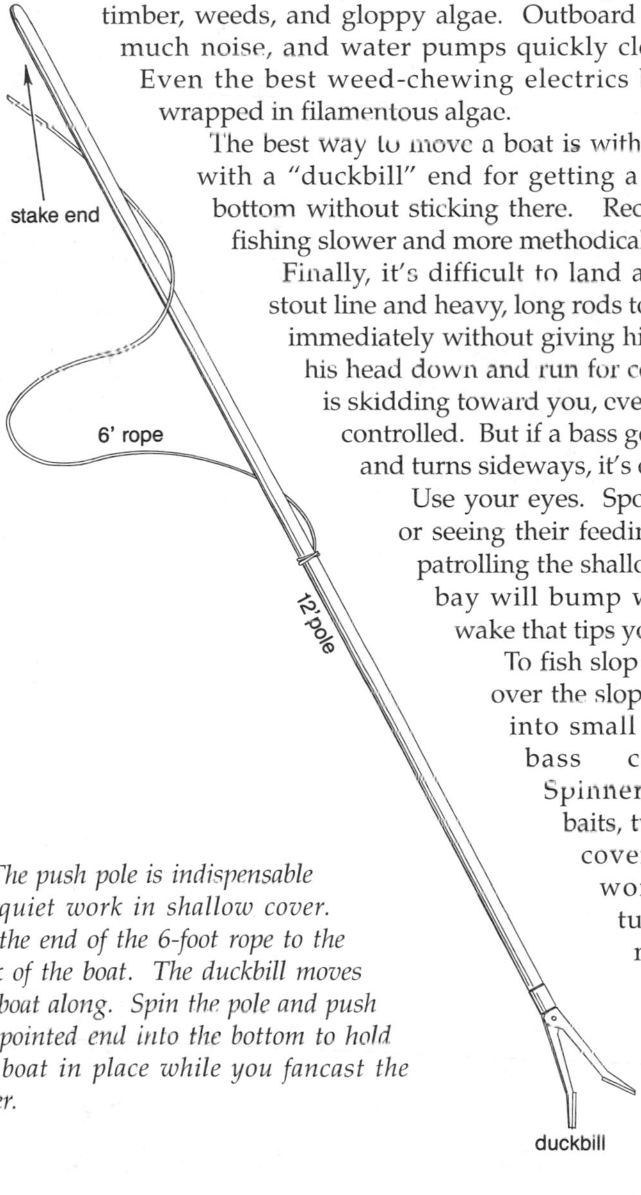

The push pole is indispensable for quiet work in shallow cover. Tie the end of the 6-foot rope to the back of the boat. The duckbill moves the boat along. Spin the pole and push the pointed end into the bottom to hold the boat in place while you fancast the cover.

weedless plastic frogs.

At the first fall cooling period, weeds in slop bays quickly begin to decay. As temperatures grow unstable in the shallows, bass leave and head for the flats to join bass that have been using that area during summer.

DOCKS

Docks provide overhead cover, shade, and vertical objects as well as sunfish and other prey. Given those attributes, it would be amazing if bass didn't live around docks and boathouses.

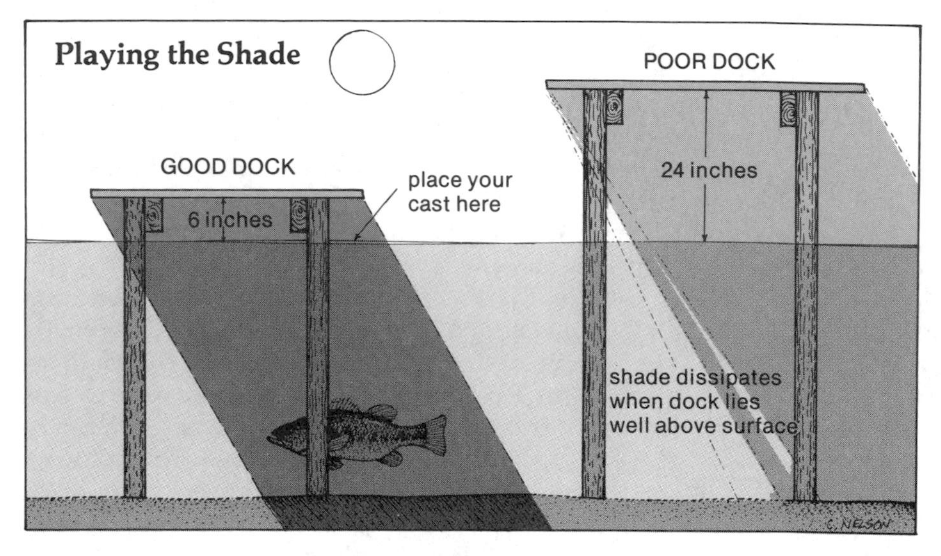

DOCKS

Prime docks for bass fishing lie close to the water and cast dark shadows, giving bass a visibility advantage over nearby prey. Shade also creates a distinct hole surrounded by weeds. Heavy pilings further enhance the area.

Cast wherever cover and shade are present. Corners and edges are prime spots. Cast as close as possible to pilings, bumping them on the retrieve. Pitch lures under the dock as far as possible if bass won't bite at the edge.

Reservoir docks are often built to float due to water level fluctuation. They often rest above deep water. While they provide overhead cover and shade, they lack pilings to concentrate bass in specific spots.

Natural lakes and some reservoirs fluctuate little, so docks are built on fixed posts. Docks may rim developed lakes, so some of them are obviously built on good bass habitat, increasing fishing potential.

Docks often run from shore to depths of 4 or 5 feet, depths bass use heavily. Sometimes docks are associated with weededges because property owners clear paths for their boats or rake out a swimming area. Many docks have deeper holes, formed when the dock owner guns his motor to run his boat onto a boat lift.

Depth is a factor, but don't assume that a deep dock is better than a shallow one. It's likely, but other factors are important.

The best docks are adjacent to weed flats that hold many bass. Some bass may remain around docks, but many move in from adjacent weeds at prime times, usually mid-day.

Docks become particularly important when several good docks festoon a section of shoreline. Bass in that area make docks a major part of their feeding program. But not all docks seem to attract bass. Subtle combinations of factors may repeatedly attract fish to one dock more than to others. You can't always tell why, but a few guidelines will help you spot the best docks.

Docks with wood pilings usually are better than docks with metal pilings. Docks low to the water offer better overhead cover than high docks. Tight decking is better than open cracks. A "T" or "L" extension on a dock makes it considerably better than a simple straight dock. Docks in good weeds usually are better than docks in shallow mixed vegetation, slop, or sand.

Big docks are better than small ones. Docks with boat bays or covered boat lifts are bigger and often more attractive to bass than docks without lifts, although bass can hold in the shade under any boat tethered to a dock. We once thought docks with deep water nearby were better than docks stranded in the shallows, but we've seen too many good docks that aren't near deeper water. What counts is the quality of cover the dock offers and the ability of the area to support fish.

Docks offer the best fishing when sun creates distinct shady areas under them. On overcast days or at dawn and dusk, bass often hold or feed on adjacent weed flats. When the sun rises, though, patterns that worked on the flats may fade. Move to the deep weedline or find a line of good docks.

Three basic approaches work for dock bass. Aggressive bass will be out on dock edges ready to chase. Retrieve spinnerbaits or crankbaits right along the dock edge, especially on the shady side. Flipping is great for fishing docks because you can drop jigs with pinpoint accuracy along dock pilings and in corners where bass hold.

Some dock fishing specialists use a spinning rod to skip plastic worms under docks. The cast is flat and powerful with a slight upswing at the moment of release. Lightly weighted plastic worms, grubs, or tube jigs will skip several times before stopping a dozen or more feet under the dock where less aggressive bass hold.

SHALLOW, MEDIUM, AND DEEP BASS

At most times of year, some bass in natural lakes are shallow, some are in middepth, and some are deep, within the depth range that bass typically inhabit. The ratio changes from one Calendar Period to another. During prespawn and spawn, most bass are shallow. In winter, most are deep. But during most of the open-water fishing season, bass can be found deep, shallow, and in between.

Bass often can be caught in each depth range during the same fishing trip. Generally, though, shallow bass often feed aggressively, but usually are the first to turn off in response to weather fronts. Deeper bass may be harder to find, but are consistent biters once they're located. More bass probably hold in middepth habitat than elsewhere, though it may take awhile to find the best spots, and fish may be scattered.

Every bass angler has certain favorite fishing patterns, but good bass fishermen learn effective approaches for each of the three major depth zones. Tournament anglers use their time during practice to identify patterns that work in each depth range. That's a good practice for any bass fisherman, particularly on an unfamiliar lake.

Because shallow bass are usually most active during low-light periods, a good general strategy is to work shallow patterns early and move to middepth flats after sunrise. Bass along the deep weedline or under docks turn on later in the day and remain active longer. As the sun goes down, reverse the cycle and finish the day fishing shallow bass at dusk.

Interpreting weeds is the key to locating largemouth bass in most natural lakes. Active bass patrol edges, along the top and sides of weedbeds. Tips of weed points are excellent because they're the junction of several types of edges. Active bass are susceptible to fast-moving horizontal presentations

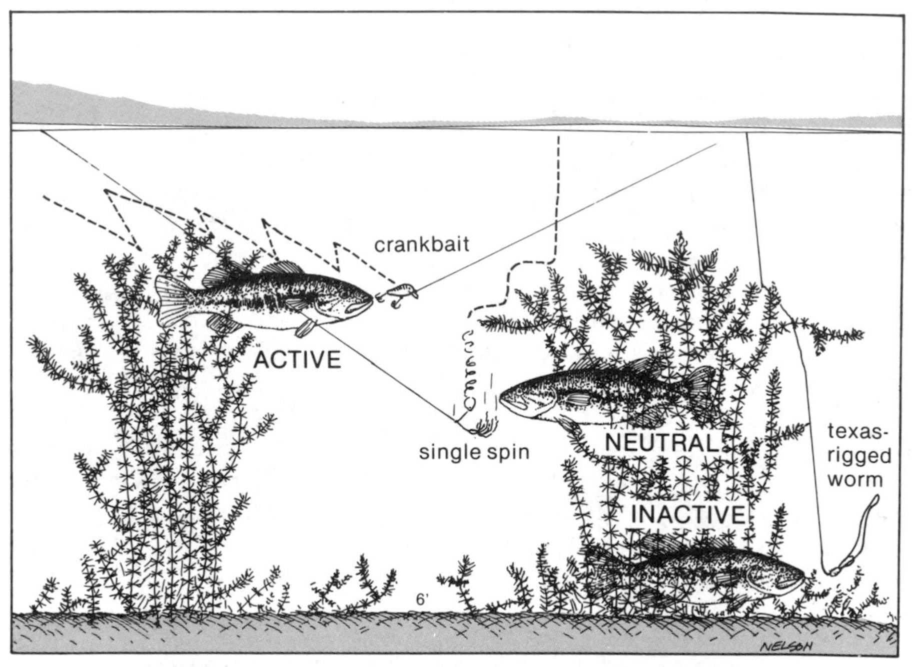

MATCHING TACTICS TO CONDITIONS

Match natural lake presentations to fish aggressiveness, position, and cover. Lures must not only reach the proper depth and move at a speed likely to trigger fish, but must also be relatively snagfree. Open-hook lures like crankbaits or jigworms work well above and along edges or in sparse cover. But switch to more weedless lures like spinnerbaits or Texas-rigged worms to penetrate weeds, particularly heavy weeds like coontail. Pads and wild rice may restrict you to weedless spoons or weightless Texas-rigged worms. Other cover may demand flippin' a weedless jig-n-pig.

Be prepared to use a variety of techniques on weedy natural lakes. Versatility is essential.

like spinnerbaits, crankbaits, buzzbaits, or weedless spoons.

Inactive bass tend to bury in weed patches. Inside corners often are better than points during inactive periods. Slow, vertical presentations like worms or jigs, or near-stationary methods like topwaters twitched above or alongside shallow cover usually are best.

Match your presentation to the type and thickness of the weeds, as well as to bass aggressiveness. Crankbaits work well next to edges or over the tops of weeds, but hangup continuously when weeds extend to the surface. Spinnerbaits or buzzbaits are a better choice over weed tops; weedless worms and jigs can be teased through dense stalks.

Open-hook jigworms work well on deep cabbage edges, where the hook momentarily hangs in weeds before you snap it clear, sometimes triggering nearby bass. But in heavy coontail use a Texas-rigged worm or jig-n-pig. Versatility is essential for consistent success.

Versatility is essential for consistent success.

Chapter 8

RESERVOIR PERSONALITY

Understanding Impoundment Characteristics Keys Successful Fishing

Reservoirs are the most diverse type of largemouth bass habitat. Bass thrive in manmade waters ranging from shallow weedy flowages to deep clear canyon reservoirs. Many reservoirs are so vast and offer so much potential habitat that they overwhelm visiting anglers.

When you're planning reservoir bass fishing strategies, consider first the biological and physical needs of bass, which we covered in Chapter 4. Next, study the characteristics of the reservoir to determine the areas where the needs of bass can be satisfied during each Calendar Period. This chapter describes reservoir characteristics that affect the abundance and location of largemouth bass.

At one extreme are impoundments formed by small dams that slightly widen and deepen streams or small rivers. Such reservoirs retain distinct currents with enough turbulence to prevent stratification. Water quality is similar at all depths, and current-related factors dominate bass fishing patterns. Largemouth habitat is limited and river-adapted black bass like smallmouths usually dominate.

At the other extreme are huge lakes formed by large dams that block major river systems. These impoundments are wide and often deep, particularly toward the dam. The ratio of the volume of incoming water to the volume of stored water is usually small and currents are local, weak, or nonexistent except near inflowing rivers. In the absence of current, water stratifies when the sun heats the surface water. Between these extremes are a wide range of reservoirs, from small to large and from shallow to deep.

Large impoundments lose riverine traits except near primary and secondary feeder rivers and during floods. Large reservoirs also often are nutrient-rich near inflows and nutrient-poor in the deepest areas near the dam. Drainage areas are large and frequently rich in both silt and nutrients. As a result, reservoirs are murky more often and for longer periods than natural lakes. In addition, heavy rain can create sudden and massive currents that swiftly and drastically change the water chemistry and level.

Major impoundments provide a variety of largemouth bass habitat at different depths and in different sections. The largest have extensive pelagic (open-water) and deep, cool areas that are marginal habitat for bass.

Many reservoirs contain riverine portions and slow-water habitats similar to oxbow lakes, river backwaters, and shallow natural marshes. Some also contain large flats with underwater vegetation, plus a variety of inundated shoreline cover. Every concept, technique, and tactic bass anglers use in rivers and natural lakes also applies to reservoir fishing.

But reservoirs offer a wider range of fishing options than rivers or natural lakes. Impounded waters inundate old river beds with scoured edges and rough terrain. They provide more bottom structure, shoreline cover, shallow-water, deep-water, and open-water bass habitat than most natural lakes.

Reservoir personality is determined by physical and biological factors that influence bass behavior. To consistently catch reservoir bass, it's necessary to understand key personality factors of each impoundment you fish.

The In-Fisherman reservoir classification system categorizes six basic reservoir types: lowland, flatland, hill-land, highland, plateau, and canyon (see Chapter 5 for details). By identifying the category a reservoir falls into, you can anticipate basic underwater structures, shoreline forms, and depths.

Key factors include size, shape, depth, current, water level, thermoclines and other clines, water clarity, water color, underwater structure, vegetation and other cover, age, climate, weather, fish population mix, purposes and uses, human impacts, and the histories of these factors. Each factor interrelates with and affects others—many items could be discussed in greater detail than we have space for here.

SIZE, SHAPE, AND DEPTH

Reservoir size, shape, and depth were classified in Chapter 5. Here we recap crucial features that aid understanding of other factors.

Clunn's Reservoir Strategy

Bass tournament champion Rick Clunn divides reservoirs into smaller, more fishable sections, and concentrates only on those sections that contain the most active bass for the time of year he is fishing.

Clunn divides the main lake into lower, middle, and upper sections. The lower 1/3 starts at the dam; the upper section includes the headwaters where the major feeder river flows in; and the middle 1/3 separates the dam area from the headwaters.

Each section has different characteristics. The lower section (1) generally has the deepest and clearest water. Headwater areas (3) are typically much shallower and more off-colored. Middle sections (2) are a blend of the two. He uses the same system (1, 2, 3) to divide major creek tributaries because they follow a similar shallow-to-deep-water progression with many of the same characteristics.

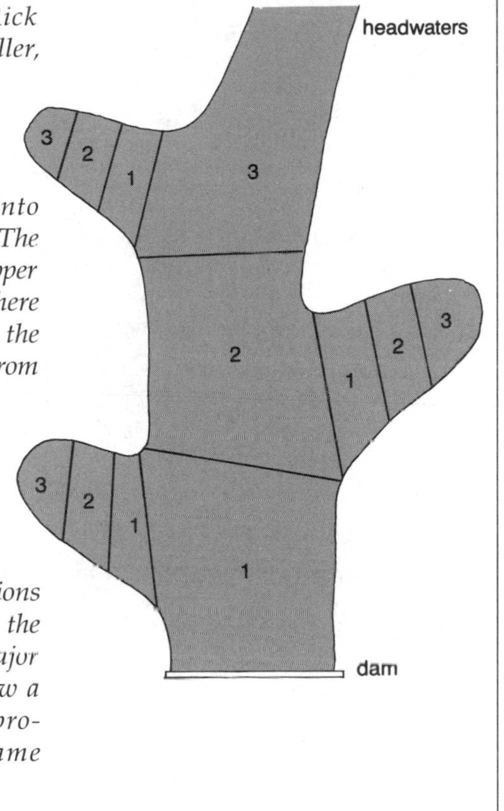

Wide shallow reservoirs warm quickly in spring, stratify early in summer, and cool rapidly in fall. Narrow, deep reservoirs warm and cool more slowly. Given similar climates, deep reservoirs usually host the spawn period later and have extended postsummer periods. In the South, deep hill-land and highland reservoirs may never cool enough to enter a true cold-water period.

When compared with large reservoirs of the same classification, small waters heat and cool faster and offer less habitat. Small waters also undergo complete water changes more quickly during rainy seasons and have less stable temperature and chemical profiles. Generally, small waters provide less consistent bassing.

Compared with deeper waters of the same size, shallow reservoirs gain and lose heat more rapidly, gather silt and age faster, remain murkier, and are more likely to have anoxic (oxygenless) areas near the bottom. Weather changes, therefore, have more immediate impact on fishing in shallow reservoirs.

CURRENT

The ratio of the amount of incoming and outgoing water to the volume of water stored, the shape of the impoundment, and directional flow toward outlets determine where currents exist in reservoirs. Wide areas in the path of inflowing water dissipate currents, while narrows concentrate and strengthen them.

Currents flowing along rough bottoms produce eddies, and currents forced to turn by structure produce vertical currents. Such mixing limits the formation of thermoclines and tends to evenly distribute nutrients, silt, and other water-born material.

Incoming water seeks its own density. Warm, and therefore "light" water flows into and mixes with warm surface water. Cold, dense incoming water sinks under warm water and mixes with cold water below the thermocline.

Salty or mineral-laden water, heavier than pure water of the same temperature, sinks deeper. Pure rain water floats on cold saltwater, and cold rain mixes with warm surface water as it sinks.

The purpose of a dam and the engineering plan dictate how water is released. Outlets near the surface drain surface water, while deeper outlets drain deeper water. Outlet depth also affects currents in reservoirs. A reservoir with outlets at 20 feet produces current at that depth when water is released; likewise, shallow drains produce surface currents.

If currents don't mix water layers, nutrients in incoming water can pass

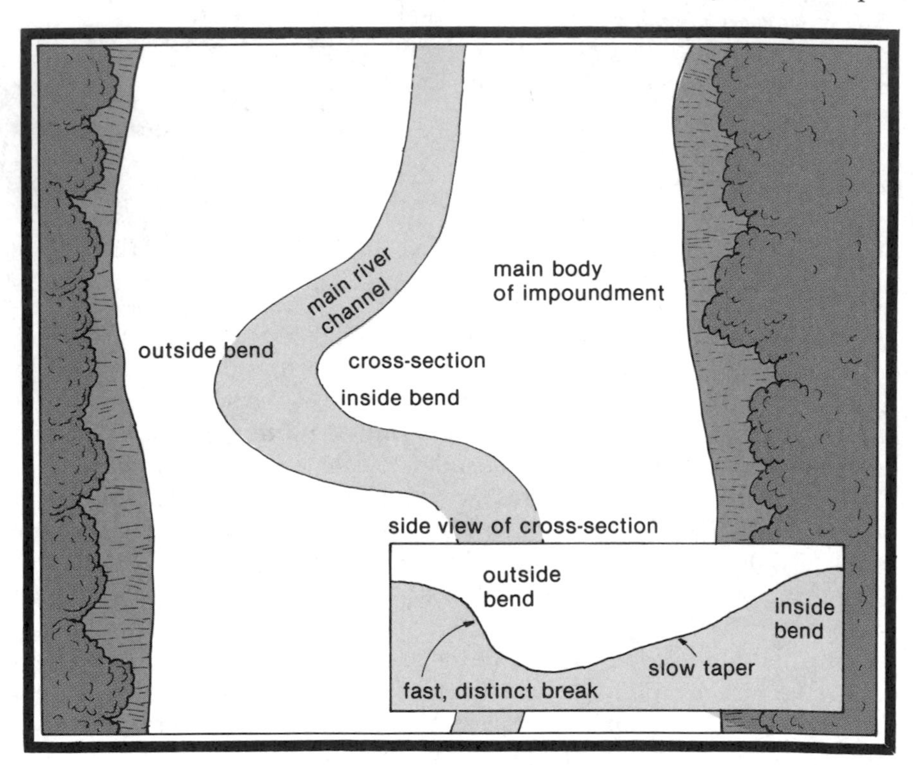

Outside Versus Inside Bends

Outside bends receive more current than inside bends. Current, or at least slight current, draws baitfish and helps facilitate feeding. Outside bends drop off more sharply than inside bends. Quick-breaking areas almost always attract more fish during the Cold Water Period.

through a reservoir quickly while relatively stagnant bottom water remains for months.

In big reservoirs, incoming flows spread and dissipate, and outflows create currents only near outlets. Large, deep-draining reservoirs may develop variable temperature profiles and may not have a distinct fall turnover. These reservoirs provide stable environments and good bassing when other reservoirs are destabilized by fall turnover.

The depth of reservoir outlets also affects water temperatures. Deep outlets remove the coldest water, raise the average temperature of deep water, and lower thermoclines. Shallow drains remove the warmest surface water, reduce the maximum temperature of shallow water, and may weaken or prevent stratification.

Currents are an important reservoir personality factor. When current is present, preyfish and bass react to it. To save energy, bass avoid strong currents by holding behind cover, though they'll face into weak flows.

In still water, bass typically stalk and flush prey along cover edges, or they attack schooling prey in open water. In current, food items drift or swim past properly positioned bass, so ambush may become a more effective feeding tactic than active hunting.

In reservoirs with strong current, smallmouths or other riverine bass species typically dominate. But regardless of species, currents determine where fish hold. When current is weak, bass may suspend and feed in open water over deep channels or move along sparsely covered shorelines and flats. They shift toward bottom or behind cover objects when flows force them to swim harder.

Bass in hydroelectric power reservoirs often match feeding periods to generation schedules. Prey species like shad school tightly and are vulnerable in currents, so bass often feed aggressively while generators are operating. Prey like sunfish and crayfish, however, seek shelter from currents; so where they're the dominant prey, bass may be more active when currents are weak.

Reservoir shape often changes current direction. Identify spots where sharp turns force currents to swerve, because baitfish and bass often concentrate there.

Deep layers of cool, dense water also mix upward at turns. Surface water becomes muddier or clearer, depending on the clarity of the deep layer. These upwellings concentrate nutrients, prey, and bass. Bass may also be more active where deep currents approach the surface.

The most obvious upwellings occur in straight reservoirs with strong currents and only a few sharp bends. Snakelike reservoirs with many bends tend to dissipate currents, so effects may be noticeable only at the first sharp turn below inflows.

WATER LEVELS

Natural lakes have stable water levels. Outflows balance inflows and depth changes only a few feet between rainy and dry seasons. It takes a drought to draw them down. In contrast, many reservoirs alternately store and release water. Inflows and outflows are seldom balanced, and the

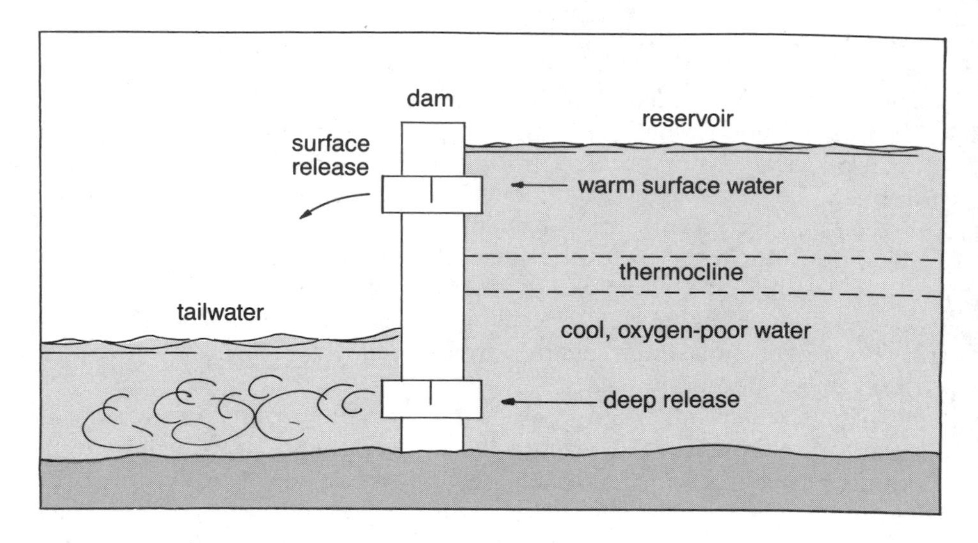

Tailwaters

Reservoirs built with surface outlets release warm water, and bass and other warm-water species often thrive in tailwaters below dams with shallow drains. Deep outlets pass cold or cool water that often holds little oxygen and may be toxic to fish until it mixes with air. Once aerated, deep-outlet water often is better suited to cold- or cool-water species like trout, walleye, or stripers than it is to bass. When bass are present in cold tailwaters, they may avoid aerated outflows and hold downstream where water has time to warm and absorb more oxygen. Some reservoirs release cold, oxygenated water that may support cold-water, cool-water, and warm-water species, respectively, as distance downstream from the dam increases and water becomes progressively warmer.

surface level is often rising or falling.

Generators operate when demands for electric power are high, and peak generation often occurs in hot months when air conditioners are used heavily in southern climates. Another seasonal peak occurs in midwinter when days are short and lights are on longer. Electric demands are highest in the late afternoon and evening, so hydropower reservoirs often have daily generation schedules.

Dams built to store municipal water supplies usually fluctuate less, but generally decline in summer and fall. In contrast, dams built for flood control or to store irrigation water may fall drastically within a few months.

Irrigation needs jump when spring rains stop. Dry seasons increase reservoir demands, while inflows decline. Wet years refill reservoirs, but extended drought forces drawdowns that can damage fisheries.

Water level reduction exposes banks to erosion that may wash away woody shoreline cover, sand, or organic material conducive to plant growth. Soft soils drift into river channels and shores remain rocky, weedless, and infertile. Such reservoirs usually have a plankton food base and bass rely heavily on pelagic preyfish. Clear reservoirs with wildly fluctuating water levels are often unproductive bass fisheries.

It's vital to know the seasonal and annual water level histories of reservoirs you fish. Low water for several years often increases fishing pressure and decreases spawning success. So bass populations decline.

High spring water levels usually produce large hatches of bass, increase cover options, and protect bass from harvest. High water often improves fishing several years later when bass have reached catchable size.

Constantly fluctuating levels often reduce spawning habitat and shoreline cover. This reduces the bass population and may prevent bass from

How Water Level Fluctuations Affect Different Reservoir Types

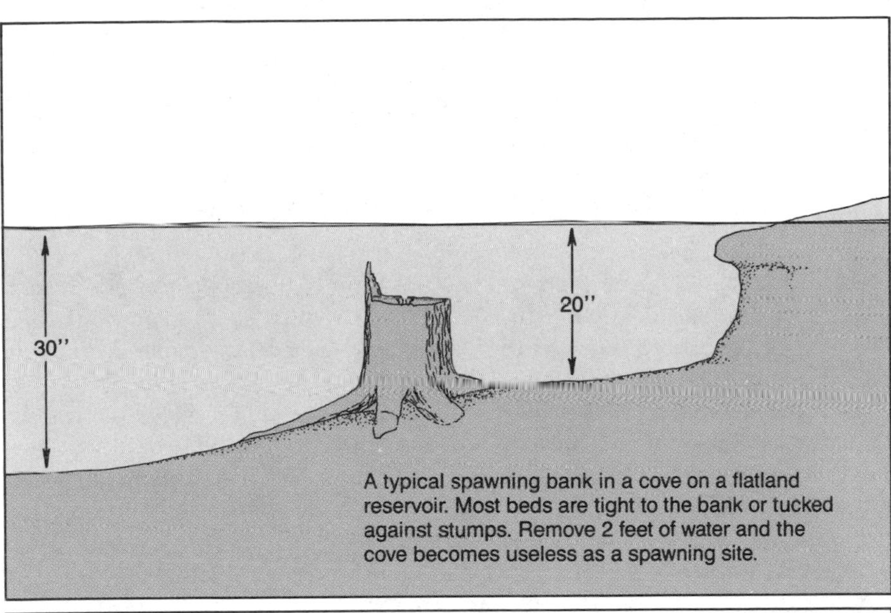

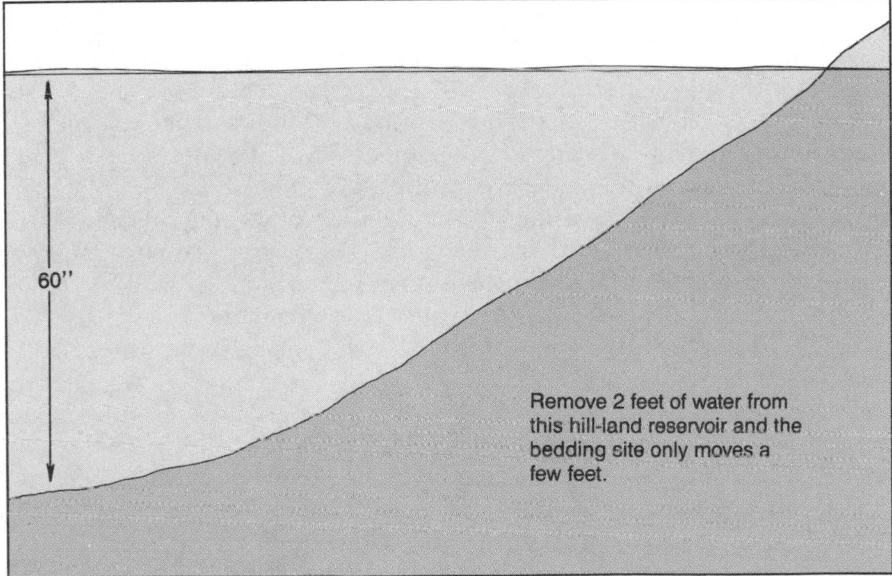

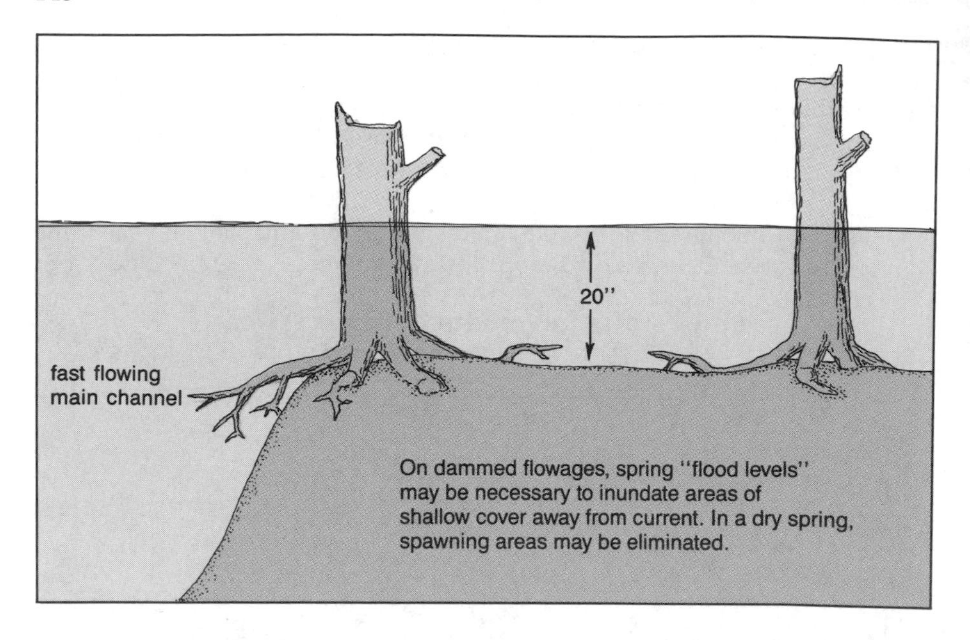

establishing stable home ranges. They are forced to move frequently and often adopt offshore feeding habits. They roam in large groups, if their numbers haven't been reduced by fishing, and they often suspend off cover and structure, particularly if other large predators aren't abundant.

Bass that establish home ranges in fluctuating waters tend to inhabit steep structures that extend from below the maximum drawdown depth to near the full-pool level. These spots provide what bass need, despite major water level changes. Steep points and bluffs are prime locations in fluctuating impoundments.

Bass in reservoirs with annual drawdowns adapt a suspended, open-water lifestyle; or they change habitats seasonally. Shallow flats and banks with gently sloping bottoms are dry too frequently to hold bass, vegetation, and prey. Flats that are frequently exposed are visited by migrant bass only when they're reflooded.

The recent water level pattern is almost as important as past history. Traditional lore suggests anglers fish shallow when water is rising and deeper when water is falling. This isn't always the best advice.

Reservoir bass move shallower, when it's advantageous. When water inundates shorelines covered with terrestrial vegetation, the new shallows often provide abundant food and cover to attract preyfish. But in reservoirs with barren shorelines above the water line, increases in level usually provide little additional food or cover. Bass most likely stay at their accustomed depths.

Dropping water levels force bass off shallow flats and away from shoreline cover, but it rarely affects bass on steep bluffs. Sudden drops may expose crayfish as they evacuate their holes, stimulating shallow feeding activity.

Periodic drawdowns that don't lower the surface enough to expose the outer edge of weedlines can form banks of offshore weeds with distinct inside edges. Vegetation near shorelines grows back slowly when water levels are raised, while the outer rings of grass remain healthy. Offshore weed rings are prime bass habitat—high-percentage fishing spots.

Drawdowns lasting only a few days may kill some shallow-water plant species, but not those resistant to drying, like water lilies and hydrilla, or those like milfoil that rapidly reseed or regenerate from broken plant parts. Indeed, milfoil may dominate reservoirs subjected to occasional brief drawdowns.

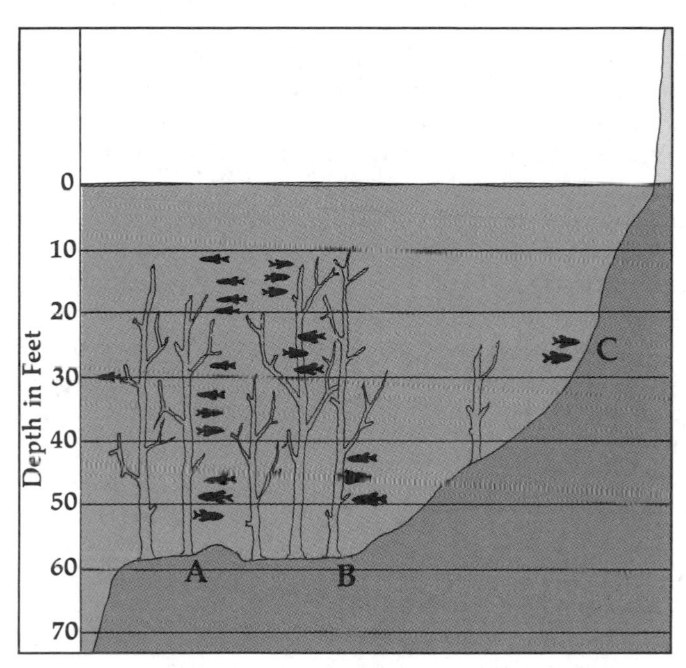

Suspended Bass

In cold water (39°F to 49°F), bass often stack up in large, deep-water schools like the fish shown in **Example A**. Vertical movement limitations mean that the bass in these vertical groups don't behave the same. Deep fish are restricted to deeper water and can't easily move to the surface. The shallowest bass may rise a few feet in response to warm sunlight, but will most likely remain near the depth they've been using.

If bass drop down from an established depth, they're forced to sink or swim actively through the long period required to re-establish equilibrium at the new depth. The low winter metabolic rate of bass makes such a move unlikely. They tend to stay near an established depth, day after day.

Vertically positioned schools break up if bass established at one depth move horizontally a few feet while the others hold in position. The result is **Example B**. Short horizontal shifts by cold-water bass are frequently misinterpreted as depth shifts. Bass that do descend, tend to move down sloping bottoms to rest without sinking farther as they get used to deeper conditions (**Example C**).

Long-term drawdowns kill most exposed weeds. Replacement plants are likely to be species that reestablish quickly by seeds or by regeneration by fragments. By allowing deeper light penetration, drawdowns between 5 and 20 feet increase the likelihood that hydrilla and other deep rooting species will colonize deeper water.

Fall drawdowns may help bass fisheries by exposing prey sheltered in shoreline cover. Drawdowns also dry and oxygenate the bottom and allow terrestrial grasses to grow. These additional cover and nutrients are available when exposed areas are again flooded.

Drawdowns during the spawn can hamper bass production, and early summer drawdowns can force bass fry from protective cover and expose them to additional predation. In general, strong bass fisheries result when water levels are stable or are drawn down in fall and raised to or above normal pool prior to the spawn and held at that level until summer.

A few reservoirs have been built for recreational purposes or to support real estate speculations. They're often held at constant levels that produce excellent fishing if prey and cover are abundant and harvest isn't excessive.

As such impoundments age, however, shallow cover rots and shorelines eventually become barren unless weeds are present. Some fixed-level reservoirs would provide better fishing if water levels were allowed to fluctuate enough to flood terrestrial vegetation during and immediately after spring spawns.

CLINES

Technically speaking, clines are slanting areas on graphs. But to bassers, clines are areas where some characteristic of the water changes rapidly. When temperatures at various depths are graphed, temperatures that change rapidly plot as slanted lines. Scientists and fishermen call areas of rapid temperature change *thermoclines*. Similar interfaces between waters with different pH, oxygen, clarity, or chemical properties are called pH-clines, oxyclines, clarity-clines, and chemoclines.

Currents mix water horizontally and vertically. The temperature and

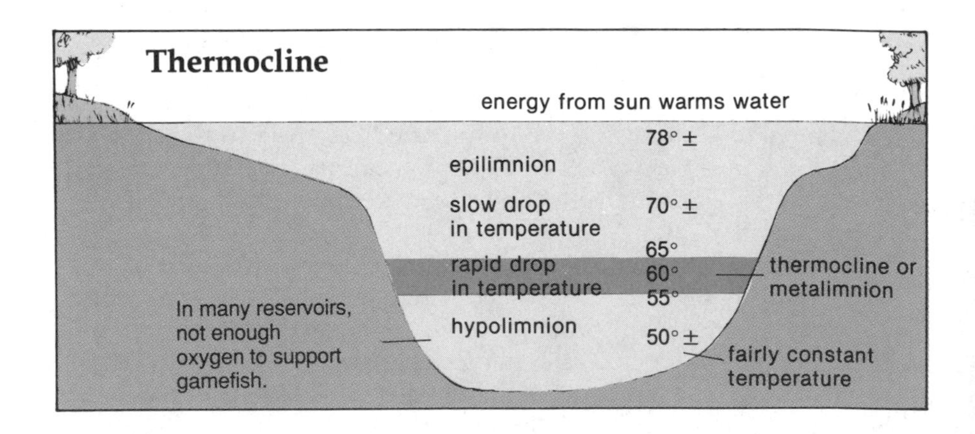

chemical content of mixed waters becomes fairly uniform, resulting in no clines.

But warm water is lighter than cool water, and the top few feet of water in lakes absorb the sun's heat. Unless the heated water is forced deeper, deep waters stay cold. Thermoclines form at depths where wind or currents aren't strong enough to mix warm, light surface water with heavier, cooler deep water.

Sheltered, murky ponds may form midsummer thermoclines at 3 to 6 feet when heat is absorbed in the top few inches and little downward mixing occurs. Clearer waters, which receive deeper light and heat penetration, form thermoclines between 15 and 30 feet. The exact depth often depends on wind. Warm, expansive reservoirs may have yet deeper thermoclines.

Strong winds can destroy shallow thermoclines and form new, deeper clines; while reduced winds may form shallower thermoclines above those formed earlier. Seasonal wind shifts combined with deep-water releases can create stair-step temperature profiles—multiple thermoclines.

When waters with different chemical qualities meet, but don't mix completely, chemoclines form. Saltwater, for example, is heavier than freshwater and may flow under or lie under freshwater and form a halocline (salt-cline). Reservoirs may contain distinct chemoclines when watersheds of feeder creeks vary chemically. Bass may prefer one side of these chemoclines over the other.

Oxygen is absorbed into surface waters from the atmosphere, generated by plant photosynthesis near the surface, or carried in by inflows. Once thermoclines form, deeper water receives no new oxygen from the surface until fall turnover. Living animals and decomposing matter below the thermocline may, therefore, use up available oxygen in deep water. Oxyclines then form.

Bass require 5 parts per million (ppm) or more of dissolved oxygen to stay in good health, and a drop below that level may stimulate movement to better conditions. Hypolimnions in many reservoirs contain less than 3 ppm oxygen by midsummer, but this usually doesn't affect shallow-water fish like largemouth bass.

In some reservoirs, buoyant decomposing particles suspend in or slightly above thermoclines. Decomposition reduces nearby oxygen and creates an oxycline far above bottom. Ample oxygen may exist above and below such low-oxygen zones. But few largemouth bass live below thermoclines or oxyclines unless they move to deep habitat before clines form in early summer.

Rotting matter also creates acidic pH layers and pH-clines near oxyclines. Given a choice, bass actively avoid a pH of less than 6 or more than 9.

Masses of water with different clarities or chemical composition form clarity-clines or chemoclines where they meet and only partially mix. Clines are important personality factors because they form semi-impermeable barriers to vertical and horizontal bass movement. When bass stop and concentrate near clines, good fishing is likely.

Meters are available to measure dissolved oxygen, pH, and light levels. These devices give important information. Once you've charted a reservoir's temperature, oxygen, and pH profile, changes usually are gradual and usually need be remeasured only when weather changes dramatically.

If you don't repeatedly measure water quality, sonar can provide a measure of important information. With the gain set high, clines may show as distinct lines. Fish sightings indicate conditions are acceptable there, while absence of fish may suggest unacceptable conditions.

WATER CLARITY

Water clarity and color are determined by plankton, dissolved organic matter, and suspended particles. In long reservoirs, inflowing water may be turbid and stained, while downstream water is clear. Water clarity gradients often alter fishing conditions over the length of reservoirs and long reservoir arms.

Water clarity determines the maximum depth bass use. Bass usually occupy depths between the surface and the point that light is too faint to see prey. The depth reached by faint light is roughly estimated by measuring the

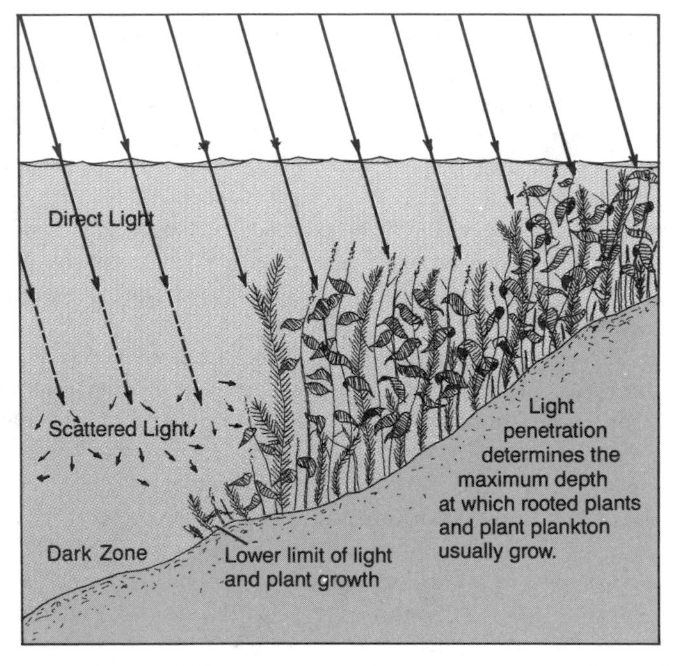

maximum depth at which contrasting objects can be seen from the surface at noon and then multiplying that depth by 4 or 5. Constantly murky water in reservoirs or sections of reservoirs usually means bass are in shallow water. Muddy reservoirs also tend to have poor bass reproduction.

Lakes produce more plankton and become greener when inflows bring nutrients like phosphorus and nitrogen. Reduced water clarity brings bass nearer to the surface. Decreased inflows, typical of midsummer, tend to clear water and allow bass to move deeper. Aquatic vegetation thrives in clear water and also clears water as it grows, since plants absorb nutrients and thus reduce the amount available to plankton.

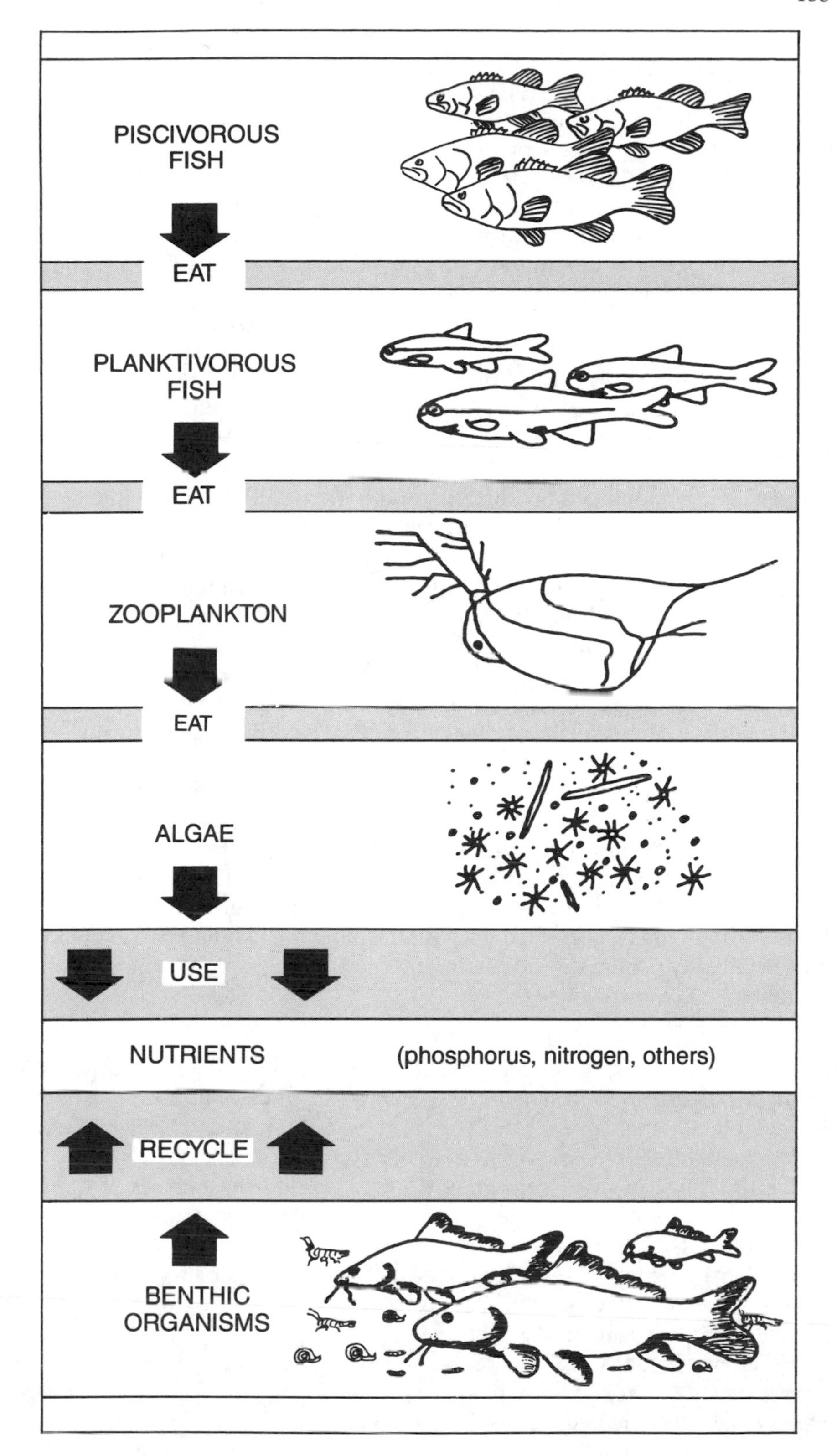
PISCIVOROUS FISH
EAT
PLANKTIVOROUS FISH
EAT
ZOOPLANKTON
EAT
ALGAE
USE
NUTRIENTS
(phosphorus, nitrogen, others)
RECYCLE
BENTHIC ORGANISMS

About Nutrients

The fertility and productivity of a reservoir is determined by the amount and types of nutrients (principally nitrogen and phosphorus) dissolved in surface waters, temporarily stored in living plants and animals, and stored in usable form in bottom materials. The least available nutrient sets the upper limit on the number of bass and other predators a reservoir can support. Phosphorus is usually more scarce than nitrogen, so the amount of phosphorus often sets the carrying capacity and productivity of reservoir bass fisheries.

Most nutrients enter reservoirs from main feeder rivers. Some nutrients are provided by smaller feeder streams; and some are absorbed from silt, rotting plants and animals, and soluble soil and rock. Upstream areas tend to hold more nutrients, produce more plant life, and hold more bass per acre than downstream areas near dams.

New reservoirs often get a massive dose of nutrients by absorption from newly inundated brush, trees, and bottom soil. But these nutrient sources are exhausted within a few years, and the fertility of most older reservoirs is dependent upon inflowing waters and release of some nutrients from the surface layer of deep-water sediment during fall turnover.

Unfortunately, nutrients buried under bottom silt can only be recycled and used by rooted plants. Nutrients that sink below the deep edge of plant lines are often covered by silt, and only the nutrients near the surface of sediments are usually redissolved during fall turnover. Most settled nutrients are permanently trapped, reducing fertility in the reservoir, the river downstream, and in any downstream reservoirs. Upstream reservoirs help purify and clear eutrophic rivers, but they usually reduce the carrying capacities of downstream fisheries.

In any event, the amount of usable nutrients in sunlit surface waters determines the carrying capacity of reservoirs, fishing quality, and how many bass can be harvested without harming the fishing. Bassers who seek quality fishing should select either fertile waters or infertile waters that aren't overharvested.

Long-term murkiness keeps bass shallow, limits spawns, reduces the number of bass, and forces fish to feed by ambush and short-range attacks. Bass can't use their more effective hunt-and-flush and schooling tactics unless they can see at least a foot or two.

Bass that live in clear water may stop feeding during periods of muddy water. When faced with sudden murk, bass may move short distances to stay on the clear side of advancing clarity-clines. But rather than move far from their home range, territorial bass will likely stop feeding and wait out brief periods of muddy water. Bass can and frequently do go without food for several weeks without ill effects.

When you're faced with suddenly muddy water, fish the clearest available water, usually near the dam; or try typically murky headwaters that have experienced little change because bass there are accustomed to poor visibility.

Bass try to move away from thick mud, just as they move away from a pH below 6, oxygen below 3 ppm, areas containing no catchable prey, or any other intolerable condition.

Plankton blooms or muddy water that lasts several months can kill underwater vegetation by shading it. The recent history of water color and clarity can be an aid to locating underwater vegetation or predicting its absence.

Once it's killed, vegetation may take weeks or years to return, depending on weed species and water conditions. Conversely, nutrients released by rotting plants may foster plankton blooms. Waves no longer dampened by surface weedbeds may stir shoreline silt and prevent light penetration that plants require.

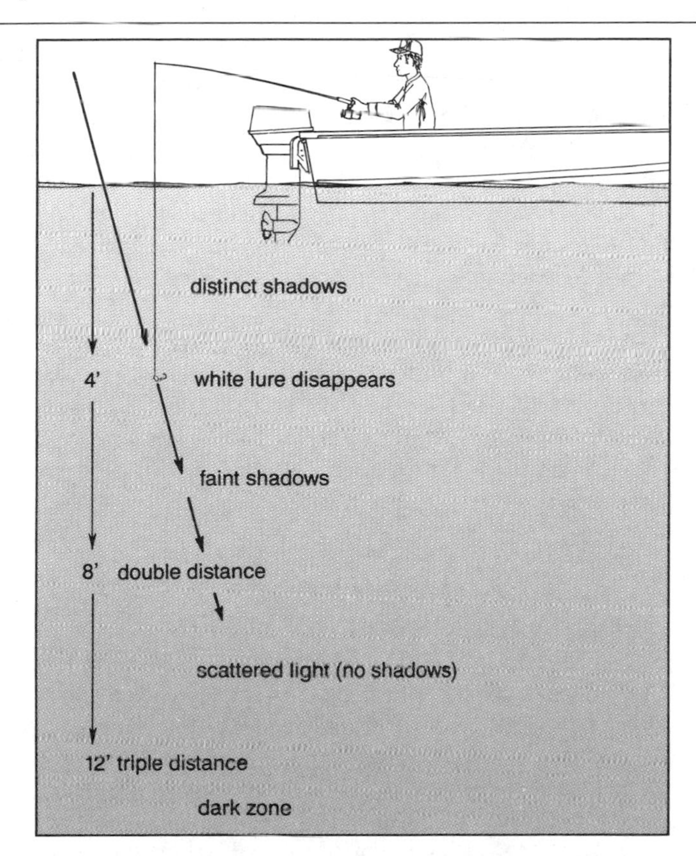

A Layman's Light Meter

Use a white or fluorescent lure to measure light penetration and make judgments about shadows. Lower a lure until it disappears. With the sun overhead, directional light will form faint shadows at up to twice this distance. At triple the original distance, only about 1 percent of the light that originally hit the surface remains. There are no shadows in this zone. Still deeper, light is insufficient to support most plant growth. Darkness prevails, although some scattered light remains.

WATER COLOR

Organic stains and particles in water reflect some colors while absorbing others. This limits the depths different wavelengths of light penetrate, and therefore determines lure color visibility at different depths.

Water in lakes or reservoirs appears blue in the absence of stains or suspended particles. As light penetrates the depths, the red-through-green parts of the spectrum are absorbed, while blue is reflected back to the surface. Water is green when green light is reflected while reds and dark blues are absorbed, as is the case when green plankton is abundant.

Lure colors similar to water colors catch and reflect scattered light. They appear brighter than lure colors that reflect absorbed wavelengths. But absorbed colors may contrast more against a light water background than matching colors. To increase lure visibility in stained water, use baits that contain both the color of the water and a contrasting dark absorbed color. Fluorescent lures are most visible, but may seem unnatural to wary bass.

Water clarity and lure colors determine how far away bass can see lures. A noisy lure tells bass something is approaching and prepares them to strike when it comes within range and appears edible. But unnatural noises may alarm bass. Noise generally seems a less effective feature in clear water where bass have longer to study approaching lures. Certainly, clarity and water color often determine which lure types work best in different portions of reservoirs.

Spinnerbaits, big noisy topwaters, and large rattling crankbaits, for example, often work better in murky or stained water where bass commit to attack before they clearly see targets. In contrast, smaller, subtle natural-colored crankbaits, topwaters, slim minnows, tube lures, and worms and jigs often work best when lures can be seen clearly. Again, different lures may work better at different ends of impoundments.

STRUCTURE

The terrain surrounding a reservoir indicates types of structure underwater. Nearby smooth and gradual rises suggest the lake bottom is similarly slick and gradual, except for eroded spots near creeks and old river beds. Bluffs, scarps, cliffs, rock slides, or steep hillsides suggest similar structures underwater.

Bass tend to move at constant depths while searching for food. They generally move parallel to shorelines and around underwater humps and points. Structures that bisect these feeding paths or force a change in direction tend to concentrate bass.

During seasonal migrations, bass follow structures that run between deep-water wintering areas and shallow spawning flats. They may follow similar structures during shorter daily feeding moves, when they shift depth only a few feet.

Gas pressure inside the swim bladder of a bass reaches equilibrium with outside water pressure after several hours at a given depth. Bass are neutrally buoyant at their holding depth, but depth shifts affect the pressure and volume of gas.

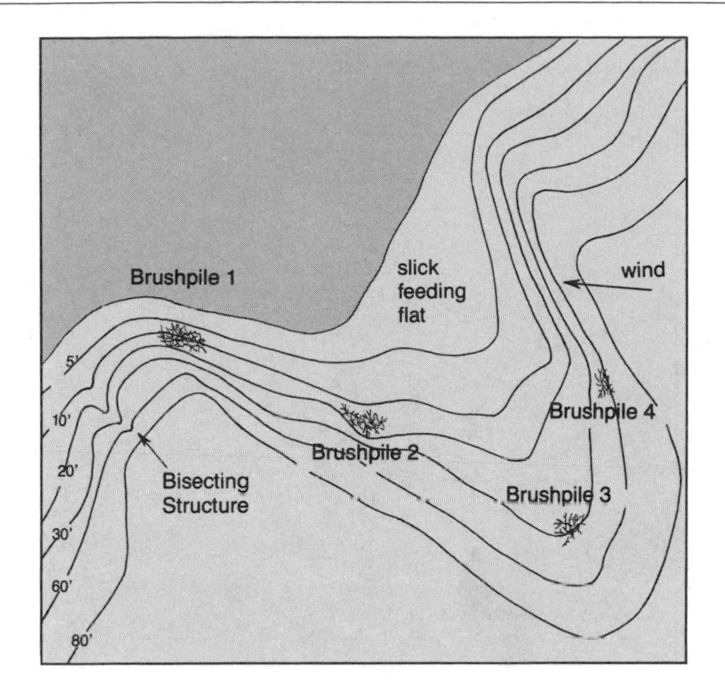

Brushpile Bass Behavior

On a typical feeding flat in a reservoir with scarce cover, active bass frequently feed on the 1- to 10-foot deep flat or suspend about 10 feet deep over deeper water on the upwind side of the flat.

The most likely area for feeding in shallow water is **Brushpile 1**, because bass can move to the flat without making a major depth change. **Brushpile 2** (at 15 to 25 feet deep) is used by bass that feed on the flat if **Brushpile 1** is occupied by large bass or consistently fished down. **Brushpile 2**, however, may be the base area for lunker bass, because they can move vertically with greater ease than average-size adult bass.

Brushpile 3 may be used by a separate group of bass that are unlikely to move to the flat. They probably suspend at 30 feet, waiting for shad to move nearby in the 15- to 30-foot depth range. **Brushpile 4** probably is used by a small group of bass that feed in the 25- to 40-foot range.

Although bass may dash upward as much as 20 feet to attack prey, they must return to equilibrium depth before their bladders expand too much. Inactive bass usually hold at their neutral-buoyancy depth. They tend to hold at the same depth day after day, making depth changes gradually.

Bass also avoid swimming into greater depths where increased pressure compresses their air bladders, making them less buoyant and forcing them to swim harder to keep from sinking to the bottom. Yet bass are often found where bottom depth changes sharply and deeper water is nearby.

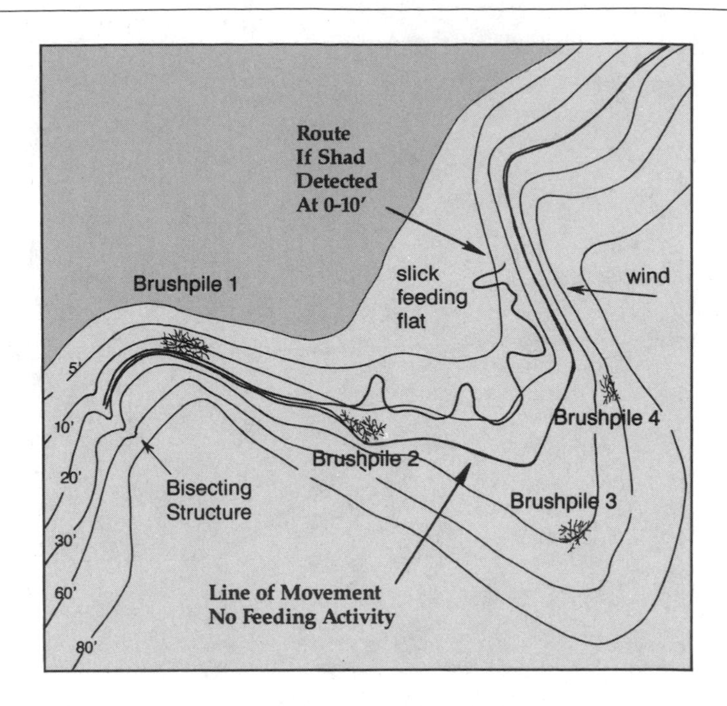

Migrant Bass Behavior

Migrant bass are accustomed to an optimum search depth rather than resting cover or base areas. Suppose migrant bass are used to 20 feet, a typical depth in reservoirs where shad swim at depths from 0 to 30 feet. They'll probably follow along the 20- to 25-foot contour line and ignore **Brushpiles 1, 3,** and **4**. Depending upon their movement as they skirt the flat, they may stop at either **Brushpile 2** or the **Bisecting Structure**. Migrants are difficult to pinpoint, but may be found by following contours at the most likely depth they're used to.

If migrant bass are usually at a 30-foot depth, **Brushpile 3** and **Bisecting Structure** would be high-percentage spots, while they'd bypass other brushpiles.

During summer, fall, and winter, structures that provide depth variation (points, ridges, bluffs, drop-offs) are more attractive to bass than gently sloping bottoms. Vertical structures also increase the odds of finding active fish because a variety of depths can be quickly checked.

In reservoirs without cover, bass relate to the bottom, often holding near the sharpest drop-offs. In reservoirs with vegetation, wood, or rock, bass utilize these cover types, particularly when the cover is on the best structure.

COVER

Cover is critical in determining bass location. Weedbeds concentrate nutrients in shallow water and provide food and cover for preyfish. Bass are

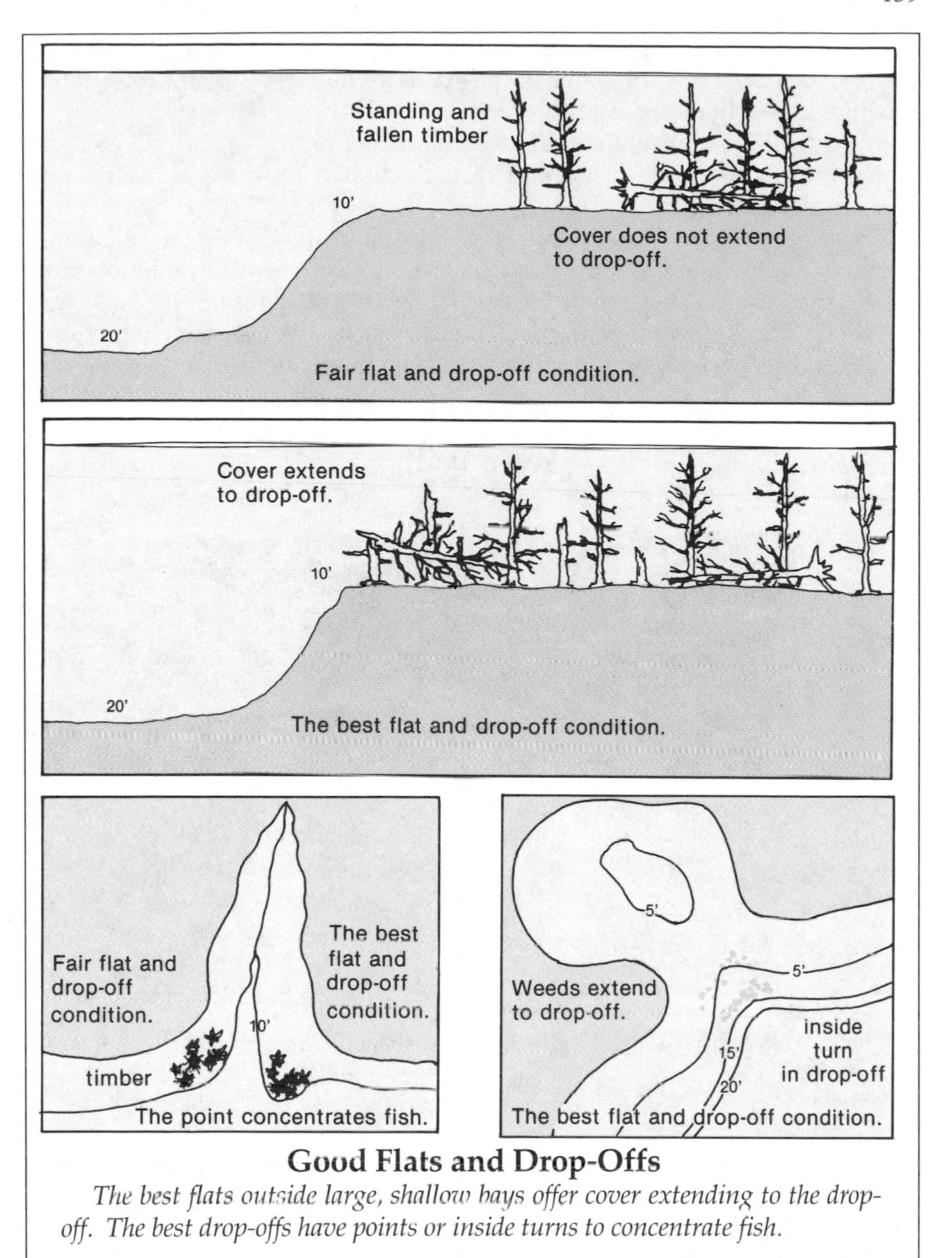

Good Flats and Drop-Offs

The best flats outside large, shallow bays offer cover extending to the drop-off. The best drop-offs have points or inside turns to concentrate fish.

attracted both to prey and to weedy cover. Where underwater vegetation is available, largemouth bass use it consistently.

Unless bass populations are near capacity, or larger and more effective predators occupy vegetation, shoreline cover like trees, brush, and rocks attract few bass when underwater weeds are nearby. Even during cold-water periods, largemouth bass often stay near weeds at moderate depths rather than moving to deeper water.

Abundant underwater plants clear water by trapping silt, blunting wave action, and reducing plankton by monopolizing nutrients. By limiting plankton and creating a food chain based more on rooted plants, vegetation modifies interactions among fish species.

Weedy reservoirs usually hold more bass and sunfishes and fewer open-water species like white bass and threadfin shad than waters with food chains based primarily on plankton.

Reservoirs that are usually murky seldom hold much vegetation because plants require sunlight. Some species of vegetation, however, tolerate more shade than others. Exotic hydrilla, since it needs little light to root and grow, thrives in dingier water than most native plants. It also roots at greater depths and seems to tolerate wider water-level fluctuations.

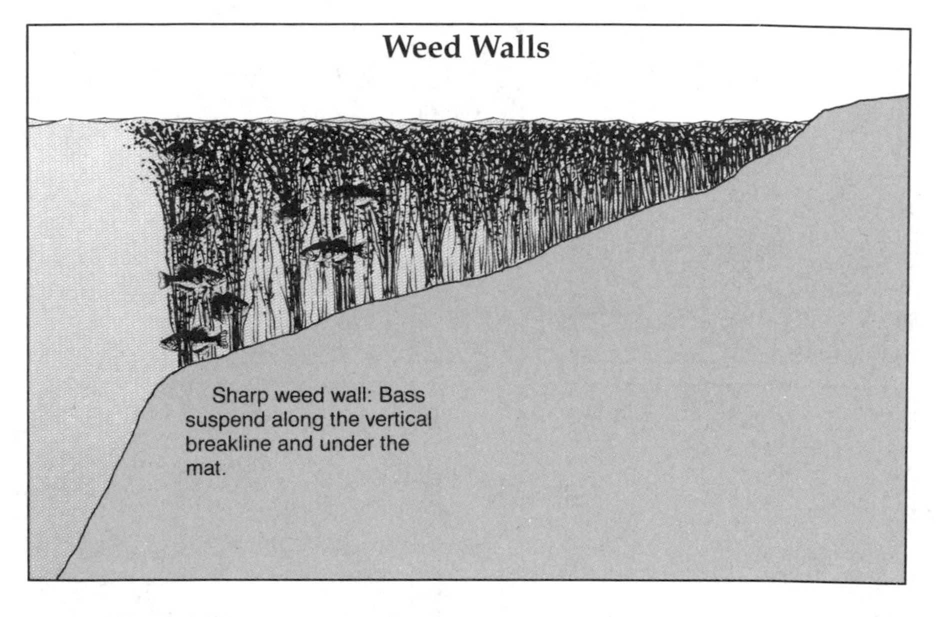

Hydrilla often forms a weed wall when a consistent light limit and drop-off create a sharp cutoff point.

Until hydrilla fills more than about 30 percent of a reservoir, it often creates excellent bass fisheries. But when it grows out of control, it clogs reservoirs and requires expensive control measures.

Native plants generally provide better habitat. Many plant species only grow in specific bottom soils like sand, silt, clay, or mud. These soils at depths reached by ample light determine which species will grow there. If you find bass in a clump of coontail at 17 feet, for example, you'll likely find other patches of coontail at similar depths in creek beds and channels where enough silt settles to form the soft bottom that coontail requires.

Few plants root in hard rock, so highland and canyon reservoirs seldom hold many underwater weeds. If weeds exist, they'll likely be in isolated flats and upstream areas where inflows drop sand and silt.

Aquatic plants trap sediment near the bottom, produce oxygen during daytime by photosynthesis, consume oxygen at night, trap surface heat, and decrease currents, creating local pH-, oxy-, thermo-, and chemoclines under large weedbeds, particularly during early morning hours. Low oxygen and acidic pH conditions often exist near the bottom under weedbeds. So bass in weeds often suspend near the canopy, although water is warmer than at the same depth away from weedbeds.

Water around weedbeds typically holds progressively more oxygen during the day and steadily loses oxygen at night. If the nighttime drop is severe, bass hold near the tops of weedbeds when dissolved oxygen is ample, but move outside the edges of beds late at night. They remain outside until photosynthesis reoxygenates the weed canopy an hour or two after sunrise.

Wood, particularly thick, branched, and horizontal wood is usually the most attractive type of cover to largemouth bass where weeds are scarce. Prime wood in shallow areas provides shade and lies on or near bottom so bass can hold near or under it. Standing timber also attracts bass that

Tom Seward

STANDING TIMBER

You're faced with searching through hundreds of trees. Only a few combinations exist where nature's work coincides with man's work to create ideal structure plus cover. Few 50- to 70-foot trees have crowns to the exact pool level of a lake, and fewer still grow along a creek channel.

These emergent half-crown trees lie along a midlake creek channel, making them distinct from other trees, suggesting that they'll attract big bass and crappies during spring. Work them from each angle, especially between the crowns and along any horizontal extension such as lodged driftwood. Don't drop lures farther than the crowns, because fish don't relate to barren trunks. These are good spots on spring nights, especially when moonlight helps you approach them.

Approach quietly and be rigged for heavy-duty work. Slide lures through the branches and use a controlled drop at the edges of the crown.

suspend to attack pelagic preyfish over deep water.

But wood inevitably rots or floats away. Most wood and brush cover that is periodically exposed to air disappears within 10 years. Tree trunks standing below the surface last longer, but once standing trees lose their branches, they're less attractive to bass. After about 30 years, only the hardest wood cover remains, and most reservoirs need habitat improvement to sustain fine-quality fishing for largemouth bass.

Rocks that provide holes and cracks where crawfish, darters, and other preyfish can hide, provide good feeding grounds, but poor bass cover. Inactive bass hold around rocks large enough to create caves and shadowed areas for protection. Boulders and rock slabs are particularly attractive.

FALLEN TREES

Fallen trees are familiar cover primarily caused by wave produced erosion from wind and boat traffic. Beavers also fell trees, plus lightning, wind, and cutting by state agencies. Fallen trees are best during spring or when trees have fallen in areas with no competing cover.

Consider how recently the tree has fallen, for it affects lure presentation. Clues to look for are the amount of sod remaining in the roots and the number of fine branches visible near the crown.

New trees resemble a broom pushed down by the handle—many small branches near the crown. Bass usually are positioned around the crown, but not in it. It's tough to get a lure down the trunk past the crown, so peg sinkers and don't let the lure bury in tight-spaced branches. A new tree offers directional wood changing to multidirectional wood at the crown.

Aged fallen trees are primarily directional wood; drop a lure down the trunk and bring worms or crankbaits through the sunken crown from 90 degrees to the side. Risks of snags increase, but this is a productive technique that drops a lure through the section of a tree that most likely holds bass.

Prime bass cover provides shade. Shade doesn't cool fish, except in very shallow and clear water, but it camouflages and hides them. Cover that consistently produces bass is usually located on distinct underwater structures, often at spots where bisecting structures encourage moving bass to hold.

AGE

New reservoirs provide unique conditions that almost always support a booming black bass population. Newly inundated land releases nutrients that support large plankton populations that in turn feed fish. If reservoirs aren't thoroughly cleared, inundated timber and brush provide additional nutrients and shallow cover conducive to dense bass populations. Lack of nest-raiding predators and limited competition with other fish allow the survival of many more young bass than is possible in older waters with established, multispecies fish communities.

Plankton blooms and prolific preyfish like shad and sunfish provide ample bass food for the first few years. Later, other species like minnows, carp, suckers, catfish, gar, white bass, and introduced predators claim a larger share of the carrying capacity (total weight of fish) of reservoirs. But fishing remains good unless anglers overharvest bass, silt clogs spawning areas, or rotting woody habitat isn't replaced by vegetation or other cover.

A reservoir's age often determines the number of bass available and where they live. When reservoirs are new and bass populations are at maximum size, population pressure forces bass to spread into all available habitats, including marginal deep water and open water.

When bass populations have stabilized at a level balanced by competitive species, bass are usually found only in better habitats. There's less competition among bass, and fish aren't as likely to be forced to live in deep water or coverless spots. Open-water schooling becomes less frequent in most older reservoirs. And bass only move to marginal shoreline cover or deep structure when unusual conditions such as highwater in spring increase spawning success.

CLIMATE AND WEATHER

Local climate determines how much solar energy reservoirs receive each year. This energy and available nutrients determine the types and amounts of primary production of plankton and aquatic weeds in the food chain. Abundance of these organisms determines zooplankton and preyfish numbers. And finally, the capacity of a reservoir to produce preyfish determines the abundance and growth rate of bass populations.

Each impoundment has a typical heating rate in spring, thermocline pattern in summer, cooling rate in fall, and plankton and prey cycles throughout the year. Yearly events, such as a prespawn bite or a midsummer slump, often recur at about the same time each year. By noting these unique cycles, anglers can plan trips to reservoirs when they usually produce good fishing. Yet yearly variations in water level or abundance of preyfish, particularly shad, mean long-term trends are more informative than "what happened last year."

Water temperature and clarity help determine where bass and preyfish are located during various seasons. Local weather patterns determine when water levels rise and fall, when inflows are muddy and clear, when winds blow, and the severity and impact of cold fronts.

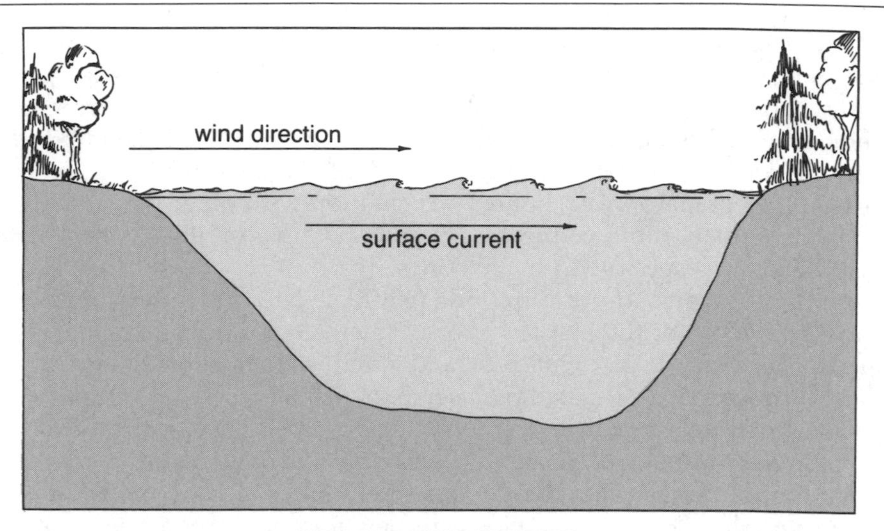

WIND CURRENTS

Currents generated by strong winds over open water flow along the surface at about two percent of wind speed. Weaker winds move water at only about one percent of wind speed. So wind blowing at 30 mph creates a 0.5 mph current, while a wind blowing at 15 mph generates a 0.1 mph current.

Floating objects like a discarded plastic worm can catch wind and move rapidly, but items suspended under the surface in current move slowly. Waves over deep water indicate water is rotating rapidly up and down, but isn't moving ahead fast.

Directional winds create currents. Although most anglers overestimate the strength of wind-induced currents, prevailing winds are important.

In giant lakes and reservoirs, constant winds blowing over open water create weak currents that flow at about a 45-degree angle to the right of the wind direction. Wind currents moving into shorelines at an angle usually turn to flow downwind along the shore. Wind currents hitting shores at about 90 degrees sometimes create a reverse current that flows back under the incoming surface flow.

In average-size reservoirs, wind-generated currents tend to follow mainlake shorelines and circle large bays in the direction of the prevailing winds. Mainlake structures that constrict this flow often attract baitfish and bass. A hump rising to within a few feet of the surface may compress and accelerate wind-driven currents enough to stimulate feeding behavior similar

SEICHE

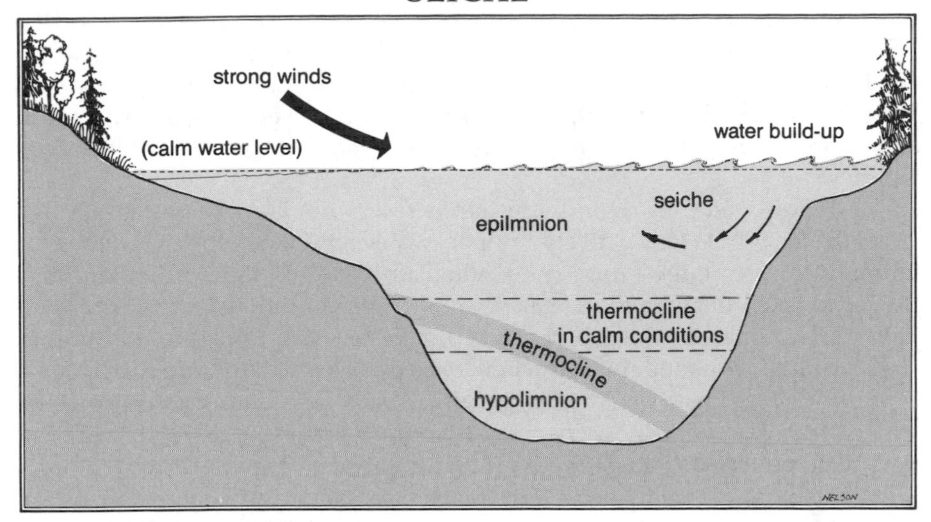

Winds from the same direction day after day eventually pile water on the downwind side of a lake. This creates a weak reverse current called a seiche; water oscillates back and forth between the two sides of the lake, often moving in a circular pattern, determined by wind direction and the shape of the reservoir.

Anglers usually can detect seiches only by noting the periodic rise and fall of thermoclines. In impoundments, seiches, like wind generated by currents, aren't as important to bass location and activity as are river currents.

to that of riverine bass.

Wind-generated currents are less important in small reservoirs, and coves usually don't have detectable wind currents. Winds lasting only a few hours create no noticeable currents and affect fishing only by creating ripples and waves that change subsurface light.

Wind currents that last several days may concentrate floating plankton near downwind shores. These concentrations sometimes attract baitfish, and prey that may stimulate bass activity. Consistent winds also push the warm surface layer of water downwind, while cooler water is drawn to the upwind side. If temperature is a critical factor, prevailing wind directions can help reservoir anglers locate warmer (downwind) or cooler (upwind) surface water.

Waves are usually more important products of wind than currents are. In clear reservoirs, waves on downwind shores can increase dissolved oxygen, reduce visibility and light penetration, and increase the feeding efficiency of bass. When skies are bright, bass on downwind shores are more likely active than bass in calmer, clearer locations.

In typically murky impoundments, where waves dirty the downwind shoreline still more, bass often leave wave-tossed shorelines. Waves produce background noise that may interfere with hearing and lateral-line senses. That's why bass feeding in murky water or at night usually select calm water.

FISH SPECIES COMBINATIONS

Each reservoir contains a mix of fish species. Riverine species, like smallmouth and spotted bass, usually do well in reservoirs with clear water and obvious currents. In reservoirs with murky water and little or no current, the best adapted native fish are nonriverine species like largemouth bass. Reservoirs with intermediate conditions accommodate any black bass species.

The open water found in many large reservoirs is marginal habitat for black basses. Bass feed actively in open water only when they're numerous enough to form large groups and when preyfish are more abundant and easier to catch offshore than near shore. These conditions only exist when lakes are at or near carrying capacity for bass, when threadfin and young gizzard shad are abundant, and when large pelagic predators are scarce.

Surface-feeding schools of large adult bass are usually found in new reservoirs, older waters experiencing a boom following a major drawdown, or waters protected from overharvest by remoteness or special limits.

White bass apparently don't force black bass away from marginal habitats. Sometimes white and black bass school together in open water; but black bass numbers often are reduced after white bass are introduced into a reservoir where prey are a limiting factor.

Joe Tomelleri

PRIMARY PREYFISH

A primary prey species in a reservoir is an important aspect of its personality. Largemouth bass are shoreline oriented if sunfish, minnows, and silversides are their most common prey.

Pelagic schooling species like alewives, threadfin shad, and gizzard shad cause bass to move onto offshore structure to intercept them. Groups of bass may also attack baitfish schools on the surface.

The introduction of striped bass into reservoirs holding black bass tends to shift bass locations. If white bass were already present, stripers and white bass compete directly for pelagic prey. The number of white bass may drop as numbers of stripers increase, but the number of black bass usually stays about the same. The black bass will, however, stop suspending over mainlake points and feeding in open water. As a result, in reservoirs they share with stripers, black bass diet often includes fewer shad and more sunfish and other shallow-water prey.

Competition or predation by pike or muskies sometimes forces largemouth bass shallow, away from outside edges of weedbeds, although mechanisms for this shift aren't known. Smallmouths may avoid both pike and largemouths by staying in rocky weedless areas.

The availability of prey in a reservoir also affects bass fishing. Bass that grow up feeding on abundant shad tend to continue chasing baits in open water. Bass that learn to feed on minnows and sunfish in shallow water sometimes stay shallow as they grow, even though open-water prey are present. In some reservoirs, however, young bass rely on sunfish, then switch to shad.

The types of preyfish in a reservoir strongly influence feeding tactics and

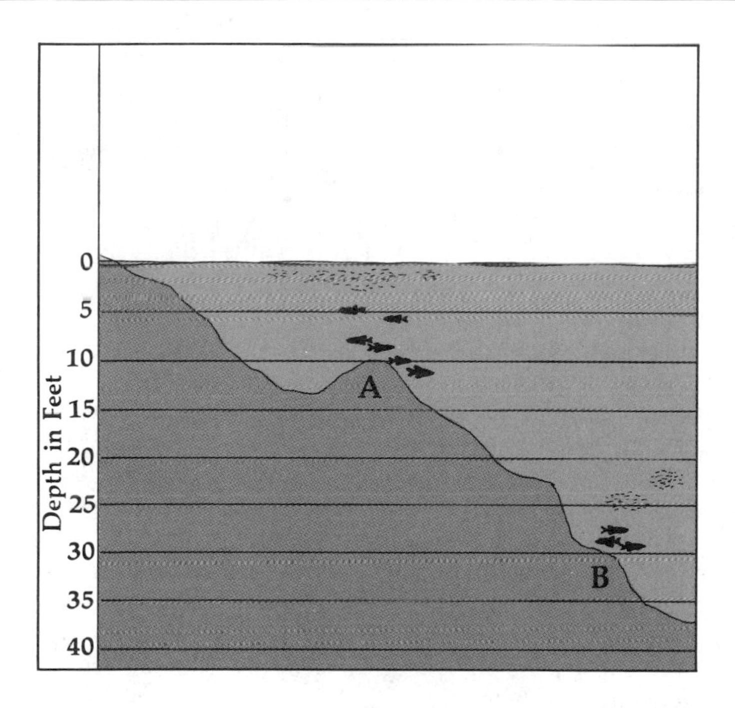

Bass Mobility

This long underwater bar shows two situations. In **Area A**, shad are concentrated at 0 to 5 feet, and bass attack them from a depth of 10 feet. If shad leave **Area A**, bass probably will move to nearby cover in the 10- to 15-foot range.

Shad have considerable depth mobility, and the same school could move down to 25 feet at **Area B**. The bass at **Area A** aren't likely to follow the shad, because a drop below the level bass are using would make them too heavy and would make swimming too difficult. The bass at 30 feet are more likely another group accustomed to the 30-foot level. This group may begin feeding as the shad move into their depth range.

bass location. Review results of food-habits studies conducted by fishery biologists on the waters you fish, and modify your lure choice and fishing locations accordingly.

Bass establish home ranges where they can catch abundant prey. If pelagic preyfish are scarce, bass stay on shorelines where minnows and sunfish thrive. The abundance of shad in most southern reservoirs encourages black bass to live in deeper water and to suspend more frequently than bass do in natural lakes.

PURPOSES AND USES

Reservoirs have been built to control floods, generate power, provide drinking or irrigation water, and occasionally to provide recreation. Recreation benefits are usually secondary, a situation often mandated by original project contracts. The quality of fishing is deemed relatively unimportant by some reservoir managers who manage waters to accomplish their primary purposes. Policies may then limit fishing.

But by altering generation and release schedules, reservoir managers could increase nutrient distribution and fish production in many reservoir and downstream fisheries. For example, authorities might limit spring drawdowns to protect bass spawns or drop water levels in fall to increase predation on shad or sunfish. Some impoundments could also be improved by fostering weedgrowth, planting artificial structures, or leaving more woody cover when reservoirs are constructed.

When anglers have organized and presented sound arguments to support policies that produce better fisheries without interference with a facility's primary mission, water authorities have sometimes modified policies. Fishery agencies, often backed by sportsmen's groups, have stopped excessive clearing of reservoirs before impoundment and have limited drawdowns during spawning seasons. We expect such cooperative efforts to increase the potential for reservoir management in the future.

Anglers aren't always able to change release policies, but they can learn release schedules and fish appropriately. By comparing releases with diaries showing times of good and slow fishing, direct relationships can be discovered. On subsequent trips, anglers can anticipate patterns associated with outlet-generated currents.

Other reservoir purposes can also influence fishing. Managers of water supply reservoirs may limit boating access or motor size, insist on sewage treatment regulations that limit nutrient inflow, or prevent fishing entirely.

In the absence of effective regulations, shoreline property owners may remove desirable shoreline cover or vegetation. Homeowners may also insist on constant lake levels, or periodic drawdowns to kill vegetation, although both actions can harm fishing quality.

Public policies are part of each reservoir's personality. Fishing regulations affect bass abundance and size. Impoundments produce long-lasting, productive bass fisheries only when they are managed with that goal in mind.

Anglers favoring species other than bass may insist predators or preyfish be stocked, even though black bass population sizes or growth rates may be reduced. Boating lobbies or the anticipation of recreational boating may force excessive clearing of timber and brush when lands are prepared for new reservoirs.

Fishery managers may also encourage harvest with liberal limits that often produce fished-down bassing waters. Or managers may limit harvest and build or sustain near-capacity bass populations. Lake managers can limit the inflow of silt, encourage weedgrowth, and replace lost habitat; or they can let reservoirs age rapidly.

You wouldn't have bought this book and read this far if you weren't a dedicated bass angler eager to learn details to improve fishing success. Do you recognize and incorporate every pertinent personality factor into your strategy when you fish a reservoir? What factors determine where and when you fish?

Make a checklist of personality factors listed in this chapter and other

Reservoirs offer fishing opportunities to over half the bass fishermen in North America. Fishermen must continue to support fisheries research that helps us better understand the dynamics of reservoir waters and the fish populations they support if reservoirs are to continue to play a vital role in bass fishing.

factors you've identified that weren't included. Fill in details. Call power company authorities to learn the depths of outlets and obtain past and present release schedules, plus water level and thermocline histories covering the last 10 to 20 years.

Ask professors of limnology and aquatic biology at a nearby university what they know about your reservoirs. Contact state fishery biologists for reports of fish population surveys and creel studies, investigations of food habits and other management activities. Talk with dock owners, guides, and other anglers to identify other personality factors. Attend tournaments to get firsthand information from a variety of top anglers. Read magazine articles on pertinent topics.

Once you have a complete picture of a reservoirs' personality, good and bad days may suddenly be explained. You're on your way to understanding why you caught bass where you did and where you missed a productive pattern. And you'll recognize similar conditions when they occur again.

Chapter 9

LARGEMOUTH BASS IN RIVERS

Where, When, and a Touch of How To

Following retreat of the Pleistocene glaciers about 30,000 years ago, largemouth bass spread northward from the warm waters of southeastern North America to populate most of the continent east of the Great Plains.

Their expansion north into southern Canada was completed between 15,000 and 20,000 years ago.

The bass travelled the vast network of rivers from the Atlantic seaboard to the Texas Gulf Coast. From their primordial home in shallow weedy lakes and sluggish rivers, bass advanced as temperature and habitat allowed. Receding waters stranded bass in enclosed basins we call lakes.

Yet despite this historical perspective, most fishermen don't think of bass as river fish. Rivers mean current. And current is associated with trout, walleyes, smallmouths, and catfish, not largemouths.

But many of North America's best largemouth bass fisheries are rivers, from the Potomac in the East, to the Sacramento in the West; from the St. Lawrence in the North to the St. Johns in the South. The largest and most important river is the Mississippi, offering prime bass water to anglers from Minnesota to Louisiana.

Largemouth bass have inhabited rivers since prehistoric times, but man's alterations have created new and different stretches of bass habitat. Major rivers have been altered with locks and dams to control flooding and aid barge and boat movement. Smaller rivers have been bridged, channelized, dredged, and dammed. The flooded backwaters that resulted have increased bass habitat in some situations, while simultaneously creating problems. Basically, though, backwaters offer largemouth bass cover, food, and relief from current.

Largemouth bass usually avoid fast current, but sometimes feed near current breaks. And they may migrate upstream or downstream through main river channels.

From late fall through the spawn, look for river bass in still, lakelike areas. During summer and fall, bass often hold near chutes and cuts with slight current or in wide and slow sections of the main river.

Not surprisingly, many species of river baitfish occupy current areas throughout the year. And bass are opportunistic feeders.

RIVER HABITAT AND SEASONAL MOVEMENTS

Research has identified five primary factors determining bass location in rivers: dissolved oxygen, current, water temperature, cover, and baitfish.

In northern rivers that freeze over, the most critical habitat for river bass is a suitable winter holding area. Backwater wintering areas sheltered from current and with adequate depth (at least five feet) tend to be slightly warmer than the main river. But as dead weeds decay under ice, they consume oxygen. This respiration and the oxygen needs of fish that concentrate in overwintering areas can drop dissolved oxygen to critical levels. If oxygen levels fall below 3 parts per million, which may occur in late winter, bass shift closer to current, where water holds more oxygen. They continue to avoid direct current, however.

Overwintering areas are scarce in some river systems. The extent of overwintering habitat may even limit the number of bass a river section can hold. Research on a 15-mile stretch of the Mississippi River between Iowa and Illinois revealed only three suitable wintering areas for largemouth bass.

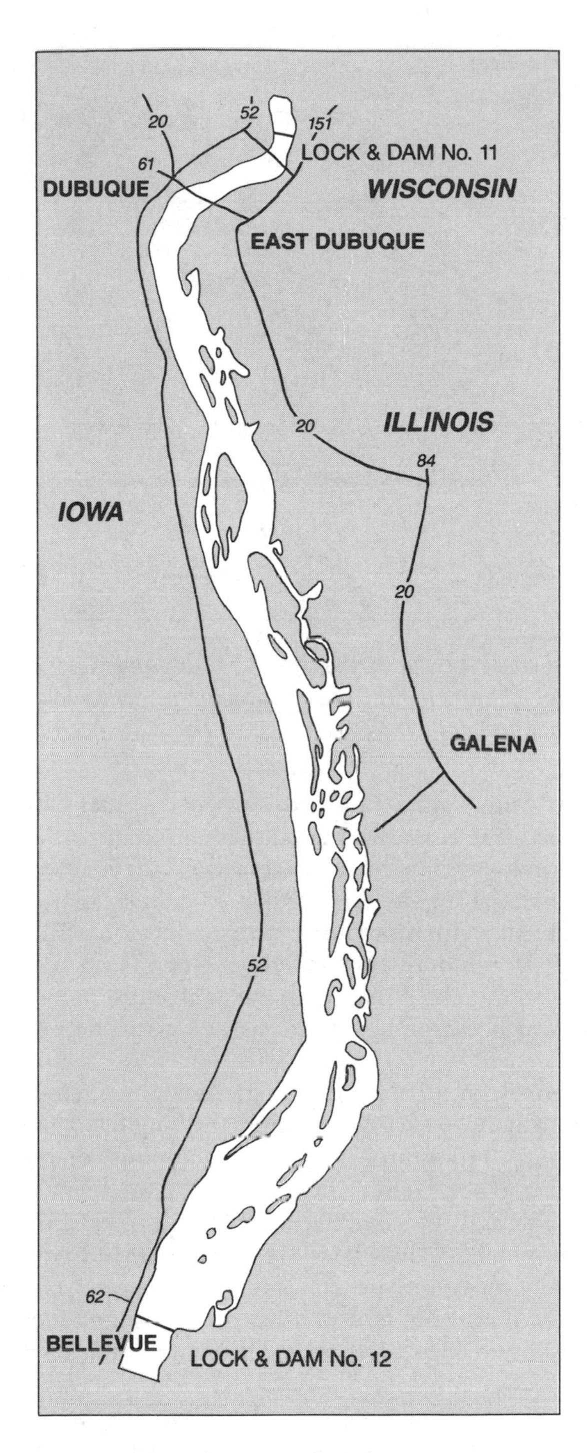

Mississippi River Pool 12 illustrates the complexity of channels, lakes, islands, and cuts that typify large navigable rivers. Backwaters are the home of the largemouth, although some bass hold on main-river structure and cover during summer and fall.

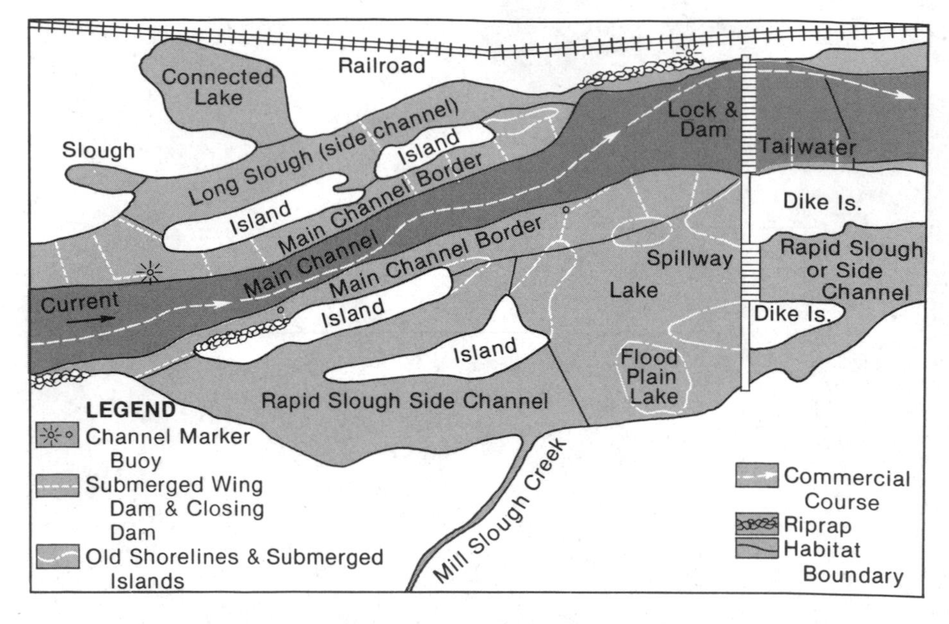

This is a hypothetical section of the upper Mississippi River showing typical habitat areas. Side channels have current, while attached lakes provide little current. Bass spend most of their lives away from the main channel.

The river possibly could support more bass if good winter habitat were more common. Excavations to create additional winter refuges are planned.

In rivers farther south where waters don't freeze, winter habitat requirements aren't as stringent. Yet similar shifts in location occur, except in south Florida where water temperatures rarely fall below 55°F.

During winter, largemouths occupy deep sloughs off the main channel where current is minimal. Areas with deep stumps, standing timber, or rocky holes may attract large aggregations of bass if the number of prime spots is limited.

Feeding is sporadic and bass aren't aggressive, but many fish in clearly defined locations can mean excellent fishing. Fishing deep, quiet backwaters with jigging spoons, tail spinners, jig-n-pig combos, or plastic craws or worms is the preferred approach.

In temperate regions, bass leave overwintering areas just prior to or at the thaw. Spring locations for river bass are more diverse than overwintering spots. Bass initially move toward shallow woody cover. High water often inundates timbered bottomlands, and bass quickly occupy those areas. They use timber, brush, and logs early in spring, switching to weeds as they develop.

During spring, bass in northern rivers don't bite aggressively while water remains ice cold and murky. They will be very shallow and tight to cover. Lures must be slowly presented close to fish to entice bites from inactive bass. Activity increases on sunny afternoons, however, in response to the sun's warmth.

Flippin' and pitchin' excel for quietly and efficiently probing cover for

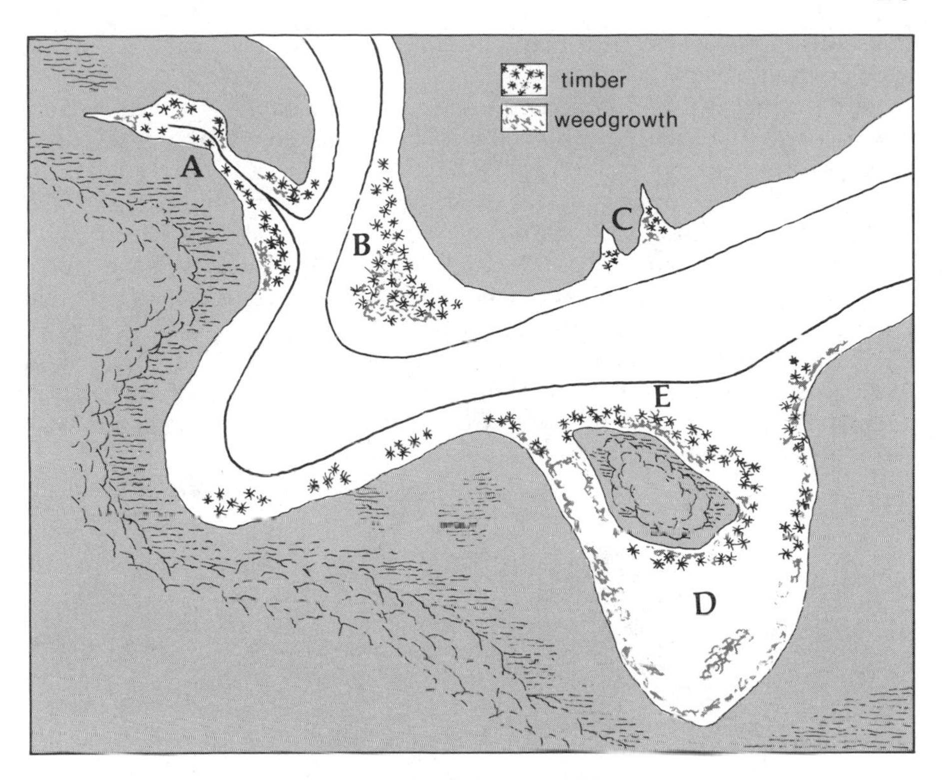

BACKWATER BASICS

Consistent fishing for largemouths in rivers rests with eliminating unsuitable river areas. Largemouths need cover away from heavy current. The obvious largemouth holding spots in this river area include ***Areas A, C, and D. Inside Bend Area B*** *may also attract fish because cover is present, and inside bends usually offer reduced current. Areas like* ***E*** *that are adjacent to good backwater areas should hold a few fish. As a rule, however, concentrate on areas away from main current.*

bass. Pitch a light (3/16- to 5/16-ounce) living-rubber jig to isolated cover—brushpiles, stumps, logs, or standing trees. Add a pork rind, grub, or craw worm as a jig trailer, for attraction and to slow the fall of the jig.

Six-inch plastic worms or craw worms pegged on 1/4-ounce bullet weights work well, too. Swim lures slowly along the length of each piece of wood. Think shallow; typical depths range from 1½ to 5 feet.

Rods from 6 ½ to 7 ½ feet long let an angler dabble a bait up and down in prime spots like the intersection of two logs, a rooty stump, a brushpile under a dock, or a thick trunk near a bank.

Choose line strength according to bass size and cover density. In most northern rivers, 14-pound test is sufficient for pitchin' in sparse cover during early spring. Use twenty where bass may exceed 9 pounds. Low stretch line aids bite detection, hooksetting, and fish control.

Switch to a flippin' rod with heavy line and a heavier lure for probing thick wood cover. Move the boat within 15 feet of the target and ease the lure into every likely hole. Bounce it a few times, then flip into another hole. In murky water, bass may bite directly under the boat. But avoid spooking them by making noise.

As the water warms, bass become active and catchable. They roam from cover toward spawning sites. Fishing can be excellent when water temperatures reach 60°F.

To locate groups of bass, cast spinnerbaits, shallow-running cranks, and rattlebaits over flats with sparse cover. Try topwater twitchin' with minnow baits like a Storm ThunderStick or Rapala minnow. Work minnow baits slowly over stumpfields, next to banks, and near weeds or algae that begin growing as water temperatures rise.

Choice of spawning areas is critical for river bass. They may travel miles to areas offering appropriate bottom type, cover, and lack of current. In general, river bass know their way around large stretches of river and may return to previous bedding sites.

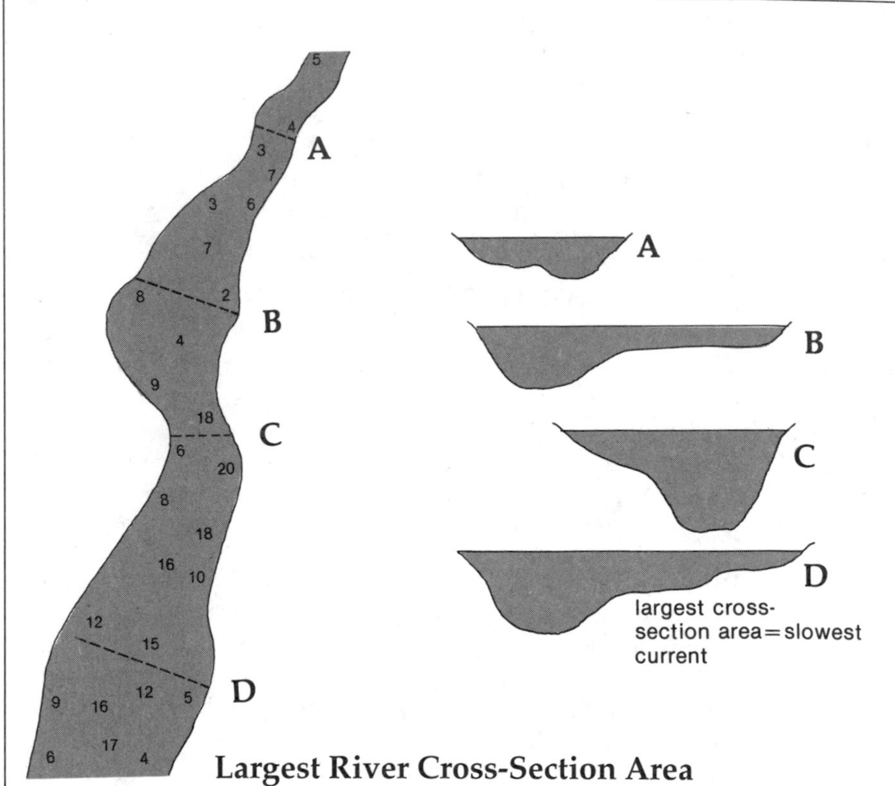

Largest River Cross-Section Area

Areas exposed to main current flow are usually not productive for largemouth bass. Main-river areas where current slows may, however, hold largemouths if cover is present. As a rule, the wider the river cross-section, the slower the current, and the more chance for largemouths.

***River Cross-Sections A** and **C** are not largemouth water. **River Cross-Sections B** and **D** most likely offer reduced current flow. But **Cross-Section D** is relatively deep and probably isn't largemouth water either. If the flat in **Area B** has cover, it may hold largemouths.*

Bass spawn in 1½- to 3-foot depths where hardpan sand or clay is covered by a few inches of silt. Sand areas may also be used, and in heavily weeded backwaters, lily pad rhizomes may suffice. Little is known about spawning behavior of river bass since murky water makes observation difficult. We assume, of course, that their behavior in rivers isn't essentially different than their behavior in lakes.

Casting small worms or tube jigs, twitching topwaters, or running spinnerbaits near isolated stickups will catch bass through the Postspawn Period. Thick wood cover always attracts bass, often big females. Flippin' and pitchin' remain important presentation approaches. Any cover between 1½ and 5 feet deserves attention.

After spawning, bass move to summer feeding areas, often backwaters or sloughs with thick cover and reduced current. They'll be cover oriented, often holding in water only a foot or two deep.

During summer, largemouths tend to be "homebodies." A bass caught from under a particular stump and then carried to a tournament weigh-in may soon return to the same spot, although the navigation process isn't well understood.

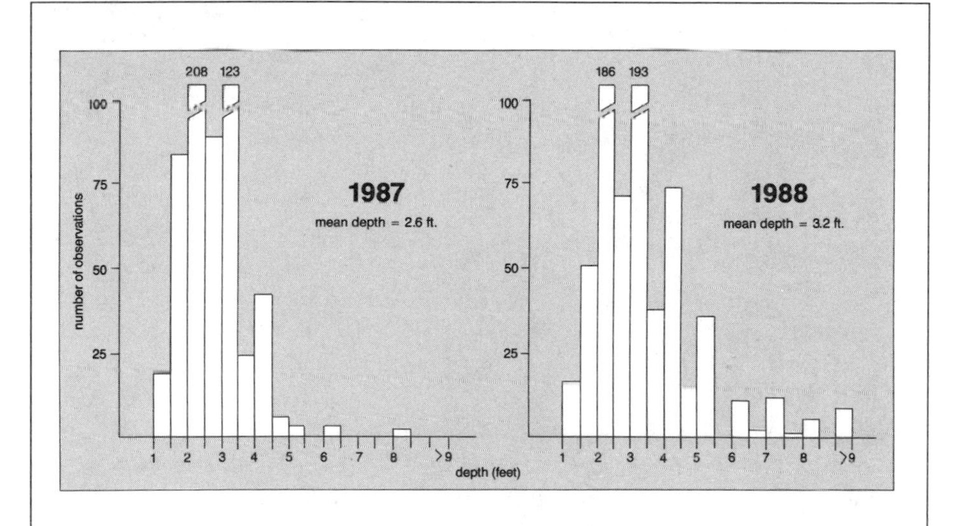

Depth Preference

John Pitlo Jr., a fishery biologist with the Iowa Department of Natural Resources, conducted a radio telemetry study of largemouth bass in Pools 12 and 13 of the Mississippi River. Largemouths selected shallow habitat throughout the year. Depth range used most often in 1987 was 2 to 2½ feet. Mean depth occupied was 2.6 feet. In 1988, the peak shifted to 3 or 3½ feet. Mean depth was 3.2 feet. Winter locations were usually deepest.

Depth of available cover, location of forage fish, water clarity, current speed, and water quality affect the depth bass occupy. Largemouths in rivers typically utilize shallow water throughout their range due to (1) abundant shoreline and backwater cover, (2) their avoidance of direct current, and (3) the similar habits of prey species.

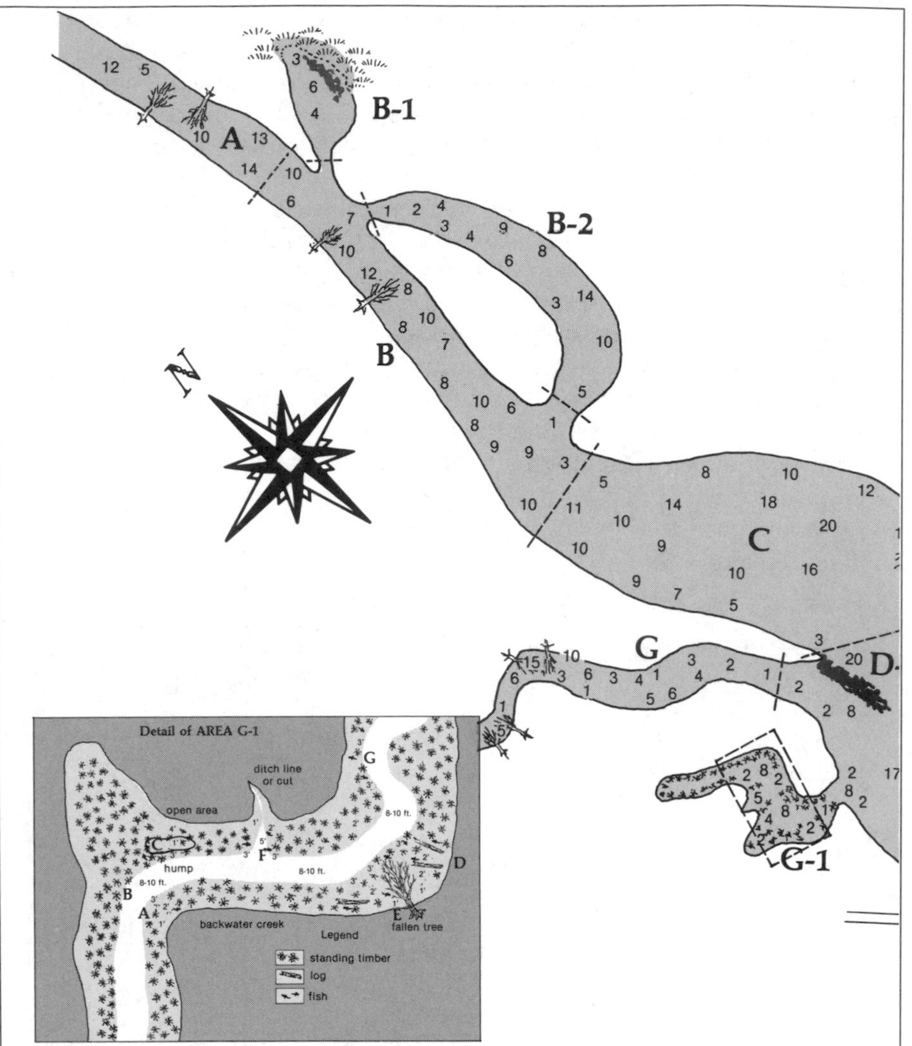

Area G-1 is a prime spot. Because the creek is full of timber, focus on areas of change in otherwise continuous timber. Where a channel meets a flat is one transition, but expect inside bends (A) and outside bends (B) to gather more fish.

Humps on a flat (C) are another transition that attract bass. Horizontal timber (D), as opposed to the abundant vertical timber, is another contrast. So are fallen trees along a continuous bank (E), and small channel cuts that merge with the main creek channel (F). Areas where a channel swings close to a bank may also hold more fish (G).

High Percentage Areas for River Largemouths

This drawing illustrates a moderate-size river stretch and some typical location options for largemouth bass.

Area A—A main-river area with adequate depth and fallen

trees to block current. This area would hold many largemouths only if flow were minimal.

Area B—A continuation of conditions in **Area A**—rates little attention.

Area B-1—A marshy backwater with good weedgrowth—may be one of the best bass areas on this river section.

Area B-2—An oxbow with a shallow ridge separating it from main current. Little cover is present to hold fish. Check it anyway.

Area C—A wide, deep riverbed with reduced current. Lacks cover. Note, however, that wide main-river areas have more potential to hold largemouths than fast-flowing narrow stretches.

Area D—A wide river area with reduced current and cover. Probably the best main-river largemouth area. Fish the weedbed at the creek point **(D-1)**, the weeds and wood on the inside bends **(D-2)**, plus the riprap and wood on the outside bend **(D-3)**. Expect cover in the

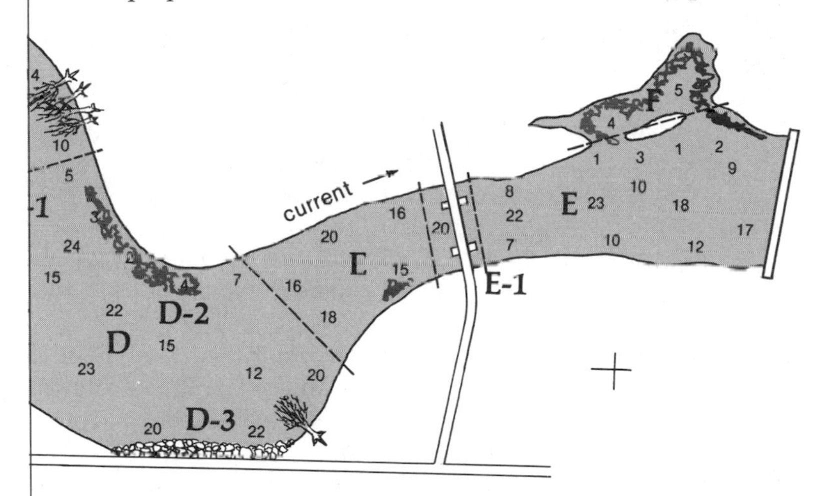

inside bend to produce the most bass.

Area E—Not good largemouth water, although the weedgrowth and bridge abutments may hold a few fish. Note the shallow flat in front of **Shallow Bay F**. If cover is available on the flat, it could be productive.

Area F—A shallow bay fronting a river section. Not enough depth to serve as year-round bass habitat, but traveling bass that hold here may stay for most of the open-water season. Also good spring and summer habitat.

Area G—A relatively shallow, barren creek. All backwater areas have potential, but some are better than others. The wood gathered at the outside bend probably means this creek floods in spring. Probably not a good spawning creek. The deep tangles provide a home for some bass, possibly big ones.

Area G-1—A creek with depth and cover. Everything you're looking for in a backwater area.

Backwater areas and cover are the keys to river bassin'. Concentrate on **Areas G-1, F, B-1,** and **D**. Slip into **Creek G** for a shot at a few large bass.

During summer, bass often hold and feed around river weeds—arrowhead, pickerelweed, cabomba, lily pads, coontail, and pepper grass. In fertile backwaters, tiny duckweed often multiplies, forming a moving canopy of cover that bass use. Bass lying under duckweed become ambush-oriented in their feeding strategies.

Fish rubber frogs, rats, or weedless spoons over thick weed mats to draw explosive strikes from bass lurking below. Work frogs slowly and steadily, using heavy flippin' tackle to present baits.

Let bass engulf the bait before setting the hook. Get the bass' head up and keep him coming to the boat. Play with him after he's landed. If a bass misses on the strike or you pull it away from him, cast back and he'll often strike again. Concentrate on edges, pockets, channels, and spots with mixed wood and weed.

In some rivers during summer, bass move to side channels and cuts that connect backwaters to the main river. Gizzard shad, minnows, and other baitfish move through cuts to feed on plankton, invertebrates, and organic material. Largemouths hold along weededges or around wood cover to attack passing prey.

Their proximity to cover makes flippin' and pitchin' worms and jigs a good option in wood and weed pockets. Spinnerbaits work, too. Run them parallel to weedlines, through weed and lily pad pockets, and over or around stumps or branches of fallen trees.

Often, submerged weedgrowth extends to within a foot of the surface. In this situation, buzzbaits and rattlebaits let you cover water quickly and create a disturbance that triggers active bass.

In rivers where water flow is moderate during summer, largemouths may hold in the main channel around objects that break current like pilings, navigation towers, and wing dams. Natural cover like fallen trees, boulders, and holes near tributary mouths hold bass, too.

As weeds recede in fall, wood cover again becomes the primary type of bass cover. Low dissolved oxygen in dying beds of submerged weeds seems to push bass out. Remaining stalks of emergent weeds like lily pads and lotus, on the other hand, provide cover and don't remove much oxygen. Easing a big willow-leaf spinnerbait through stems can produce big bass when temperatures range down to about 50°F.

For fishing near wood, cast jig-n-pig combos, worms, and craws to deeper blowdowns and stumps. Bass roam the edge of cover during fall more than they do during summer; so a pinpoint presentation like flippin' isn't critical, except under adverse conditions like cold fronts, falling water levels, or heavy fishing pressure.

Weed stalks on the outside edge of expansive flats continue to hold bass until they move to overwintering areas. Look for inside bends in weedlines that lie in 4 to 10 feet of water. Cast and slowly retrieve Texas-rigged worms and crawfish through stalks.

When the bait catches a stalk, shake it in place. Plastic baits impregnated with salt or amino-acid formulas seem to work well for slow cold-water presentations. Scent and taste additives may induce bass to hold baits longer, allowing more time for a solid hookset.

Moving in stages, bass filter toward overwintering areas, arriving before ice-up in northern latitudes. They may move 10 miles or more in some systems.

Bass also inhabit small slow-moving creeks, particularly in the Southeast. Streams no more than a cast across can hold big bass.

In small streams, deep holes frequently located at sharp outside bends are prime habitat, particularly when they're enhanced with wood cover. Deep holes give bass space and also attract a variety of prey.

Creek bass typically hold downstream from cover even though current is slight. During rainy periods when current increases, bass move to more protected areas. Stumps, boulders, snags, rock piles, bridge abutments, cypress trees, and other objects blunt current. Bass lie tight to these objects, ready to seize food.

In small creeks, fish small crawfish-color crankbaits, 6-inch Texas-rigged plastic worms, 1/4-ounce jig-n-pork combos, and topwaters. Spinning tackle and 10-pound test will usually suffice, except where bigger bass and cover combine to require stout tackle.

TIDAL SYSTEMS

In some systems, particularly along the Atlantic and Gulf coasts, tidal rivers and associated marshes offer good bass fishing. Many of these areas are vast and receive less fishing pressure than nearby lakes and reservoirs. Bass in tidal marshes don't live as long or grow as large as bass in still

Largemouth Bass Locations in Tidal Rivers

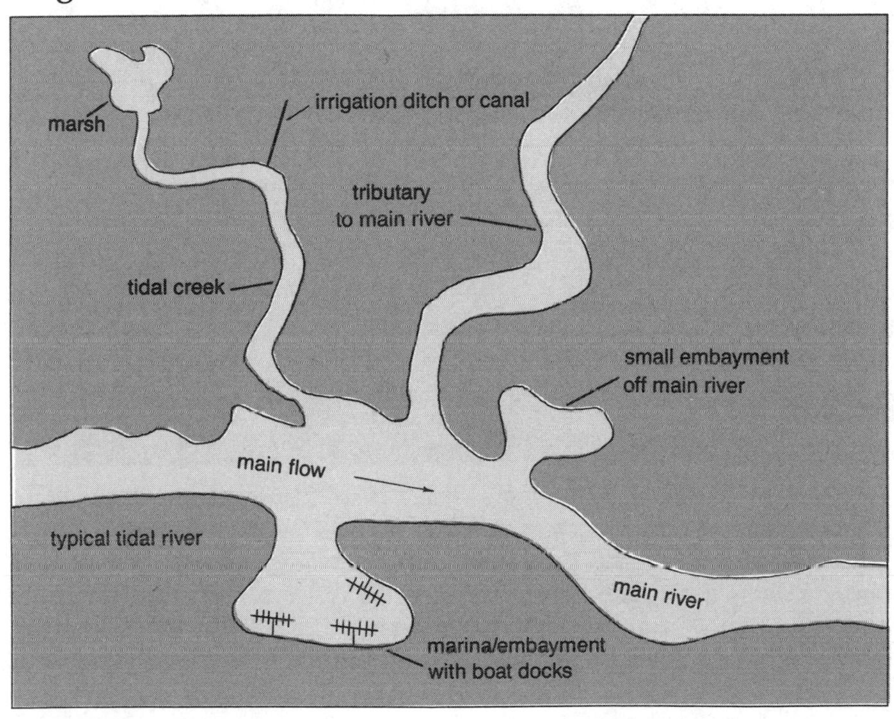

waters, yet they grow strong and fight hard.

Nearly any estuary from New England to Washington may contain a good largemouth bass population in areas where salinity is less than 8 to 10 parts per thousand. In spring, when freshwater runoff pushes saltwater downstream, bass follow and occupy marshes or sloughs that become too saline in summer. As river discharge declines, the "salt wedge" moves upstream, hugging the bottom because saltwater is denser than fresh.

Position of Bass in Weeds

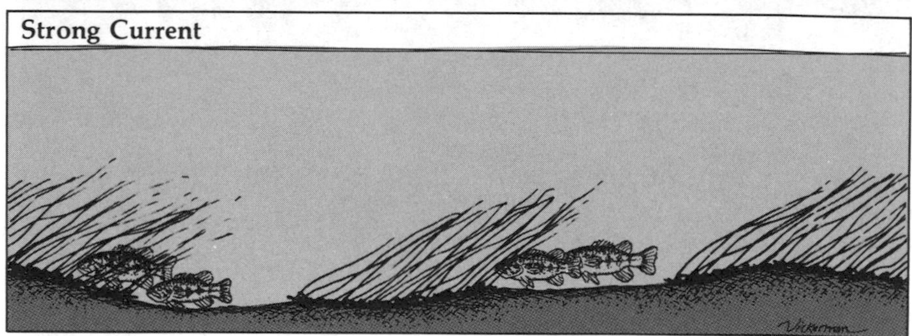

In backwaters without current, bass relate to weed cover much as they do in natural lakes. Active fish usually relate to edge areas and tend to ride high.

In moderate current, bass usually face into it, and again, active fish ride high. When current is heavier, bass hunker behind vegetation, using it as cover to break the force of current. No current or mild current is best. Where timber exists instead of weeds, bass relate to it and the varying degrees of current much as they do to weeds.

A typical tidal marsh is a pondlike area ringed with marshy emergent weeds and connected to a tidal river by a creek. The river, which flows into the ocean, is termed tidal because its lower reaches are affected by twice daily oceanic tide cycles.

Most bass fishermen aren't accustomed to thinking about tides, but they're central to catching bass in coastal marshes. Twice a day at high tide, salty ocean water moves inland and fills tidal marshes with saltwater or freshwater; salinity depends on river discharge and proximity to the river mouth. The flow of incoming water can be strong enough to reverse the flow of some tidal rivers.

Visualize a combat zone, with rivers trying to push water seaward and the ocean pushing water inland. The contest goes back and forth as tides rise and fall. Fish react to changing conditions by moving, though many species of tidewater fish are euryhaline—tolerant of a wide range of salinities.

When the tides recede, a heavy flow of water moves toward the ocean. Marshes rapidly lose volume and become too shallow for bass. Bass seem to have an instinctive concern about being caught in shallow water. They evacuate to avoid being trapped in isolated pools. And by moving

Tidal Positioning

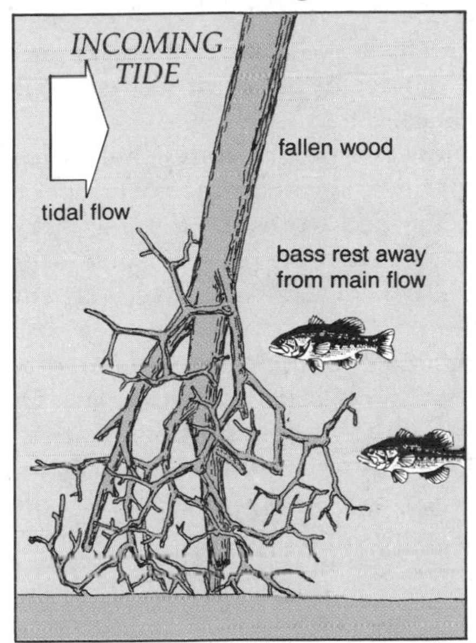

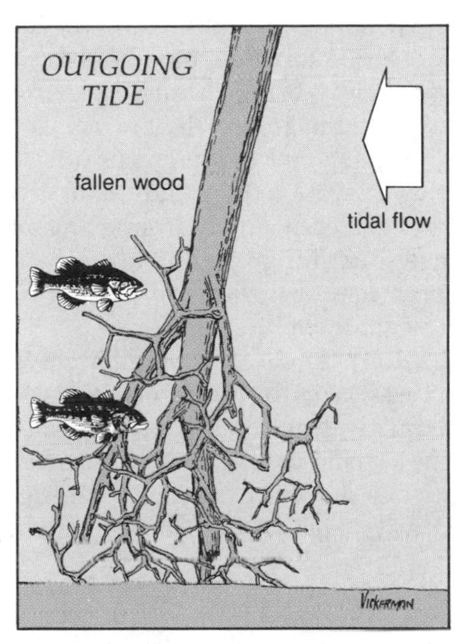

Incoming tide*—As the tidal surge sweeps in from low tide, small baitfish, crustaceans, and grass shrimp move with the flow. Bass become active and hold behind and tight to wood cover that deflects current. The last two hours of an incoming tide usually provide the heaviest feeding activity.*

Outgoing tide*—Bass move with the current to the opposite side of wood cover. The first two hours of the outgoing tide usually provide the best fishing. Bass taken on dead-high or dead-low tides (little water movement) are bonuses.*

downstream, they can utilize food that the seawater swept in. Tides make marine creatures available to bass—sand worms, eels, crabs, and saltwater baitfish such as juvenile shad, herring, killifish, and Atlantic silversides.

Tides, of course, rise and fall in response to the combined gravitational effects of the sun and moon. Tide tables predict these fluctuations, but the impact inland, where bass live, is delayed. Tidal strength is affected by moon phase as well as moon position, so predicting water levels and their effects on bass is tricky. The best times to fish are between heavy tidal flows when the water is moving, but not running heavily one way or the other.

When tides raise water levels in marshes, bass scatter in heavy shoreline marsh cover. They may congregate around the marsh inlet, facing toward the incoming water that brings baitfish. Tidal flows position bass downstream of cover where they dart out for prey.

Bass often hold in little holes or dips in marshes or tidal creeks. Emergent and submerged vegetation provide obvious cover. Quickly run a spinnerbait or weedless spoon through weeds. On the other hand, slowly probe fallen timber, pilings, or bridge holes with worms and jigs.

When water levels drop, bass leave emptying marshes and move to the river or locate in twisting feeder creeks. You should leave, too, unless you like the prospect of 6 hours in a muddy hole. Bass may move as far as several miles or stay close to the inlet mouth.

During low tide, bass hold in rivers or creeks along current breaks such as stumps, bridge abutments, or rocks. Undercut banks in feeder creeks also hold them, but they're usually not concentrated.

Fishing for bass in creeks or rivers at low tide differs from fishing when they're scattered around a marsh at high tide. Locate prime cover objects and fish each slowly from many angles. Jigs and worms on flipping tackle are ideal for pinpoint lure placement. In current, present lures a bit upstream of where you suspect bass will be; current will move your bait toward them.

Rivers are a pleasant alternative to the more familiar habitat offered by ponds, lakes, or reservoirs. Creeks can be waded or fished from shore. On larger waters, canoes and jonboats allow a pleasant float far from the noise and bustle of usual water recreation. On big rivers, on the other hand, you'll share the waters with tugs, barges, and foreign freighters. But always there are bass, if you know where, when, and how.

Chapter 10

PATTERN FISHING

Environmental Variables Plus Presentation Variables=Pattern

During the 1970s, tournament angling radically transformed bass fishing.

Countless new lures and presentation techniques were devised for specific fishing situations. But perhaps most notable was the concept of "pattern fishing," usually attributed to Roland Martin. We'll give Roland credit for the name, but observant anglers have long used the method to find and catch bass.

A pattern is a fishing formula that incorporates environmental and presentation variables into a bassin' equation. Apply the proper formula in similar situations and the answer's bass action.

Thus, fishermen often refer to a fall dock pattern, or a summer slop pattern, or a spring canal pattern. Each pattern involves a set of fishing tools and techniques. But in a larger sense, pattern fishing is a process of observation and analytical thought. The pattern fisherman matches environmental observations with techniques and lures, then tests the formula on wily *Micropterus*.

"Eliminate that which is false, and what remains must be the truth."
Sherlock Holmes

A pattern includes three basic components: (1) *circumstances* such as season, time of day, cover, water clarity, and other factors; (2) *location*, or types of areas to fish (specific spots in waters); and (3) *presentation* including lure type, tackle, and mode of presentation. A proven pattern states: "If certain conditions exist, bass will be active in a particular habitat and I can catch them by fishing a prescribed way."

Patterns and their components range from simple to complex. For example, a common summer pattern in weedy natural lakes is to cast small plastic worms on light jigheads along the front face of dense weeds. The worm falls vertically and draws strikes from active bass cruising the edge

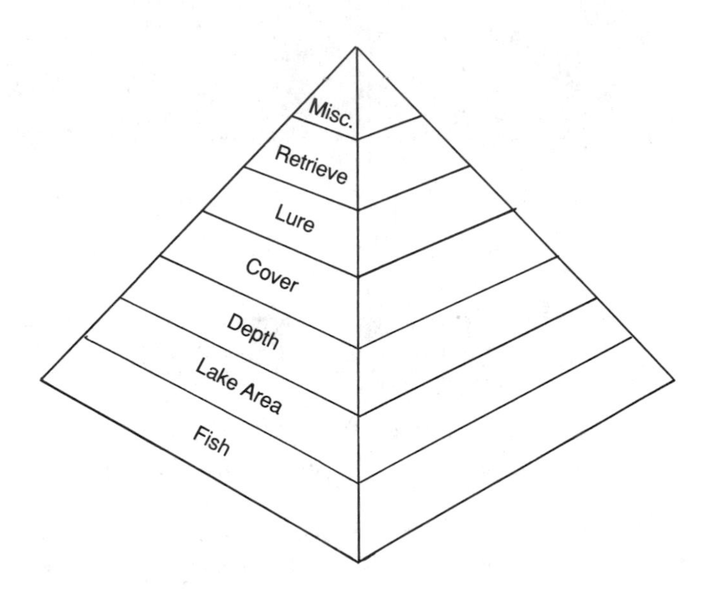

Constructing a pattern is similar to building a pyramid. Begin with a solid foundation of general or basic information, and add layers of supporting material. Every succeeding layer may be smaller and consist chiefly of little things—fine-tuning what you've already built. Yet each level raises you to new heights and can be just as important as the supporting foundation.

Level 1—For instance, say you begin with an understanding of the fish's basic nature. In this case, it's bass. Predict what bass need at this time of year.

Level 2—Pick the likely areas or sections of a lake, river, or reservoir and less active bass holding near the bottom. The pattern can be refined to specify points instead of inside turns, and one weed type instead of another, but fishing jigworms along the outside edges of weedlines generally nabs a lot of bass.

Patterns can also be specific. During adverse conditions like cold water or the passing of a front, patterns tend to be more complex and demanding. Say you're fishing a typical spawning bay during early prespawn. Spring weather has been blustery and changeable. Today is sunny, but a minor cold front just passed. Many anglers are out, but nobody's catching much.

The front probably pushed bass slightly deeper and made them less active. You look for stumps or weed clumps located between a shallow bay with cover and deeper water, say 8 to 10 feet deep. Weed clumps in the shallows won't necessarily hold fish. Nor will stumps in deep water without shallows nearby, because bass that were shallow don't abruptly move to deep water. So you fish cover in a transition area between the shallows and deeper water.

---

that provide suitable bass habitat at this time of year. It still encompasses a broad area, but you're beginning to focus on your objective.

Level 3—Zero in on a productive depth range by fishing several likely spots.

Level 4—Note the forms of cover that produce best. Is it weeds in general, or a specific weed type? Brush, standing timber, or fallen logs? A specific type of tree?

Level 5—Which style of lure best matches the type of cover? Spinnerbaits? Crankbaits? Worms? Must it be weedless?

Level 6—What type of retrieve best matches the cover and fish's aggressiveness? Cover water fast? Or slow down and strain? Stop and go? Pump and flutter? Let is sit dead still? Combinations?

Level 7-8-9—Color of plastic worm? Body type—curly-tail, lizard body, grub? Does it make a difference? Does 6-pound-test line draw more strikes than 10 without excessive breakoffs and lost fish? Does time of day or do weather conditions make a difference? Is this the best pattern or just one of many?

Get the idea? Infinite number of levels exist. Each successive step may seem almost inconsequential by itself. But a little edge—extra step —may raise you a notch above the competition once you have established all the other necessary factors.

You may hear a tournament angler credit his recent victory to using a "modified XYZ lure with a mylar skirt," but that's but a tiny part of what put bass in the boat. Establishing a solid pattern or set of patterns, fine-tuned down to the skirt color, put all the elements together for a successful catch.

To reach new heights, don't just build the top of a pyramid. Build a solid base to work from.

You might have to use a "quiet" lure, a subtle lure that provides few distinct signals—a smoke grub on a 1/8-ounce jighead and 6-pound line, perhaps. You might add a scent or taste formula and move the jig with slight hops and long pauses. That's all part of the pattern. Even then, you might find that fishing is good only during the warmest part of the day. That pattern is narrow and demanding. But when enough bays with cover at the right depth let you reproduce the pattern, you might have a great day despite adverse conditions.

Patterns are composed of many factors: rising or falling water levels, water clarity, fallen trees, species of aquatic weeds, oxygen levels, thermocline depth, wind direction or strength, cloud cover, structural elements, cover objects, current, direction of the sun, and the presence of baitfish. The list seems infinite. Depth generally is a major component, though depth by itself means little. Usually, specific combinations of elements must be present.

A pattern isn't important if it only applies once in ten years on one arm of one impoundment. The power of patterns is repeatability. A strong pattern specifies important conditions and requirements, and nothing more.

For example, during late fall bass sometimes congregate along steep banks with no current. Small grubs and sensitive spinning tackle let you fish successfully despite the cold. Yet these pre-ice bass concentrations may be scattered along the bank at various depths, say 5 to 50 feet. Depth isn't a critical part of this unusual pattern. Instead, the pattern involves seasonal timing, refuge areas, and subtle baits. It's a versatile pattern that can help you catch bass wherever you fish.

Look for the key factor in a pattern. A pattern often contains several elements that can change, and one or more that must be present. Unfavorable conditions like adverse water temperatures or low oxygen can dictate where bass will be. These "worst factors" can be a condition bass can't adapt to or can't live without. A key factor is often so pronounced that bass must react to it.

Don't hang onto minor details unless they make a difference. Look for variables in location and presentation that count. Identifying weed species is interesting, but is it critical? Or do any weeds with broad green leaves growing in 8 feet of water hold bass? And does a plastic worm really have to be purple? Exact lure color isn't usually an important part of a pattern.

Start with general patterns based on season and lake or reservoir type. The bass will tell you if your pattern's mostly right or wrong. Then refine it.

More than one good pattern usually exists for a given day. Several ways usually exist to catch bass—creek arm patterns and main lake patterns, morning patterns and mid-day patterns, hydrilla patterns and riprap patterns. Lakes may have several eutrophic bays and mesotrophic basins, for example. The hot pattern for one area may not work in another.

Patterns get hot and grow cold as conditions change. Bass react to environmental changes; so must you.

Pattern fishing is more than having a recipe file for success. It emphasizes observation and analytical thinking. The process eliminates unimportant factors and isolates those that put fish on your line.

PERCENTAGE FISHING

The search for patterns should begin with fast, broadly appealing presentations. Hope to find a situation where aggressive methods work, because it usually means more bass.

Identify the critical parts of a pattern. Then work it hard. Here, active bass had moved to the edge of heavy cover in slop bays. The buzzbait allowed Al Lindner to quickly cover water and maximize his catch of bass. When bass activity slowed later in the day, he slowed his approach, too, concentrating on heavy shallow cover with a Moss Boss, or on weed patches or flats with a Texas-rigged worm. Patterns change as conditions change. The percentage chance that certain patterns will produce bass also change.

All bass aren't at the same activity level at the same time, though, even in a small pond. Then, too, some bass are smarter (warier) than others. Can you draw a strike from inactive bass tucked tight in cover? Probably. But don't accept slow fishing without checking other alternatives.

Start with the assumption that some bass are easy—somewhere. Fishing quickly over a lot of water puts your bait in front of more bass, increasing your odds of contacting aggressive fish.

Identify a pattern that works, then work it hard. Say the location part of a pattern involves fishing secondary creek arms of an impoundment where large milfoil beds meet a sandy shore. Don't bother with other places—milfoil without sand, or sand without milfoil. Do what works, then do it again. If it works, it's a pattern.

PRESSURED BASS

The principles of pattern fishing are as true today as when Roland Martin coined the term. But the amount of fishing pressure has changed. Pressure makes surviving bass harder to catch. Slow, precise fishing often is necessary.

FINE-TUNING A PATTERN

The guy at the bait shop said they're hittin' spinnerbaits. That's the pattern?

Wrong!

Spinnerbaits are but one element of a successful pattern. If you toss them in many different areas of a lake, chances are you'll catch something.

But if you eliminate water in an orderly fashion, refining the "spinnerbait pattern," what you're left with is a successful approach, a real pattern.

Select a section of the lake that has potential. Bass anglers often break a large reservoir into thirds—upper, center, and lower—since impoundment characteristics vary from one end to the other. Water clarity, predominant depth, cover or seasonal habitat may favor one region over others. Use your experience or ask questions before you begin fishing.

If recent success with spinnerbaits suggests that a bait worked across shallow cover is producing in the middle portion of the lake, start fishing likely areas there.

Are you predominantly catching bass in main coves or in secondary coves off the main ones? Secondary ones? Good. Key on those.

Are the fish mostly coming at the back ends of the coves, along the center sections, or at the mouth where the secondary coves meet the main cove? Halfway out? Good. Concentrate there.

Are bass on points, flats, steep shorelines, bluffs, or channel edges? Points? Good. Sloping points? Even better. Sounds like bass are dropping toward the main lake after spawning, but haven't fully penetrated the main coves in heavy numbers.

Spinnerbaits on points—with what kind of cover? Weeds, wood, rock, gravel, shale—what? Wood? Not surprising. Spinnerbaits are good "wood lures." Open rocks might have popularized a crankbait pattern.

Brush, logs, stumps, standing trees? Stumps *and* logs? Both are producing in the 3- to 5-foot range. OK, so you can't narrow it any further. Both are easily fished with spinnerbaits.

Buzzed, slow-rolled, pumped and fluttered—what retrieve is best? Slow-rolled? Good. Don't waste time fluttering baits if the bass will hit a steadily moving subsurface lure, even though they tend to ignore a rapidly moving one buzzed at the surface.

Skirt color? Blade color? Lure size? Tandem or single? A 3/8-ounce white single-spin with nickel blades? Excellent. A trailer hook caught some short strikers? Outstanding.

Son, a pattern. Slow-rolled 3/8-ounce white single-spins in 3 to 5 feet on sloping wood points halfway out secondary coves in the central portion of the lake.

Now . . . is it best in morning or evening? Cloudy or sunny weather? Wind or no wind? For big fish or numbers . . .

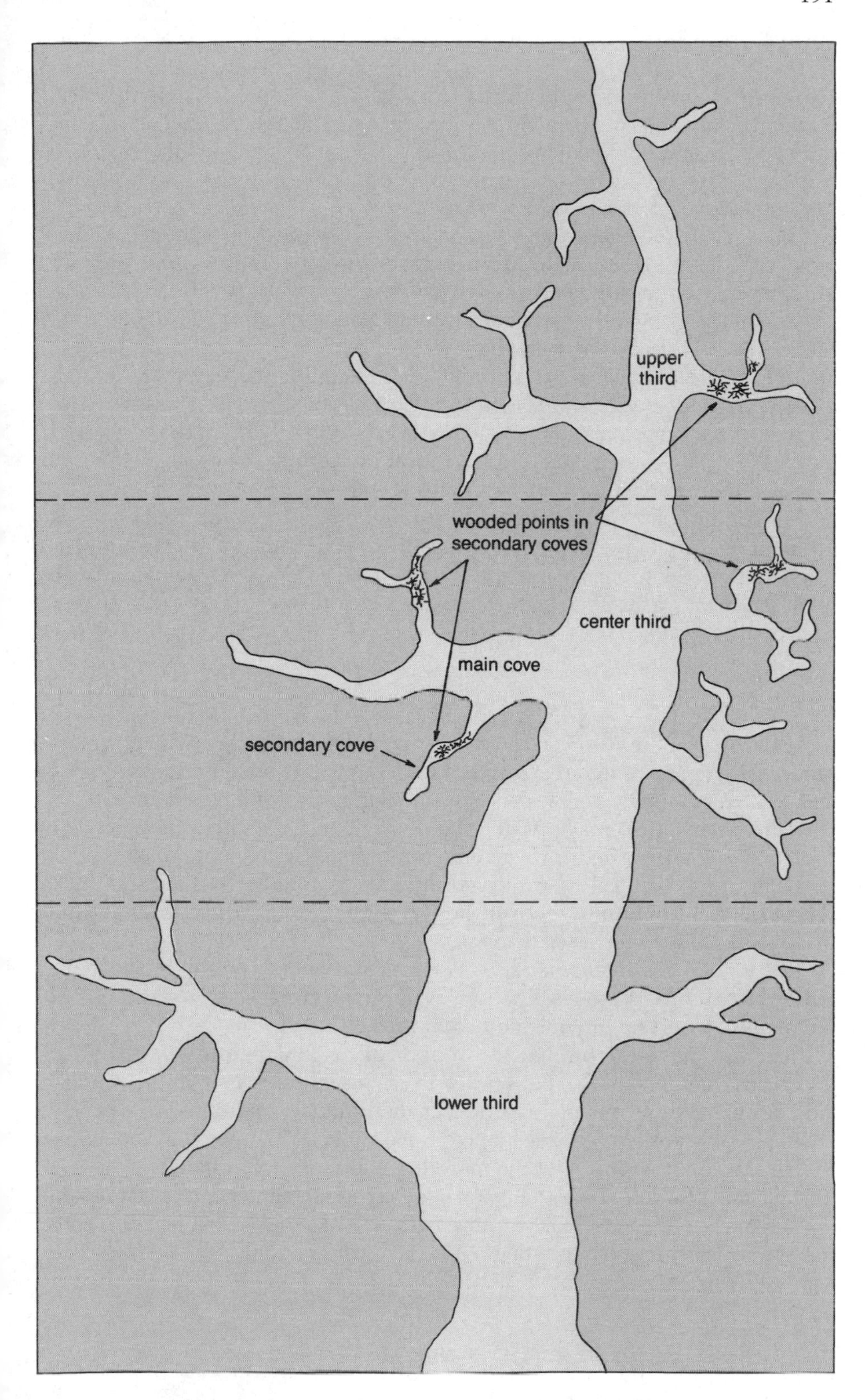
upper third
wooded points in secondary coves
center third
main cove
secondary cove
lower third

What everyone else is doing may be a low-percentage approach.

For example, during summer there are usually bass in shallow, weed-choked bays. But working lures through dense weeds is hard work. Cranking rattlebaits over emerging weedlines can be easier and quicker. But after anglers pound weedlines all summer, percentages may change. Slop bays usually receive less pressure, so bass there may be less lure shy. Fighting the vegetation may be worthwhile.

Today's bass often become conditioned to certain lure types. When Al and Ron Lindner first moved to Minnesota in the '60s, they caught bass all summer by cranking spinnerbaits across flats. Spinnerbaits still catch bass in many situations, but bass more often demand slower finesse presentations.

Percentage bass fishing has shifted toward lures and presentations that are harder for bass to become conditioned to. Anglers now rely more on soft plastics or pork presented slower and more vertically. Early tournaments were often won by competitors who raced around and caught the easy, most active fish. Now, they're often won by locating a group of good-size fish and working them patiently with the right presentation.

The concept of pattern fishing and working percentages still applies. Look for patterns. Try to find a pattern to maximize your catch in size or numbers. Try fast horizontal presentations to locate bass. Then slow down and fish more precisely with subtle baits that don't give off warning signals that bass are conditioned to.

TIME ON THE WATER

Patterns aren't recipes you can read and apply. Percentage fishing is more than a game plan. Without experience to demonstrate what percentages may be, you won't know where to concentrate your efforts with which lures.

Patterns and percentage fishing are empty concepts without time on the water. Experience is necessary before you start seeing the sense of repetition, or before you can easily separate unimportant variables from critical ones. The ability to evaluate environmental signals and adapt to changing conditions leads to consistent success.

Every good bass fisherman uses patterns and percentages to improve the odds of catching bass—a few fish when everyone else is skunked, or fabulous catches that provide fond memories.

You may have to eliminate a number of options before you arrive at productive combinations. But it's worth it. You'll catch fish on them today and be able to draw on your experience when similar conditions arise.

Repeatable patterns are like money in the bank. When you start out, your bank account is slim. But the more time and effort you invest, the larger the available fund to draw from. Yet even a veteran angler can't live only off his savings. He has to look for new patterns and make new goals. That's what makes fishing so interesting. More is never enough!

"Poor devil, got one of those new reels. . .you know, magnetic drag, left or right hand retrieve, flippin' switch, free floating levelwind, fightin' drag, hawg handles, palming sideplate. . .just couldn't handle it."

Chapter 11

EQUIPMENT

Boats, Motors, Electronics, Rods, Reels, and More

Knowledge remains the key to fishing success. Equipment alone, therefore, can never be the key. You can't buy fishing success by buying gadgets. Yet knowledge of proper equipment is an integral part of the total body of bass fishing knowledge.

Today's competitive fishing market contains a broad range of good equipment at a broad range of prices. With so much equipment available, and so many changes constantly taking place, understanding tackle trends and general guidelines for choosing equipment keys making choices that can help you fish comfortably, efficiently, and successfully.

RODS

Combinations of graphite and fiberglass have emerged as the most workable materials for rods. Ultracheap "graphite" rod blanks don't contain enough graphite to gain the advantages of graphite. But small differences in graphite and glass percentages among the best blanks of top manufacturers aren't that important. The construction of the blanks and one step beyond, the construction of the rod—ferrules, wraps, and handle—are important.

Rod design has benefited from graphite's strength and light weight. Sensitivity is a by-product of light weight. Today's best general-purpose 5 ½-foot graphite rods weigh less than ultralight fiberglass rods once weighed, yet are gutsy enough to drive a worm hook home. Fishing with plastic worms and jigs requires sensitivity and power. But sensitivity and power are almost as important for working spinnerbaits and crankbaits.

Because graphite is so strong for its weight, rod designers have been able to create effective longer rods. Long fiberglass rods once were heavy and soggy—buggywhip actions. Today, rod makers produce rods in light, medium, or heavy actions at any practical length.

Fine graphite rods make fishing more effective. Perhaps more importantly, though, they make fishing more fun.

The trend is to longer rods. Good baitcasting rods over 6 feet long didn't exist before the mid-1970s. Modern flipping rods measure 7 ½ feet. Pitching rods run 7 feet. Good crankbait rods are available from 6 ½ to 7 feet long. And each of these longer rods offers advantages.

Length can increase casting distance, allow a wider range of horizontal lure manipulation, and help set hooks better at long distances. Long rods can also offer vertical leverage to help fishermen quickly pull bass up from cover. And long rods offer more total "bend," more total rod material in contact with line once a fish is hooked, decreasing the chance a fish will get slack line.

Yet with length comes trade-offs fishermen must consider. Long rods magnify torque, the force of a fish on the fisherman. Torque increases with rod length. A 2-pound force pulling on a 9-foot rod produces 18 pounds of torque. But the same 2-pound force on a 6-foot rod is 12 pounds; 8 pounds with a 4-footer. "Longer" may be better in many situations, but "longer" must be "longer" for you.

In simple terms, you need to match the length of the rods you fish to your body physique. A good "pitching" combo for a small woman might measure 6 ¼ feet, while the standard for the average male is 7 feet. Yet a tall, strong man might find a 7 ½-foot rod a better performer.

Short rods offer advantages, too. One advantage is the opportunity to cast more accurately. Short rods also excel at powering fish from tough cover. To be completely outfitted, the versatile bass angler will probably need short, long, and medium-length rods in several actions for different situations.

Rods with slower actions are easier to cast accurately. Early graphite rods were ultrastiff from butt to tip, but softer tips are better for pinpoint lure placement. Give in a tip also prevents pulling away a crankbait before a bass has engulfed it.

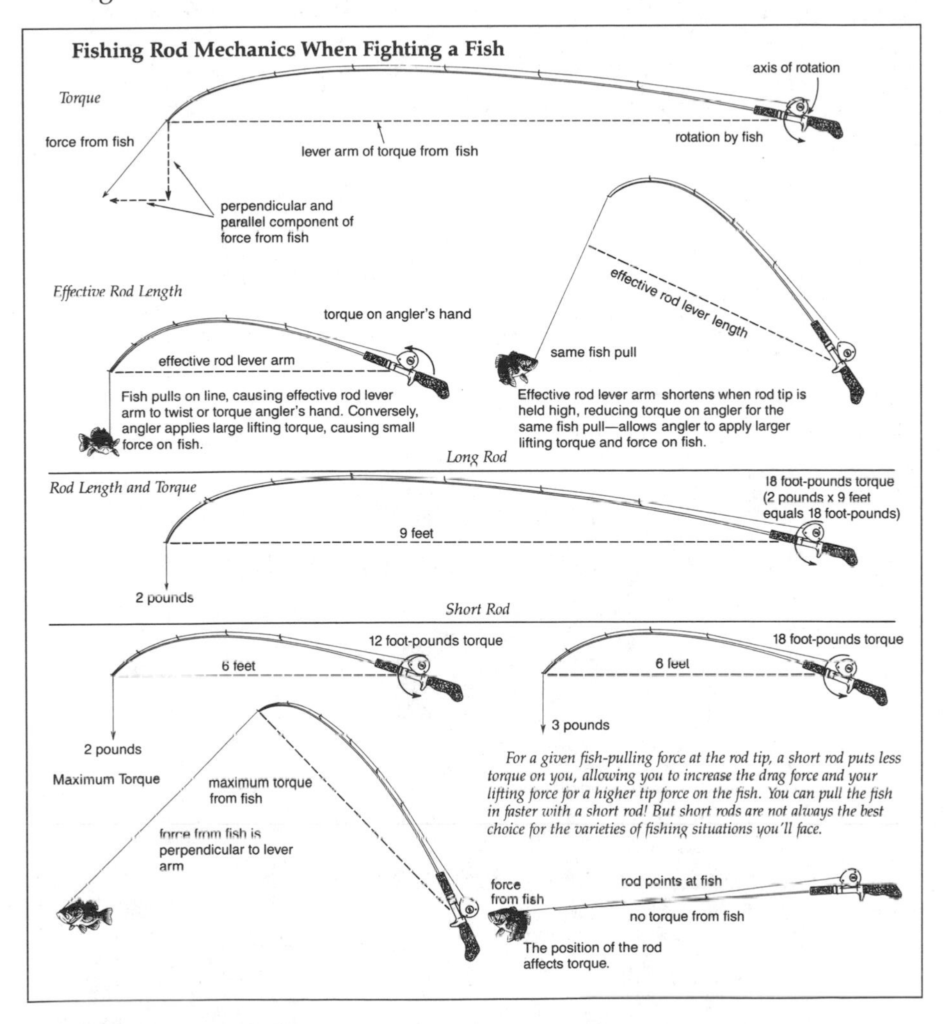

Rod choice—length and action—is more like politics than science, an exercise in compromise more than a physics equation. But given similar length and action, lighter-weight rods are more sensitive. And given your ability to handle them, longer rods offer advantages for many situations.

The best rods from different companies weigh about the same, with little difference in sensitivity. A fine-quality rod from one of at least six major manufacturers, when it matches the fishing situation, will provide pleasant fishing and the opportunity to catch more fish than ever before.

Grips have changed, too. Blanks often run through the rod handles with portions of the blanks exposed. This design offers strength and sensitivity. The biggest change in grips, however, is the trend to two-handed grips or "trigger grips" on casting rods, not traditional pistol grips. Two-handed grips allow powerful easy two-handed casts and greater leverage on sets. Long handles also ease wrist strain for fishermen who use crankbaits or spinnerbaits that pull hard.

Bass anglers usually have several rods, each rigged with a lure for specific situations. A typical selection of six rods might include:

- A 7 ½-foot flippin' stick rigged with either a big spinnerbait or

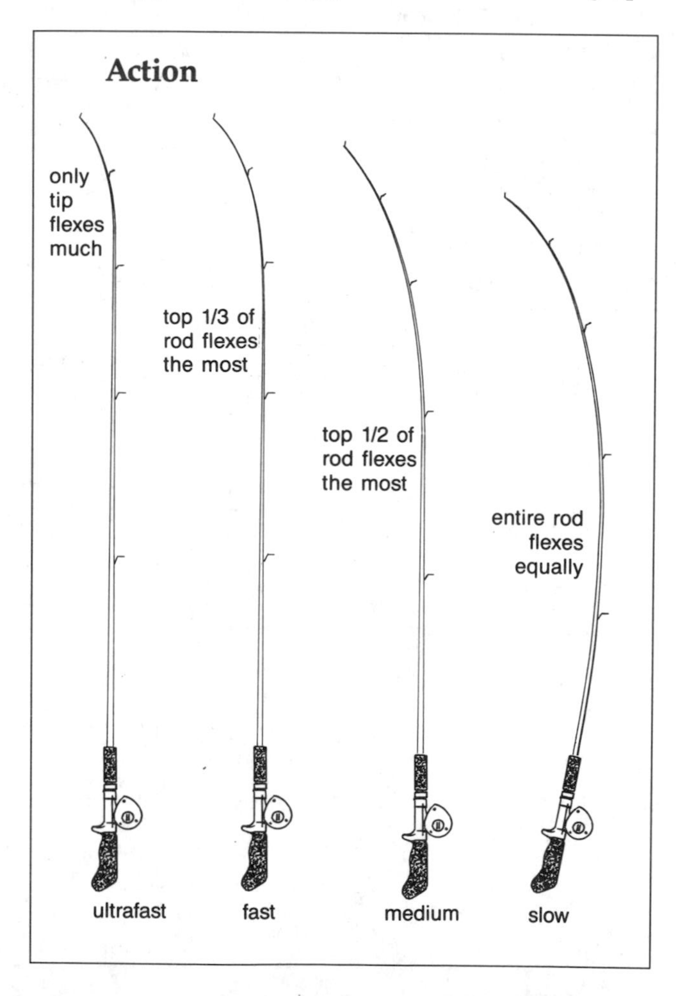

buzzbait—for working quickly over, around, or through heavy shallow cover (17- to 25-pound-test line).

• Another 7½-foot flippin' stick rigged with a 1/2- or 5/8-ounce rubberlegged jig tipped with a plastic trailer or a pork chunk—for flippin' to shallow cover or working deeper in heavy cover on flats (17- to 25-pound-test).

• A 7-foot pitching rod rigged with a 3/8- or 1/2-ounce rubberlegged jig or a Texas-rigged worm and a 1/4- to 1/2-ounce bullet weight—for working edges of heavy cover, open pockets in cover, or around docks (17-pound test).

• A 6½- or 7-foot casting rod with plenty of backbone, but a fast tip rigged with a spinnerbait or rattlebait—for working quickly over flats (14- or 17-pound test).

• A 6- or 6½-foot casting rod with moderate action throughout and a soft tip, rigged with a crankbait—for working outside weededges or along timber (14- or 17-pound test).

• A 6-foot fast-action spinning rod rigged with a 1/8- or 1/4-ounce jig rigged jigworm style—for working edges of cover (8- or 10-pound test).

Choose the proper rod and lure for the situation, just as a golfer would choose the right club. When you've determined the pattern, stow the extra rods. You may want to retrieve a rod or two from the rod box to further fine-tune options for the pattern. For example, you may want two fast-action spinning rods on hand, one with an 1/8-ounce head and the other with a 1/4-ounce head. Or rig both with 1/4-ounce heads, but rig one with a straight 4-inch worm and the other with a 5-inch worm with a curly tail.

A bit more about standards for bass rods. Flipping rods are one of the oldest specialty rods. Their length allows precise lure placement with a flip and their heavy actions provide power for hauling big bass from heavy cover. The entire rod, including the tip, is moderately stiff for better hooksets. The parabolic action—bending farther down the blank than other styles—is effective because the tip isn't used for casting small lures. Flipping rods have long grips.

Heavy-action spinning rods are also popular for flipping. Even a sensitive baitcasting reel can't let out line as easily as a spinning reel. Disadvantages exist, but spinning flipping rods are a popular new element in this presentation.

Worm rods, either spinning rods or casting rods, need backbone to drive a large hook through the body of a worm and into the mouth of a bass. Most worm rods measure 5½ to 6¼ feet—more power—but long-handled models up to 7 feet are available. The best worm rods are light—sensitive—and stiff except for a fast-action tip.

Specialized crankbait rods usually are longer than worm rods —6¼ to 7 feet, as opposed to 5½ to 6¼ feet—and have two-handed grips. Their action is slower throughout the rod, with a slightly faster tip to give a final zing to a crankbait. Tip flexibility improves hookups and reduces escapes when bass leap and shake a big crankbait. Some manufacturers bond a fiberglass tip to graphite to increase tip flexibility.

Fifteen years ago, a "bass rod" was a medium-heavy baitcasting rod. Today, we have at least five basic styles of standard bass rods, plus special-

"You wanna talk backbone *in a rod..!!?"*

purpose bass rods for vertical jigging, jigging with pork trailers, jigging with grubs, spinnerbaiting, split-shotting, topwater fishing, and shiner fishing. Many new models of spinning rods are designed for light-line finesse techniques. Some bass specialists, however, still can't find what they want and turn to custom rod makers for rods with the qualities they're looking for.

REELS

Modern baitcasting reels are less prone to backlash than older reels (with their heavy spools and excessive line capacity). Centrifugal brakes and magnetic backlash controls almost eliminate backlashes for experienced casters—except when casting into wind, of course.

Modern baitcasters offer gear ratios from about 3.8:1 to 6.3:1. During the 1980s, manufacturers sold "faster is better." But high gear ratios make it difficult to work lures slowly; cranking leverage is sacrificed, too. The trend is to moderate ratios or to reels that offer two or more gears for changing speed. Other improvements include shapes that are easy to palm, quieter actions, more ball bearings for smoother operation, and lighter overall reel weights. Freespool buttons are also more easily reached.

Unfortunately, some reel makers still feel they must complicate reels with tricky features often compromising strength and function. A choice of features is fine. But don't forego mechanical simplicity and good old-fashioned rugged construction.

Designers of spinning reels also have entered the gimmick game. Some reels feature complex drag-adjustment systems that could confuse an aerospace engineer. And do we really need "trigger fingers" in order to cast? Most experienced anglers consider them at best just one more thing that can break.

Improvements include quieter actions, more reliable drag systems, conveniently located antireverse switches, and lighter construction. Long

SUPER TUNING REELS*

This process can result in a reel so smooth you hardly know you're turning the handle. Super-smooth reels transfer underwater information from lure to line to rod to . . . reel! The reel's often the forgotten link.

This process only works with top-quality reels. Even then, some reels have flaws that interfere with super-tuning.

Materials and tools needed for super-tuning include an air-driven speed wrench, toothpaste, lapping compound (option), WD-40, and a compound of moly coat and grease.

Remove centrifugal brakes because they'll burn under the stress of rapid spinning.

Remove the faceplate to reveal the gear system, which you'll first coat with a polishing compound and later with moly-coat grease.

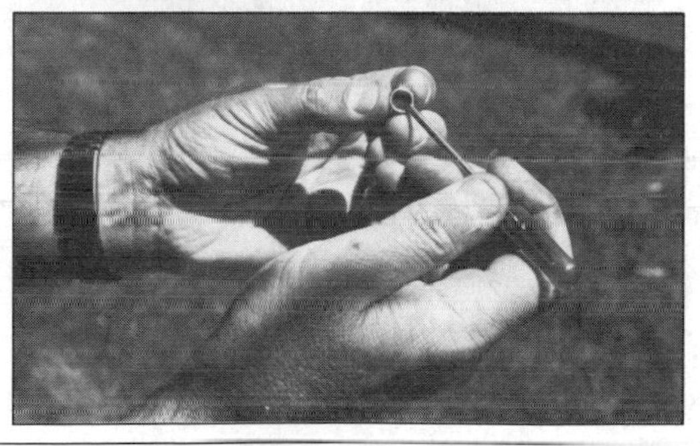

Cushion the cap nut that holds the star drag and handle in place with a rubber, leather, or cardboard shim to prevent excessive tightening during the speed-tuning pro cess.

Remove the pawl to disengage the level-wind system.

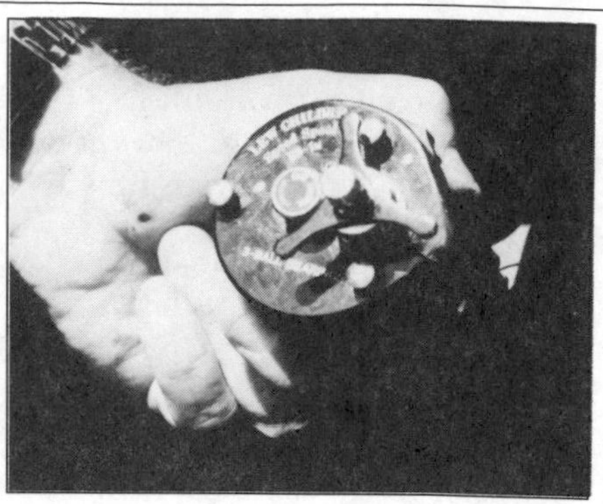

The reel, minus its handle, is ready for spinning with the speed wrench. The polishing compound fine-tunes the gear system.

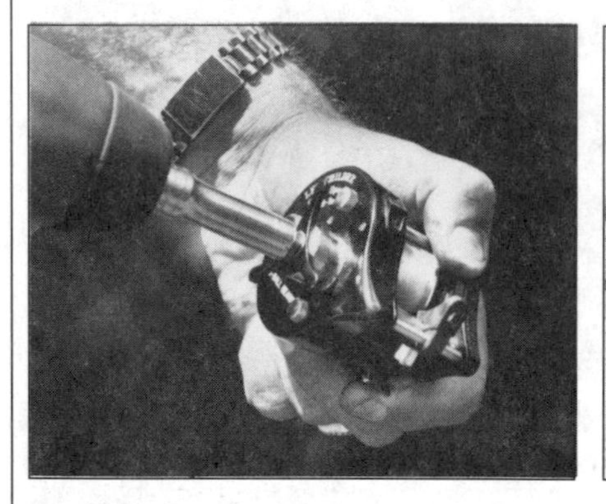

Spin the reel no longer than 45 seconds with the speed wrench at 4,500 rpm. The toothpaste polishing compound fine-tunes the gear system.

Mix moly coat, a molybdenum-based compound, with general-purpose grease.

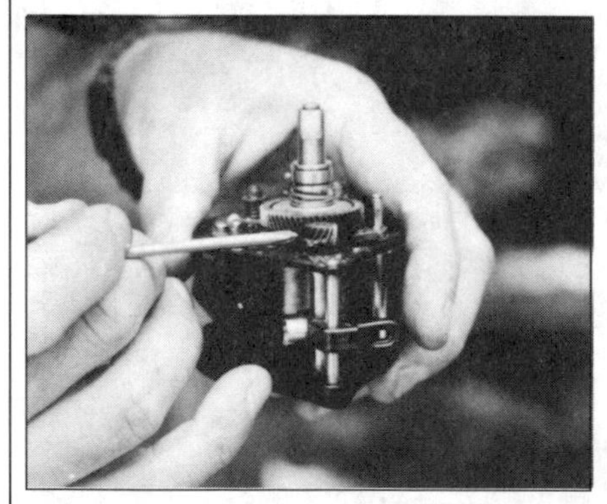

After polishing, apply a thin paste of moly grease to all gears.

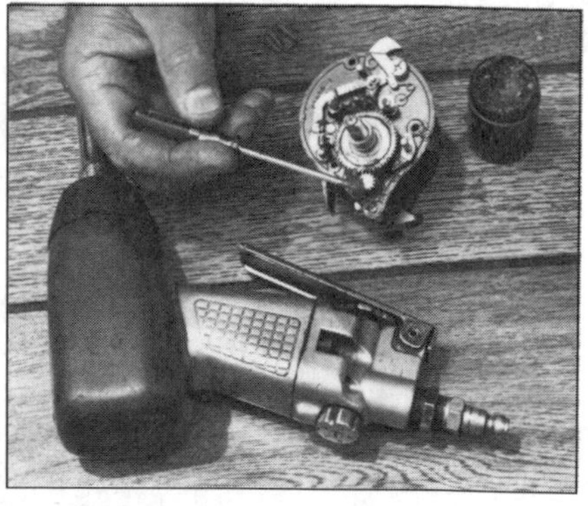

Apply moly coat to the pawl gear.

**by Gregg Meyer, Lakewood, Colorado.*

A fine reel is as beautiful to behold as the bass it helps deliver.

spools increase line capacity and facilitate long casts without adding size and weight to the reel.

Spincast reels are rarely seen on fishing shows or on the tournament circuit, but they have a place in bass fishing. Push-button reels are easy to operate and can be mounted on top-quality baitcasting rods. Several companies offer models with dependable star drags and midrange gear ratios.

Spincasters work well for casting crankbaits and spinnerbaits. They allow long-distance casts with the wind and won't backlash when cast against the wind. Because line release on spincasting reels is mechanical, they're not subject to centrifugal brake failure that plagues baitcasters in heavy rain.

When buying a reel, look for durability and simple fine-quality construction. Hold the spool with one hand while you turn the handle back and forth to check for "slop" in the gears. Consider gear ratio and line capacity. You're going to get what you pay for, so make sure you know what you need.

LINES

In the past two decades, lines, primarily monofilaments, have been vastly improved. Lines are stronger for their diameter, hold knots better, and quality control is tighter. And many more line choices are available.

If you fish six rods rigged with different lures, you might want six different lines on those rods. Lines enhance the performance of a rod-and-reel combo with the chosen lure. A soft supple line like Berkley Trilene XL, for example, might be the choice for fishing crankbaits (1) because you want the bait to run as deep as possible (XL is thin line) and (2) you want the forgiveness of a line with moderate stretch combined with a stiff rod. Another choice that offers more "feel" is a low-stretch cofilament like Stren Prime that many fishermen believe transfers more vibration from the lure along the line to the rod and to your hand.

Dozens of options exist for changing bait performance, given the many line options available. Certainly, no single line excels at all tasks, although lines like Stren and Berkley Trilene XL are all-around good choices. Fine-quality line is important, but expect to pay more to get the best. So start with good line. Then retie often and replace line frequently.

Monofilament lines are either limp or abrasion resistant, which isn't a problem for fishermen with several rods rigged for different situations. Limp lines cast better on spinning reels and perform well in finesse presentations. Tough lines cast well on baitcasting tackle and perform well around cover.

Again, though, no single line is perfect for each situation. But tough, abrasion-resistant line is necessary for fishing stumps, rocks, timber, brush, and weeds that nick monofilament, drastically reducing strength. While no industry-wide standard measures abrasion resistance, generally abrasion-resistant line is wiry and resists denting with a fingernail.

Limp, shock-resistant line with no stretch hasn't been developed. The most sensitive lines with the least stretch are more brittle and may break on the set and coil in cold weather. Dropping tube jigs down a steep bluff bank calls for limp, thin, but strong line like Trilene XL, DuPont's Magna Thin, or Bagley's Blue Label Silver Thread. But they don't resist abrasion in cover.

Different situations also call for different colored line. High-visibility fluorescent line is easy for fish and fishermen to see in clear water. Use fluorescent line for murky water or at night. Clear water calls for thin-diameter lines in subtle colors—clear, gray, or green.

The most visible lines are fluorescent or "optically brightened." The least visible lines probably are light green rather than clear. When low visibility is critical, camouflage line with a brown or green marking pen by running narrow stripes across the line while it's on the reel. This breaks up its cord-like appearance underwater.

To avoid heavy steel leaders, tie on lures directly. But in some situations, a 14- to 25-pound test short single-strand wire leader can prevent losing lures to toothy predators like pike. Wire leaders also cut through weeds easier.

Many crankbaits, rattlebaits, and topwaters work best attached with a split ring or wire snap. Spoons and in-line spinners sometimes require a snap swivel rather than being tied directly to your line. Good-quality hardware is worth paying extra for the service and reliability it provides.

Sharpening Hooks

STAGE 1.

CUT A BLADE ON BOTH SIDES OF INNER POINT. THIS IS WHAT CUTS THRU MEMBRANES. YOU MUST DEBURR THE BARB. THIS OCCURS WHEN FILE DOES NOT STUTTER OR SKIP ACROSS BARB.

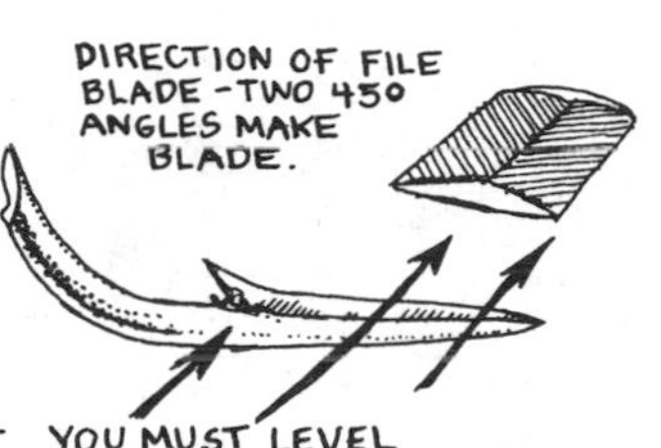

STAGE II

EACH SIDE OF POINT MUST RECEIVE A LONG TAPERING ENTRY RAMP. ALWAYS HOLD FILE AT ANGLE YOU WANT ON HOOK. YOUR HANDS ARE LIKE JIGS IN THAT THEY HOLD WORK AND TOOL AT CORRECT ANGLES.

STAGE III

SHARPENING WILL NOT OCCUR UNTIL THE OUTER-TOP OF POINT RECEIVES IT'S OWN TAPERING, DOUBLE EDGE POINT. THIS IS THE CRITICAL CUT.

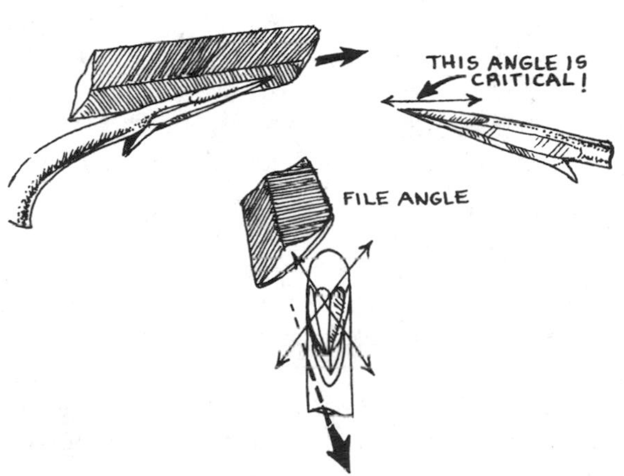

Tom Seward

SHARPENING HOOKS

The use of lighter line is one important trend in bass fishing, whether for finesse techniques or with heavier line in cover. Sharp hooks slip easily into fish flesh, making it possible to use lighter line.

BASS BOATS

Bass boats are highly evolved machines. Bass fishing is primarily a casting game that requires moving rapidly between fishing spots, maneuvering efficiently around cover, and casting from a stable platform. Most bass boats

"I just said we'd get there first, I didn't say we'd be able to stop."

are built on flared V-hulls that handle waves well and are stable at rest. Low sides expose little "sail area" that makes boats difficult to handle in wind. Hull lengths range from 15 to 21 feet, with 17- and 18-foot models the most popular.

The race for more horsepower has declined, mostly because 150 hp will move a boat as fast as is safe on most waters. Accordingly, some tournament organizations restrict motor size to 150 hp. With hydraulic or electric jack plates, a motor can be adjusted vertically to run in shallower water as well as being trimmed and tilted.

Boat interiors have changed, too. The popularity of flipping led to larger bow decks, so two anglers can stand up front for an equal shot at prime cover. Rod lockers accommodate longer rods. Those changes have consumed storage space, so fewer boats can hold large tackle boxes, one reason for the popularity of smaller soft-sided tackle packs. Velcro rod fastening systems hold rods safely without the hassle of stowing them in a locker.

A high-performance boat requires a lot of electricity. Small boats need two batteries, one to start the outboard and power the electronics, and a deep-cycle battery to power the bow-mount trolling motor. Bigger boats with 24-volt systems use two deep-cycle batteries, plus a battery to crank the motor. Some larger boats house five batteries—a "marine" battery to start the outboard and run electronics, plus two sets of paired deep-cycle batteries for the electric motor. When the power in one pair is exhausted, a switch brings on two fresh batteries.

Bigger isn't always better. Bigger bass boats are too heavy to launch at unimproved ramps, draw too much water to fish extremely shallow cover, and are too wide to maneuver in dense timber or narrow culverts. Many serious bass anglers own a deluxe fiberglass boat and a light aluminum. Other serious bassers reject the price of high-performance rigs, choosing less

Small waters with limited access offer the opportunity for fine bass fishing. Small boats often key access to this fishing.

In many areas of North America, multispecies fisheries call for V-hull boats and the option for fishermen to work from a front casting platform or the rear of the boat—trolling, backtrolling, or casting.

The bass boat—design, speed, and all—that bass fishermen everywhere dream of owning. Get there fast, fish from a stable platform, and do it in style.

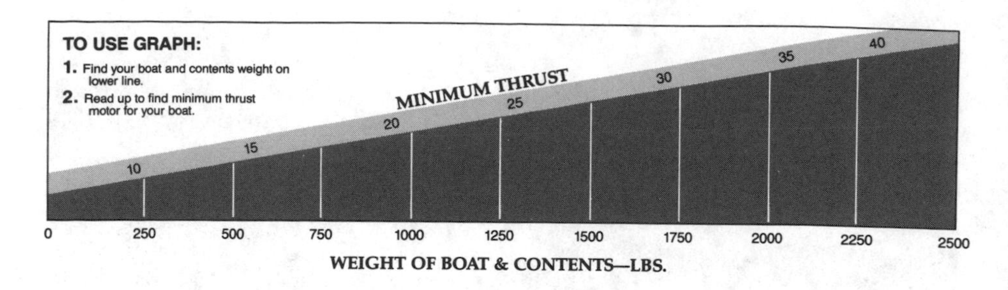

Size of Boat Versus Electric Motor Thrust

Minn Kota provides this graph to determine the minimum thrust needed to move a boat. Fishing in wind, waves, and weeds requires additional thrust.

expensive midsize aluminum rigs that tow easily behind six-cylinder vehicles and burn less gas in smaller outboards.

The industry trend is to prerigged boat packages that include boat, motor, trailer, trolling motor, sonar, batteries, instruments, and accessories. Prerigged boats, however, don't allow for individual choice of accessories. But package deals usually cost less than the same equipment purchased separately. And prerigged consoles often look better because gauges fit in dashes molded to hold them. Complex electrical systems also require special skills and tools for rigging.

Many bass boats are also equipped with push poles for moving through heavy cover or for driving into the bottom to anchor to. Most bassers also carry anchors, another trend to slower, more thorough fishing.

Although livewells were improved during the early 1980s, many companies have failed to further refine their systems. Most tournaments follow a catch-and-release format that penalizes for dead bass. Studies of delayed mortality also show that livewells must be improved to ensure that bass weighed alive don't die later from the stress of their captivity. Tests show that the volume of water moved through a livewell is important. Aeration and recirculation, temperature control, and livewell shape all are vital in keeping bass healthy. Many bassers also add chemicals to sustain the health of bass in livewells.

Despite test results and catch-and-release consciousness among bass anglers, most bass boat livewells are inadequate. For a catch of five bass, a 20-gallon capacity is minimal, and two such livewells are required for boats in tournament competition. Rear deck placement is essential due to weight constraints. Rear placement also cushions the ride bass get.

Rounded livewells and livewells with padded tops also reduce damage to fish. Livewells with small windows in the top allow adding fish without drastically changing the light level. Recirculating pumps, lake-water aeration systems, and timers are essential equipment.

Cooling systems and bottled oxygen systems are experimental, but will become standard in pro-style boats. Anglers must demand such features from manufacturers, because at the cost of even midrange boats, bass fishermen and their quarry deserve them.

SONAR

Depth, a key component of most bass fishing patterns, requires a sonar system. But sonar plays a different role in bass fishing than it does in walleye or salmon fishing, where you actually see fish on the screen. Bass in heavy cover, shallow water, or on the bottom are difficult to detect on sonar. Exceptions include aggregations of winter bass on reservoir structure in deep water and bass holding outside deep weedlines. But bass fishing must not be at the wrong depth, and sonar is critical for detecting deep weeds or timber even if it doesn't show individual fish.

Paper graphs remain unmatched for presenting baits on structural elements in deep water where maximum resolution is important. And in newer units, switching paper isn't a problem.

Liquid crystal display (LCD) units continue to improve. They're easy to operate, durable, easily read in sunlight, and display objects well.

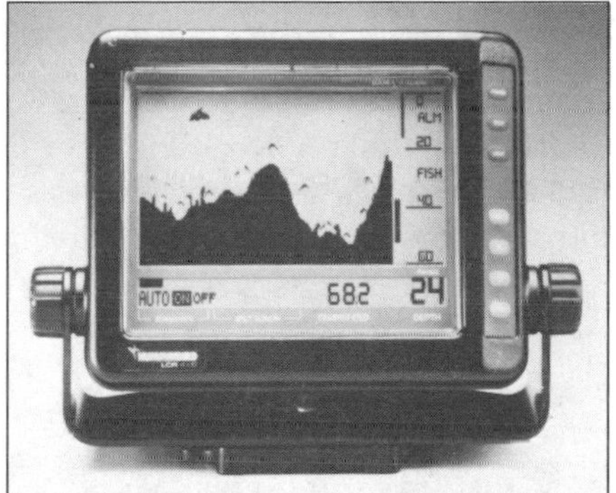

Most bass boats are rigged with three sonar units: An in-depth flasher and either a paper graph or LCD mounted on the dash; and a flasher or LCD mounted on the bow.

Many boats are rigged with three sonar units: (1) A flasher built into the console to give fast, continuous bottom readings. The transducer reads through the hull when mounted in the bilge area. (2) A large LCD with a high pixel count or a paper graph mounted on the console or on a swing bracket to give detailed pictures of structure, cover, baitfish, and bass while motoring to find a spot. In this case, transducer placement on the transom provides optimum detail. And (3) another LCD on the bow platform for bottom readings while running with the bow-mount electric. This transducer is mounted on the lower unit of the trolling motor.

Bass anglers who fish large reservoirs and lakes often use lorans to electronically mark hot spots so they can return to them. A full complement of satellites, projected for the mid-1990s, will allow an even more precise navigational system.

TROLLING MOTORS

Nothing matches a bow-mount electric for maneuvering through timber or holding along a weedline. Bass fishing is a casting game, and electric motors are the caster's ally. Power seems to be what most anglers look for in a trolling motor. Two factors determine power requirements. Heavier boats

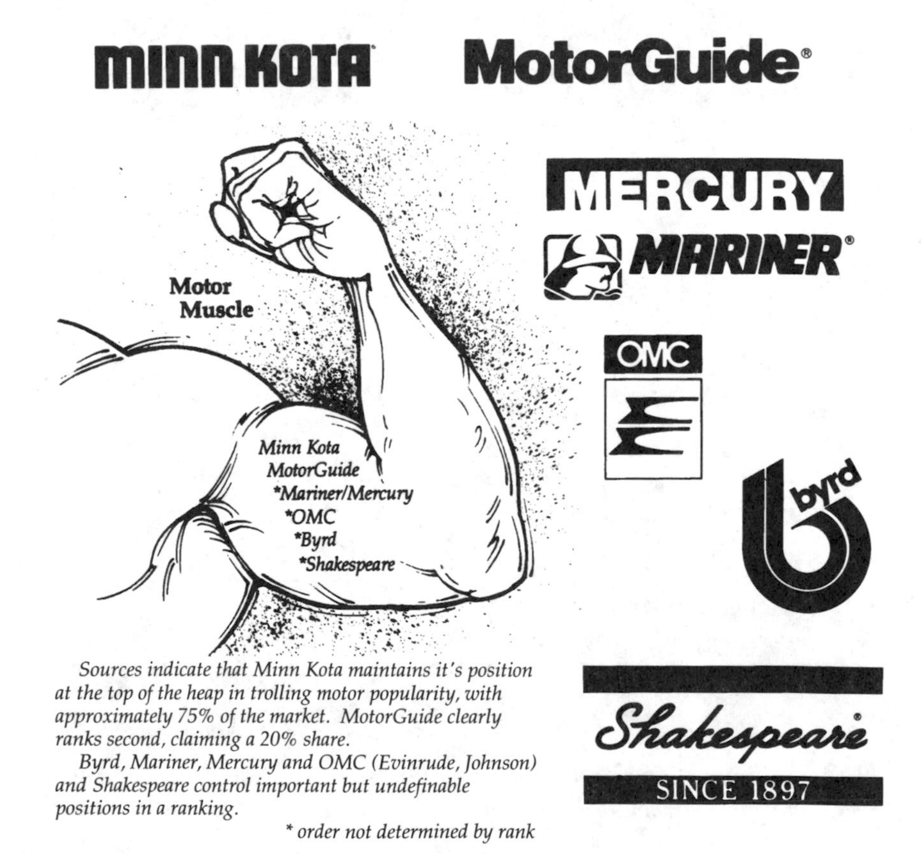

Sources indicate that Minn Kota maintains it's position at the top of the heap in trolling motor popularity, with approximately 75% of the market. MotorGuide clearly ranks second, claiming a 20% share.

Byrd, Mariner, Mercury and OMC (Evinrude, Johnson) and Shakespeare control important but undefinable positions in a ranking.

** order not determined by rank*

(18- and 20-footers) require stronger electric motors. Some manufacturers offer guidelines to match power with boat weight, but also consult other fishermen about how much power it takes to move various boat models in wind and waves during a long fishing day.

Today's weedless trolling motor props: the Minn Kota "Weed Invader" and MotorGuide "Hannon System" 2-blade prop and 4-blade "Ninja" prop.

To move a boat through a weedbed, the prop must chop weeds and operate with weeds wrapped around the shaft and lower unit. This quickly drains power. Standard semi-V-hull aluminum boats with high sides also require extra power to compensate for their high sail area.

Unfortunately, it's difficult to compare the power of motors from different companies. Although thrust readings may be inflated, ratings usually suggest comparative power ratings within a manufacturer's line. Ultimately, experience is the best judge.

Which electrical system do you need—12-volt, 12/24, or 24? The choice used to be easy. The 12-volt system was inexpensive, light, and easy to rig since it required only one battery. On the other hand, 24-volt systems offered maximum power. Then the Mercury 12-volt Thruster proved that a 12-volt system could adequately move a big boat. Other powerful 12-volts followed, but high amp draw required two batteries wired parallel.

For a large, heavy boat, we recommend a 24-volt system. The 12-volt models with huge props can handle heavy boats, but they punish batteries. For lighter boats, 12-volt systems are fine, especially if they aren't used in heavy weeds. A 12/24 system allows switching from series to parallel wiring. Fewer amps are drawn, but power is available when it's needed.

Pulse modulation, a major advancement in trolling motor technology, turns the trolling motor on and off thousands of times per second—20,000

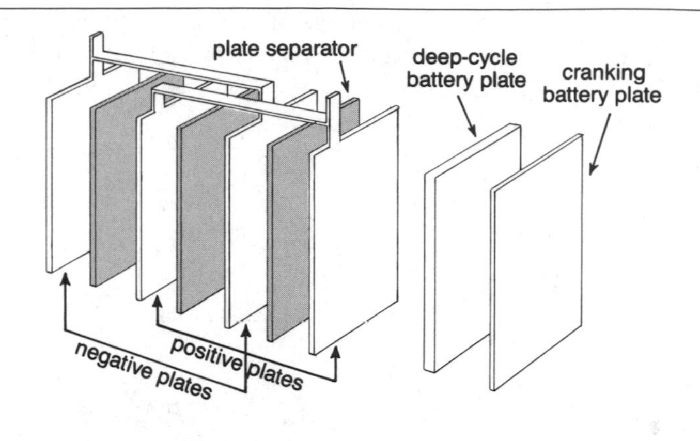

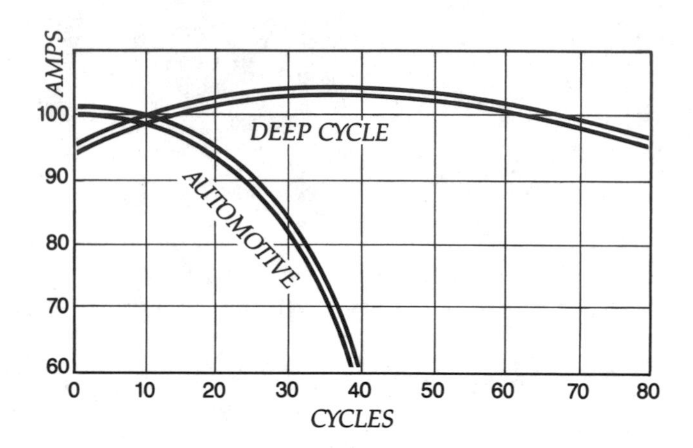

Deep Cycle-Automotive Battery Comparison

Metals on positive and negative battery plates react chemically when immersed in sulfuric acid, the most common battery electrolyte. The reaction creates voltage that coats the plates with lead sulfate and dilutes the acid. Discharge, as this process is referred to, can vary from a few minutes of cranking a car to more than 12 hours of running a small trolling motor with a powerful deep-cycle battery.

Automotive batteries, needed primarily to start (crank) the engine, have many thin plates to provide a large surface area, since many amps are required simultaneously and only the material near the plate surfaces reacts chemically. Cranking batteries are not meant to be discharged below 90 percent of full capacity; several discharges below this level reduces performance.

Deep-cycle batteries are designed to be discharged and charged many times. Thicker plates produce fewer amps, but the charge is held for a longer time.

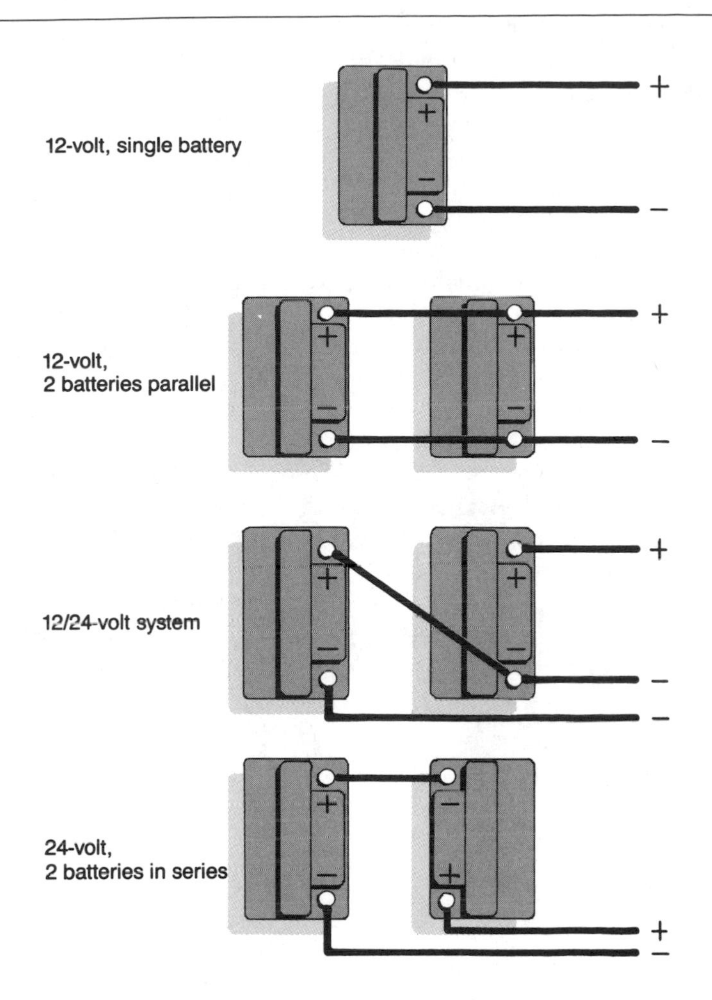

Voltage Options & Rigging

A 12-volt one-battery system is simple and works fine for light-duty applications. But more powerful motors that move heavier boats in adverse conditions quickly discharge the battery, especially on high-speed settings.

Available amp hours can be doubled and voltage maintained by hooking a second battery in parallel—positive to positive, negative to negative—with jumper wires. Use 6-gauge to minimize current loss.

Two batteries hooked in series—positive to negative, negative to positive, or to the motor—provide 24 volts.

A 24-volt system offers maximum power for trolling motors, but isn't as efficient as a 12-volt system. Amp hours of service aren't doubled.

The 12/24-volt systems, popular for trolling motors, offer the option of high power or long service. A switch, usually located on the powerhead or foot-control panel, changes the system from series to parallel.

times in the case of the Minn Kota Maximizer. Direct current from the battery is pulsed, which reduces draw on the battery and increases its life—3 to 5 times as long with systems available from Minn Kota and MotorGuide. These systems often last several fishing days without charging. Early pulse modulated motors interfered with some bow-mount sonar units, but proper rigging has eliminated the problem. Although props with extra blades and alternative blade positioning have increased weed resistance, a totally weedless prop doesn't exist.

Many anglers favor manual-control bow-mount electrics, but the trend is to foot-controls. Better engineering has eliminated the stiff cables that often broke in foot-control units. And stand-up "bike" bow seats have made standing and running a foot control more comfortable.

Hand-control units still excel for directional fishing—parallel to a straight weededge, bluff bank, or into wind. New wiring systems, with on-off switches placed at several spots in the front deck, also increase positioning options. Personal preference and habit are important in choosing a steering mode. But with practice, a foot-control model frees both hands, which isn't possible with hand-controls.

You can't buy fishing success. Success is based on knowledge, not gadgets. But knowledge of good equipment, as we've said so often in this chapter, helps good fishermen fish more efficiently, more comfortably, and therefore, more successfully. The right tackle makes fishing more fun.

Chapter 12

CRANKBAITS

Shake, Rattle, and Roll!

In 1967, Fred Young's hand-carved forerunner of the Big O spurred a major innovation in bass fishing. Although diving, wobbling "plugs" like the Heddon River Runt, Bomber, and Hellbender had existed for years, this new-style fat "alphabet" bait quickly gained popularity. Cordell's Big O, Bill Norman's N, Bagley's Balsa B, and Rebel's R were among the first snag-resistant diving baits that crashed and crawled their way through timber and across weed tops. This characteristic made them ideal for use in snag-

Row 1: Crankbaits like the River Runt, Bomber, and Hellbender predate the newer plastic-lipped lures. Interestingly, the old metal-lipped lures with the diving lip in-line with the long axis of the lure (Hellbender and Bomber) generally dive deeper than their more modern angle-lipped cousins.

Row 2: Shallow divers come in a wide variety of shapes and sizes. Long thin lures like the Bagley Bang-O-Lure, shad-shaped baits like the Shad Rap, and fat-bodied "alphabet" models like the Bill Norman "N" series provide a wealth of different actions. Bass love 'em all. Walleyes, on the other hand, seem to prefer thinner-shaped lures like the minnow or shad baits. Whether it's the difference in profile, action, or a combination of both is contendable, but it's a good rule.

Row 3: Deep divers come in sizes from minuscule to mammoth. The long lip digs into the water and makes the lure dive deep. Shown are a Mann's 15+Plus and Poe's 1200 series. The Rebel Suspend-R, meanwhile, looks like a floating lure, but is weighted to remain at a stationary depth when the retrieve is stopped.

Row 4: Sinking, weighted "rattle" lures like the Bill Lewis Rat-L-Trap sink until the retrieve begins and then run at a constant depth. Blade baits like the Heddon Sonar perform somewhat like rattlebaits, but lack the high-frequency vibrations of an internal rattle chamber. The metal-bodied Spoonplug enjoys popularity among a handful of trolling enthusiasts, yet is also effective when cast, allowed to sink, and retrieved across deep structure.

infested reservoirs just coming into their heyday.

The diving bills common to most crankbaits provide a trio of bass-triggering effects: (1) varying the length, position, and shape of the bill varies running depth (longer bills dive deeper); (2) the combination of bill and body shape gives each lure a distinctive rolling wobble; and (3) the forward bill position deflects snags. Actually, the bill contacts snags first, flipping the lure around them while the body shields the treble hooks from snagging. "Crankbaits," as they were named by southern guides, were easy to use effectively, so they were an instant hit.

The basic design has been modified through the years into a variety of shapes and diving effects. Long, thin minnow-imitators like the Rapala are most popular in short-lipped, shallow-running models also ideal for surface twitching. Intermediate body shapes—not so round and flat, yet not long and thin, either—are equally effective on bass, walleyes and pike. These are often referred to as shad baits (the Shad Rap, for example) because of their similarity to the triangular body profile of gizzard shad.

Running depth has long been a popular topic of contention, as each manufacturer repeatedly brought out larger, longer-lipped models proclaimed to dive deeper than the competition's. Today's diving champions claim to achieve the 20-foot-plus range when cast on light (8- to 12-pound-test) line. Generally expect lures to run considerably shallower, however, than the manufacturer's claims. For casting, deep-diving crankbaits are effective down to perhaps 15 feet, with 12 feet being a more realistic norm.

Since crankbaits work well in and around cover, most anglers prefer powerful casting tackle and heavier 12- to 20-pound-test line to withstand the abuse of object fishing and to muscle fish out of cover. That's part of the reason they seldom achieve their maximum claimed running depth. A few crankbait specialists like Tom Seward, however, prefer lighter line and spinning gear in minimal snag or clear water situations, such as highland reservoirs or strip pits. They trade increased depth and casting distance for

COMPARISON OF POPULAR CRANKBAITS UNDER VARIED CONDITIONS*

Lure	Casting Depth (ft.) (12-pound-test line)	Trolling Depth (ft.) (8-pound-test line)	Trolling Depth (ft.) (14-pound-test line)	Prime Trolling Speed Range (mph)
Bagley DB-3	12	26	21	2.6
Cordell C27 Ratt'l Spot	5	12	9	3.0
Rebel Wee-R	6	12	10	2.3
Rapala #7 Shallow Shad Rap	5	8	5	3.0
Poe's 1200 Series	17	41	35	3.0

Different styles and sizes of crankbaits provide a variety of effective running depths and speeds. Each model, however, is most effective under its own range of conditions. Switch lures and sizes to best match the situations you're faced with.

*Adapted from *Crankbaits*, Fishing Enterprises Press, Box 7108, Pierre, SD 57501.

the greater likelihood of losing a lure to snags, wear and tear, or a big bass.

In preparation for his book *Crankbaits*, walleye tournament angler Mike McClelland and his associates tested the running depths of over 200 different lures under a variety of conditions. As expected, long casts and lighter line increased the running depths of most crankbaits.

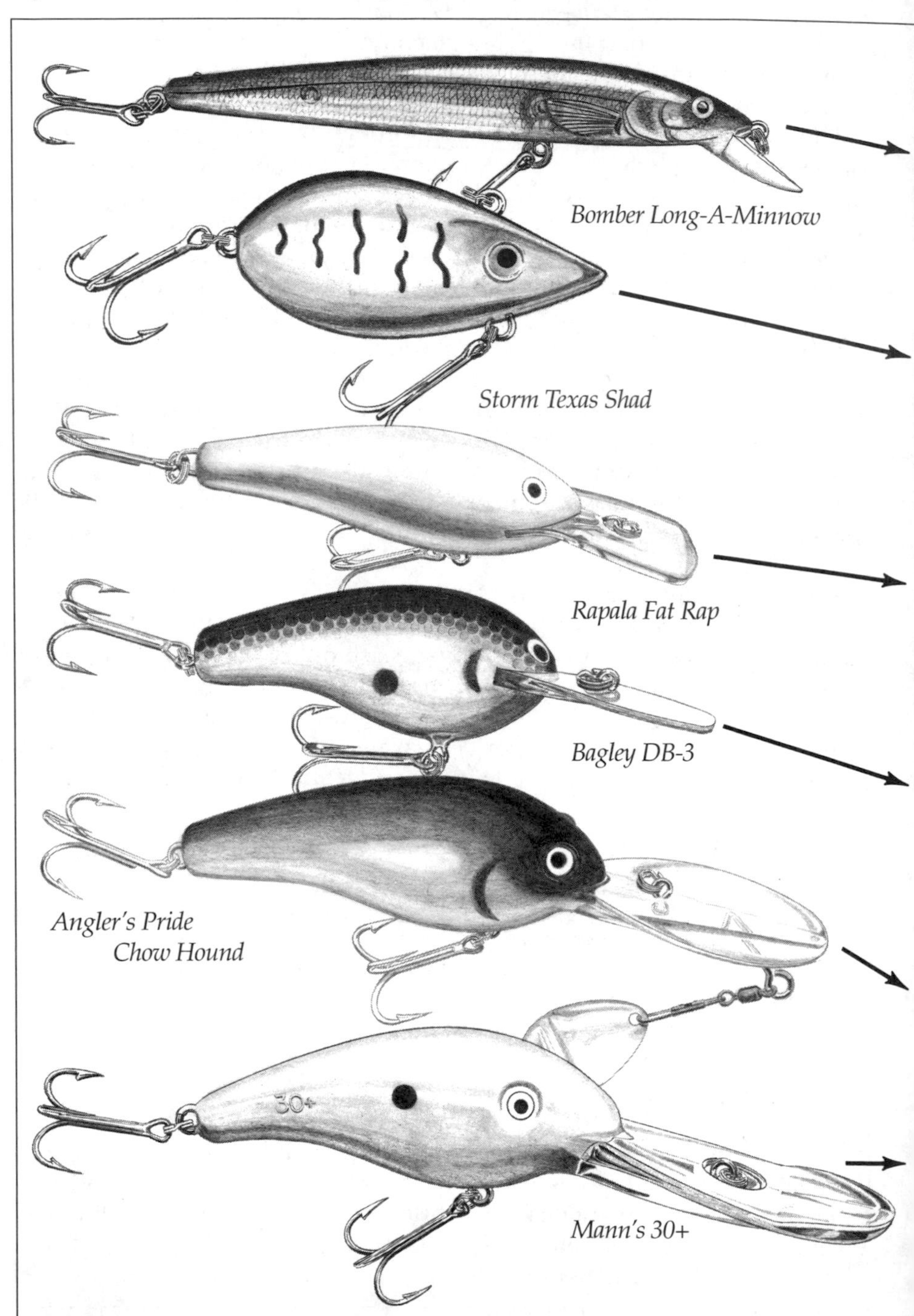

In general, both cast and trolled lures ran about a foot deeper for every line size decrease (for example, switching from 14- to 12-pound-test line). The maximum running depth and most effective speed were chiefly a function of lure shape and design, although lure depth can be varied slightly by changing retrieve speed. Holding the rod tip down beneath the

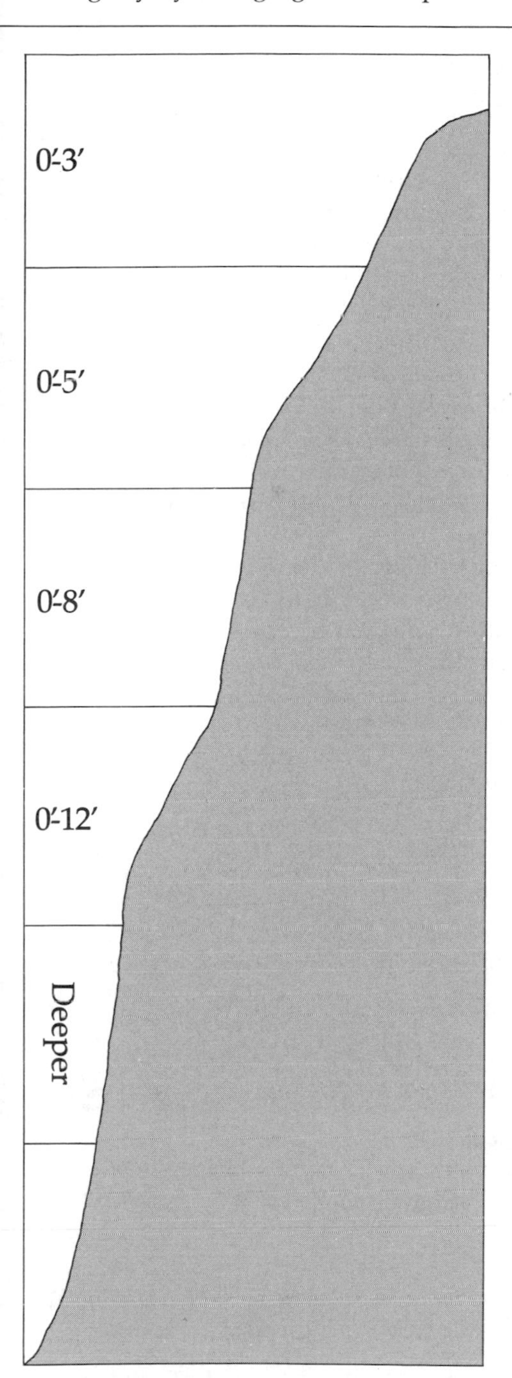

A complete selection of crankbaits lets you cover each depth level. Try natural-patterned baits in clear water, "hot-bellied" natural patterns in stained water, and fluorescent-colored baits in dirty water.

surface didn't appreciably affect the running depth—a popular misconception.

One general rule in crankbait fishing for bass is to contact cover. This changes lure speed and direction, and typically triggers bass strikes more than a free-running lure. Reel a few quick turns to make the lure dive, then back off to a slower crawl. Keep your rod tip low, in position to pump the rod tip, pause, or set the hook. Vary your speed with a stop-and-go motion, using just enough speed to tickle weed tops or contact wood or rocks. Cast parallel to fast-dropping shorelines, distinctive weedlines or channel edges, and manmade structures like riprap, to maximize the time the lure contacts bottom and remains in the fish zone on the retrieve.

If you hang up momentarily, give the lure some slack. If the bill is wedged across a rock or limb, natural buoyancy often lifts the lure toward the surface. Wood-bodied or injected foam lures have the most buoyancy and rise the fastest. Plastic-bodied lures usually rise slower, yet generally survive contact punishment best due to their tougher construction.

If a pause doesn't free the lure, try a series of sharp jerks or wrist snaps followed by slack line. No luck? Move the boat to the other side of the snag and pop the lure off in the direction it approached the snag. Still stuck? Use a lure retriever to reach down and rip the lure off the snag by straightening the hooks or breaking the snag. In any case, bang cover, because that's where the bass usually are.

Neutral buoyancy baits like the Rebel Suspend-R are better suited for more open-water conditions. Stop the retrieve and let the bait hang instead of rising to the surface. This application works well in cold water or for neutral fish, but not so well in heavy cover.

A family of sinking crankbaits, known as "rattlebaits" due to their

Up and Away

A Lo'Contact retrieve triggers big bass in a wide range of activity moods. Short intervals of bottom contact reduce hang-ups and allow a better feel of bottom features.

Light line and lure components allow plastic lures to rise backwards quickly from stumps and debris. The rod tip must be instantly pushed forward to back the lure off as you make stump contact. Weight and length of line controls lure rise time.

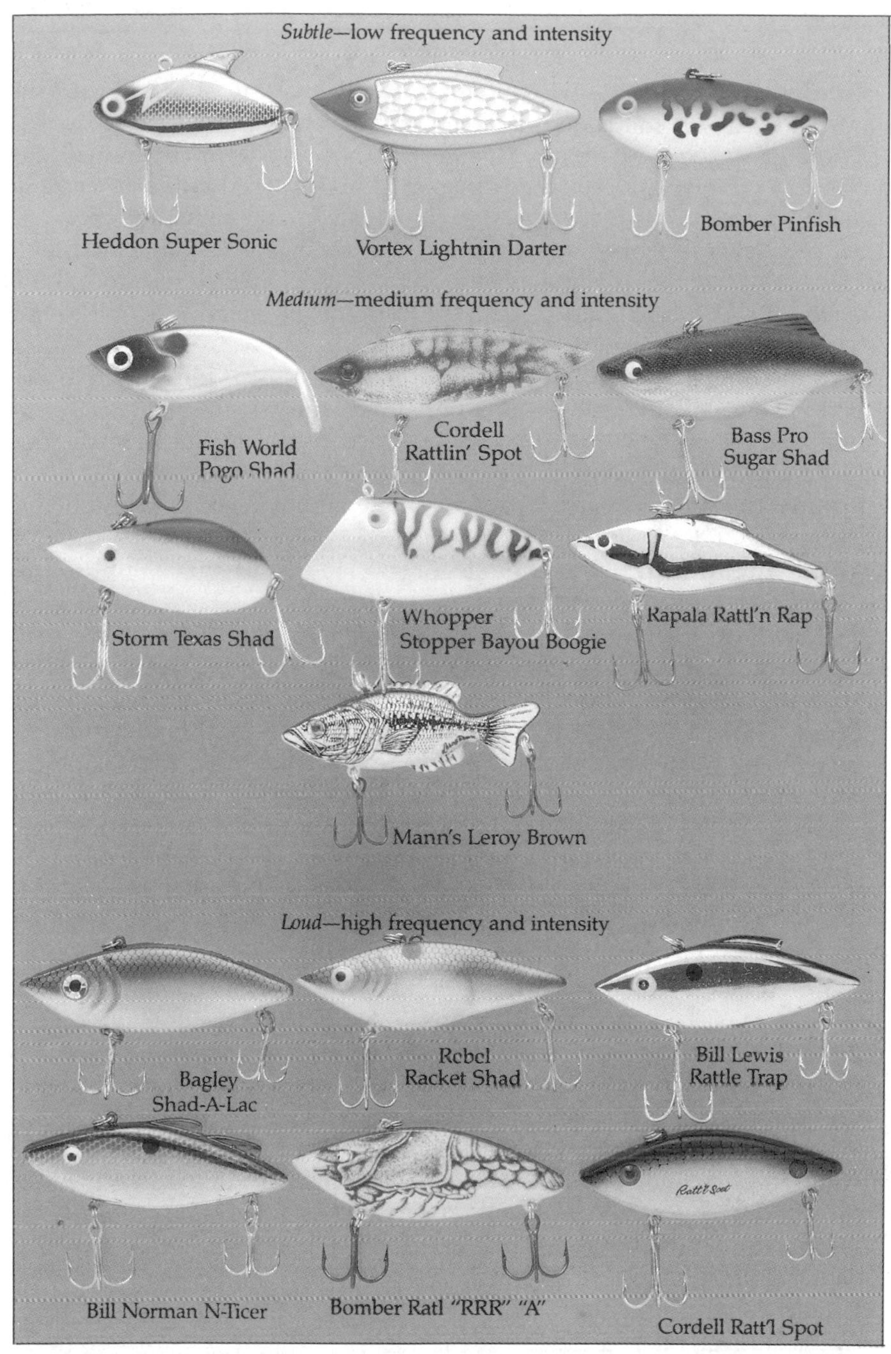

Rattlebaits are not all alike. Some produce simple, subtle low-frequency "thuds," while others produce loud low-frequency thuds. Others produce moderately loud combination low-thuds and high-frequency rattles, while some produce loud low thuds in combination with loud high-frequency rattles.

This scale represents our unscientific characterization of some rattlebaits on the market.

RATTLEBAITS

Cordell Rattlin' Spot—Three Sizes. Flat lead head slug. Loud low-frequency thuds. Overall sound: loud and low.

Cordell Ratt'l Spot— One size. Flat lead head slug plus multiple small shot in body. Loud low-frequency thuds plus loud high-pitched rattle. Body rattle dominates sound. Overall sound: loud, combination low and high pitch.

Mann's Leroy Brown—One size. First cousin to Mann's Slidin' Finn-Mann. Flat lead head slug plus multiple small shot in body. Loud low-frequency thuds plus loud higher-pitched rattle. Head thuds dominate sound. Overall sound: moderately loud combination low and high pitch.

Bass Pro Shops Sugar Shad—One size. Lead head slug plus multiple shot in body. Loud low-frequency thuds plus loud high-pitched rattle. Overall sound: higher-pitched head rattle, lower-pitched body rattle; moderately loud combination low and high pitch.

Fishing World Pogo Shad—One size. Multiple shot in body. Medium loud medium pitch. Overall sound: moderately loud medium pitch.

Vortex Lightnin Darter—One size. Flat lead head slug. Subtle low-frequency thuds. Overall sound: subtle low pitch.

Bomber Ratl "RRR" "A"—One size. Flat lead head slug plus multiple small shot in body. Loud low-frequency thuds plus loud higher-pitched rattle. Head thuds dominate sound. Overall sound: loud combination low and high pitch.

Bomber Pinfish—One size. Large body slug. Low-frequency rattle. Overall sound: moderately loud low pitch.

Bill Norman N-Ticer—Two sizes. Flat lead head slug plus multiple small shot in body. Loud low-frequency thuds plus higher-pitched rattle. Body rattle dominates sound. Overall sound: loud combination low and high pitch.

Bill Lewis Rat-L-Trap—Three sizes. Flathead slug plus multiple small shot in body. Loud high-pitched rattle plus subtle low-pitched thuds. Overall sound: combination of loud high pitch with low-pitched background thuds.

Storm Texas Shad—Two sizes. Multiple small shot in body. Moderately loud medium pitched rattle. Overall sound: medium loud medium pitch.

Rebel Racket Shad—One size. Flathead slug plus multiple small shot in body. Loud low-pitched thuds plus loud moderately high-frequency rattle. Overall sound: loud combination low and medium-high pitch.

Whopper Stopper Bayou Boogie—One size. Multiple small shot in body. Medium-loud medium-pitch rattle. Overall sound: medium loud, medium pitch.

Heddon Super Sonic—Two sizes. One large shot in body. Subtle low-pitch rattle. Overall sound: Subtle low pitch.

Bagley's Shad-A-Lac—One size. Flathead slug plus multiple small shot in body. Loud low-pitched thuds plus moderately high-pitched body rattle. Overall sound: loud combination low and medium-high pitch.

Rapala Rattl'n Rap—One size. Flathead slug plus multiple small shot in body. Moderately loud thuds and high-pitched rattle. Overall sound: moderately loud combination low pitch and moderately high pitch.

hollow-bodied lipless design, contain weights that rattle against the body and each other. Examples are the Bill Lewis Rat-L-Trap and the Cordell Spot. These heavy baits sink until you begin your retrieve. Then they run at a consistent depth unless you stop to pump and flutter them into holes in weedbeds or down the sides of wood cover. While the bait has no diving bill, the slanted nose deflects it over snags. These traits make rattlebaits versatile lures for everything from high-speed shallow retrieves to deep-water jigging.

The *rattle* in rattlebaits is more than just a gimmick designed to catch more tackle buyers than fish. Rattles alert fish more than silent crankbaits do. Some lures like the Ratt'l Spot produce loud vibrations, while others like the Rattlin' Rap are more subtle. Carry a variety of lures and experiment to determine which is best for conditions you're fishing.

Moving lures of *any* kind push water and send out low-frequency vibrations that fish sense through their lateral line. Bass may hear high-frequency vibrations of a moving crankbait as far as 100 feet away, though the vibrations may blend with other underwater sounds until the lure gets close to the fish. Once a rattlebait approaches the fish, however, the high-pitched vibrations of the rattles are heard through the bass's inner ear. At close range, bass sense lower frequency sound waves with their lateral line. So the fish may begin zeroing in on an approaching bait even before it's visible.

At some point, the lure also becomes visible to the bass. If it passes near enough—in the strike zone—the fish may decide to strike. The final decision is based primarily on sight, yet vibration and sound may trigger bass into striking even though the lure isn't a perfect imitation of natural forage. It sounds interesting, moves enticingly, and looks edible, though.

Metal-bodied "blade" baits like the Heddon Sonar, Cordell Gay Blade or Silver Buddy are technically not crankbaits, but function similar to rattlebaits—minus the rattle. The thin, heavy metal bodies that send out distinct vibrations have long been popular vertical jigging lures for walleyes. Yet they can be effectively fished in nearly any situation you'd fish a rattlebait. They'll even take a beating on rocks without being knocked out of tune. Their small size makes them prime lures for smallmouths, too.

Trolling lipped crankbaits is an effective method for covering a lot of water. Baits that float high usually work best around weeds, because you can pause and float the bait above high clumps that would otherwise snag. Wood or rocks are best trolled with punishment-resistant plastic lures, and especially metal-bodied lures like the Spoonplug. If you snag a limb, just jiggle the Spoonplug up and down; it's negative buoyancy flops the lure up and down and often off the snag without the use of a lure retriever.

Effective speeds run the gamut from high-speed trolling approaches to stop-and-go crawls. Higher speeds are usually best in warm water; slower speeds when water is cold. Some anglers prefer low-speed (3-to-1 ratio) casting reels to force a slow retrieve, while others swear by high-speed (6-to-1) reels for a crank-and-burn approach. In most cases, a standard (4.5-to 1) reel is a good compromise. Just vary your retrieve speed or change lure style.

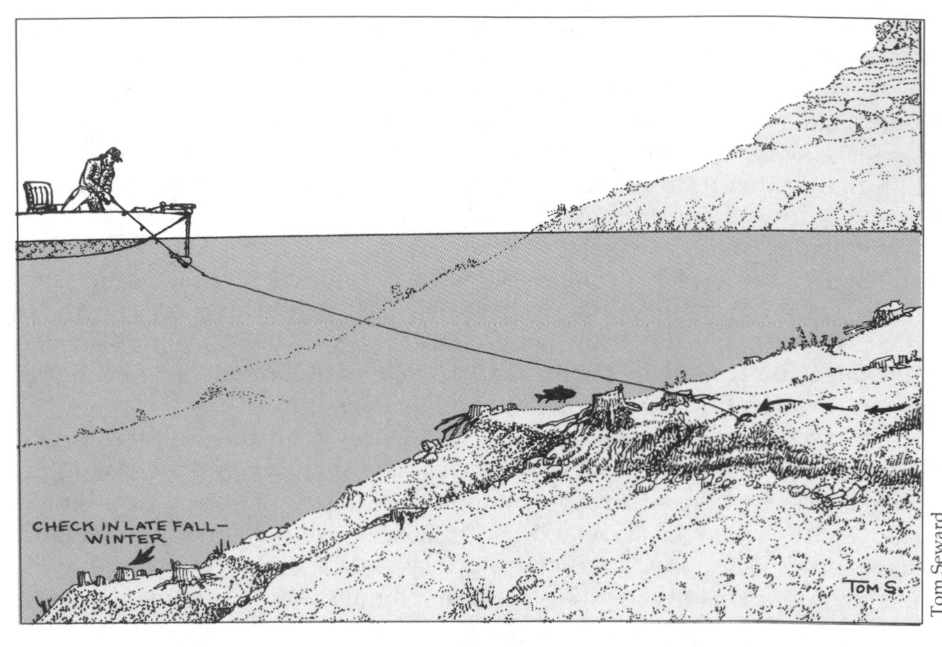

Positioning

This angler accurately brings his lure down the deep-water edge of a 14-foot shelf. Using sonar to position the boat, reposition to cover the outside deep-water stumps on the other side of the shelf. Casting angles are important.

For example, say you've been using a shallow diver that runs at 2 to 4 feet. Switch to a deep diver designed to run at 6 to 9 feet; just retrieve it slower, with frequent pauses. It'll run 2 to 4 feet deep if you retrieve slower. The result is a slow presentation at a shallow depth.

The deepest divers are generally large compared to their shallower-running counterparts. Increased lure size usually presents no problem unless bass are spooky, such as in clear water or during unfavorable weather conditions. The general principle, however, is to use smaller lures in spring and to switch to progressively larger lures as the forage species grow during the year. Active largemouths will eat a *big* crankbait.

Color and color patterns are largely personal choices that depend most on confidence and personal success. Try matching natural forage like crawfish, shad, or bluegills; lots of good natural imitations are available. Yet a moving crankbait blurs the exact color pattern, often presenting a colored profile rather than an exact replica of a forage species.

Thus, it's usually best to select a lure for its proper size and diving ability rather than its color. Clear water, however, calls for subtle natural colors like white or silver—natural forage patterns. Dark or dirty water calls for high-vis colors or combinations of colors that reflect light and color—chartreuse, fire orange, copper, or gold. Color should help the fish find the bait in dark water, but not spook them in clear water.

Tying your line directly to the wire clasp usually stifles lure action and may cause the bait to run to one side. A snap, O-ring, or loop knot

Tuned Lures Catch More Fish

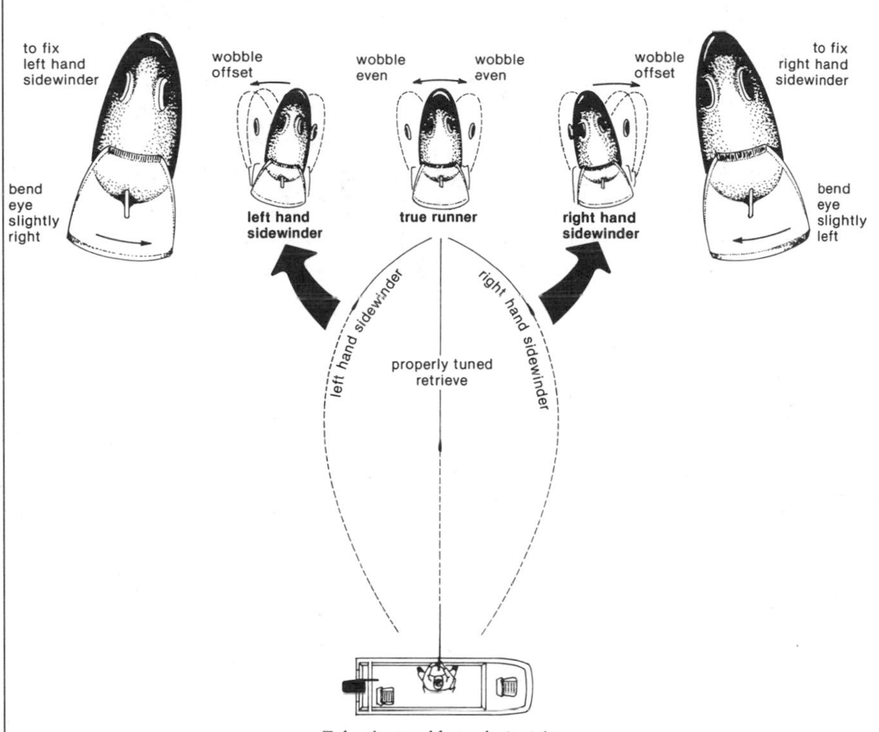

Take the trouble to do it right

Many new crankbaits don't run true. Even a perfectly tuned lure can become a "sidewinder" after it has bumped rocks and logs or hooked a big fish. A bait that rides to the side won't reach proper depth and will foul weeds more easily—no fish. A properly tuned crankbait is essential.

To tune a crankbait, first make sure all hook attachments are on straight and that nothing is obviously out of balance. Next, inspect the eyelet. On some models it will be an imbedded wire in the nose or lip. On others, a screweye is threaded in the plastic.

If the lure (see drawings) runs to your left, move the eyelet (ever so slightly) to the right. If the lure runs to your right, move the eyelet to the left. If the eyelet is made of imbedded wire, nudge it with needlenose pliers. But be careful with the screweye types. Carefully bend the entire screweye. Don't turn it.

It is better to "undertune" the lure several times than "overtune" it. Bend the connection too much and you can loosen it and ruin the bait. Some lures can't be tuned if imbalance is due to a manufacturing defect. Return them or write them off as a bad investment.

generally lets the lure reach its maximum potential, both in wobble and depth.

Many baits don't run straight and must be tuned for proper results. Even an old favorite can be knocked out of tune by repeatedly banging into cover or after hooking a big fish.

Proper tuning is easy and requires minimum effort. Hold the lure in one hand and face it toward you. Grasp the metal attachment clasp or screweye with a long-nose pliers. If the lure ran to the left as it approached you, *bend* the clasp slightly to the right. (Don't *turn* a screweye—bend it). If the lure ran to the right, bend it to the left. Then make a sample cast, and retrieve the bait. If you undertuned or overtuned on your first try, repeat the process. Eventually, it will run straight and dive to its maximum depth potential.

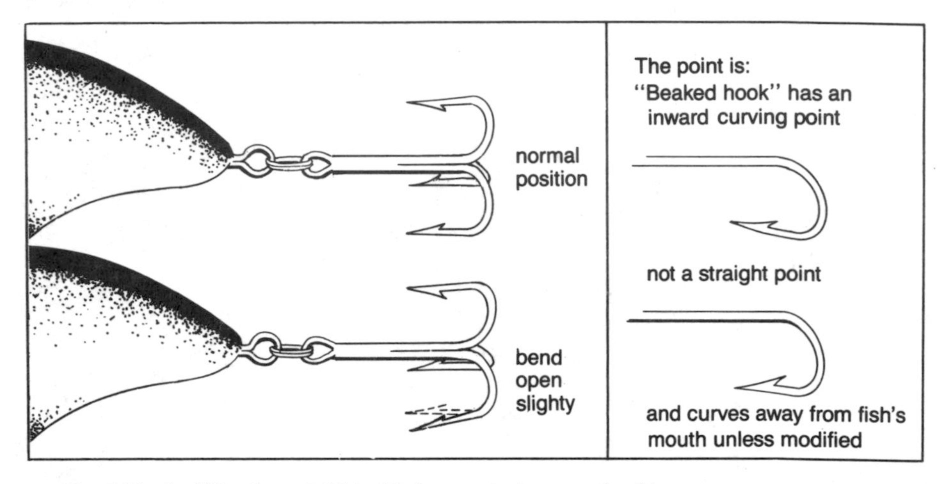

Bend "beaked" hooks out 10 to 15 degrees to improve hooking success.

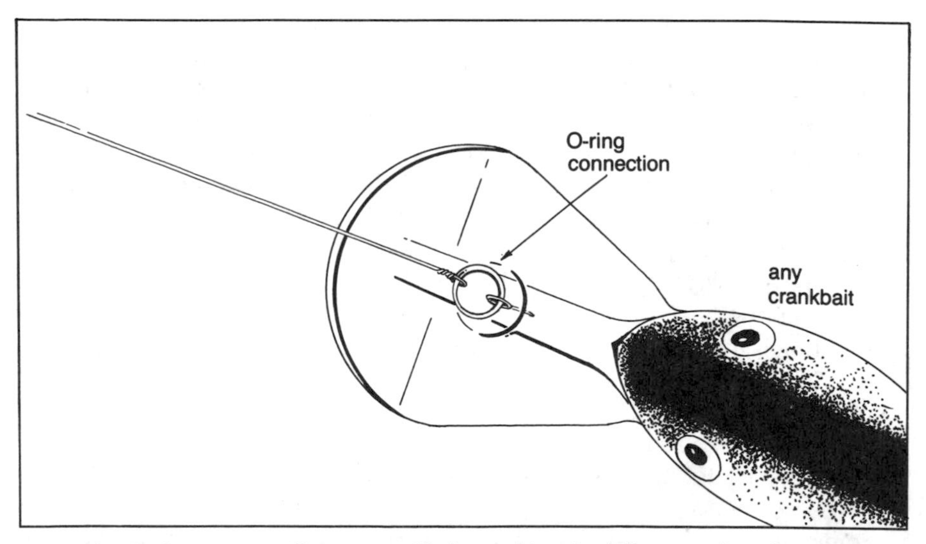

An O-ring or snap allows a crankbait to achieve its full range of motion. Tight knots, however, stifle bait action.

Even if you can't tune a bait to perfection, don't throw it away. Keep a few "sidewinders" on hand for dock fishing. A lure that runs *slightly* to one side will dig around pilings and under a dock on the retrieve. Just cast as close and parallel to the dock as possible, and let the lure poke underneath. You'll sacrifice a little depth, but perhaps make up for it in effectiveness—even though the bait only works along one edge of the dock. Approach the dock from that direction for best results.

Crankbait strikes range from slamming runs that threaten to tear the rod from your hands to subtle bumps that barely disturb the lure's natural vibration. Be prepared to set the hook—hard—at the slightest feel of anything unnatural.

Ultrasharp hooks are critical to begin penetration even before you feel a fish, because bass can inhale and exhale the bait in an instant. A soft-tipped 6-foot straight-handled casting rod lets you set the hook with authority, yet has enough "give" to maintain tension and prevent ripping a hook out when a fish jumps. Clasp the rod handle between your forearm and side during the retrieve to reduce strain on your arm. Numerous manufacturers feature "crankin'" rods designed specifically for this style of fishing.

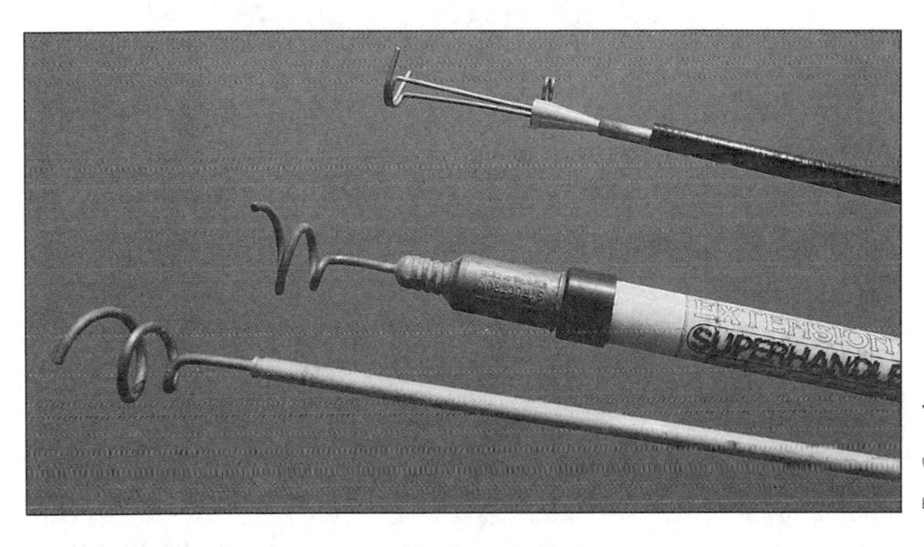

Tom Seward

A trio of lure retrievers. Items like these pay for themselves in a week! Modify them or invent your own. All are extendable.

Top: Brand X, which is effective and light, has a 15-foot extendable glass telescopic body. Line threads through the small loop at the tip, and the hoop pushes the lure off.

Middle: A Lur-Pal coil, epoxied to a 16-foot extendable painter's fiberglass pole, is drilled at the coil end to drain water. Good for deep hang-ups.

Bottom: Original Lur-Pal retriever with extendable aluminum sections. Line is "screwed" into the center of the coil as the pole is slid down to push off the lure. Coil could be wound larger.

Today's standard crankbait rod: Long handle for two-handed casting and leverage when setting ands fighting fish; backbone through the middle of the blank; and a soft tip.

Crankbaits are so easy to use that they're almost impossible to misuse. That doesn't mean that all you have to do is pitch them out and reel them in. Selecting the best combination of size, running depth, and color for water color and cover conditions takes practice. Then experiment with different retrieve speeds and motions to determine the best combination. The result is a highly effective, relatively snagfree presentation geared to trigger neutral to aggressive bass, while efficiently eliminating large areas of unproductive water.

Crankbaits are highly effective *search* lures. Use them to find productive areas. Then switch to slower moving lures that penetrate deeper into cover for less aggressive bass. Crankbaits are an important part of your bass arsenal and should be an integral part of your bass fishing approach.

And don't be surprised if you catch more than bass. The infinite array of crankbait shapes, sizes and colors also appeal to walleyes, pike, muskies, stripers, trout, salmon, and panfish, plus catfish and a host of saltwater dynamos. They're a bait for all seasons and species, often the best choice.

Chapter 13

SPINNERBAITS

Flashing Wonder, Shallow Magic

Spinnerbaits probably account for more bass than any other lure. And when you consider 20 million bass fishermen tossing spinnerbaits because they work so well, it's easy to credit spinnerbaits for a billion bass each year.

Is spinnerbait flash the flash of an injured baitfish? Or does the vibration attract bass? What about the profile of the bait? Is it one of these or the combination that apparently creates a universal feeding stimulus that causes bass to strike?

Spinnerbaits are versatile. Designs vary, and components can be switched to match fishing conditions. Blade colors, sizes, and shapes can be changed as well as skirts and trailers. The overhead position of the wire arm deflects obstructions for fewer snags through weeds, rocks, and wood. As a result, spinnerbaits fish effectively from the surface to more than 30 feet deep, the maximum depth bass typically use.

Big-bass specialist Doug Hannon, who has caught hundreds of bass weighing more than 10 pounds, considers spinnerbaits one of the top-four big-bass lures because they're quiet, natural-acting baits. That is, they fit into the static world of big bass. Spinnerbaits, though, probably don't resemble a natural food so much as a combination of elements attractive to bass.

Forerunners of modern spinnerbaits were crafted in the early 20th century. The Shannon Twin Spinner, produced by the former W. J. Jamison Company of Chicago, Illinois, caught bass deep and shallow with modifications in head weight and blade size and shape. The Shannon design was modified by other companies, some that still produce twin-arm models.

The 1970s was the decade of the spinnerbait, a time for innovative designs. During these years, tournament anglers found that casting a flashy lure to as many shoreline cover objects as tournament time permitted was an effective way to catch bass. Many tournaments were won with spinnerbaits. Rising tournament stars like Rick Clunn, Ricky Green, Tommy Martin, and Jimmy Houston gained fame by tossing blades. But as bass became conditioned to spinnerbaits in heavily fished waters, many bass fishermen began relying on additional lure types for most fishing situations.

This is as it should be. Spinnerbaits aren't magic lures, but they are an essential tool for catching bass when their style and size are matched to fishing conditions.

SPINNERBAIT CATEGORIES

A bent wire on a spinnerbait holds the spinner over a lead body, basically a jig. That sets spinnerbaits apart from straight-shaft spinners, such as the Mepps or Vibrax. Paint, hardware and colorful skirts are added for more attraction. The three basic spinnerbait types are the single-spin, tandem-spin, and twin-spin:

Single-spin—Single-spins, spinnerbaits with one blade, usually an Indiana, are the most basic and versatile. They can be fished deep or shallow, with a straight retrieve, a stop-and-go, or helicoptered vertically.

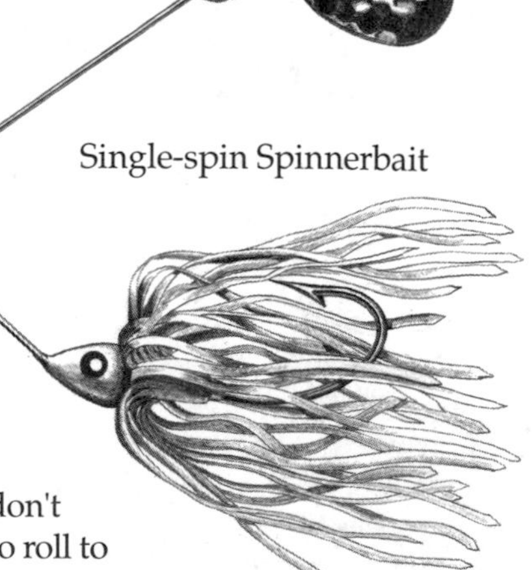
Single-spin Spinnerbait

The single-spin's clean design fishes through cover with minimal snags. Single-spins relay a distinct thumping vibration that makes it easy to stay in touch with the lure; soft strikes are telegraphed immediately. But single-spins don't work well at high speed because they tend to roll to the side.

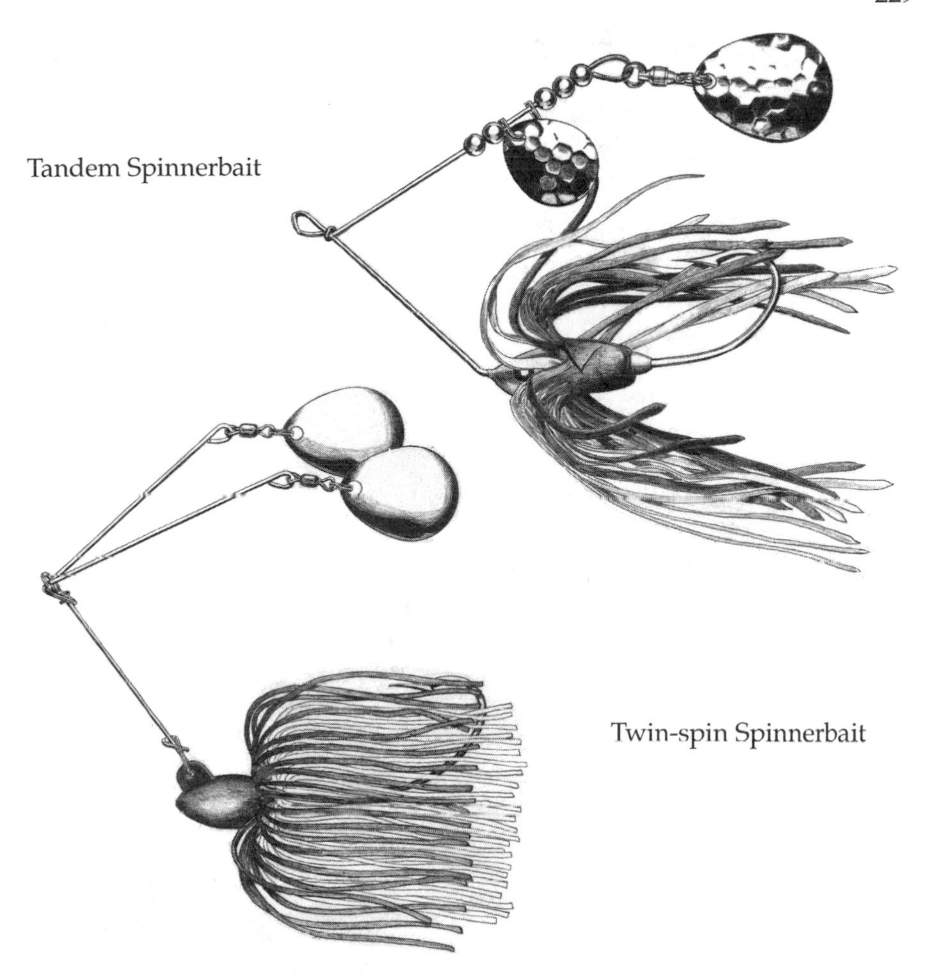

Tandem-spin—Tandem-spins have two spinners on the same shaft for more flash and lift than single spins. Tandem-spins emphasize the spinner as much as the jig. They can be worked quickly through shallow cover for bass in an active feeding mood. Tandems are also excellent for buzzing under the surface—pushing a bulge. But they're difficult to fish effectively in deep water, and they don't spin well on a vertical drop. They also lack the distinct thump of a single-spin blade.

Some bass fishermen believe the extra flash of a second blade is unnecessary. Tandems, however, will continue to be popular when they're at their best—worked quickly for shallow bass.

Twin-spins—The twin-spin is a flashy form of jig with rocker arms that hinge at the jig eye. They usually have a heavier head and smaller spinners than other spinners. A lift-fall jigging retrieve is usually the best presentation in situations when you'd otherwise use a jig-and-pig.

Try fishing twin-spins with a pork or plastic dressing. Or use livebait, particularly minnows or waterdogs (larval salamanders). Twin-spins offer little lift and don't work well near the surface, but they're a good choice around middepth weed clumps during fall.

Blade Shape and Rotation

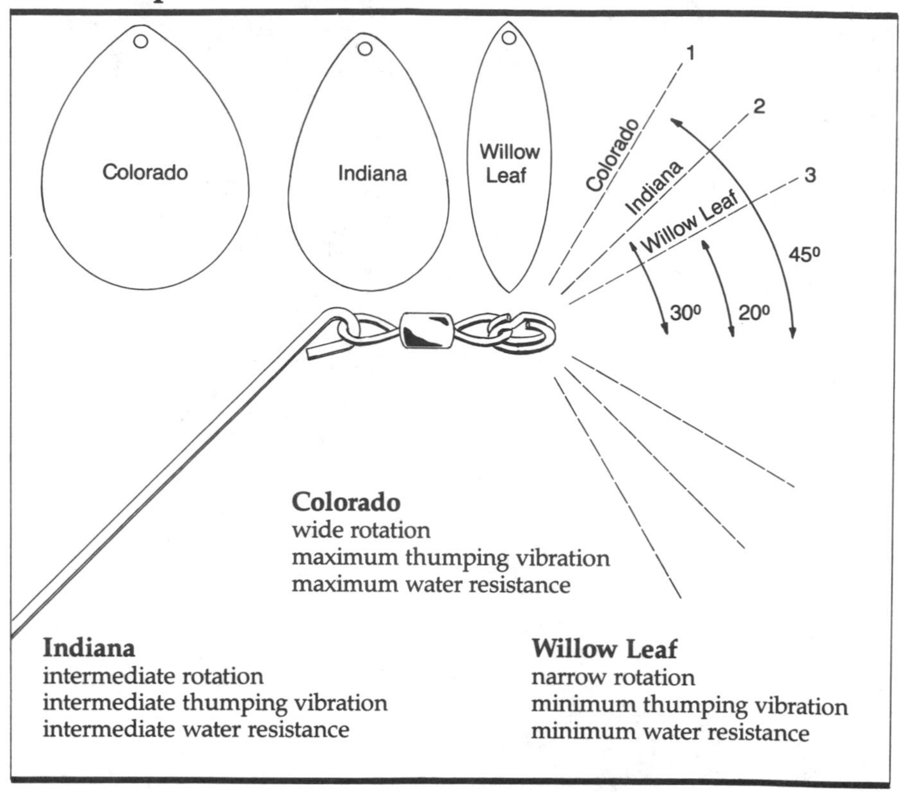

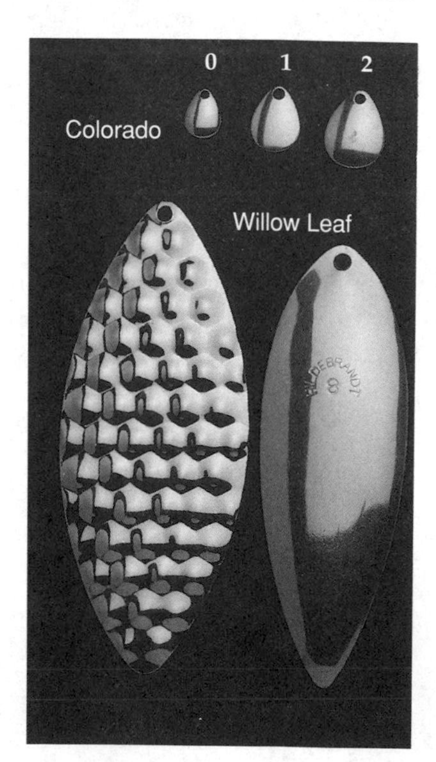

Blades

Blades come in different shapes, sizes, and colors. Each has strengths and weaknesses. Experiment, but blade size and type must balance with the rest of the lure. If it doesn't, the lure will spin in a circle, fall too rapidly, or hold too high.

WEIGHT

Common spinnerbait weights are 1/4, 3/8, and 1/2 ounces. Less popular weights are 1/8-, 5/8-, and 3/4-ounce sizes.

Follow two general guidelines for choosing size.

• In clear water, use a small bait; in dark or dingy water, go bigger. The 3/8-ouncer is the best all-around size.

• Switch size with the season. During spring, you can take trophy bass on a 1/8-ouncer. Throughout summer, a 3/8-ouncer is most popular. During late summer and into the fall Cold Water Period, switch to heavy spinnerbaits with large blades.

BLADES

Blades add flash and vibration and determine how fast and deep the bait can be worked. The blade probably suggests injured baitfish. But bass probably don't clearly see a rapidly spinning blade; scuba divers report the blade looks like a hazy aura of light. Instead, bass hear spinnerbaits bumping cover, and they feel the thump of the rotating blade with their lateral line.

Three basic blade categories include: Colorado, a rounded blade; Indiana, a moderately wide and long blade; and Willow Leaf, a long thin blade. An industry standard for blade shape doesn't exist, though, just as none exist for hook sizes (or shirt sizes, for that matter).

Colorado blades fall slowly and produce a subtle flash, good characteristics for bass early in prespawn, for pressured bass, and for sluggish bass in shallow water. Smaller models work well in rivers for smallmouths and spotted bass.

Large Colorado's on heavy heads excel for bass holding in deep water during fall.

Retrieve big blades slowly to keep the spinnerbait from turning sideways in the water. Heavy heads add stability, and compact Colorados are the best for casting distance and accuracy.

On safety pin spinnerbaits, Colorado blades revolve on a swivel and rotate on an axis as they're retrieved. Rotation creates underwater vibrations you can feel through a sensitive rod and see in the thumping rod tip. The slower the retrieve, the wider the rotation and the lower the frequency of thumps.

Cupped blades produce more vibration. Their following edge is bent farther toward the concave side of the blade, like a cupped propeller blade, so they catch and push water better than any other design, making them a good choice for fishing deep, in murky water, or at night.

As blades narrow from rounder to pear-shape, they become "Indianas." Narrower blades revolve faster and rotate in a smaller arc, but present a longer visual profile from the side, which adds flash and decreases vibration. Narrower blades also fall faster, pass through stick-ups and weeds easier, and can be retrieved faster without turning a bait to the side. The intermediate-shape Indiana is effective in most situations that call for spinnerbaits, but they aren't always the best choice.

Blades continue to narrow to cucumber-shape Willow Leaf designs. The Willow Leaf spins fast and therefore creates little distinct vibration. Long blades present a distinct flashy visual profile from the side. They also make lures snag-resistant and weed-resistant, but long blades don't spin well on the fall. It's also harder to start them spinning once they stall because they don't catch water as well as wider blades. Long blades also sail in the air, causing inaccurate casts.

Blade size—Colorados are available in sizes from #00 (small enough for bluegills) to #8 (a mouthful for a muskie). Willow Leafs run from #1 to #8; #3

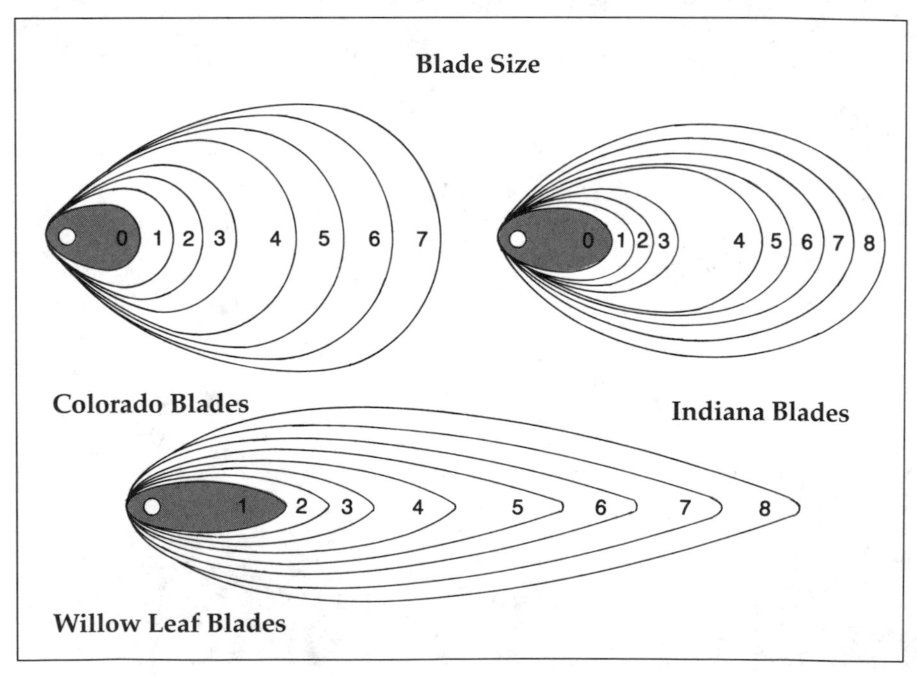

through #8 commonly appear on spinnerbaits. Numbers are arbitrary, however; most #3 Willow Leafs are smaller than #3 Colorados.

On most spinnerbaits, blades can be switched to provide different combinations of size, color, depth, and flash. No absolute rules exist for matching blade size to head weight. Decide what you want to accomplish, then match blade size to the bait, speed of presentation, and feeding mood of bass.

Larger blades amplify spinnerbait features for better or worse. The largest Colorados run upright only at the slowest speed. And their loud splash, heavy vibration, and large profile may spook more bass than they attract. On the other hand, a small Indiana won't attract attention in murky water and is hard to feel in windy conditions.

As a rule, start with small blades in spring, moving to larger blades as the season progresses. Try #2 and #3 blades for prespawn bass. For trophy bass during fall, #4s are a minimum, #8s an option.

Blade finish—In general, fish spinnerbaits fairly fast in heavy cover, so blade color and finish are less important than on baits bass have a longer time to study.

Blade finishes are painted, flat metallic, or hammered. They may also be fluted or plastic. Certain colors work better in particular waters, often for no obvious reason. Personal preference plays an important role in choice of finishes.

Most fishermen begin with silver blades in clear water and gold or copper blades in murky water. The additional reflecting angles on hammered and fluted blades make them slightly flashier than smooth blades. Certainly, though, tiny individual flashes are less pronounced than a single flash produced by a larger surface.

Clear water and shallow fish may require a switch to white blades to reduce flash. Or try plastic blades with a hint of metal flake. Some anglers use a candle to "smoke" blades and reduce flash.

Black blades may work at night; but in our experience, they don't work noticeably better than other colors. Try orange, pink, and blue if you want howls of laughter from your fishing buddies. One never knows.

OTHER COMPONENTS

Skirts—Living rubber is the most popular skirt material because it doesn't gum up and can be tied with a simple tool. Alternating long and short strands adds action. Create your own color combinations.

Tinsel, Mylar, and metal-flake skirts are popular, too. They're active and add flash. Substitute materials or colors to modify lure appearance and action. Tinsel and Mylar, for example, create a "thin" bait that moves easily through water. Thin baits often work well during early season. Later, though, they may not offer enough profile to trigger big bass. Switch to a combination of Mylar for flash with a bulkier material like living rubber.

Like blade color, skirt color often isn't critical. Most fishermen match or contrast skirt colors with blade colors. White and chartreuse are popular; mixtures of white and chartreuse with pink, blue, black, and lime seem to work well on many waters.

Combinations

As the most popular spinner dressing, hair like Mepps' squirrel tail gave way to vinyl, shown on this Bass Buster Scorpion. Vinyl was durable and colorful, but not as supple as the rubber strands on Northland's Reed Runner. Living-rubber skirts are easily made at home and give a lively look (Toledo Tackle's Pro Series). More rubber strands provide bulk and slow drop-rate. Metal-flake skirts provide action and sparkle (Tournament Lures Weapon spinnerbait). Add a few tinsel strips, or go for total flash with an all-Mylar skirt (Heron Lures). Firetail skirts add color variation, too (Stanley Vibra-Shaft).

Trailers add a final color or wiggle that means extra strikes. They also slow a lure's fall and provide balance. Worm tails, grubs, or crawdads can be impaled on the hook. Hook them on the trailer if you're using one.

Shown are Burke's Split Tail Trailer, Brother's Limberneck trailer, Mann's tail and Stanley's Pro Trailer (with rattlers). Dri-Rind chamois trailers are available in many styles and colors. Or try HMS Compound's "Electric Eel," a polymeric semiconductor that's said to add a positive charge to your lure to attract strikes.

Uncle Josh's pork rind is cut in several trailer styles: pork skirt (#170), crawfrog (#27), little crawdad (#33), pork grub (#CL42), and twin tail (#U2) among others. Hog hair offers other rind styles: split tail, lizard, and large rind.

Skirts on many commercial baits are so long that they invite short strikes. A little thinning will get your bait down faster without hurting its appeal and may reduce missed fish.

Rubber, living rubber, and plastic skirts must dry thoroughly to lengthen their usefulness. Avoid laying them in direct sunlight. Rubber quality varies, so look for lures with supple nonstick skirts. Replacement skirts in various colors, glued on short sections of flexible tubing, are available.

Arms, Heads, Hooks—Long arms make spinnerbaits snagproof, but can lead to short strikes. Spinnerbaits with long arms also don't fall true. When you stop your retrieve, the bait slides to one side. Long-armed baits, however, are effective in heavy cover.

SPINNERBAIT PRESENTATIONS

Standard Retrieves

Run a variety of baits at the same steady speed. Tandem-spins run the shallowest. Single-spins run at various depths, depending on blade style—Colorados shallowest, Indianas deeper, and Willow Leafs the deepest. Even though a twin-spin has two blades, it runs deeper than a single-spin, since twin-spin blades are usually small.

A single Willow Leaf will hang on the surface, but you have to reel like crazy. A tandem-spin will also run deep, but you have to reel so slowly that the blades probably won't turn properly.

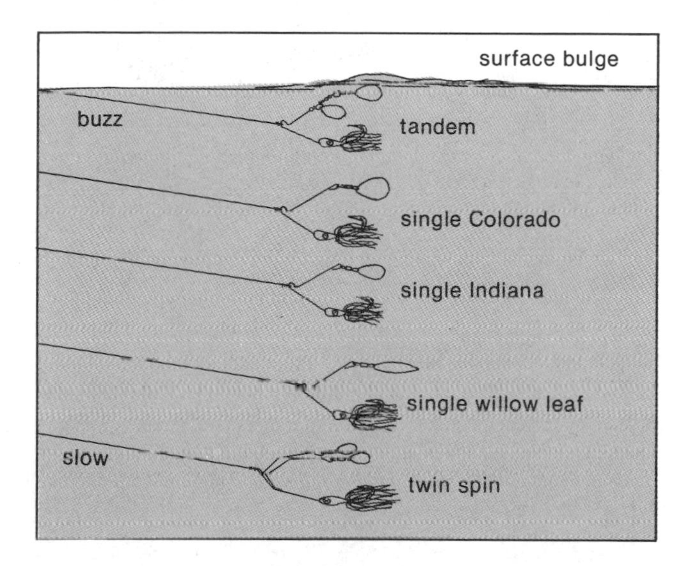

Mix the possible combinations, and you have many options. But choosing the proper combination lets you efficiently probe various depths—strain water from shallow back bays, to middepth flats, to deep drop-offs.

Watch your line carefully for the slightest twitch that may signal a strike. Concentrate on "feeling" the blade vibrating as it moves. Set the hook if the blade stops vibrating or if the lure feels weightless. Many strikes go undetected because anglers aren't alert. If in doubt, set the hook.

Short-arm models are better for jigging presentations that include lifts and falls. A short arm coupled with a Colorado blade and a heavy head is best for deep vertical fishing or slow cranking in deep water.

The gauge of wire in spinners varies. Thin wire transmits vibrations well, but bends when stretched between an eager 200-pound basser and a determined 6-pound bass. Springy wire arms also collapse on the strike for better hooking, and they run straighter during fast retrieves. Wire that tapers from a heavy gauge at the head to thin wire at the blade (Stanley's Vibra-Shaft models) provides durability and sensitivity—thin wire on the upper arm bends as the lure is retrieved, adding stability and snag resistance.

Most spinnerbait heads are conical, a shape that moves easily through the

Flutter or Yo-Yo

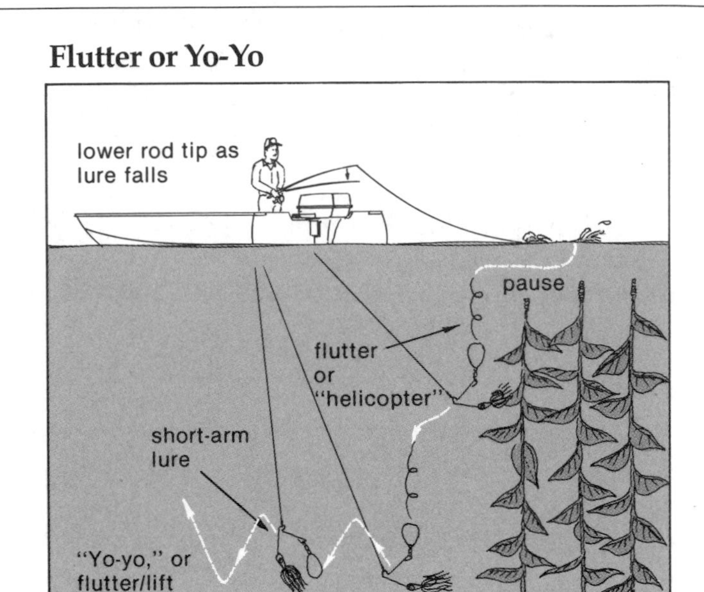

Crawl or Slow Roll

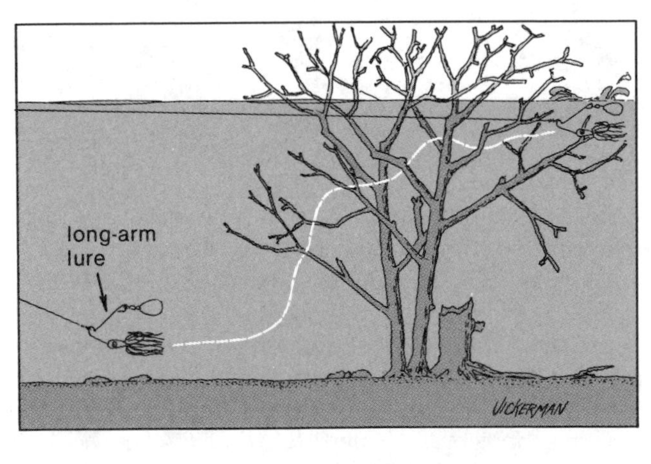

water while minimizing hang-ups. Models without a crevice between the head and wire-tie catch fewer weeds or twigs. But a wider head in combination with larger blades adds stability.

Wobbling spinnerbaits are a recent change. Some have cupped heads, while others have action bills molded into the head. A wobble adds attraction to the combination of blades and skirts.

But wobbling spinnerbaits aren't as snagfree as traditional baits because traditional narrow heads must be modified to achieve a wobble. But bass accustomed to standard designs can sometimes be tempted with wobblers.

Strong O'Shaughnessy hooks remain the norm on spinnerbaits, although some manufacturers are offering extra-sharp premium hooks or hooks with a

Bump the Stump

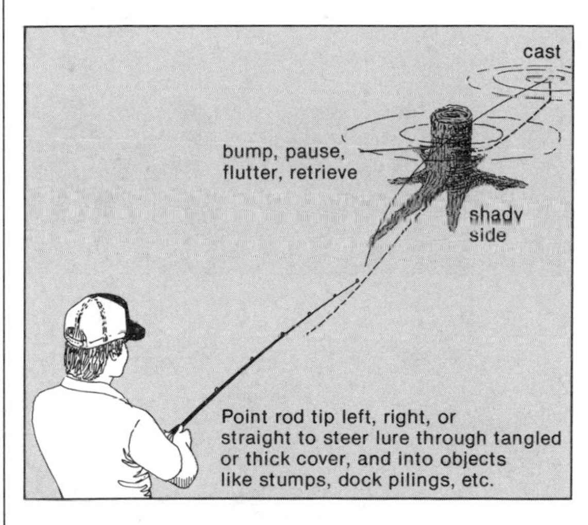

Always try to bump or bang something—weeds, reeds, docks, stumps, logs, trees. If you can bump it, you can probably catch a bass there sometime during the year. Free-swimming retrieves usually work only on aggressive fish.

Paralleling

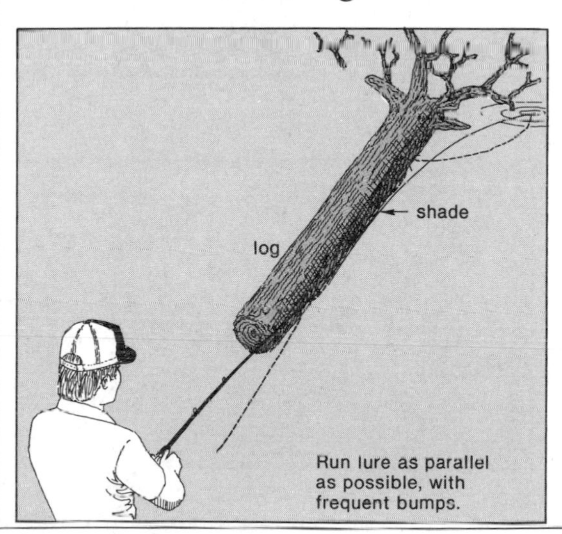

For fishing along edges, like the edge of a log or the edge of a weedline, cast parallel to cover. Retrieve the lure as close as possible to cover, occasionally touching it.

wider gap for better hooking. Many spinnerbait hooks have large barbs. Filing barbs eases hook penetration and creates a smaller hole that holds fish without tearing tissue. The safety pin design generally eliminates the need for a weedguard, but a few companies offer models with guards for flippin' heavy brush.

Because spinnerbaits often move quickly, bass may hit behind them; you feel a bump or the blades stop turning, but no hookup. Trailer hooks often help catch those short strikers. But trailers slipped over the barb increase both hookups and snags.

Trailers that point up are more snag resistant, and try trebles as trailers on schooling bass in open water. Sections of surgical or aquarium tubing about

Combination Retrieve

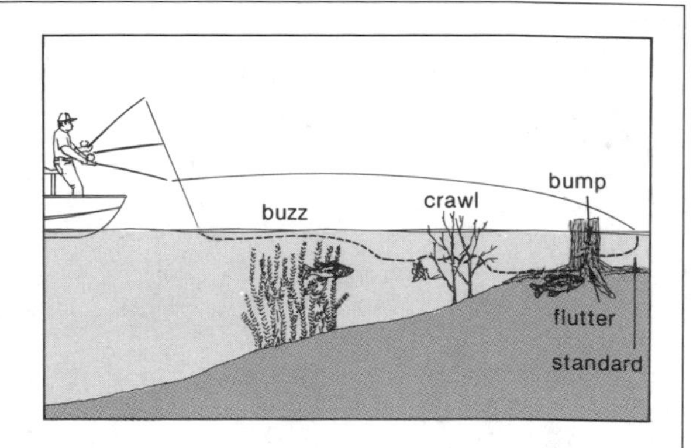

Buzzing

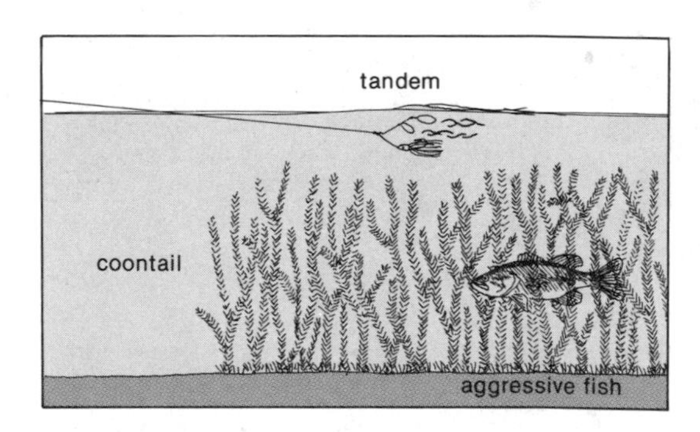

Tips for Reeds

Target the heaviest clumps of reeds. Use a long-arm spinnerbait and position the boat so you can cast in the direction the reeds are bent. Don't cast across bent reeds. Keep your rod tip high and horse 'em out.

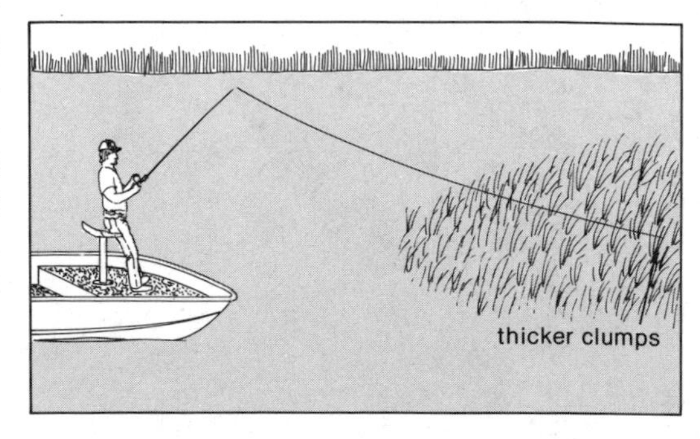

Wobblers

Not satisfied with flashing, vibrating blades; colorful fluttering skirt; and trembling trailer? Manufacturers offer spinnerbaits that wobble from side to side, adding more action to the package.

These baits at times prove tantalizing to largemouths, smallmouths, pike, and even walleyes. Options include (top) Lunker Lure's Spring Bil with a flexible spinner arm and Heron Lure's Hot Cheeks with a concave face to make the head vibrate, and a spinner arm attached with a split ring to allow freedom of motion.

Flying Lure's UnderCover spinnerbait falls back under cover on the drop, due to its head design.

More Blades

When choosing spinnerbaits, consider blade shape, size, and finish. Stock a variety, from round Colorados to narrow Willow Leafs. Tandems allow mixing and matching colors and shapes.

Options today include (left to right) Blue Fox's Roland Martin Okeechobee Special, a big bass lure with a #1 copper Colorado and a #8 silver Willow. Blade length calls for a trailer hook. Hart Tackle's Guy Eaker model combines a gold and silver willow. Cabela's single Colorado and tandem Zorro Aggravator create a thumping vibration, plus flash amplified by a hammered finish. The blades are cupped for maximum vibration. Brother's Short-Arm Limberneck lets the head pivot for working in brush.

Strike King's Diamond Leaf finish on a broad Willow Leaf and Great American Fishing Supply's wide Indiana with fluting increase reflective angles. Fleck's Weed Wader with tandem Indianas provides versatility for fishing the surface down to 8 feet. Gopher Tackle's twin-spin features a pair of Colorados on a harness that lets the lure pivot. Unconventional designs include Hart's Shaker with three knife-shape blades, Bass Pro Shops Cajun Rattler with a sound chamber, Bumble Bee's Chopper Bee (by Hart Tackle) with a pear-shape Alabama blade, and Mepps Adjustable-Blade Bass Killer.

Carry extra blades, skirts, and trailer hooks to make adjustments.

1/4 inch long can be slipped on the trailer hook eye to hold its rearward position when it's impaled on the main hook.

Or dip trailer hook eyes in "tool-grip" plastic compound and let it harden. Then slip it over the rear hook. Trailers should be slightly smaller than the main hook to reduce snagging and maintain lure action. Use trailer hooks, however, only if you're missing fish.

TRAILERS

Right from the package, most spinnerbaits work well once hooks are sharpened. But the addition of trailers adds another attraction factor. Two-tail trailers help balance spinners that tend to tip. For added bulk and wiggle, a single grub with an action-tail works well. Trailers also reduce the rate of fall to help keep spinnerbaits nearer the surface or buzzbaits on top during slower retrieves.

Pork chunks also add buoyancy and bulk, but pork must be removed when the lure's not in use. Chamois-like leathers, available in a variety of colors and trailer shapes, need no special attention.

In-Line Spinners

In-line spinners were "the" spinnerbaits for most bass anglers through the mid-1960s. They remain popular because they run true and hook fish well. They spin at slow retrieves and have a small profile, ideal for rivers and other clear waters with dense cover.

Options for today include the Mepps Aglia and Long Aglia; Panther Martin; Helin's Angel; Kurachi's spinner; Blue Fox Vibrax; Yakima Bait's Roostertail; Hildebrandt's Snagless Sally and gold willow.

IN-LINE SPINNERS

In-line spinners, invented in France to match post-World War II spinning tackle breakthroughs, also work for bass. The steady flash of Mepps Aglias attracts gamefish from trout to muskies. In-line spinners are particularly effective on bass in shallow flats during spring and fall.

In-line spinner design has changed little over 40 years, a testament to the bait's effectiveness. But they tend to snag in cover. Hildebrandt's Snagless Sally, an example of a bait combining a single hook and wire weedguard, is a weedbed mainstay, though.

Spinnerbaits are a mainstay bass bait. Become familiar with the role the component parts play in the performance of spinnerbaits. Become familiar, too, with which conditions call for which baits. And learn the spinnerbait presentations that bass respond to.

Weeks may pass without wetting them, but under the right conditions, spinnerbaits put bass in the boat like nothing else. And the best part is, fishing them is so easy . . . and so much fun.

Chapter 14

WORMS AND JIGS

Subtle Steps To Sweet Success

Plastic worms have as colorful a history as the assortment in your local tackle shop. Every imaginable size, shape, color and texture adorn wall displays. But it wasn't always so. Not long ago, soft plastics were in their infancy.

The origin of the plastic or rubber worm can be traced back to the late 1800s when several visionary bassers molded styles of prerigged worms.

These were little more than curiosities until Bill Norton of Marion, Indiana, rigged a rubber worm on a harness devised for live nightcrawlers. His Sportsman's Products worm was one of the first commercially successful worms.

Nick Creme, an Akron, Ohio, livebait angler who tired of late-night worm hunting produced a plastic imitation in a mold made from a live worm. The immediate, though localized success of these and other fake crawlers made by Charles Burke, Dave Delong, and other midwestern lure designers began a plastic worm craze that continues today.

The reason for worm popularity is no secret; they catch more bass in a wider variety of situations than any lure yet devised. Yet many anglers regard wormin' as the most difficult presentation to learn. To master the versatile worm requires study, an open mind, and lots of time on the water. This chapter details how to manipulate variables like shape, worm size, hook size, sinker weight, and rigging to maximize your bass catch. We'll also cover the worm's closest relative, the jig, and how they complement each other.

Bass love worms; why is a mystery. Though the first worms mimicked nightcrawlers, a bass rarely sees a live crawler. Adult bass primarily eat small fish or crayfish. A skinny piece of plastic doesn't seem to resemble natural foods.

Worms do, however, look attractive and vulnerable. The natural action of a worm—wiggling, twisting, jerking, falling, bumping—perfectly depicts distressed and vulnerable prey. A worm doesn't resemble any particular food form, but produces cues typical of a creature in death throes.

It seems alive, but barely. Remember, bass are opportunistic and don't have tight definitions of food. If potential food is near and looks catchable, bass usually grab it.

Worms don't give off many negative signals. Bass become conditioned to lures, but not as easily to worms. Spooky bass that reject other baits can often be taken by careful wormin'. But minor differences in worm rigging and retrieves can produce major consequences in the catch.

In the 1960s, worms became popular with southern anglers who fished thick timber in newly impounded reservoirs. The "Texas rig" was devised for reducing snags in dense cover. Stereotyped worm tackle included a pool-cue baitcasting rod, a reel with the drag screwed down tightly, thick fluorescent line, and a big bullet sinker to take the worm through heavy timber.

That tackle still takes bass, but is outdated on many waters. Northern bass anglers have added weedline techniques dependent on the jigworm, a jig coupled with a worm, leaving the hook exposed. And western bass anglers win tournaments with worm systems consisting of unusual rigs, spinning rods, and lines as light as 4-pound test.

Plastic worms are amazingly versatile. Are bass in 6 inches of water or 60 feet? Worm 'em! Are they roaming weedy flats, suspended off ledges on a creek channel, or huddled at the base of flooded brush? Worm 'em! Are they inactive or chasing bait? Worm 'em! Is it hot enough to melt your boat or cold enough to freeze your guides? Tie on a worm! Quicker and more

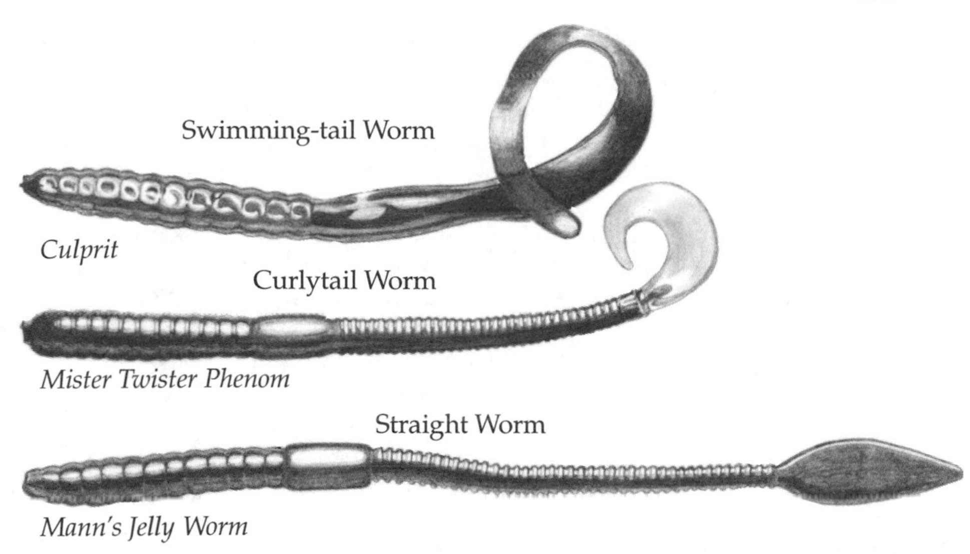

Worms come in many shapes, sizes and colors, from tiny 4-inch subtleties to 12-inch-plus monsters. The three most common varieties are swimming tails, curlytails, and straight tails. Each offers a different degree of action and drop speed.

Craw worms and lizards can be fished much the same as regular worms, but offer a different profile. They're not meant to replace typical worms—just add to the possible combinations.

efficient ways to catch bass may exist in certain situations, but no bait works as well in so many places. If you want to consistently catch bass, you must master worms.

Fishermen once assumed worms had to look just like the real thing. But blue, grape, and other unnatural colors soon became bass killers. Experimentation produced wild colors and combinations—some by accident and some on purpose. And they all caught bass. Though today's market offers an amazing range of colors and styles, the hottest worms in the next decade may include colors and patterns not yet invented.

The same is true of worm action and rigging. Original straight-tailed worms weighted with bullet sinkers have been reshaped and rigged for new, effective actions. Most bass anglers, even serious wormers, have barely scratched the surface of worm presentation.

WHICH WORM?

When choosing a worm, consider length, thickness, toughness, density (whether a worm floats or sinks), action, appearance (color and pattern) and taste.

Worm length should suit the bass's metabolism and mood. Short worms are often best for inactive or spooky bass. Cold fronts, ultraclear water, and heavy fishing pressure may also call for small offerings. When bass are active in warmer or murkier water, go with large worms. Large worms often catch the biggest bass, although numbers of fish may be sacrificed.

The most popular worm sizes nationwide are 6- and 7-inchers. Early in the year or for dealing with finicky bass, 4- or 5-inch worms may work best. During summer, 8- or 9-inch models shine. In thick cover or stained water, bass see 7- to 9-inch worms more easily. Due to widespread increases in fishing pressure, the trend is to smaller worms.

Similar guidelines apply to worm thickness. Thin worms work best early in the year. Thick worms are best when bass are looking for larger prey later in the season. The Mister Twister Phenom is a thin worm that appeals to early season bass. The meatier Culprit is deadly in midsummer. Since longer worms are generally thicker than short worms, you can make a short fat worm by biting an inch or two off the head of a long worm. Fat worms drop slower and stand up to thick cover and hooksets better than thin worms.

Worms also differ in toughness. Soft worms usually have more action, but tear quicker. Tougher worms require a harder hookset, especially with Texas rigs. When fishing through cover like reeds or timber, select a worm that doesn't shred easily.

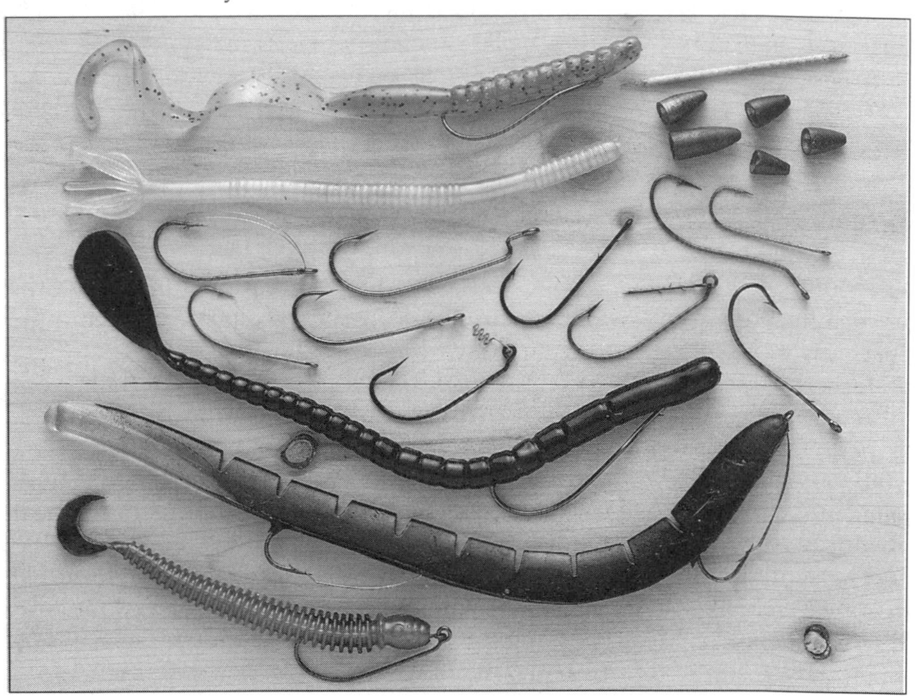

The Texas Rig

Texas rigs are designed to crawl in and around cover without snagging: Culprit's Sticky Worm and Pen Worm, J.W.'s Ding-A-Ling and Hawg Hunter for large fish or dark-water conditions, and Larew's ringworm-style worm. Carry assorted sizes of hooks and sinkers to match the size of your worm.

Options include: Gamakatsu's colored worm hooks; Eagle Claw's popular 95JB; Tru-Turn's Cam-action Brute and EZ Link; Klein's Black Weapon Hook; Mister Twister's Keeper Hook; Mustad's central draught #3777; Owner's triple edged hook, and Razorback's Auto Barb.

Most worms are dense enough to sink slowly, but floating worms have remained popular, especially on Carolina or split-shot rigs. Floating worms fished Texas-style or with a weedless hook are also effective surface baits in shallow cover.

The three basic worm shapes are straight, curlytail, and swimming-tail. No simple rule exists for choosing worm shape. Straight worms fall quickly and fish through cover easier than swimming-tail worms that often wrap their tails around twigs or weed stalks. The subtle action of straight worms sometimes works best on inactive bass. A straight worm isn't without action, however; you give it the action. Straight worms are versatile, all-around choices, like single-spin spinnerbaits with Indiana blades.

Swimming-tail worms have more built-in action and slower drop speeds. They're most effective in clear open water where bass can see worms well. Aggressive bass may grab a swimming-tail worm as if it were a crankbait. Use swimming-tail worms in moderately heavy cover for a slower drop, such as along the face of a bluff or down a sharp weededge.

In dingy water, a worm with an action or paddletail, like the Ding-A-Ling, Ditto Gator Tail, or Mister Twister Thunder Worm creates more vibration to help bass find it.

Curlytail worms are an intermediate choice. They fall slower than straight worms and pass through cover better than swimming-tails. They're often used on light jigs around cabbage and other weedline growth. If they have a fault, it's that panfish often nip at the tail, particularly firetail versions.

Does color matter? Anytime you fish a slow-moving lure that bass get a good look at, color can be important. Every bass fisherman will run into a situation where one color—and it can be a strange color—outfishes everything else three-to-one. But color isn't always critical. In most situations, casting precision and retrieve are more important.

When does color matter? The slower the presentation, the less active the bass, the clearer the water, and the more open the cover, the more color becomes a factor. And vice versa—fast presentations, active bass, warm water, and thick cover make color less critical.

Nationwide, black may still be the number-one confidence color, followed by blue, purple, and red. But every year, new colors get hot. Recent hot colors or patterns include moccasin, bubble gum, tequila sunrise, junebug, and pumpkinseed. "California" worms popular on clear western reservoirs are subtle earth-tone in coloration and are short, thin, soft, and salty. They appeal to spooky bass in clear water.

In dark water, dark colors like black or grape work well. Perk up your worm in murky water by using a firetail, or go with glitter patterns. In clear water, single colors in varying shades often work best. Translucent colors like smoke or bloodline worms are also top choices in clear water, or when bass are inactive.

Many good worm fishermen match the color of the forage. For bass feeding on shad along a bluff bank, pearlescent worms like red shad, black shad, or blue shad are good choices. For bass feeding on crayfish, go with reddish-orange, brown, or olive. Blue-black-green mixtures work well where bluegills are common. But color rules are made to be broken, so don't

Impregnated Baits

Many plastics manufacturers now inject salt into their plastic baits (Gene Larew Salty Dawg). Berkley has taken a different approach and mixed amino acids in their Power Baits.

hesitate to experiment or play hunches.

Taste and scent are potential factors to consider when choosing a worm. Taste at times seems to make a difference—mainly in cold water or for inactive bass. A flavorful worm encourages bass to hang on longer, making it easier to get a good hookset. Many worms are impregnated with salt, and Berkley's Power Worms are flavored with amino acids. Scent sprays and scent sticks also mean extra fish at times, although taste, not scent, may remain the critical factor. Fishing reports suggest this interaction of science and fishing could produce important worm innovations in the future.

PROFILE

Bass in heavily fished waters see lots of worms. So give them an unfamiliar profile. Switch to a craw worm or a lizard body. Plastic salamanders are touted to resemble egg-stealing amphibians, and may therefore produce strikes from bass during the spawning cycle. Crayfish are a preferred bass forage in many waters, and bass often hit plastic crayfish mimics better than any other lure.

Different Profiles

Give bass a different profile than they're used to seeing: **(Column 1)** *A Zetabait Gillraker (Texas-rigged); Ditto Fire Claw; Harvelle Crawfish; Culprit Softy Craw; and (**Column 2**) Mister Twister Lizard; Slug-Go (see Chapter 16); and a combo rig using a Gopher Worm Dancer, Mister Twister Keeper Hook and Phenom Worm; and an Uncle Josh Pork Crawdad (detach part of the worm if you wish).*

DROP SPEED

Active bass often take a worm on the drop. Whether you fish a jigworm or a Texas rig, one key is the right drop-speed. Worm color, length, thickness, and action are important; but drop-speed often is the difference between fishin' and catchin'.

Adjust drop-speed mainly by matching your weight to the other worm characteristics that affect drop-speed. Use enough weight to work cover properly and maintain a feel for what's happening underwater. Balance worm size, body type, and density to make drop-speed match conditions and the mood of bass.

Bass in cover can often see only a few inches away. A worm tumbling into a hole may be visible for only a second. If the worm drops too fast, bass may not see it long enough to decide to strike. On the other hand, if your weight is too light, the worm might not get down to where bass are holding.

Aggressive bass respond well to fast-dropping worms. You can also fish a quick-dropping worm faster, to cover more water. But inactive bass ignore fast-dropping worms. When bass are touchy, give them time to respond by slowly drifting the worm down to them.

It's a balancing act or compromise. You want to fish quickly and effectively, but conditions sometimes require slower drops and more patient presentations. The trend over the past decade has been toward slower presentations. We want to fish as fast as we can to show the worm to more bass, but pressured bass grow increasingly touchy and harder to trigger, making slower presentations more important.

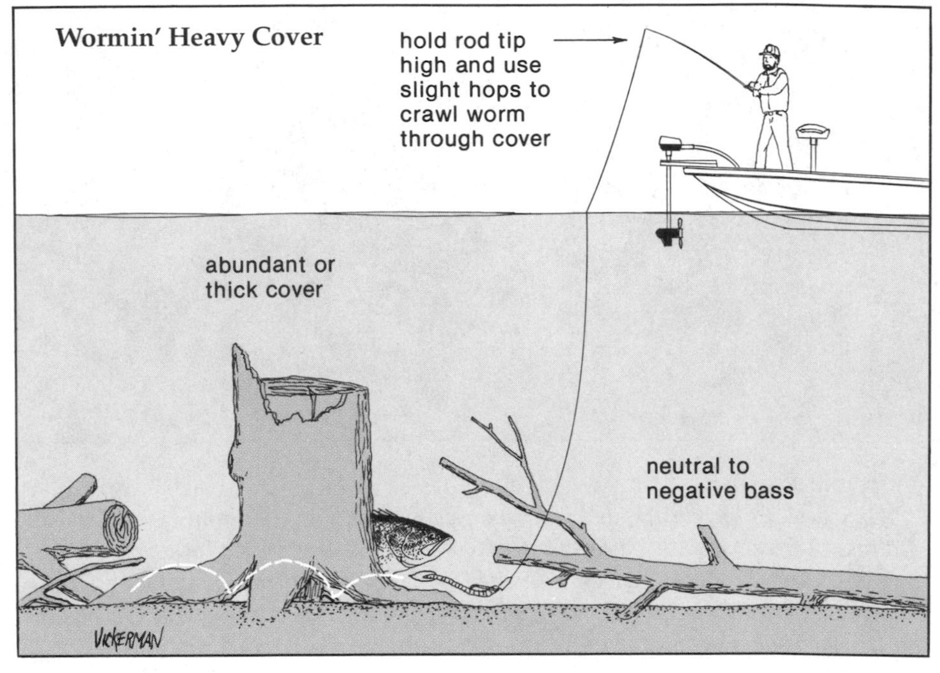

Texas rigs work best for penetrating heavy cover, when open-hook lures will snag, or when fish are nonaggressive. Sparser cover and more aggressive bass may be fished with quicker approaches.

THE TEXAS RIG

The Texas rig is the most basic and most popular worm rig. It's simple and clean, and fishes in the most difficult cover. It gets down to neutral bass lying under weed clumps or at the base of wood. It's also designed to be fished with frequent pauses, allowing the worm to remain motionless between hops. Short upward lifts of the rod tip impart a wiggling action or slide the worm over or through cover.

Other rigs may be more attractive at times, but nothing beats the Texas rig for fishing where bass live, and that's usually what counts. A 7-inch Texas-rigged worm is the number-one producer just about anywhere bass swim.

Prepare the rig carefully. Balance hook size to worm size to preserve worm action. Thread the hook through so the worm hangs absolutely straight or you'll get poor action and line twist. Either bury the hook point deep into the body or push it almost all the way through, depending on how much snag resistance is needed and how tough the worm body is.

Rigging A Keeper

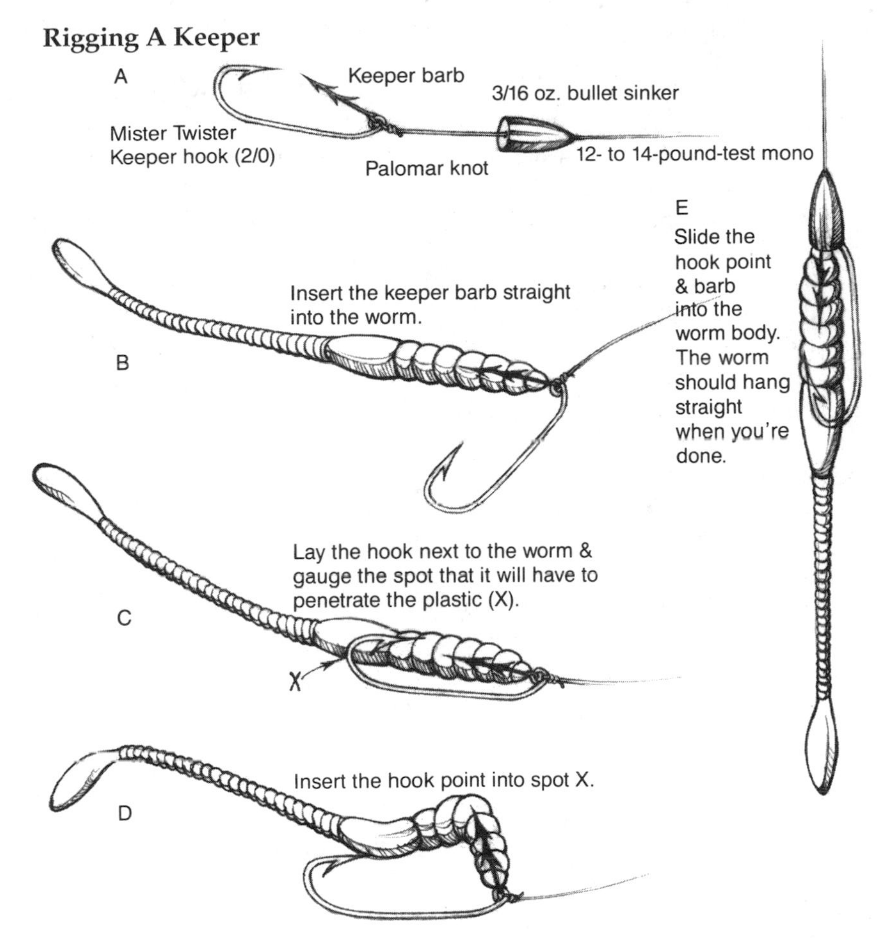

When the hook point is buried in the worm, you must drive it through plastic to penetrate a bass's jaw. If the fish inhales the worm in a coiled gob, you might need to drive the hook through multiple layers of plastic before it sinks home. Texas-rigging, therefore, usually requires line of at least 12-pound test. At times, 17-, 20-, 25-, or 30-pound test is required. You also need a rod with a lot of backbone to generate a powerful hookset and pull bass up and out of cover.

Texas rigs require large specialized hooks. Cam-action hooks (Tru-Turn Cam-action Brute, Eagle Claw 45) twist upward and grab a solid hold in a bass's jaw. Premium hooks—Gamakatsu, Mustad AccuPoint, Stanley Pro Point, Eagle Claw Diamond Point and Lazer Sharp, Klein Black Weapon and triple-point Owner hooks—have extra-sharp points that produce solid hookups. Some anglers prefer hooks with extra-wide gaps, like Owner's Magnum Gap.

Carry a selection of hooks in sizes from #2 to 5/0 to cover different worm sizes. Premium hooks are sharp enough to fish "as shipped." Others should be touched up with a hook file. But always touch up any hook after catching fish or snagging wood or rock.

Carry a broad selection of bullet sinkers to match conditions. The 1/8-, 1/4-, and 1/2-ounce sizes are most popular, but carry 1/16-, 3/16-, 5/16-, 3/8-, 5/8-, and 1-ounce sizes too.

In general, sinker weight should be as light as possible while still letting you feel cover and getting the worm where you want it to go. Shallow depths and light cover call for lighter weights. Wind, deep water, and heavy cover call for heavier weights. You may need a heavy weight to penetrate an overhead mat of vegetation, yet fish the worm almost motionless once it reaches the bass zone.

The classic Texas rig has a sliding bullet sinker. In heavy cover, peg the sinker in place by inserting a toothpick between the line and the sinker. Then break off the tip. Stanley makes a rubber-coated, self-pegging sinker. Fixed sinkers tend to snag less than sliding sinkers that may separate from the worm and wrap around twigs or weed stalks.

Worm rattles have been around for years, and occasionally seem to pay off in more strikes. Rattles are most effective in murky water or heavy cover like hydrilla, where bass don't have much time to see and respond to a worm. Painted worm weights are available, though plain lead works fine most of the time.

The hookset is extremely important with Texas rigs. Early riggers let the bass run with the worm before setting, but that led to missed strikes. When you feel a bass take, drop the rod tip, take up most but not all the slack, and snap the rod up with a sharp crack. Don't use enough power to lift an anchor, but crack the rod quickly with authority to drive the hook in.

THE JIGWORM

If the Texas rig is the ultimate cover bait, the jigworm is the ultimate edge bait. A jigworm is a worm rigged on a plain jighead with an exposed hook point. Jigworms excel for picking bass off weededges. They aren't designed for use in heavy weeds like coontail or milfoil, but they're ideal in sparse growth like cabbage or along sharp hydrilla walls.

The exposed hook hangs up on sparse weeds now and then, which can work to your advantage. Feel the texture of the weeds as you pull through them. (Texas rigs sometimes slide through sparse weeds so easily that you can't learn much about the shape and feel of the cover.) And when you pop a jigworm off a weed, the worm explodes forward before settling toward bottom. If a bass is watching, this may trigger a strike.

Because jigworms have sharp, thin exposed hooks, powerful hooksets aren't necessary. Jigworming is a finesse game, featuring medium-action rods, lines about 8-pound test, and a delicate sense of feel. Set the hook by bending your wrist to tighten the line. No need to rush.

Though you can fish a worm on a heavy jig, the classic jigworm technique involves light or even ultralight heads. The most useful weights are 1/16-, 3/32-, 1/8-, and 3/16-ounce. Carry 5/16- and 1/4-ounce heads, too, to adjust drop speed and compensate for wind and current.

The Gopher mushroom jighead, which fits flush to a worm, is a popular head style. Yet almost any small jighead will do, especially if it has a lead

Jigworms are outstanding drop-lures when snags aren't a major factor: Kalin's Western Worm on a darter head; a Mister Twister Phenom (firetail) with a 1/8-ounce Gopher Mushroom Head; a Zetabait Gillraker on a fibre weedguard jighead; a Perma-Glo Worm on a 1/16-ounce Mushroom Head; and a Charlie Brewer Slider rigged weedless.

barb to secure the worm to the head. They slip through weeds well and give the worm an attractive spiralling action as it drops. Most strikes occur on the drop as the worm descends with a slow, teasing action.

Jigworms are usually 4- to 6-inchers, but don't hesitate to fish bulky 7- to 9-inchers for big bass. Straight, swimming-tail, or curlytail worms all work on jigheads. Choose body styles based on the cover you're fishing, the rate of drop you want, and the mood of the bass.

The jigworm isn't designed for casting far up into weeds. It's best fished nearly parallel to a distinct edge. Cast the worm slightly up on top of a weedline and then tease it toward deep water with a series of short pulls, letting it drop as far as possible after each drop. If it hangs up, give it a quick wrist snap to break the weed stalk, rather than a steady pull that uproots weeds and fouls the lure. Done properly, the light worm works its way along the top and front edge of the weeds, falling into little cracks and crawling up again before falling deeper. Eventually it reaches the deep edge where it falls to the bottom outside the weeds.

Most jigworm anglers in natural lakes let the bait sink on a semi-slack line with no added action. West Coast reservoir anglers, however, have popularized a shakin' approach, using frequent upward flicks of the rod tip to impart a quivering action. Pop 10 or 12 times, release 5 feet of line, hold the line with your trigger finger, and pop 10 or 12 more times as you follow the line down with your rod tip. Don't close the bail on the spinning reel until the worm reaches bottom or you get a strike. It's an alternate reservoir tactic that's effective down to 40 feet or more.

We've mainly discussed light jigheads with exposed hooks fished with medium-size worms, but all sorts of combinations are possible. Try a worm on a jig with a fiber or plastic weedguard. Standup jigheads are popular because they keep a worm visible right on the bottom. The Charlie Brewer "Do Nothin' " jigworms are both a lure and a system. These 4-inch worms can be rigged weedless, and they're equally productive when fish are suspended.

The use and appreciation of jigworms has been limited to weedy lakes in the North and Midwest, and to deep, more clear reservoirs in the West and mid-South. But as weeds become more important in aging impoundments, more anglers are discovering jigworm techniques. While exposed hook points on jigworms are best suited to soft cover like weeds, there are applications for light timber and rocks.

THE CAROLINA RIG

The Carolina rig was mostly used in southern waters until western anglers modified it to suit their clear impoundments. This rig is similar to livebait rigs popular in the Midwest, but with a floating worm (instead of livebait) behind a slip weight. The lure floats up off the bottom and is free to wiggle and drift. A typical rig involves a sliding bullet sinker, a swivel, and a 24- to 30-inch leader attached to a hook and worm. The hook can be buried in the worm Texas-style or fished exposed, depending on the cover it's fished in. Some specially designed Carolina rig worms have two small hooks with small plastic appendages that fit over hookpoints to reduce snags.

The Carolina rig isn't as snagfree in brush or timber as the Texas rig and isn't as suitable for weeds as a jigworm. But it excels in deep water or sparse cover. Carolina rigs are unwieldy to cast, but can be drifted or slowly trolled, keeping the worm down where the fish are.

There are many variations. Jack Chancellor won the 1985 BASS Masters Classic with his Do Nothin' worms—short worms with two hooks fished Carolina style.

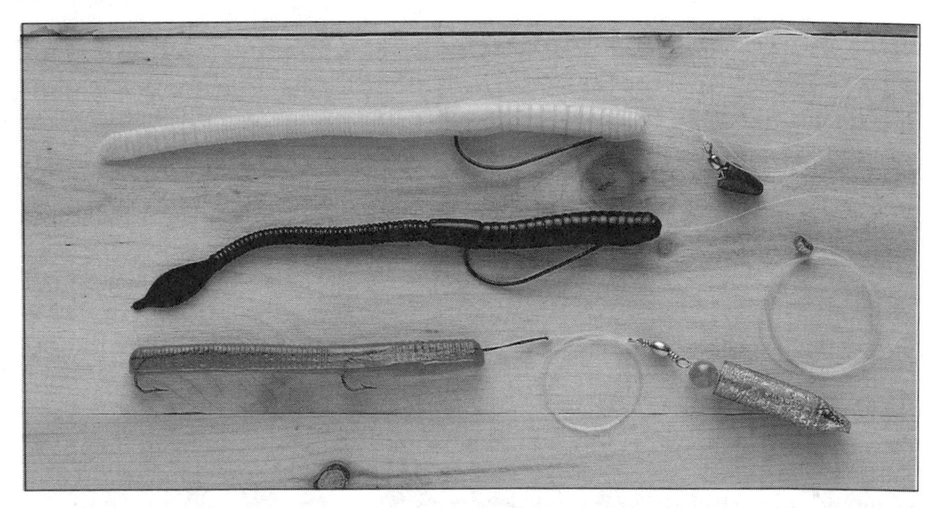

The Carolina rig is a sliding sinker arrangement designed to float a worm off the bottom: bubble gum worm rigged on a standard Carolina rig; Mann's Jelly Worm with a lead shot for weight; and Jack Chancellor's Do-Nothing rig.

Western anglers who work clear open reservoirs win tournaments with finesse variations of Carolina rigs. The Split Shottin' technique is an adaptation that uses a fixed split shot instead of a sliding weight, or a small sliding weight with a plastic bead above the swivel or stop as an attractor.

The worm (or other plastic bait) is usually "skin hooked." Bury the hook point just under the outside edge of the bait so it doesn't have to sink through much plastic before hitting the fish. Sharp hooks are absolutely necessary. In open water, fish Carolina rigs with an exposed hook.

Leaders can be shortened to as little as 6 inches when bass feed tight to the

Finesse Retrieves

3 move lure
2 pick-up slack
1 slackline sink
Nearly vertical lure drop achieved by slack-line sink. Allows lure to reach inside creases of structural configurations.

Lift & Drop

Nearly vertical lure drop achieved by slack-line sink. Allows lure to reach inside creases of structural configurations. (1) As soon as lure hits water, drop rod tip; leave bail open. (2) When lure hits bottom, reel in slack. Then slowly raise rod tip. (3) Move lure with rod. (4) Drop rod tip to allow lure to sink on slack line. Maintain finger contact with line to detect subtle hits as lure sinks.

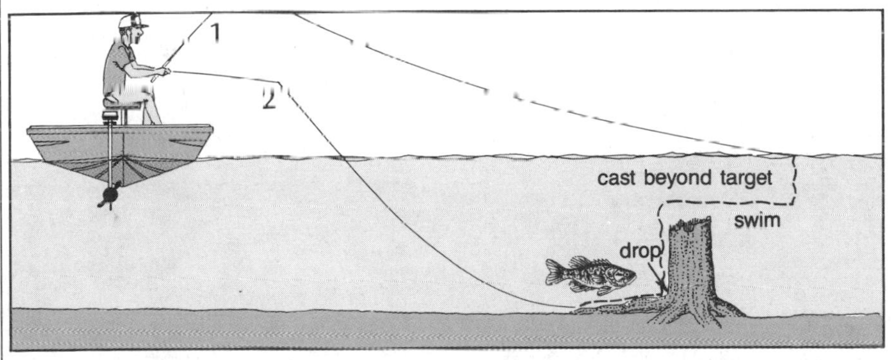

Swim & Drop

(1) With rod held high, use reel to swim lure just under the surface. (2) When lure reaches target, quickly drop rod tip. This allows the lure a straight, nearly vertical drop into the prime crease or inside turn areas.

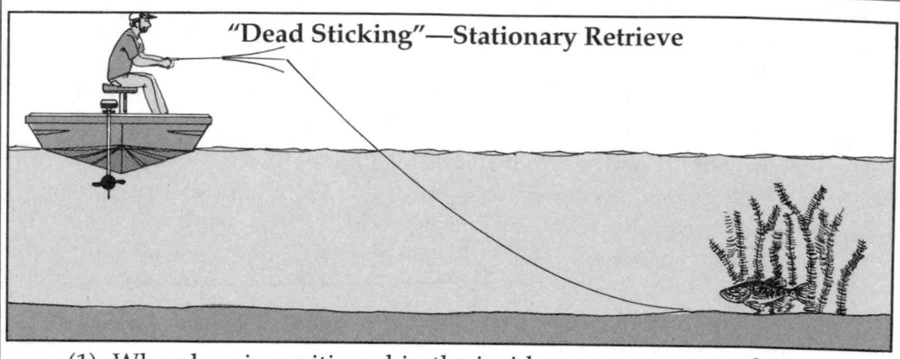

(1) When lure is positioned in the inside corner or crease, leave line slack. (2) Continue to leave line slack. (3) Continue to leave line slack. (4) After what seems like an eon, crank in *most* slack line. (5) While maintaining finger contact with line, lift rod tip slowly to remove last bit of slack. "Feel" for lure or fish. (6) Gently shaking the rod tip with the line nearly tight will make the lure quiver, possibly provoking a strike. (7) Pause. Either retrieve and cast again or use lift and drop retrieve.

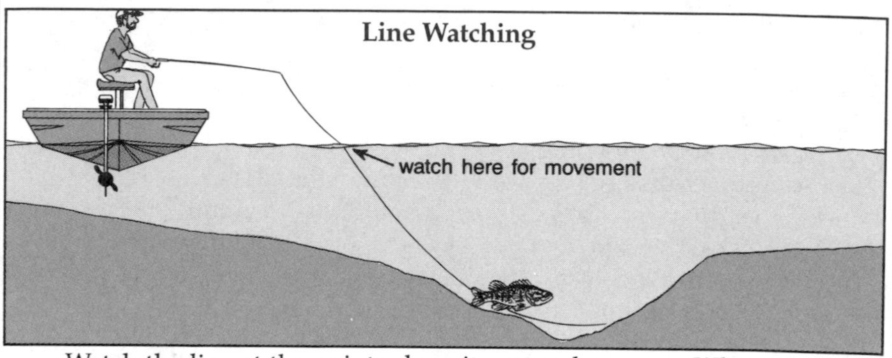

Watch the line at the point where it enters the water. When you see any movement—no matter how slight—set the hook.

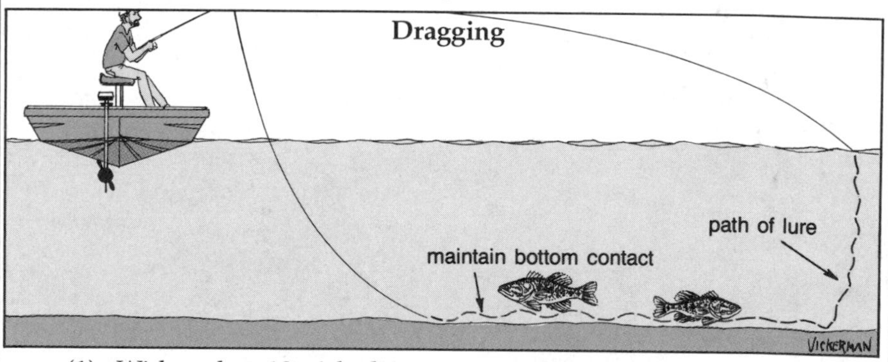

(1) With rod at 10 o'clock position, S-L-O-W-L-Y move lure with reel—*do not* lift lure from bottom. Just slide it along. (2) Many times a hit is subtle. Sometimes a slight additional weight or a very subtle throbbing sensation are the only clues to a hit. A well developed sense of feel is a must!

bottom. The "California rig" features a movable rubber stop instead of a fixed swivel, so leader length can be adjusted easily. Float the worm higher by fishing it on a floating jighead. Experiment for best results.

The worm floats up at rest, moving downward when the rig is pulled. Aggressive fish often like the jerkier up-down action of a short leader. Inactive bass prefer the slower glide of a worm on a long leader. Try different sinker colors, rattles, or colored beads as attractors.

Use a long rod for Carolina rigs because there's a lot of slack line to pick up before setting the hook. Southern anglers use long baitcasting or stiff spinning rods. Since western desert impoundments are often clear and open, bass are spooky. Some anglers use 4- to 6-pound clear monofilament on 7-foot light-action spinning rods.

Try Carolina rig adaptations to fish grubs and other soft plastic baits. Reaper bodies, curlytailed grubs, crawdads, tube jigs, and western innovations like Haddock's 18-Tail and the Slinkee are examples. The basic rule is to use straight worms when fish are inactive; action bodies when bass are aggressive.

OTHER WORM RIGS

A few less-used but effective worm rigs include:

Swimming worm—Rig worms with a bend in the middle so the bait rolls. Burke's swimming worm and the Touchdown worm are examples. Barrel swivels are generally rigged in-line above the worm to reduce line twist. The spinning, rolling action works in deep water on Carolina rigs, but is best noted for producing trophy bass in shallow cover.

Wacky worm—This curious rig was apparently devised by upstate New York bassers who called it a "twink worm" or "Helderberg rig." Hook a straight worm once through the egg sac. Use no weight or insert a finishing nail into the worm head for better casting and a faster drop. Soft tugs cause the worm to writhe like a diseased leech. It also slightly resembles a fleeing crayfish.

Wacky worms are specialized, but deadly when they're used properly. They're obviously not snagless, but in shallow water, you can steer the worm into open pockets and watch the action as it's worked. Wriggle wacky worms in front of inactive bass, or let them sit in holes on a "deadsticking" presentation. Tweaking them in vegetation often draws bites. Watch your line carefully because strikes may show only as a twitch or slight pull.

Wacky worm styles can't cover a lot of water like a Texas rig or jigworm, but are effective in areas where you're sure bass are holding. Try them under docks, where they fall slowly and squirm tantalizingly in front of bass that ignore faster-moving baits.

Floating (weightless) worm—These are usually Texas-rigged or fished on hooks with weedguards. They're a natural bait that fishes well over shallow weedy cover. They're weightless, so they don't spook bass when they hit the water. Fish them with alternate twitches and pauses. Bubble gum, white, and chartreuse are popular and easy to watch during lowlight periods and in murky water.

Doodle Rigging

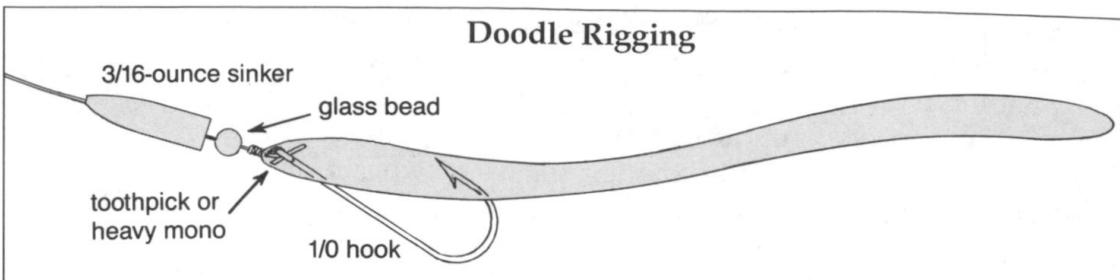

Doodle worms run 4 to 6 inches long, the colors are muted, and the worms feel soft and natural. The worm tail is straight, which produces an enticing action when doodled.

Doodle worms spiral on the sink, an action that often proves more effective than curlytail worms that dive straight down.

Doodle worms are also impregnated with salt. Some experts say bass hold them longer because they taste natural.

A 3/16-ounce bullet sinker balances well on 6-pound-test line for shaking doodle worms. Sinkers are painted to match worm colors and slide freely on the line above the hook.

Don Iovino sells custom-painted sinkers, including ones made of brass. He also adds a glass bead between the sinker and hook for more sound. (Plastic beads don't make as much sound.) According to Iovino, the banging of weight on the bead improves his strike ratio in extra deep water and at night.

Both Gary Klein and Iovino use 1/0 "Black Weapon Worm Hooks" that Klein's tackle company imports from England. Weapon hooks feature a round bend and needle point to penetrate without tearing flesh as conventional file-point hooks do. A piece of heavy monofilament or toothpick is placed through the hook eye to prevent slipping when the hook's inserted into the worm.

Vertical Doodling

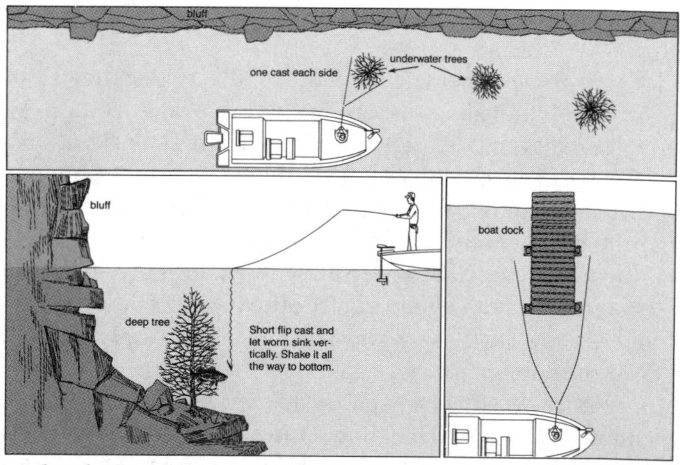

For better hooking, couple 2 ½-inch tube jigs with a leadhead jig with a 1/0 hook. Four- and five-inch baits need 2/0 and 3/0 hooks, respectively. Solid-bodied "Gitzit type" baits like Lucky Strike's G2 require external rigging; hollow bodies can be rigged either way.

JIGS

Like worms, jigs are critically important in modern bass fishing. They fish with precision in nearly any kind of cover, with any action you impart. Jigs also are versatile. Select and mix components to create something fresh and attractive, so bass don't become conditioned to them.

Jigs account for many of the biggest fish caught each year. For example, 17-pound 11-ounce "Ethyl", the largest bass ever caught in Texas, fell for a black, brown, and pink Stanley jig. For years, the heaviest 5-bass limit taken in a B.A.S.S. sanctioned event was a 34½-pound Massachusetts catch taken on a jig-and-pig. Jigs are assuming an even greater role as anglers learn to use them to catch bass in dense weeds like hydrilla and milfoil.

WEIGHT AND SIZE

With most lures, weight and size are linked so a bigger lure is a heavier one. Not so with jigs. Size often results from the fullness of the skirt and the profile of the dressing. Weight is determined by the amount of lead in the head, which makes little difference in size. You can, therefore, control size and weight independently.

"Bass jigs" come in sizes from 1/8 to 1 ounce. The most frequently used sizes are from 1/4 to 5/8 ounce. How heavy should your jig be?

Heavy jigs offer these advantages:

- They cast well and are easy to flip and pitch.
- They sink quickly to deep fish, making them efficient.
- They can be fished faster.
- They provide a better sense of feel, providing more information about what your jig is contacting underwater.
- They fish better in high winds.
- They can punch through canopy cover to bass that rarely see a lure.

Light jigs offer these advantages:

- They drop slower, remaining in the fish zone longer to give neutral or inactive bass an extra second to strike.
- They have smoother action that is more attractive to neutral or inactive fish than the jerky action of heavier jigs.
- They land softer, spooking fish less.
- They work better for swimming presentations.

Obviously, you must compromise and choose jigs according to bass activity, depth, wind, current, and cover type.

ANATOMY OF A JIG

Jigs are perhaps the simplest lure. They're comprised of a head, a hook, and dressings—hair, rubber, plastic, or livebait. Many bass jigs have weedguards for fishing dense cover. That's it. Simple and inexpensive.

The basic head design of modern bass jigheads is a modified banana. This shape slides through weeds and other cover well and has a good kicking

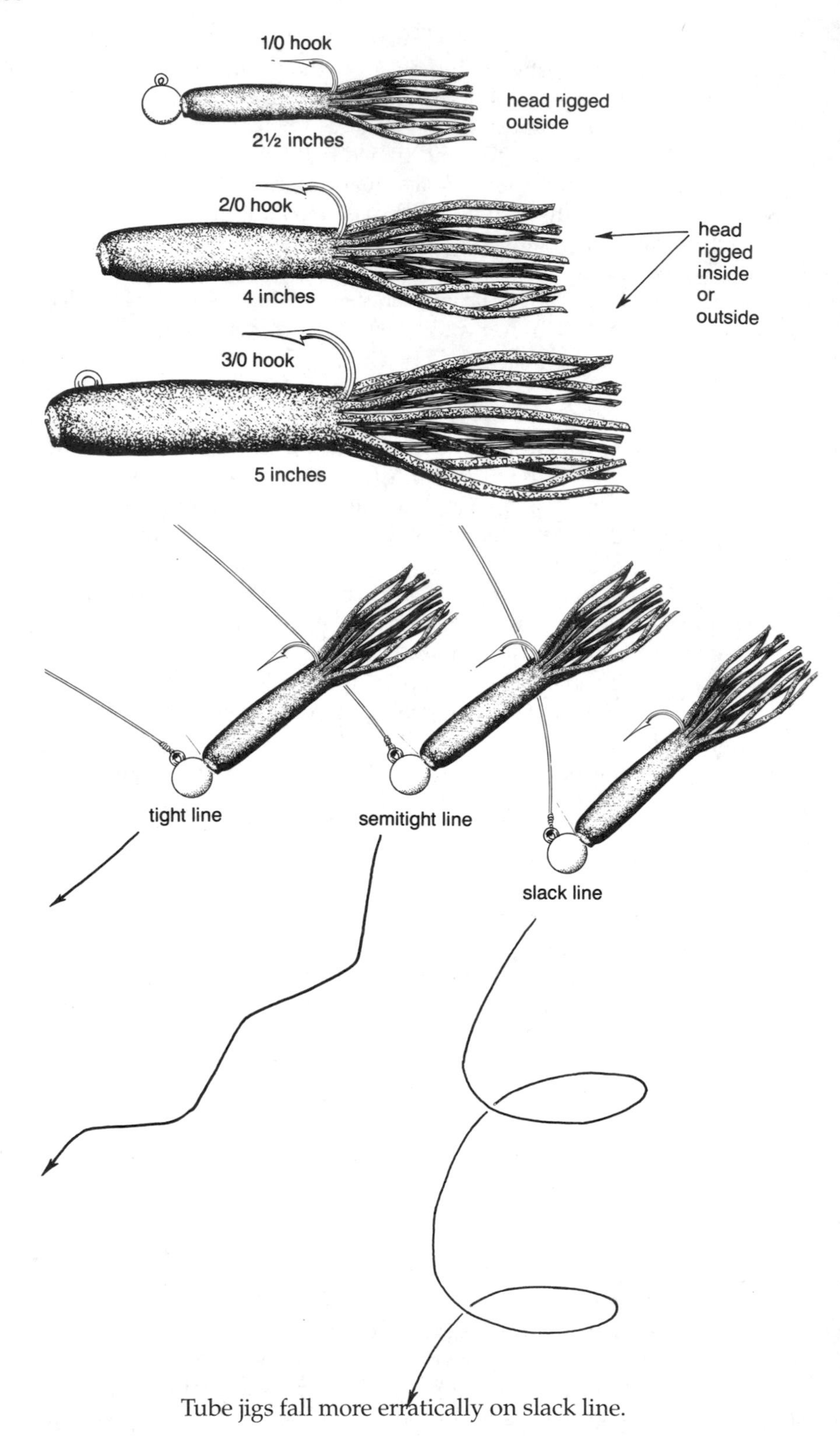

Tube jigs fall more erratically on slack line.

action when it's twitched. Most jig-and-pig jigs have bulbous banana heads that bounce off brush. But jigs fished in weeds should have the hookeye placed as far forward as possible and a tapered head approaching a coneshape to reduce fouling strands of weeds.

But other head styles work, too. Jigs that glide or are fished vertically below the boat in open water have hook eyes located on top of the head. Gitzit type jigs are an example. While less snag-resistant, they swim naturally when fished vertically.

Standup heads are best in some situations because they keep the most attractive part of the jig up where it's visible, and they have good action. Perfectly round heads are best for fishing deep water. They drop faster than other shapes. A relatively new design, the Slo-Poke, concentrates the weight of the jig back toward the hook bend, causing the bait to fall in a horizontal attitude. This seems to trigger bass that have seen worms falling nose-down. Kalin's cone-shaped dart heads give worms or grubs an erratic glide.

Jig hooks have historically been large and stout—1/0 to 5/0—and have required sharpening to be effective. That's changing. Some jigs come with extremely sharp premium hooks. Others have wide-gap hooks for better hookups when adding tough, bulky pork dressings. You can increase hooking percentages by offsetting your hooks—bending them slightly left or right. But don't lose the protection of the weedguard, if the jig has one.

Skirts were originally made from bucktail. Though it appears a little old-fashioned today, bucktail is a superb material that looks appealing and is trouble-free. The dominant skirt material for bass jigs, however, is "living rubber," which ties easily and has excellent action, even at rest. Mylar skirts offer flash that's often effective.

Most bass jigs are tied with more skirt material than is needed, because full skirts look good in a tackle store. You may want to thin out or shorten them.

Both plastic "Y" and fiber weedguards work well, but neither should be used directly from the manufacturer because they're often stiff enough to reduce hookups. Hold a knife at the base of the underside of a Y-shape guard, then slide the knife toward the end of the guard, thinning and shaping it.

Check the tension needed to depress a fiber weedguard. If it's too stiff or if you're fishing light cover and need less protection, thin the guard by eliminating fibers with a line clipper. Spreading the fibers with thumb pressure also helps hook penetration.

TRAILERS

Bass fishermen usually fish jigs with a trailer. But a black marabou jig with no dressing will take fussy bass during the postspawn transition. Jigs with mylar skirts are attractive without any dressing, and cranking a white bucktail jig can turn on reservoir bass holding on offshore humps.

But a jig is usually best with some dressing, and only pork and plastic get much use.

The complaint against both worms and soft plastics has been that they get stiff in cold water, killing the action of the bait. Frequent In-Fisherman contributor Tom Seward finds that soft plastics remain soft and active at all temperatures, contrary to popular theory. Some of the most popular versions include:

Shad—Shad baits have vibrating tails. Examples include the Mister Twister Sassy Shad and the Renosky Shad. Slip the bodies on ballhead jigs with no skirts. Keeper spikes hold the body in place.

Grubs—These short plastic bodies are real fish-foolers. Some grubs have broad, but thin tails for added action; others have action tails like shad lures.

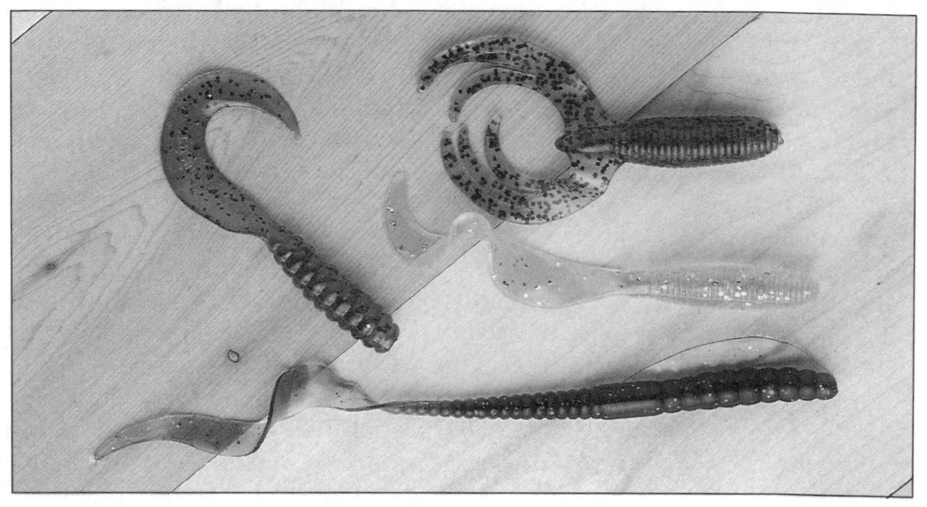

Plastic baits complement bass jigs. The best plastic trailers have action tails. Trim your favorite plastic worms or use shorter grubs.

When a bass grabs a pork bait it thinks it's real meat! Options include (left to right) Uncle Josh's black #11 Pork Frog—an old favorite; Josh's new option—two-tone Pork Crawdad; Hog Hair—pork bait that includes the pig's stiff hair in the rind to simulate spines; Berkley's Strike Rind—scented pork that isn't ruined by dehydration; and Dri Rind—tanned deer hide cut into trailers of various shapes.

Still others have flat beavertails that undulate.

Frequent In-Fisherman contributor Rich Zaleski counts the smoke grub on a 1/8-ounce jighead an ultimate "confidence" lure for negative bass. If bass won't take that bait, he knows they won't take anything. A translucent grub is one lure bass don't seem to get conditioned to. They're also killers on bass suspended in trees during winter.

Curlytails—They're grubs with active tails, and they're great bass baits. In fact, they'll catch just about anything that swims. Curlytail grubs appeal to active bass, although they also work for finesse presentations like doodling. (See sidebar.) Mister Twister invented the curlytail concept; and recent innovations include thin, but wide sickle-shape tails for added wiggle. They're also impregnated with salt and amino acids.

Gitzits—Invented by Bobby Garland, these fat, tube-body jigs provide unique action. The jighead inserts inside the body and is usually fished with an exposed hook. The key to the Gitzit's effectiveness is its slow, spiralling fall. The hollow body traps air, causing it to drop slowly.

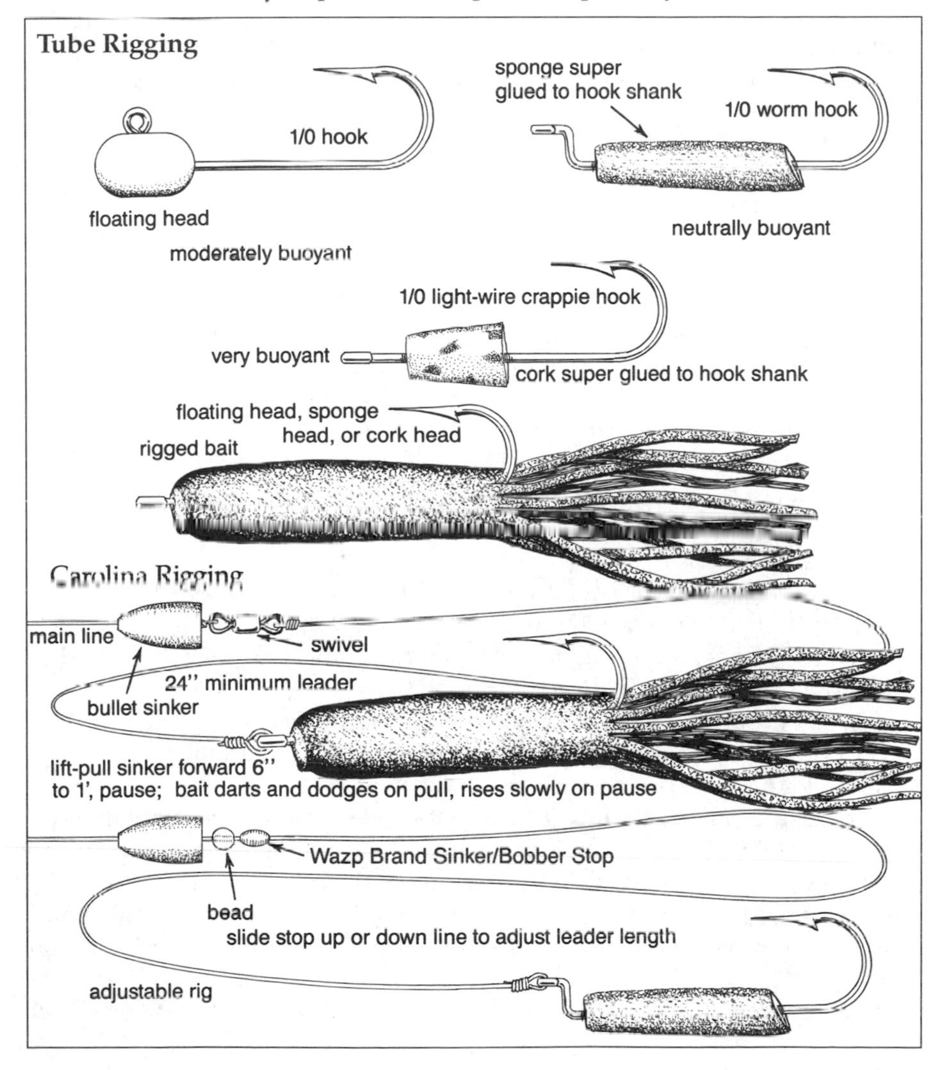

Action depends on the weight of the jig and how tight you hold your line while the bait drops. Gitzits and other tube baits are almost always fished on light jigheads weighing 1/4 ounce or less. A Gitzit dropping on semi-slack instead of taut line will glide in slow circles as it descends. Rig them up in endless ways for presentation variations.

Gitzits often work in tough conditions--bass in cold, clear water after a front, or following heavy fishing pressure. They're also deadly on prespawn, spawning, and postspawn bass, or anytime bass hold in clear shallow water.

Because they fall so slowly, tube jigs are great for bass holding under floating docks. The lure remains visible as it slowly drops, and a light Gitzit can be skip-cast under a dock to get to bass farther back.

Reapers—Reapers have been around for a long time, but have recently been rediscovered by California anglers. They're flat, eel-like soft plastic baits that catch all species of fish. Western anglers fish 3-inch reapers on Carolina rigs. But midwestern anglers have long known that a 5-inch reaper body on a wedge-shaped jig is an excellent weedline bait. Reapers on standup 3/8-ounce jigheads can be fished quickly along and through sparse cabbage weedlines. They rip through weeds with vigorous action. Rig them with the tail vertical for side-to-side action or horizontal for a slower descent in open water.

Large plastic bodies like the 5-inch reaper generally work best on 1/4- to 3/8-ounce standup jigheads. Smaller 3-inch grubs and curlytails generally match up best with 1/16- to 1/8-ounce jigheads similar to those used with jigworms. Mushroom heads, round heads, heads with wire or fibre weedguards, and standup heads all have their place. Light wire hooks will bend open to free snags if you use 10-pound-test line, though most tiny baits perform better with 6- or 8-pound line, especially in deep water.

Carry assorted jighead shapes and sizes, and match them to individual baits and conditions. You'll be surprised how much difference a subtle change in drop-speed or body shape and color can make.

Plastics excel at fishing cover edges and open water. But for the tough stuff, break out the jig-and-pig.

JIG-AND-PIG

A weedless rubber-legged jig with a pork rind dressing is the ultimate big bass bait for many bass anglers. At times, a plastic craw worm or other trailer can be substituted with equally good results.

The jig-and-pig is a big, meaty mouthful with irresistible action. It has that certain something that triggers big bass—bulk, taste, and tantalizing action that mimics bottom-dwelling fish and crayfish.

Early in the year, 1/4-ounce jigs are just right for fishing developing weed flats and shallow wood cover. Once weeds are fully established, the 3/8- to 5/8-ounce sizes give the punch needed to fish deep and in thick cover. You can fish a jig-and-pig through brush and tree limbs, letting it tumble and crawl through cover. It's also a first-class flippin' bait. But jighead selection is important.

Bass jigs were originally designed for fishing in timber. The bulbous head

The leadhead jig and pork was the hot bait of the early 1980s. No longer a sensation, it's still one of the most versatile lures .

on most jigs bounces off wood. The line-tie on top of the head allows it to be lifted over large limbs, especially with a vertical presentation like flippin' or pitchin'. But thin-branched trees like cedars and pines snag jigs when the line and jig wrap over and under twigs. Stringy weeds wrap around hook eyes when there's even a slight crease between the eye and head. For such conditions, pointed wedge-shape heads are far more snagfree and a must for effective angling.

The heavy Penetrator jig is specifically designed to cut through surface cover like milfoil. It's a weedless bullet head from 5/8 ounce to 2 ounces that punches through the surface canopy to bass below. Try bouncing Penetrators or other heavy jigs along the base of weedlines; the jig kicks up silt to attract attention.

Bass jigs have large, premium-quality hooks with wide gaps. Smaller hooks are inadequate because the added pork attractor is so fat. They come with either fiber or plastic "Y" weedguards to minimize snags. Jig balance is critical. A balanced lure descends straight and stands up once it reaches the bottom, sticking the trailer directly in the bass's face.

The most popular jig and pork colors are somber and natural, with black,

Jigheads are shaped to suit different fishing applications. The Lindy Dingo Jig was one of the earliest bass jigs. Its stand-up head, often tipped with live bait, was designed to fish weededges and drop-offs. The line-tie is on top, making the lure jump off the bottom when twitched.

Rich Zaleski's Marsh Invader, manufactured by Hankie Jigs, is designed for fishing thick shallow vegetation. The forward position of the line-tie and spoon-shape head facilitate this.

Flippin' jigs have heavy banana-shape heads like the Bass Pro Shops 5/8-ounce Master Flippin' jig. The head must be narrow to slide through thick cover. The position of the line-tie is not crucial because the jig is presented vertically.

Balance is the key for casting jigs like the 7/16-ounce Stanley. They must drop straight and stand on the bottom. The forward position of the line-tie is a compromise. Good dropping action must be maintained, but should be as snagless as possible.

brown, orange, or green being top performers. You may want to use a bright piece of pork like white or orange on a dark jig. In murky water, try a dark jig with a skirt of two contrasting colors (like black and chartreuse). Experiment with colors, although they don't seem as significant as they are in worm fishing.

Numerous pork baits work well on these jigs. The Uncle Josh U-3 Twin Tail strip lets the bait fall quickly to get into cover or down to a deep weedline. The #11 Pork Frog is a classic, but try the #1 or #10 for bulky profile and slow drop. Several companies including Berkley and Hog Hair offer other pork styles that work well on weedless jigs.

Carry a sharp knife to trim pork baits or split the tails to fine-tune drop speed and action. Pare the fat off pork to make it drop faster. A series of

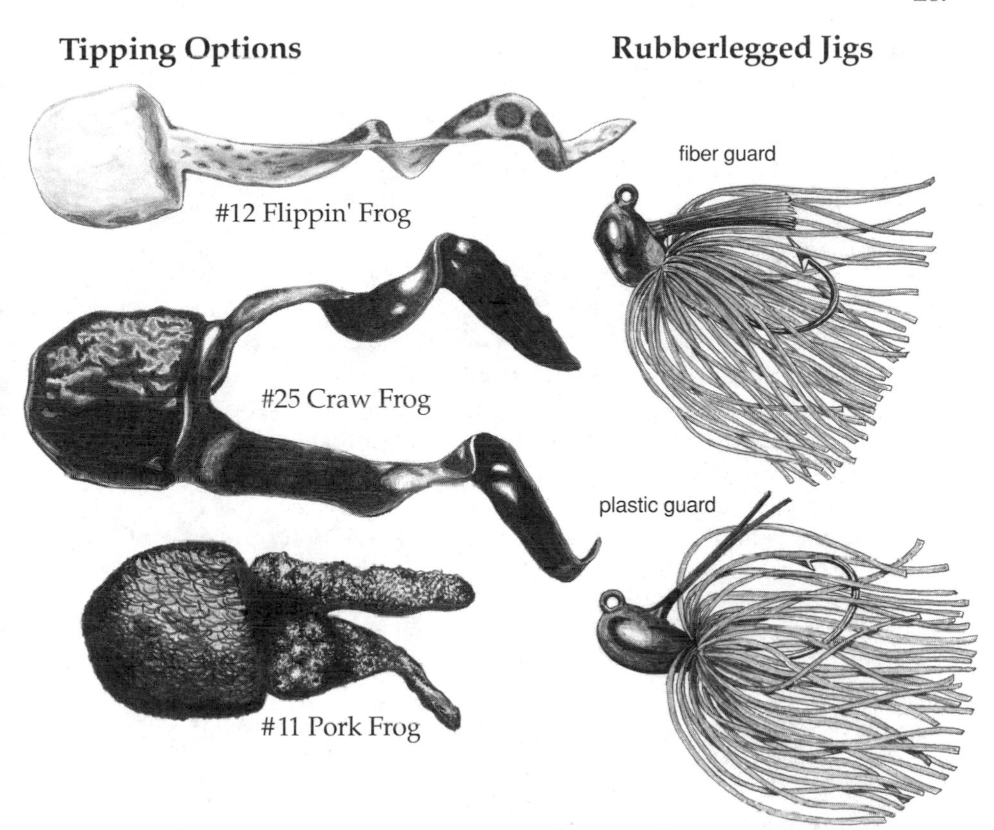

shallow slits along the underside of the fleshy pork body increases action. Slicing the tails of pork frogs or crayfish can increase their flutter. Adding a 1-inch section of plastic worm on the hook shank keeps pork chunks from turning and catching the hook point, which can be a problem with jig-and-pig combos.

Pork would be even more popular if it didn't dry when exposed to the air. A dried pork dressing is both ruined and a nuisance to cut off your jig. Plunk your pork-dressed jig in a livewell to keep it wet or use foam filled pig pouches. Or try Berkley's Strike Rind, which isn't ruined by dehydration, or porklike dressings made from tanned leather like Dri Rind.

PRESENTATION

Jigs and worms can be cast, pitched, or flipped. The thicker the cover, the closer you must get to fish it effectively. This is due to: (1) the nature of the lure, (2) the nature of the cover, and (3) the position of fish within cover. Flippin' requires the closest approach to cover. You're less than 15 feet from the object and fish. Pitchin' gives a little more room—up to 30 feet or so. Casting is applicable in many situations.

Flippin' is the best approach in dense timber or thick weeds. You can't retrieve a jig horizontally through vertical stalks or branches without frustration. The broad jighead and its density will grab and snag. Fish the lure vertically in thick vertical cover.

Jig and Pig Principles

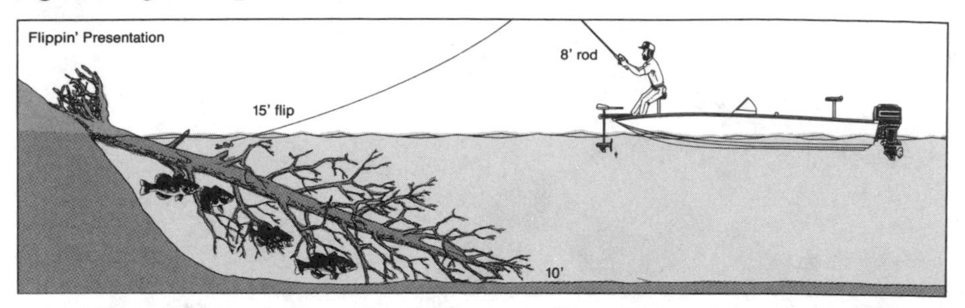

When inactive bass are in thick cover, flip a jig or worm through the branches to fish below. Vertical jigging presentations keep the lure in the strike zone for extended periods to trigger fish. The tree can be fished thoroughly by jigging through the branches. A vertical presentation minimizes hang-ups.

Flippin' calls for at least a 7-foot rod. An 8-footer is best unless there's too much overhead cover. Heavy line is mandatory.

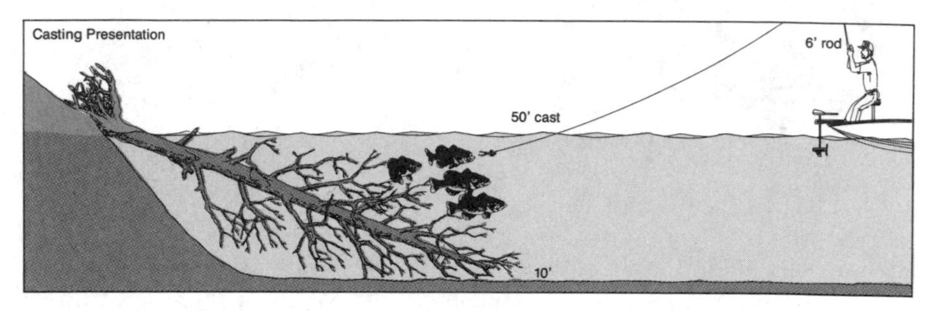

Active fish stay on the edge of cover. They're watchful and may be spooked by a close approach. Stay back and cast lures to edges.

Jigs and worms won't hang up often if you let them drop through outer branches. Spinnerbaits and crankbaits work in outer edges, but jigs often take bigger bass. Shorter rods cast more accurately, and you can drop to 12- to 17-pound-test line.

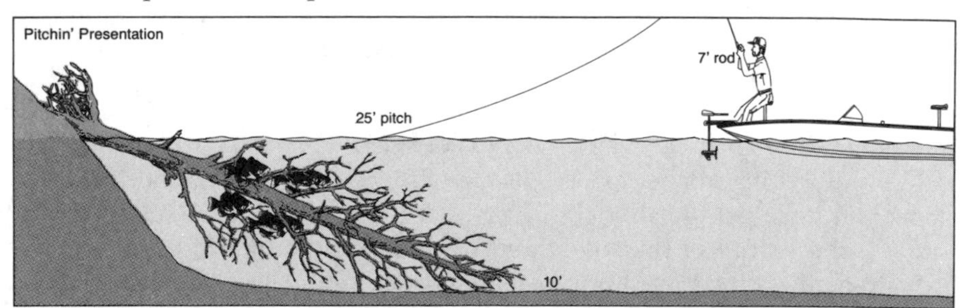

Pitchin' is a compromise that gives more vertical control than casting, but less than flippin'. It's the best choice if the water is clear or the fish are more active and holding in the outer branches.

The underhanded pitch is accurate up to 30 feet. Use a 6 ½- to 7-foot rod for longer pitches and better vertical control. Choice of line depends on cover and size of fish. The key to pitchin'—practice, practice!

Bass occupying such cover are neutral or negative—resting. To get a bite, present the lure quietly and precisely right in front of the bass. Ultraslow flippin', known as doodlesockin' in Texas, may be required.

Pitchin' is a faster presentation to cover more water. Thinner cover permits a more horizontal presentation without hanging up too much. More active bass stay near cover edges like weed pockets and outer tree limbs. They'll hit the faster-moving bait and won't be turned off by a little splash.

Casting works for edge fish. Drop the lure at the edge of cover and let it fall vertically by dropping your rod tip or stripping line.

Edge fish are usually active and will grab the lure as it drops. Active fish are also spooked by angler activity because they tend to be close to the surface and alert. Casting lets you present lures from a distance to avoid scaring fish. If cover is sparse—small patches of grass or a stump field—casting is most efficient because you can work the jig through several high-percentage spots on the same cast.

Use 12- to 17-pound line for most casting. Pitchin' calls for 17- to 20-pound test, and flippin' works with 20- to 30-pound test.

The jig and worm families are perhaps the most versatile bass lures. They can be fished from top to bottom in cover or open water all year long. You can't say the same for any other lure.

Combinations of size, shape, color, texture, drop speed, and snag resistance, are endless. Carry a variety of components and mix and match them to suit prevailing conditions. A versatile approach including jigs or worms will catch bass at times when nothing else seems to work.

Chapter 15

TOPWATERS

The Explosion Factor

Topwater fishing for bass began when James Heddon whittled the first topwater lure in 1894. Early topwaters were chunky wooden plugs with two or three sets of trebles—very effective in shallow, weedy natural lakes where Heddon, Fred Arbogast, and other early lure designers tested their baits. The explosive strikes attracted by the baits made them the preferred lure type for

TOPWATERS SIMPLY AREN'T IN FASHION

OLD MAN AND BASS

I met a grizzled fisherman, his skin like wrinkled leather,
He fished for lunker bass all day, regardless of the weather.
When I asked him how he caught those hawgs, he told me what to do:
''Jus' toss a topwater at 'em, son, them bass'll come to you!''
''But mister,'' I protested, ''I'm a master at flipping jigs in heavy grass.
I'm an artist with a plastic worm; topwaters are so crass.
I'd rather stick with the hottest trends whenever I'm out there bassin',
And topwater lures, my dear sir, they simply aren't in fashion.''

''Here's what I think of fashion!'' he replied with a spit,
And proceeded to tie on a big wooden plug with paint chipped off of it.
It had whirling props at either end like an Arkansas crop duster,
And he said with a wink of one good eye, ''Just watch and you'll learn somethin', buster!''
He chucked said plug next to a log and it sat for like a year,
Then he slowly drew back his old metal rod to put trusty Pfleuger in gear.
The black line slowly wound 'round the spool till all the slack was gathered,
Then he gave a jerk as I watched bait lurch and props churn water to lather.

From the corner of my eye I saw a great wake move from the weeds,
My heart skipped a beat as the plug came to rest and the ripples began to recede.
Then the old man spit and braced himself and I swear I heard him say,
''Hit it, you big ol' mossy-backed mule! Go ahead'n make my day!''
With that, he gave the lure a twitch, so propellers barely spun,
And the surface erupted in a watery blast, like the end of the world had begun.
The old man reared back as plug disappeared in swirl and suck and flush,
And hooks sank home and the bass jumped and shook, and my knees just turned to mush.

Bass pulled hard, old man pulled harder, and soon he had her boated,
A big-mouthed behemoth of 21 pounds, all slimy, bugeyed and bloated.
Then he turned the bass loose, gave me the plug, saying ''Take all your worms, jigs, and spinners,
And sink 'em down into the sea, 'cause HERE'S what bass want for dinner.''
Now whenever I fish for big-mouthed bass, I forget flippin' and pitchin',
Leave my worms on dock, my jigs under lock and crankbaits in the kitchen!
So forget what's vogue with hotshot pros, take a tip from that crusty old man,
Once you catch 'em on the top, you're a tried 'n true topwater fan!

—author unknown

Don Wirth

many fishermen. That's why they're popular today, too, although it hasn't always been the case.

Bass tournament fishing of the 1970s rejected surface fishing in most situations, turning to bass on deeper structure and in dense cover. Topwater fishing demands slow careful fishing, and missed or lost bass are common. Such characteristics were incompatible with the run-and-gun, high-percentage approach of many tournament pros.

Recently, though, topwater bass fishing is enjoying a revival because new topwater baits are easy to use in dense cover, and bass fishermen have rediscovered bass in shallow cover. Tracking studies verify what a few canny bass men have long known: A substantial portion of the bass population remains in shallow cover from early spring to late summer.

Recent tournament wins with topwaters have given them new respectability. As timber in old reservoirs has rotted away and weed cover has grown thicker, baits designed for bass lurking in dense weeds like milfoil and hydrilla have been developed.

Topwaters usually work best on bass in fairly warm, calm, shallow water. But a slowly twitched topwater will also take bass early in spring, and they work later into fall than most anglers realize. Topwaters catch bass in one-foot waves, too. And two types of topwaters—buzzers and jump baits—often pull bass from the bottom in 15 feet of water. So even though shallow bass in warm, calm water are the ideal for topwaters, don't automatically reject them when conditions are less than perfect.

The most consistently productive temperature range for topwaters is from about 60°F to 90°F. They're especially effective during low light periods of dusk and dawn or on overcast days. Bass hit topwaters any time of day, however, from under milfoil, lily pads, and other thick cover where light levels are reduced.

A big bass busts through a carpet of duckweed to attack your plastic frog. Now that's bass fishing—fun!

But topwaters also are ideal for catching bass most anglers ignore. Even given an awareness of shallow-water bass populations, most bass fishermen prefer to move freely in open water. They avoid slop bays and milfoil flats where moving a boat is difficult. There's a jungle back there; but a world of bass fishing awaits you if you're prepared.

For bass in shallow cover, the old "bait and switch" routine often works: Work the water with a fast-moving topwater like a spoon or buzzbait. Have another rod rigged with a rubber frog, a Texas-rigged floating worm, or a jig-n-pig combo. Bass often boil at fast lures, but miss them. Drop the slow bait onto the spot before the ripples fade. Bass often continue to look for the meal they missed. Make a good cast, and the bass will do the rest.

But what is a topwater bait? A tandem spinnerbait could be called a topwater when you buzz it so the blades bulge the surface. And we call weedless spoons topwaters even though they're often fluttered into holes in cover. We categorize topwaters this way: buzzbaits, prop baits, jump baits, minnow baits, chuggers, spoons, and slop baits.

BUZZBAITS

Buzzbaits are modifications of spinnerbaits. No bait is more fun to use. Bass don't hit buzzbaits; they kill them. Strikes are awesome.

Too, buzzbaits are great for covering water quickly. They're ideal for bass scattered over a big shallow flat with weeds tucked just under the surface. Or use a buzzer to move through a stump field, again showing the bait to a lot of bass in a hurry.

But buzzbaits also take bass by casting on spots. "Bump the stump" around standing timber or use a long rod to weave buzzers through holes in beds of lily pads. They also work in choppy water, and they sometimes attract fish from deep water.

But buzzbaits aren't for inactive bass. Stop a buzzbait or slow it down and it sinks and loses its appeal. Many fishermen bypass negative fish, assuming a few eager biters are always out there somewhere.

Size, noise, and speed are three important variables when choosing a buzzbait. Go small in spring, bigger later on. Consider total profile and length as well as blade size.

Though all buzzers are noisy, some are noisier than others. Sometimes the noisiest buzzer isn't too loud. Other times, a softer steady splash is better. Experiment by bending the lure so the blade whacks the head or wire shank to produce a clatter as well as a splash.

Speed's important. Many times bass bust a buzzbait if it's fished slowly, but still chews the surface. Multiblade buzzbaits or twin-arm buzzbaits like Blue Fox's Double Buzzer can be worked slower than standard buzzers. Carry buzzers for fast work and slow work.

Add a trailer hook for bass that strike short. Trailer hooks increase

To boat on a buzzer! Buzzbaits work best over weed flats or, as is illustrated here, worked through sparse surface cover leading into heavy cover.

hookups, and they don't often snag when they're positioned upright with a piece of surgical tubing or aquarium hose.

Buzzers are snag-resistant in most wood and weed cover. Cast them with a longer rod, 6 ½ to 7 ½ feet, and maneuver the tip to steer the buzzbait into logs and along emergent weed clumps. Long rods let you easily keep the bait on top, and they provide powerful long-range hooksets and leverage to pull bass from heavy cover. Use 14- to 20-pound-test line for fishing buzzbaits.

PROP BAITS

Prop baits are cigar-shape plugs typically with a propeller fore and aft. Many have blades that look like smaller versions of the flat blades on buzzers. Others have blades like airplane props. Since they float, prop baits can be worked slowly with varying retrieves. As you crank, the prop bait gurgles across the water like a quiet buzzer. Stop a prop bait beside a stump and let it sit, then twitch it to entice a bass holding there.

Prop baits are favored by many topwater specialists because they're so versatile. Fish them fast or slow, quiet or loud. They work in moderately choppy water. And unlike buzzbaits, you add action to the bait, which gives

WHY BASS HIT TOPWATERS

For years, fishermen have mentally misclassified the bass as a bottom feeder, probably because of the popularity of bottom-bumping lures such as jigs and plastic worms. But look at the orientation of the eyes of bass and the strong underbite of its mouth. The fish is suited to surface feeding.

The eyes are set far forward and closer to the top of its head than to the bottom. Its best field of view is approximately 15 degrees upward and 30 degrees forward. Within this spectrum, the bass has excellent vision and depth perception, both essential to a predator.

Add the ability to change body color to match background, a body type that can maneuver to catch prey efficiently, and a mouth large enough to take a variety of prey.

Doug Hannon

The bass isn't just a fine topwater feeder, but perhaps the best adapted predator in freshwater.

you control. Stop-and-go retrieves often are better than straight retrieves.

The blades must spin freely. Check them for weeds or algae. Experienced ears can detect a lure that's out of tune. Blades should spin freely when you blow on them. To break in new prop baits or buzzers, hang them outside the car window on your way to the lake.

Fish prop baits with stiff line in the 12- to 20-pound-test range. Light, thin line breaks easily in heavy cover. It also drops down in the water too easily, getting under lily pads and upsetting the proper action of the lure.

Unfortunately, prop baits and other topwater plugs with exposed treble hooks often snag weeds and wood. Snipping off the leading treble reduces snagging and won't seriously affect hooking percentage.

JUMP BAITS

Jump baits are rounded plastic or wood plugs, weighted to float nose-up, tail-down. After becoming popular in the mid-20th century, the Heddon Zara Spook, a typical jump bait faded, becoming just another plug. Rediscovery came first out west on vast, clear canyon impoundments like Mead and Powell. Today, the bait's popular from Maine to Florida. And like the jig-n-pig, Spooks have special appeal for trophy bass.

Bass usually respond to a variety of retrieves. "Walking the dog" is an exception. In this retrieve, which is inextricably tied to the Zara Spook, retrieve speed is steady and the lure moves in side-to-side lunges that don't vary. The visual and sound appeal of this retrieve often attracts bass better than anything else.

To walk the dog, hold your rod tip at the 10 o'clock position. Give it a rhythmic set of 6- to 12-inch jerks as you crank by letting the line go slack in between cranks. Takes practice, but it's worth mastering.

Several Spook imitations, plus other jump baits move in unique ways. These lures key on the opportunistic nature of bass by imitating dying fish. Colors are generally natural, with a dark back and a light belly to increase the deception.

Jump baits work best in moderately clear water. Fish them over flats, submerged stumps, weeds, treetops and even over steep drops. Bass have been known to come from 15 or 20 feet of water to bust a jump bait, although such aggression isn't typical.

MINNOW BAITS

Minnow baits are long, thin crankbaits with a small lip for shallow running at a steady retrieve. They're often called "twitch baits," because of how they're fished as topwaters.

The Prespawn Calendar Period is prime time for minnow baits. When water temperatures rise into the 50°F range, bass move shallow and begin feeding steadily. They're not ready to chase fast-moving lures, but can be tempted with vulnerable-looking baits. Minnow baits are deadly from then until the spawn.

Prespawn bass in bays tuck tight to shoreline cover or hold over relatively

Walking the Dog

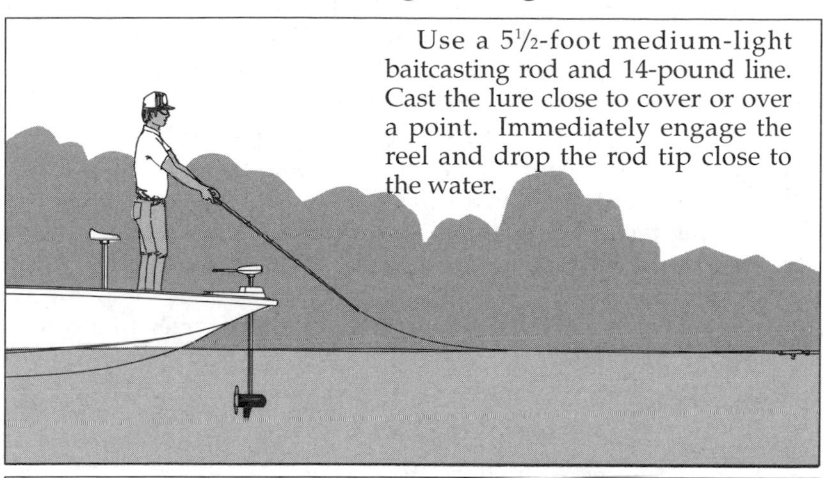

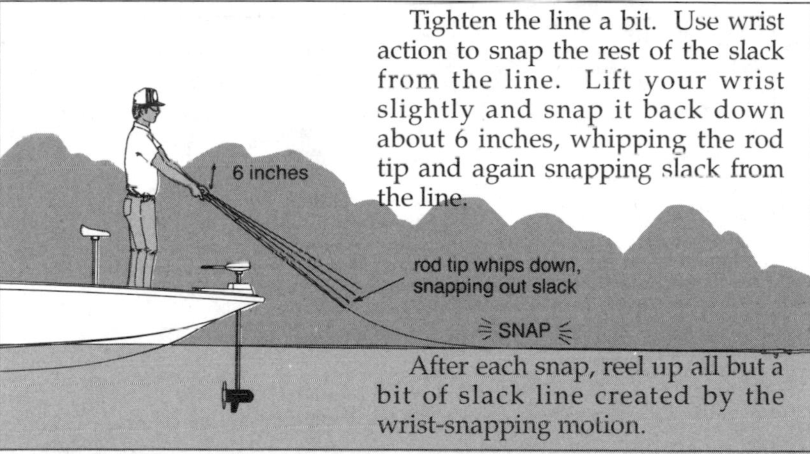

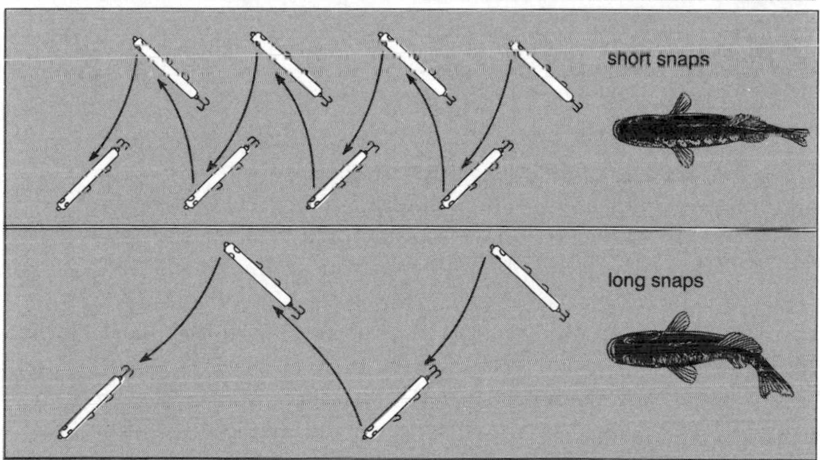

Repeat, using your wrists to move the bait The lure will dart erratically side to side.

open shallow water where lily pad stems or other sparse cover remains. That's when twitching a minnow bait can be deadly.

Balsa minnows land on the water gently, and when lightly twitched, appear to quiver like a dying minnow. Careful rod manipulation with spinning tackle or light baitcasting tackle keeps the lure moving slowly, attracting bass. Twitching can be excruciatingly slow or brisk, almost like walking the dog. Match your retrieve to the mood of bass.

If twitching doesn't work, minnow baits dive shallow on a steady retrieve. When you bring the lure by a weed clump, stump, or rock that might hold bass, stop the retrieve to let the bait rise to the surface. Give it a few twitches before moving it again.

Minnow baits also work for fishing over shallow cover like emerging weedbeds or around clumps of emergent grasses. A small spinnerbait would be more weedless, but a minnow bait twitched slowly with a stop-and-go

Topwater Data Center

	MINNOW LURE	STICKBAIT	PROP BAIT	POPPER	CRAWLER	WEEDLESS TOPWATER
ROD, REEL	5 1/2' to 6' bait-caster; light-med. action; 6' to 7' spinning; light-med. action	5 1/2' to 6' bait-caster; light-med. action	5 1/2' to 6' bait-caster; med. action	6' to 7' bait caster, med. action 6' to 7' spinning med. action	6' baitcaster; med.-heavy action	7' to 8' bait-caster; med.-heavy action
LINE	10- to 14-lb. baitcaster 6- to 10-lb. spinning	14 lb.	12 to 14 lb.	10- to 14-lb. baitcaster 6- to 10-lb. spinning	14 to 20 lb.	14 to 30 lb.
WATER CLARITY	clear	clear-murky	murky-muddy	clear-murky	clear-muddy	clear-murky
BEST RETREIVE	extremely slow w/occasional weak twitch	slow, steady twitches slow, erratic twitches	moderate, no long pauses	moderate, steady pops	slow, very steady	slow, short pauses
BEST COLORS	black back/silver or gold side bone/orange	black, chrome, blue, perch, yellow	black, brown, frog	bass, bone, perch, bluegill	black	black, char-treuse, green w/hot secondary color (yellow, red, orange)
WHERE TO FISH	weedlines, shallow creek ends, points sloping banks	points, sloping banks, weed-edges, brush	river bars, brush, weededges, stumps, logs submerged grass	weedholes, weededges, submerged grass	ponds, pits, small lakes; weedlines, shorelines	dense surface lily pads, milfoil, hydrilla, other thick vegetation

retrieve often is more productive early in the year.

Balsa minnow baits are best fished on open-face spinning equipment with 8- to 10-pound line. The baits are light for their size and often frustrate baitcasters. Yet their soft splat and buoyant action produce bass. Plastic minnows like Smithwick's Rogue or Bomber's Long A cast farther and can be used on heavier spinning tackle or baitcasting combos, particularly rods with a soft tip.

Plastics provide a faster-moving, flashier look that may appeal to more aggressive bass. Work them fast with harder twitches to stimulate bites. Tying minnow baits directly to the nose ring dampens their action, although some fishermen maintain tying directly provides a more controllable action. To maintain maximum wobble, however, install an O-ring or snap, or tie on with a loop knot.

CHUGGERS

We lump chuggers with poppers, one of the oldest and most traditional bass plugs. They have cupped faces that make a loud noisy splash when you pop them.

Like the Zara Spook, Rebel's Pop-R was a classic bait that regained popularity following success on the tournament circuit. Chuggers are sometimes best worked slowly, because the splash of a fast retrieve may spook neutral bass. Slow retrieves are best when you want a lure to stay in one spot for a while to tease bass into busting it.

Topwater Types

Topwaters (top, left to right): Roland Martin Double Buzz; Heddon Torpedo; Arbogast Hula Popper; Zara Spook. (Bottom left to right): Johnson Silver Minnow; Heddon Moss Boss; weedless hook plus Big Daddy Pork Frog; Superfrog.

Use chuggers to fish a specific spot or confined area you think holds bass--a tree, stump, weed clump, or the front edge of bulrushes, for example. Chuggers also are a fine option for fishing at night. Some chuggers, like the Pop-R are best fished with rapid twitches or a jerk-jerk-pause cadence over flats or along weedlines. Bass accustomed to attacking near-surface schools of shad find this retrieve hard to resist.

How hard should you chug a bait? Depends on the aggressiveness of the fish and the clarity of the water. In clear water or for less active bass, keep chugging away at a moderate clip and let the lure sit still longer. In dark water or when bass are feeding aggressively, chug away noisily.

Some chuggers are noisier than others. If you want to fish slowly, but still attract attention, try cup-face lures like the Hula Popper. Whup! Whup! To work a little quicker without spooking bass, try a flat-faced chugger. Wuck, wuck, wuck!

Crawler-type topwaters like the Jitterbug and Crazy Crawler, baits that wobble on top during a steady retrieve, are a subcategory of chuggers—great topwaters for small lakes, farm ponds, and strip pits, especially in low light.

Reel them in slowly without varying the speed or stopping the lure. Sometimes a bass will strike four or five times before it gets the bait. Don't flinch or jerk the lure until you feel the fish on the bait.

WEEDLESS SPOONS

The Johnson Silver Minnow is yet another traditional bass bait, one we consider a topwater. Use it for fishing quickly over and through moderately heavy cover—too thick for a spinnerbait, but open enough so you don't have to resort to a "slop" bait. A Silver Minnow may work better than a spinnerbait in emergent cover like reed beds.

Heavy cover. Heavy bass. On a Heddon Moss Boss, one of the best heavy-cover baits of all time.

Silver Minnows are heavy and offer a narrow profile; so move them quickly to keep them on top and minimize snags. Spoons flash attractively through openings in cover, crawl on top of pads or other obstructions, then flutter down when they hit open water. Bass may follow a spoon while it's skidding over weedtops, ready to bust it when it tumbles off the edge. A pork chunk, plastic trailer, or skirt adds wiggle and lift to a spoon, and also slows the drop speed. But don't use a dressing so long that bass strike too far back on the lure.

Other weedless spoons like Strike King's Timber King are fatter and lighter and work best with slower retrieves in thicker cover. A light-wire weedguard aids snag resistance, although these spoons are weighted so the single hook lands and rides up. Hooks and skirts can be replaced on several models. Strike King, Johnson, and other companies have added a Colorado spinner in front of the weedless spoon to increase attraction when it's retrieved across pockets. In lily pads or other surface vegetation, the blade clacks on the spoon for added acoustic attraction.

SLOP BAITS

This increasingly important category includes three types of bait: (1) slop spoons like the Heddon Moss Boss or Bagley Grass Rat; (2) hollow-bodied "rats" or frog baits like the Scum Frog; and (3) solid foam-bodied baits like Bill Plummer's Superfrog or Burke's Skitterfish.

These baits work over cover like algae, lily pads, duckweed, Eurasian milfoil, or hydrilla. Slop fishing is gaining popularity as lakes and reservoirs age and become weedier. Bass fishermen generally ignored thick cover after the advent of deep-water structure fishing, but a number of slop specialists have gained national prominence recently. And slop fishing is so much fun, once you're properly equipped, that anglers everywhere are testing it.

To work heavy weedmats, fish light, wide-bodied weedless lures. The bait should be smooth so it skids along the weedy surface, giving off vibrations. Action or color usually isn't important because bass don't have a chance to study the lure. Bass bust anything that seems to be the right size, often blowing up through the slop to grab a lure they haven't seen.

Plastic spoons like the Moss Boss work best dragged slowly and steadily over heavy cover like pads, wild rice, milfoil, duckweed, or matted algae. Norman's Weed Walker adds a propeller in the spoon body for added buzzing action in open pockets.

Hollow-bodied frog baits work in many of the same weed spots. Many have skirts instead of legs and double hooks with the points buried in the soft body of the bait. Since they're light, they can be difficult to cast. Serious rat and frog casters often slip pieces of plastic worm, glass beads, or leadshot into the bait to add weight that adds casting distance. Weights rolling around in the frog give it a natural head-up posture and a quivering action when it hits an opening.

Solid foam-bodied frogs have been available since shortly after World War II when Bill Plummer invented his famous Superfrog. Plummer's frog has been improved with recent plastics technology, but it remains much the same

MAT STRATEGY

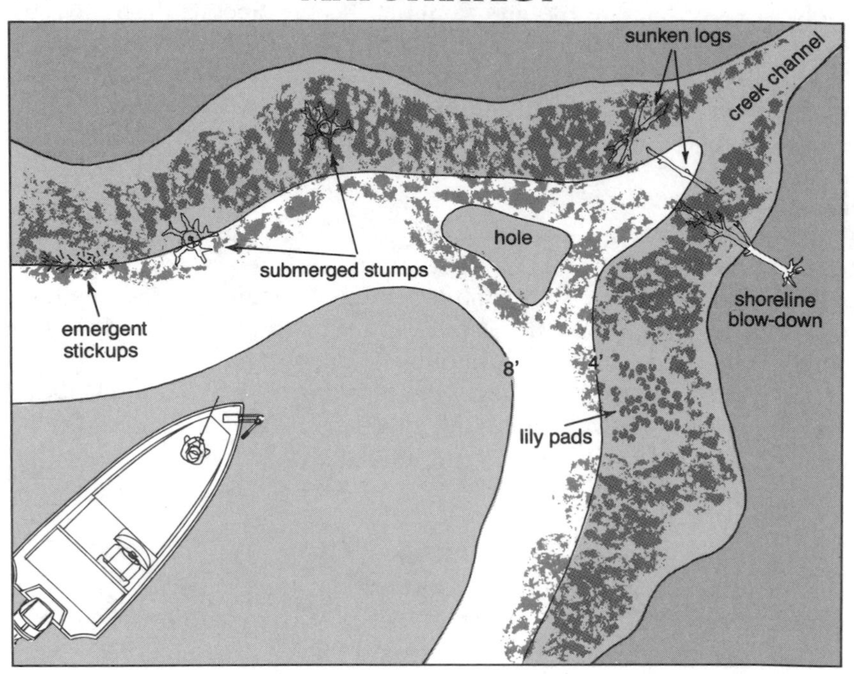

Casting frogs or other slop baits randomly over surface vegetation draws strikes from bass lurking below. The key, though, is identifying specific spots that hold the most bass.

Vegetation obscures cover and structure; so to find key spots, rely on homework, observation, and instinct. A contour map suggests spots where vegetation might form thick cover if bottom type is appropriate.

Identification of weed species or types and knowledge of their characteristics aids frog fishing. Weed species vary in preferred bottom, depth, current, water color, and water chemistry. Observe shoreline features that give clues to underwater features.

Stumps, logs, stickups, and fallen trees are high-percentage areas within a weed-choked bay. Bass use this cover in spring and fall when weeds are sparse, and they remain there when vegetation is dense.

Flowing water from a creek forms a weededge that may lower temperature and raise the level of dissolved oxygen. A key spot for a big fish, perhaps. Weeds in holes are usually sparser than on the surrounding flat. Bass ambush prey along these cover breaks.

Patches of a weed species within a larger colony of another species represent another edge because stem and leaf characteristics differ.

Lily pads surrounded by submerged weeds are particularly productive. Pads shade sunlight, preventing weedgrowth below. Bass sit in the holes, ready to attack prey from below.

Weededges are obvious and consistently hold bass. Cast to edges before pushing into the thick stuff. When push-poling, note rocks, stumps, or holes that you feel. Cast to them next time, though.

deadly bait.

To fish slop baits effectively, use strong tackle and tough low-stretch 20- to 30-pound monofilament. Long rods help lift a bass' head on top of the canopy of weeds after the strike. A slop rod should also have a long butt so you can bury it in your stomach to provide leverage. Flipping sticks work well. Fighting a fish in slop isn't fancy. Stick the fish hard, lift harder to get the fish up and coming, and then make sure he keeps coming. If a bass gets enough relief from pressure to get its head back into dense weeds, it usually escapes by shaking the hook or tearing loose. And even tough line will break in abrasive grasses.

COLOR

Color usually isn't an important factor in choosing a surface bait. Carry a few of your favorite topwaters in shad, perch, shiner, or other light colors, plus a few dark models.

In clear water where cover isn't dense, natural colors like rainbow trout, baby bass, or natural minnow hues usually work well. In dark water, try big dark baits that give bass a bulky silhouette to spot. White, chartreuse, and black work well in slop, because they're easy to watch as you work the bait. Bass use lateral line cues and surface disturbance to attack baits, often without seeing them.

HOOKING

When a big bass bombs through a layer of algae to crush a frog, even topwater specialists make mistakes. Set the hook as you would a Texas worm. Drop your rod tip and pause just a moment to let the bass turn his head, then hammer him. You need to set hard with weedless topwaters like spoons or frogs; not so hard with treble-hooked baits. But don't jerk too soon.

Missed strikes are common in topwater fishing over heavy cover. Always cast back to a fish that misses a bait or one that hits a bait but misses the hook. When a bass misses a fast-moving bait, throw a frog or another floating topwater to the spot. Cast back four or five times to rekindle interest.

If a bass misses a topwater in cover, casting a worm or jig-n-pig into the blow-up hole sometimes works best. The key is getting a bait there quickly. If a bass steadfastly refuses all offerings, note the spot and try later.

SURFACE FISHING AT NIGHT

Night fishing with surface baits can be a heart-stopping experience that produces lots of bass. Don't expect fast fishing. Slow periods happen at night, just as during the day. But night fishing can be fun and productive, especially on calm, muggy summer nights when daytime fishing is uncomfortable. Night fishing may also be effective on lakes that host heavy boat traffic.

While bass respond to worms, spinnerbaits, or crankbaits at night, topwaters are top producers. Bass often feed in shallow water at night, so they'll bust surface baits. They also often leave dense cover and roam open flats to feed, making them easier targets.

A good night bait should be easy for bass to see and strike. Move lures

Hollow Body Baits

When bass strike hollow rubber baits, they compress the body, exposing the heavy double hook tucked against the body to avoid snagging weeds. Snag Proof was an early pioneer in this lure style and now offers a variety of shapes and colors, including (top row) frogs in two sizes, a skirted frog, and Moss Mouse. Southern Lure's line includes (from left) Scum Frog, Scum Frog Jr., and Bassrat. Lloyd Tallent's Rat and Frog are made by Mann's Bait Co.

steadily without jerks or pauses so they make enough surface commotion to attract bass.

Choices include prop baits, buzzers, and crawlers. The black Jitterbug is the most famous night bass bait and has accounted for some tremendous bass. The bait offers bass a big meaty profile, moves slowly and steadily, and makes a ruckus.

Finally, try inserting a cyalume light stick in translucent hollow frog baits. Never know what you might shine on.

Chapter 16

MISCELLANEOUS LURES AND BAIT RIGS

Alternative Presentation Packages for Tough Times

This book can't cover every bait that's ever caught a bass. But even excluding oddballs, several important lures don't fit the typical categories. "Jigging" lures—spoons, tailspinners, and blade baits—are metal lures that can help you catch bass in lakes, rivers, and reservoirs. These versatile baits also work on fish species like white bass, stripers, crappies, walleyes, smallmouths, lake trout, and marine species. Then we want to be sure you consider a soft plastic stickbait that's uncannily productive at times. And finally, livebait rigs continue to play an important role in bass fishing, especially for larger bass.

JIGGING SPOONS

Jigging spoons are underused in the South and almost totally unknown in the North. Coastal anglers have relied on spoons for casting and vertical jigging for stripers, blues, and other marine species. Inland fishing guides, on the other hand, have long relied on them because they're easy to use and often outperform other bass lures.

Perhaps they'd be more popular if they weren't so simple. A jigging spoon is a bar of metal with a hook (usually a treble) on a split ring. They don't look impressive hanging on a peg in a baitshop.

The "classic" jigging spoon is the narrow, straight Hopkins with a hammered finish. That's the type of spoon we'll target, though other spoons

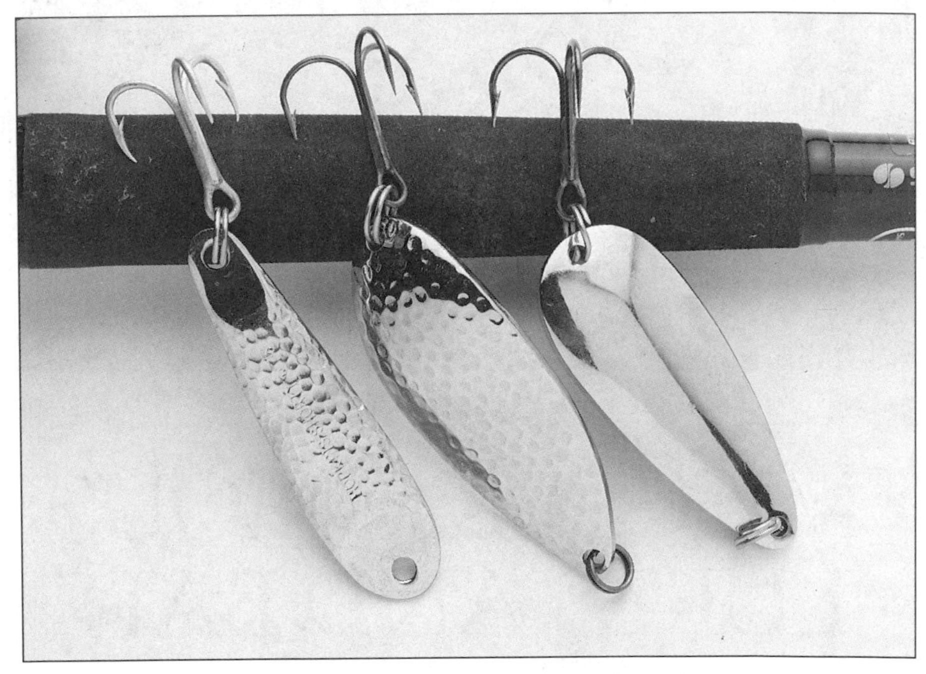

The Hopkins spoon (left) is a traditional spoon for vertical jigging. Traditional casting spoons like Luhr Jensen's "Krocodile Stubby" (center) and Bass Pro Shops' "Dixie Jet" work well for cast and retrieve presentations. Chrome baits that weigh 3/4 ounce are most popular, but gold, fluorescent and various painted patterns outproduce them at times.

Vertical Jigging

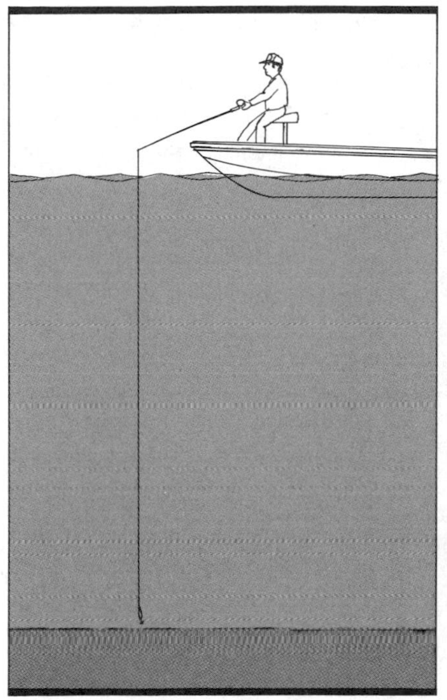

Drop the lure to the bottom and begin vertically jigging with your rod tip at about 8 o'clock.

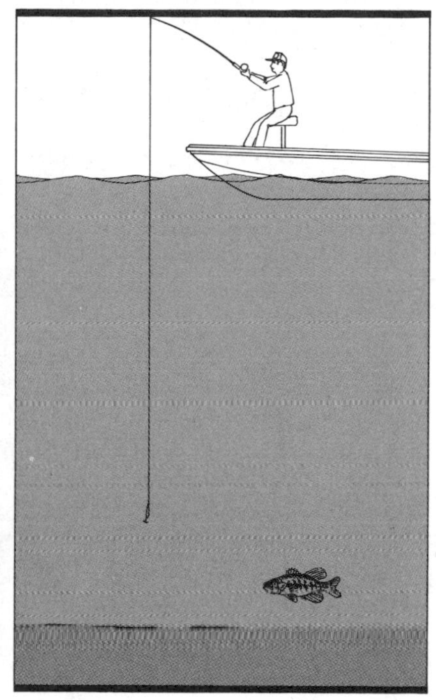

Snap the rod tip sharply to 11 o'clock.

Follow the lure back to the bottom with your rod tip. The line should't be too slack or too tight. Most strikes occur as the lure falls back to the bottom.

can also be jigged. Bomber's Slab, the Luhr Jensen Krocodile, Eppinger Dardevle, Acme's Kastmaster, and Jig-A-Whopper's Hawger Spoon work for deep presentations. These wider or more curved spoons fall more slowly and with more flutter.

The jigging spoon is versatile and efficient. Fish it vertically or cast it and fish it horizontally. Spoons have an attractive tumbling action that can be altered with twitches, jerks, or pauses. Fish it fast or slow, deep or shallow. Jigging spoons work well in current, too.

Few lures match a jigging spoon for pure efficiency, for quickly dropping to where bass are and drawing strikes. This is especially important for bass in deep water. A spoon's weight lets you fish precise structural elements in wind or current while maintaining a feel of the lure to ensure a quick hookset. Or when a distant school of shad is ravaged by largemouths, fire a spoon 75 yards to reach them.

Jigging spoons come in several styles and colors, but the solid metal spoon with a hammered silver finish is most popular. The best all-around weight is 3/4 ounce.

Many spoons come with heavy cadmium hooks. Remove them and add a bronzed 2/0 Mustad treble that can be readily sharpened, yet has just the right amount of spring—land a big bass with it, but straighten the hook and save the spoon if you snag sunken timber.

Match a jigging spoon with a 7-foot graphite rod and abrasion-resistant 12- to 17-pound-test mono. Low-stretch line is best. Jigging spoons imitate crippled shad, but dressings of pork, bucktail, or rubber skirts sometimes add appeal.

Jigging spoons are most acclaimed for use when concentrations of bass are holding deep in timber during winter. Use a paper graph or high-resolution LCD sonar to locate schools of shad and bass or other predators suspended below them. Work them with a spoon. Old roadbeds, humps, points, bluffs, ledges, and other structural elements are also ideal for spooning. And don't overlook spoons for probing ledges, creek channels, standing timber, and bluffs in summer and fall.

Try casting a jigging spoon across a hump or weedbed and retrieving quickly to the vertical edge. Then let it tumble down the front face. Strikes may be jarring, slight bumps, or a weightless feeling.

The basic vertical retrieve is a sharp snap that jumps the spoon upward, followed by a quick return of the rod tip to its starting position as the spoon falls. Most strikes come on the drop. Follow the dropping spoon with your rod tip, barely maintaining contact. A tight line reduces attractive tumbling action. A slack line leads to missed fish.

TAILSPIN BAITS

According to lure legend, Alabama conservation officer Tom Mann's first lure invention was a lead-bodied bait with a small Colorado blade on the tail. He named it Little George in honor of former governor George C. Wallace. Mann made fabulous catches with the bait on Lake Walter F. George (commonly known as Eufaula), and its local popularity led to the

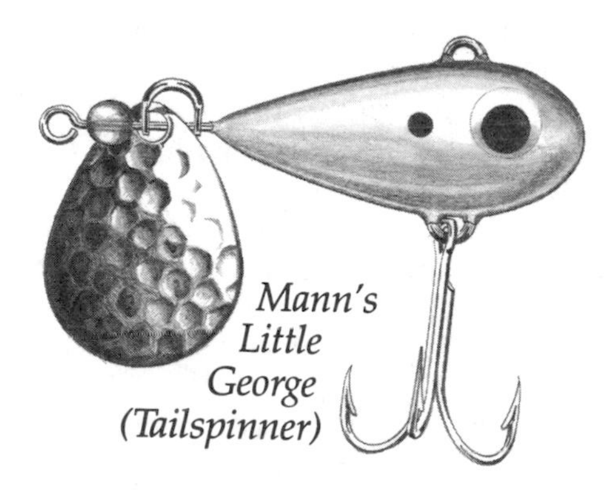

Horizontal Retrieves For Tailspinners

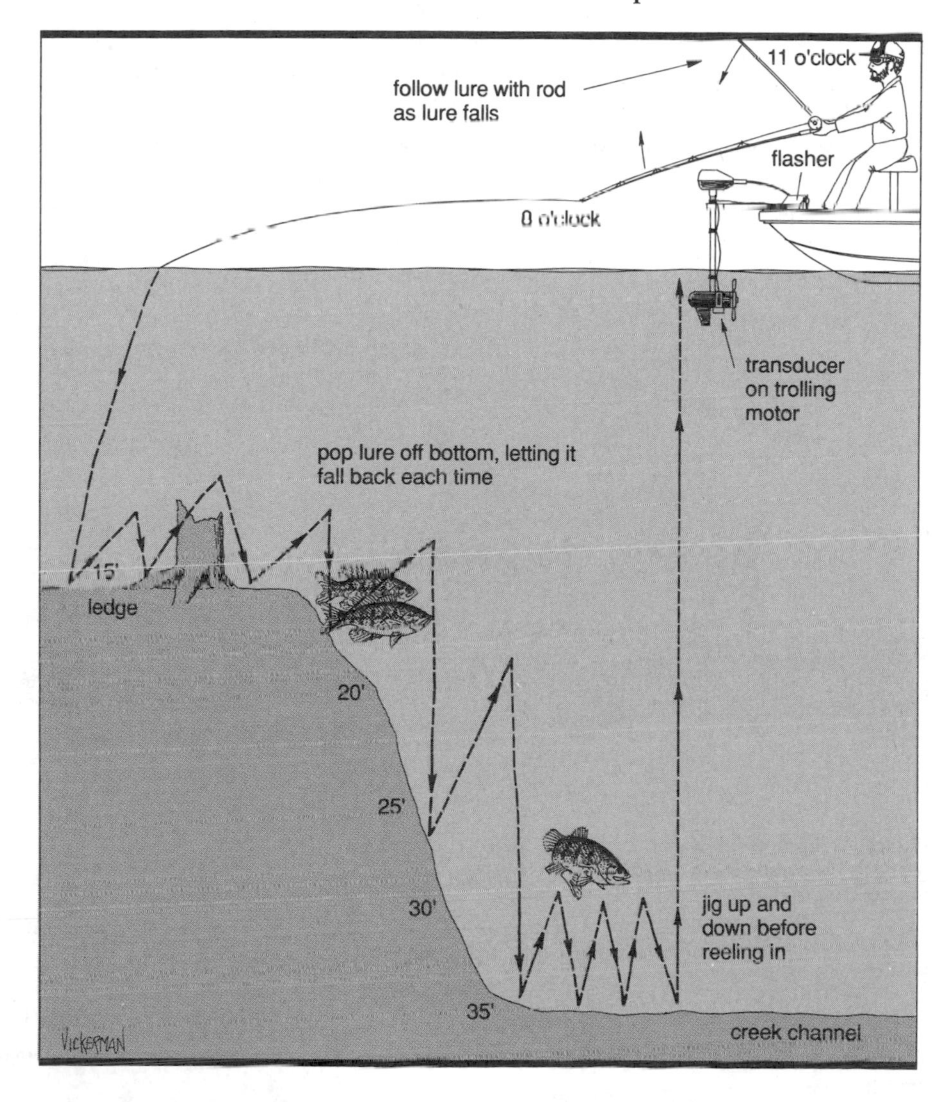

establishment of Mann's Bait Company in Eufaula.

Tailspins are fished similar to jigging spoons, but because of the tail blade, they rise or fall slower than a spoon. The Colorado blade parachutes the lead body, providing flash and a thumping that sends out sound waves. Tailspinners can be jigged vertically, fished with a lift-drop retrieve, or reeled steadily like a crankbait.

Bass scattered deep in standing timber, along creek channels, or on middepth (15 to 25 feet) ledges can be suckers for tailspinners. A controlled drift combined with a lift-drop retrieve is a deadly combination, summer and winter. And tailspinners cast like a bullet, so you can fire them to a distant school of frenzied bass.

The most versatile sizes are 3/8 and 1/2 ounce, but for probing vertical structure in deep water, carry 3/4 and 1 ounce models as well. Replace the hooks with bronzed Mustads or Eagle Lazer Sharp trebles.

Use a sensitive rod and line as light as possible, given cover density and fish size. Medium casting or medium-heavy spinning rigs handle tailspinners well. Tying directly onto the metal loop enhances feel of the lure. But check line often because tailspinners can twist line and nicks are inevitable around rock and timber.

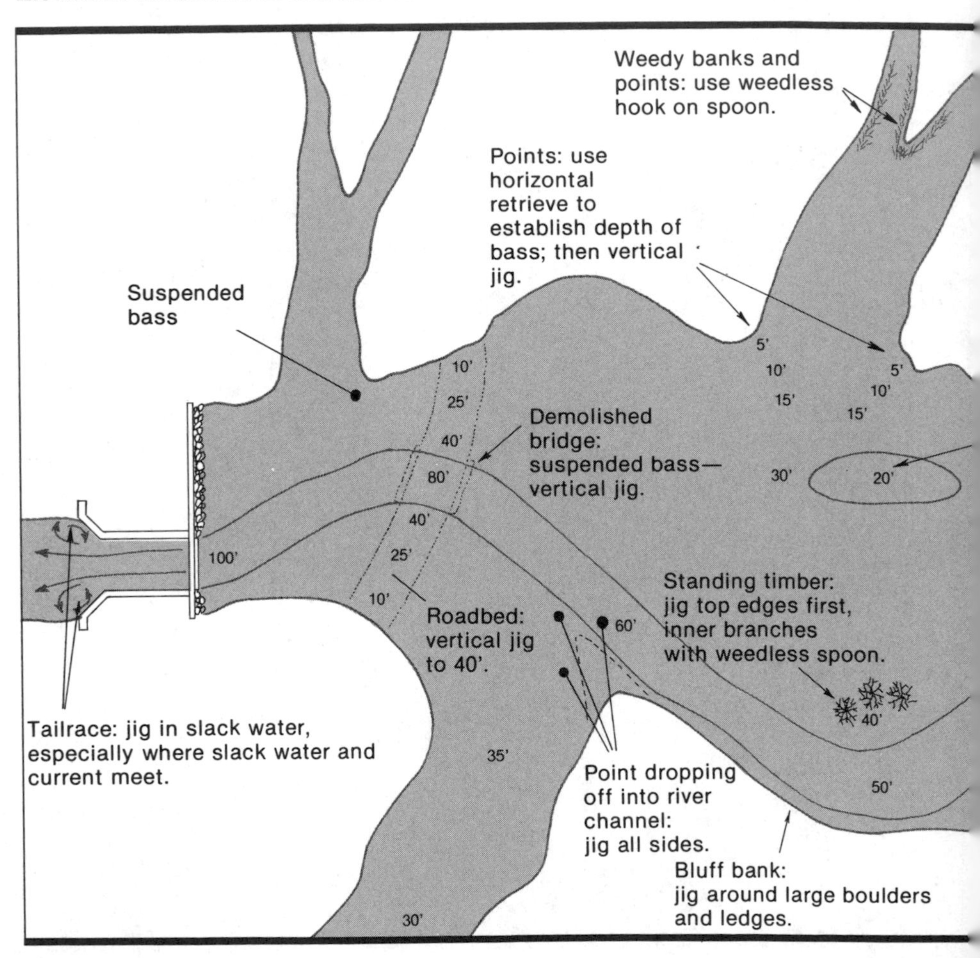

BLADE BAITS

Blade baits are thin metal baits, weighted toward the bottom with tie-on holes on the middle of their backs—metal cousins of rattlebaits like the Rat-L-Trap, without the rattle. Examples include Cordell's Gay Blade, Heddon's Sonar, Reef Runner's Cicada, Bullet Bait, and the Silver Buddy.

All-metal blades tend to run deeper and send strong vibrations when retrieved. Like tailspinners and spoons, blade baits can be fished horizontally, vertically, or in between. Blade baits can also be cast far.

A few blade baits have two or three line attachment holes on their backs that produce different lure actions and running depths. The forward hole gives the tightest vibration and the greatest depth. The rear hole produces a wide wiggle, strong vibrations, and runs closest to the surface.

Blade baits often hook the line on the cast, particularly when tied to the rear hole. That isn't a problem when you vertically jig them. Work blades with a moderate jigging action. Or try ripping them when bass are aggressive or as an attracting mechanism for neutral fish.

Blade baits are highly underappreciated as bass lures, though they're locally popular in specific regions for specific species—lake trout in Canadian lakes, white bass in reservoirs, smallmouths in highland reservoirs, walleyes

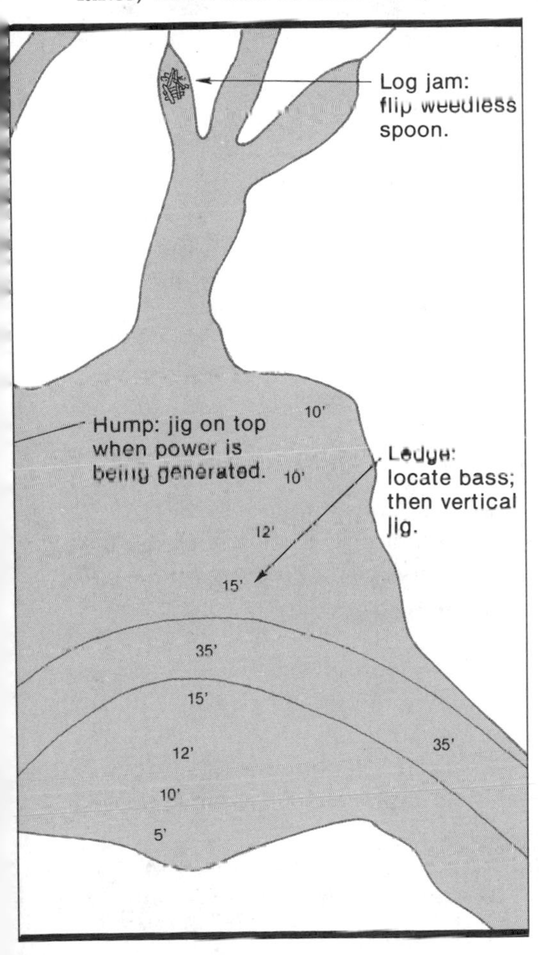

Vertical Jigging Options in Reservoirs

Options such as fishing a ledge drop-off call for horizontal casting to locate bass, and vertical jigging once they're pinpointed.

Blade baits - - Cordell Gay Blade; Reef Runner Cicada; and Heddon Sonar, Bullet Bait and Silver Buddy.

in rivers. Blade baits are ideal for fishing down a stair-step ledge. But though blade baits are usually jigged in the depths, they can also be fished in surprisingly shallow water. Change your retrieve speed to work a blade bait over shallow weedtops, then let it fall down the edge.

A limitation of blade baits is that they snag heavy cover. But they come through weeds better than you'd expect. One bait, the Cicada, instead of trebles, has double hooks that point rearward making it easier to fish in cover.

Don't tie directly to the line attachment holes. For best knot strength and action, use a small snap or a split ring.

SLUG-GO

Slug-Go is a most unusual bait and one of the most fun to use. Slug-Go is a soft plastic stickbait that looks like a short, fat worm. In the water, though, Slug-Go acts like nothing you or a bass have ever seen. Properly rigged and manipulated, Slug-Go becomes the sickest, most distressed baitfish imaginable.

Slug-Go's erratic wandering action is the key to its effectiveness. Designer Herb Reed studied baits and concluded that two things make a bait stable in the water: weight placement near the nose and an action tail. So Slug-Go was designed with the weight centrally located and a tapered tail that doesn't stabilize the bait. The result is a bait with an unpredictable action that fools bass and just about any other predator fish.

Rigging is critical, and most bass fishermen get it wrong at first because the basic rig is almost, but not quite like standard Texas rigging. Slug-Go

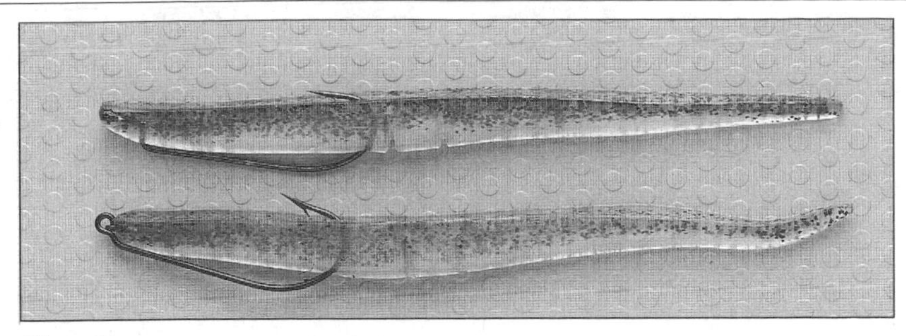

Slug-Go

Depending on your preference and the density of cover, Slug-Go can be fished on either spinning or casting tackle with 8- to 20-pound-test line. Slug-Go must be rigged perfectly straight or its erratic enticing action is lost. Pay *exact* attention to how far back in the lure the hook passes through. Pass the point and barb through *perpendicular* to the lure body, coming out on top *exactly opposite* the point at which it enters the bottom. Failure to do this correctly creates "Swanback Slug-Go" or "Humpback Slug-Go," and neither works.

When fishing heavy cover with a stiff rod, pegging a toothpick through the eye of the hook keeps Slug-Go rigged straight and performing properly. Or try a drop of Super Glue on the kink in the hook shank before sliding it into the lure.

Adding a slip sinker or lead shot to the line *inhibits* the erratic action. Instead, insert a piece of lead wire directly into the lure for getting deeper. Experiment with the position of added weight to alter the effect.

comes in two sizes, the standard and the Baby Slug-Go. For the standard, use a 4/0 Eagle Claw "J" series hook (95JB or 95JBL) or the somewhat lighter 5/0 Gamakatsu kinked-shaft hook. Baby Slug-Go takes a 2/0 Eagle Claw or 3/0 Gamakatsu.

An improperly rigged Slug-Go will roll and twist your line instead of blundering about in its special goofy action. Start by running the hook point through the nose of the bait. Don't run the hook far back before bringing it out again. Roll the hook a half-turn, then run the point completely through perpendicular to the body on a straight line. When the hook is just through, pull Slug-Go down until the hook point rests just outside the body. This has been called "Texsposed" rigging—rigging Texas-style but with an exposed hook point.

Slug-Go is mainly a shallow to medium-shallow bait. Use heavier hooks to get the bait deeper, or insert a finishing nail into the body. The bait moves through medium cover well and is ideal for fishing an expansive weed flat or inside weededges. Even when baitfish are abundant, Slug-Go's erratic action attracts bass from afar.

Slug-Go comes to life when you twitch it, then allow it to coast between twitches. Regular "walking the dog" twitches make the bait wander. Hard

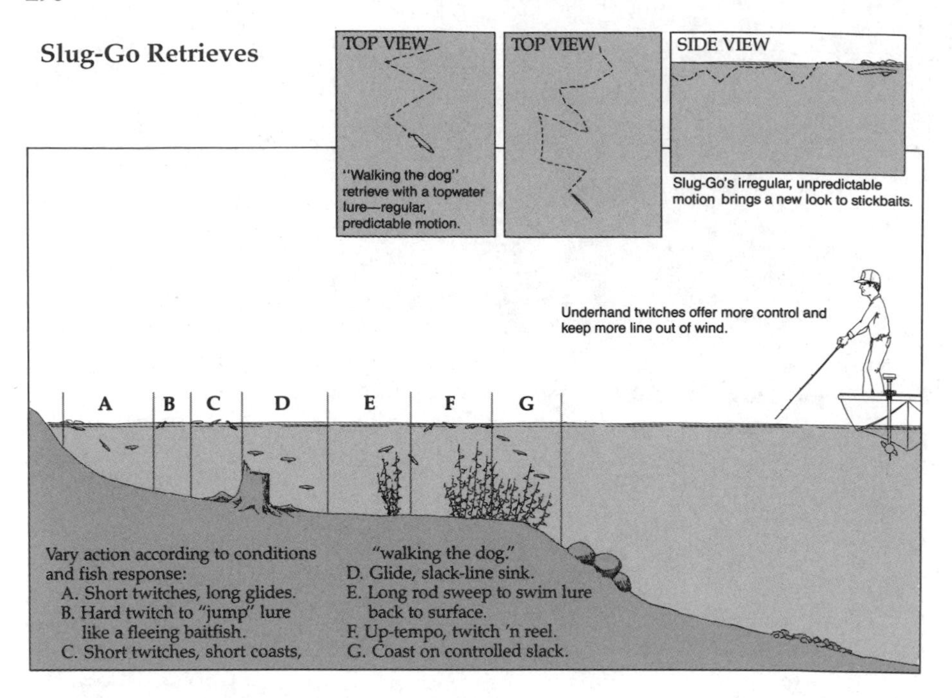

twitches squirt it along like a fleeing baitfish.

Let Slug-Go drop into weed pockets or along stumps. If a bass follows but doesn't strike, let Slug-Go fall to the bottom. Tighten up slowly and strike if something feels odd. If the bass hasn't struck, kick Slug-Go toward the surface with hard twitches.

Slug-Go, though still a secret in many areas, is doing big business with bass all around North America.

LIVEBAIT

In Chapter 4, we described the feeding habits of the largemouth bass as opportunistic. They attack and eat animals ranging from near-microscopic water fleas to small mammals and birds.

The diversity of acceptable prey and the hearty appetite of bass mean great fishing opportunities with livebait. Nineteenth-century bass anglers relied primarily on frogs and shiners for the incredible catches depicted on faded photos in historical archives. Vast improvements in tackle and lure technology made casting artificials the favorite technique of millions of modern bass anglers.

Many anglers prefer the fascinating natural interplay between predator and prey that's only possible with livebait. And when conditions are tough—cold fronts, wintry weather, high wind, suspended bass—livebait often is the best way to a good catch.

It would take several chapters or even an entire book to cover the diverse bait-fishing techniques for largemouth bass, so we'll cover several standard methods as well as several special techniques. Imagination and experience are critical to fishing bait successfully.

When fishing livebaits for bass, remember that bass engulf or overtake all but the largest prey. When you feel a strike, the bass has the bait, so set the hook. Delaying may cause a bass to reject a bait. Or more often, a bass quickly swallows the bait and is gut-hooked and difficult to release.

Gut-hooking causes serious damage to the esophagus, gills, or other organs. It's almost impossible to remove the hook without causing mortal injury. Cutting the line and leaving the hook embedded usually gives the best chance for survival, since hooks rust and fish have great healing powers.

Most bass fishermen voluntarily release a large portion of their annual catch. Special regulations also restrict bass harvest within various size ranges. These measures are essential for continued good-quality fishing in waters everywhere.

Livebait fishing has been banned from many trout waters because of excessive mortality in areas where populations can't withstand high harvest. Experience shows that bait fishermen can release bass successfully if they use appropriate rigs and handle fish carefully.

SHINERS

Shiners take all sizes of bass, even some not much bigger than the shiner, but shiners are the best way to take a trophy in lakes where they're native. In many waters, big bass get big by learning to avoid artificial baits. Bass that are wary of lures often go for a live shiner presented in a natural way.

But you won't nail a trophy just because you soak a shiner. Serious shiner fishermen monitor the quality of their baits; use heavy, top-quality tackle;

Hooking Techniques for Wild Shiners

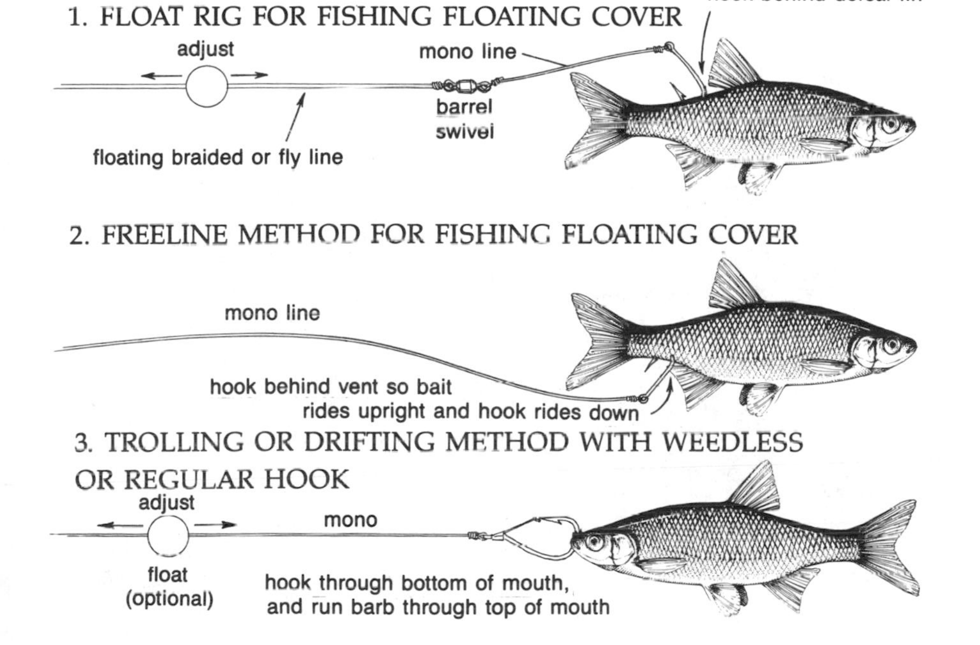

study bass location; and work baits actively—go to bass rather than waiting for the bass to come to them.

Use tackle heavy enough to bull big bass from heavy cover. Long rods—from 8 to 10 feet—are needed for firm hooksets, sometimes at a long distance. Many shiner rods are custom built, some from heavy saltwater blanks. The rod must have an ample foregrip and a long butt for the leverage needed to power a bass away from snags and pads. The most popular reels are the Ambassadeur 7000 or 6500, spooled with 17- to 40-pound-test line, depending on cover density and abrasiveness and potential bass size.

Choose a hook that matches the size of the shiner. Small shiners call for hooks as small as 1/0; big shiners call for 5/0 or 6/0 hooks. Strong, sharp hooks are needed. The Eagle Claw 84, 84RP or 84 Lazer Sharp are the most popular.

For weedy cover, use an Eagle Claw hook with a weedguard. Doug Hannon, a master at bait fishing, spends as much time on his hooks as many anglers spend prettying their boats. He recommends grinding a four-cornered point with a dental grinder or similar tool, then frequently refinishing the point with a stone.

Floats often are useful to keep the shiner near the surface. They also help transfer information on what's happening underwater by the behavior of your shiner. Large styrofoam or cork floats with tapered ends work well. Partially inflated balloons easily slide up or down your line and slip through dense cover. Inflate the balloon, knot it, and tie the tag end onto your line.

Fish shiners by stillfishing, casting or trolling. Casting is the least popular, for shiners are expensive and they'll have to be replaced after every few casts. For casting, shiners are usually rigged on a jig, a Carolina rig, or on a flasher rig (with the shiner on a snell behind a spoon with the hooks

Fishing Floating Cover

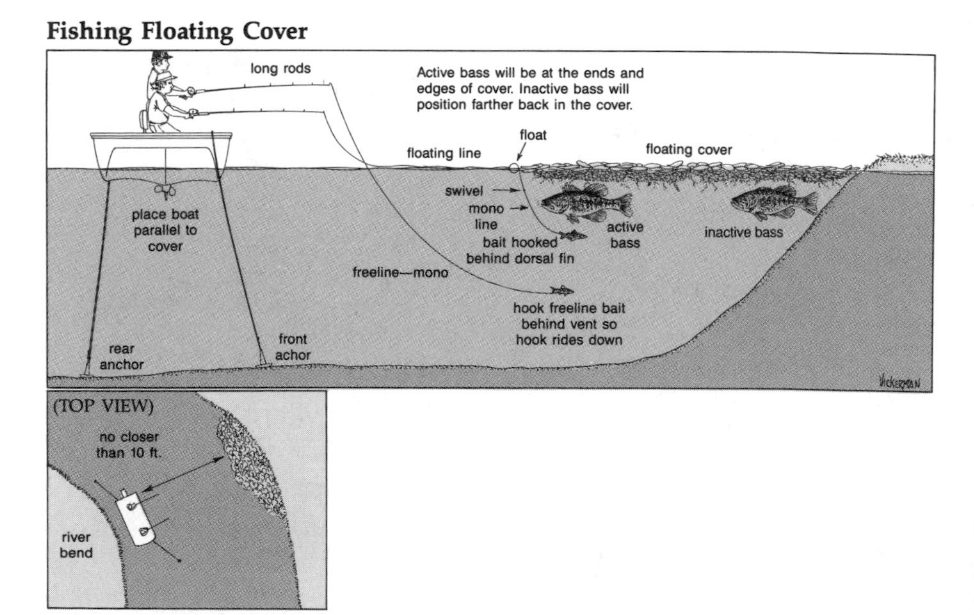

removed, much like a Great Lakes dodger rig).

Stillfishing is especially effective for fishing under canopy cover like water hyacinths. Rig a shiner with or without a float. Under a float, hook the shiner through the back, behind the dorsal fin. Without a float, hook a shiner behind the vent. Position the boat, anchored at both ends to prevent swinging, at least 10 feet from the cover being fished. Cast the bait near cover, then tug on the line to encourage the shiner to move into thicker cover, the lunker's lair.

The most productive shiner technique in most lakes is trolling or drifting. Often you have enough wind to drift at the right speed, and drifting is always quieter than trolling. Use a trolling motor as needed to correct the drift.

Without wind, run your trolling motor at constant low speed because turning the motor on and off can spook shallow bass. Hook the shiners in the mouth from the bottom up, using weedless hooks for weedy cover. Floats are optional. Use long rods to spread lines and cover more water.

CONVENTIONAL RIGS

Bass occupy such a wide range of habitat and eat so many prey types that successful livebait rigging is diverse, ranging from a simple hook and bait to intricately balanced systems involving floats, sinkers, shot, swivels, beads, and leaders.

Livebait Rig—Livebait rigs are especially good for locating inactive bass in deep water. Lip-hook a lively 3- or 4-inch chub or shiner and slowly troll or drift the base of drop-offs and weedlines. The sinker should slip on your line. Use a bullet weight or a walking sinker. Carefully lift and drop the sinker, feeling for the transition from hard to soft bottom where the drop-off levels out and meets the lake basin. This is where inactive bass often hold when weeds are scarce. Try this rig in reservoirs without dense cover.

Livebait Rig

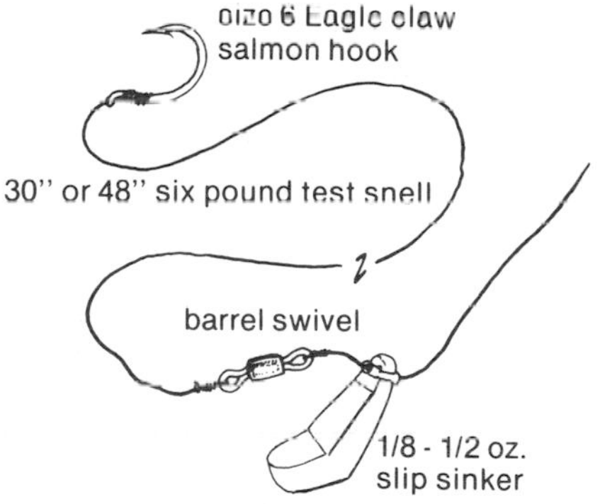

size 6 Eagle claw
salmon hook
30" or 48" six pound test snell
barrel swivel
1/8 - 1/2 oz.
slip sinker

depth	recom-mended sinker weight	distance from boat
15′ or less	1/8 or 1/4 oz.	45′-60′
15′ to 25′	1/4 or 3/8 oz.	30′-60′
25′ to 45′	3/8-1/2 oz.	fish almost directly beneath boat
beyond 45′	3/4 oz.	″

Set Rig—Set rigging means casting a bait into a set position where it stays until a bass finds it (in rivers it often drifts before it gets there).

The basic set rig is a "slip rig" consisting of an egg sinker sliding on the main line, held in place usually 6 inches to a foot above the bait by shot pinched on the line. A drawback to the egg sinker is that it easily rolls and drags in current. Add a bell sinker or walking slip sinker such as the Lindy-

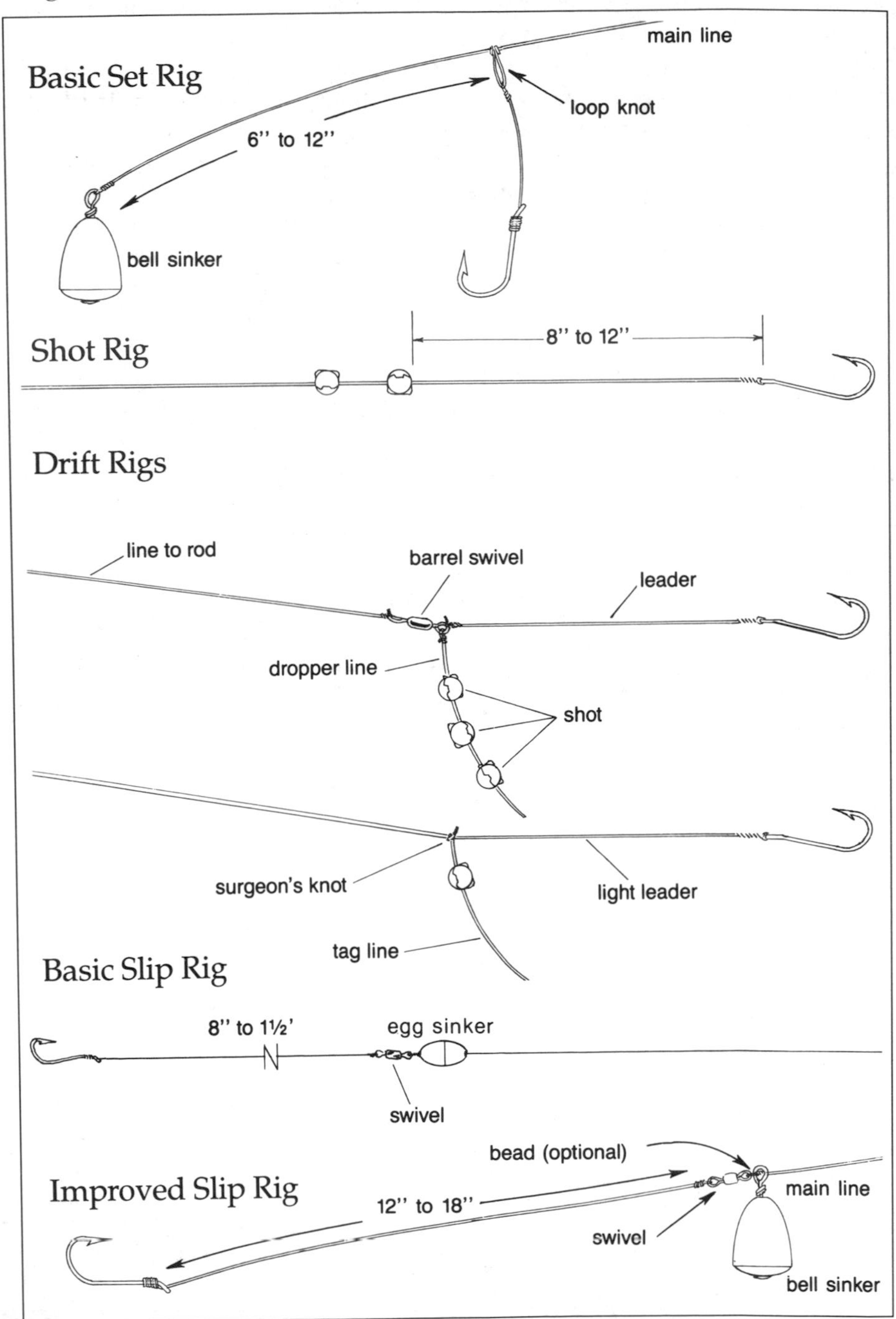

Little Joe Lindy Rig sinker to your line to improve the efficiency of this basic rig. Instantly adjust snell length by adding a neoprene float stop instead of shot to stop the sinker.

3-Way Rig—Slip rigs aren't usually adequate in current. Try rigging with a stationary sinker. A 3-way swivel rig is a traditional river standby. Tie the main line to one rung on the 3-way swivel. Add a 6- to 12-inch dropline—add a weight like a bell sinker to this line. Tie a leader—18 to 36 inches of mono complete with a hook—to the final rung on the swivel.

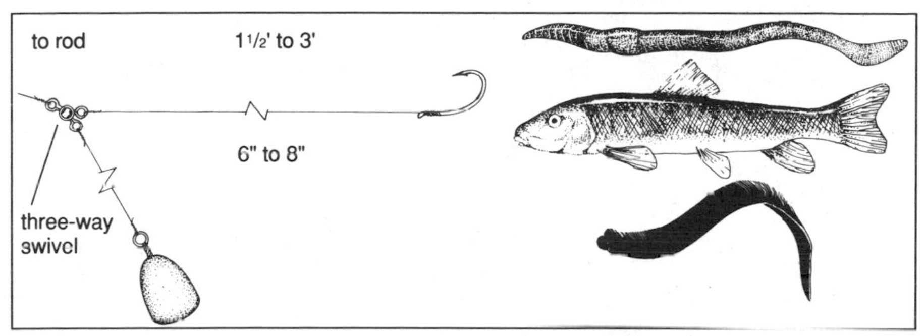

Slip-Float Rig—Slip-float rigs work to drift baits across flats, for drifting baits through or along holes in rivers, and for most situations where baitfish need to be fished from shore. The rig consists of a stop knot or neoprene float stop on your main line above the float (bobber) to set depth. A bead on the line prevents the stop from sliding through the top of the float. A hook and several shot 6 inches to a foot above the hook complete the rig.

To facilitate casting, the float stop reels through your rod guides onto the reel as the float slips down to the shot. The bait drops to the predetermined depth when it hits the water. Float rigs excel for shiner fishing, but also work with nightcrawlers and leeches where aggressive panfish aren't a problem.

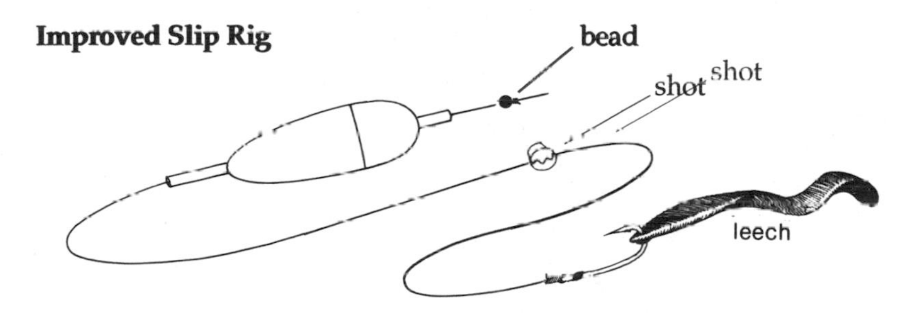

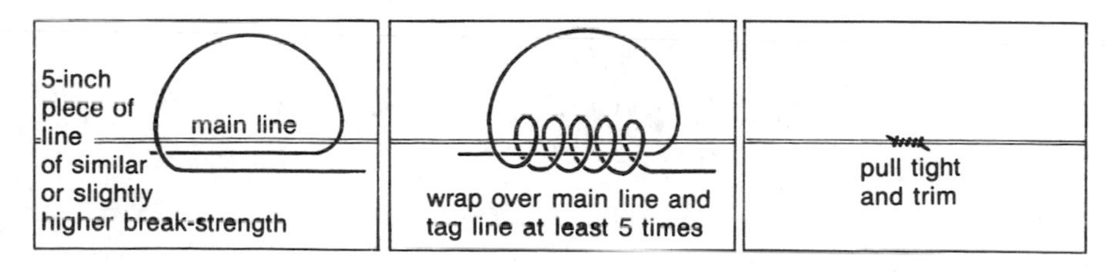

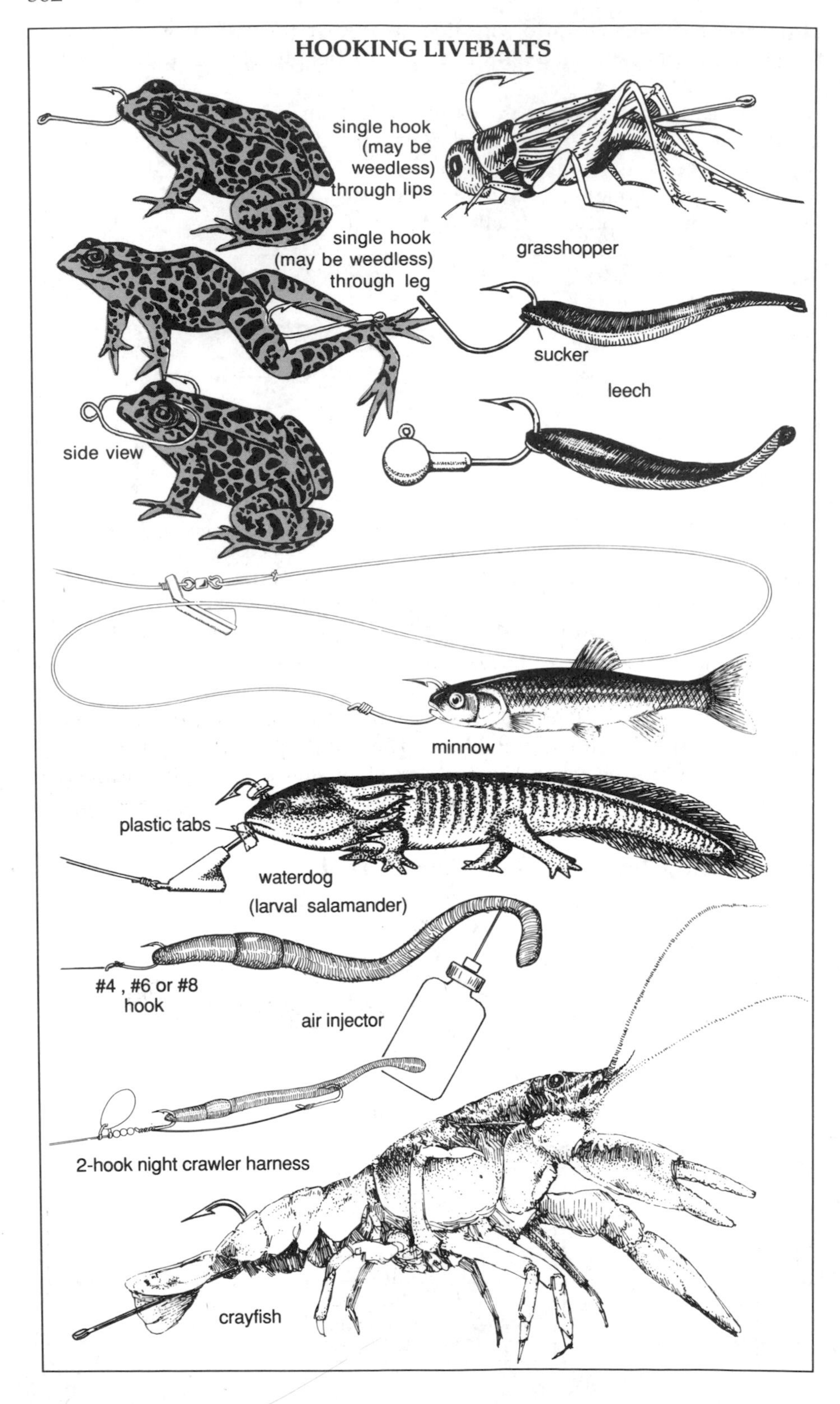
HOOKING LIVEBAITS
single hook
(may be
weedless)
through lips
grasshopper
single hook
(may be weedless)
through leg
sucker
leech
side view
minnow
plastic tabs
waterdog
(larval salamander)
#4 , #6 or #8
hook
air injector
2-hook night crawler harness
crayfish

QUICK STRIKE RIGGING

Quick-strike rigs are superior to conventional livebait bass rigs in three ways. First, they almost invariably hook a bass in the jaw, which lets you release bass in good condition. Shiner fishing with conventional tackle all too often hooks a bass in the gills or the gut.

Quick-strike rigs hook bass better than conventional rigs, too, especially when you use baits like sunfish that are hard to use on conventional rigs. With conventional rigs, you often have to play a waiting game when a bass bites. That leads to a lot of missed or injured fish, and the problem is worse if you use sunfish because bass mouth them longer than they do shiners. With quick strike rigs, you can hit the fish as soon as it touches your bait. The result is a high rate of solid hookups.

With quick-strike rigs, you also have the flexibility to choose somewhat

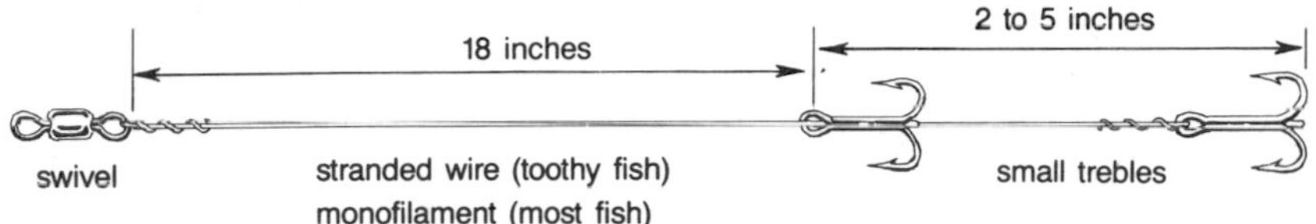

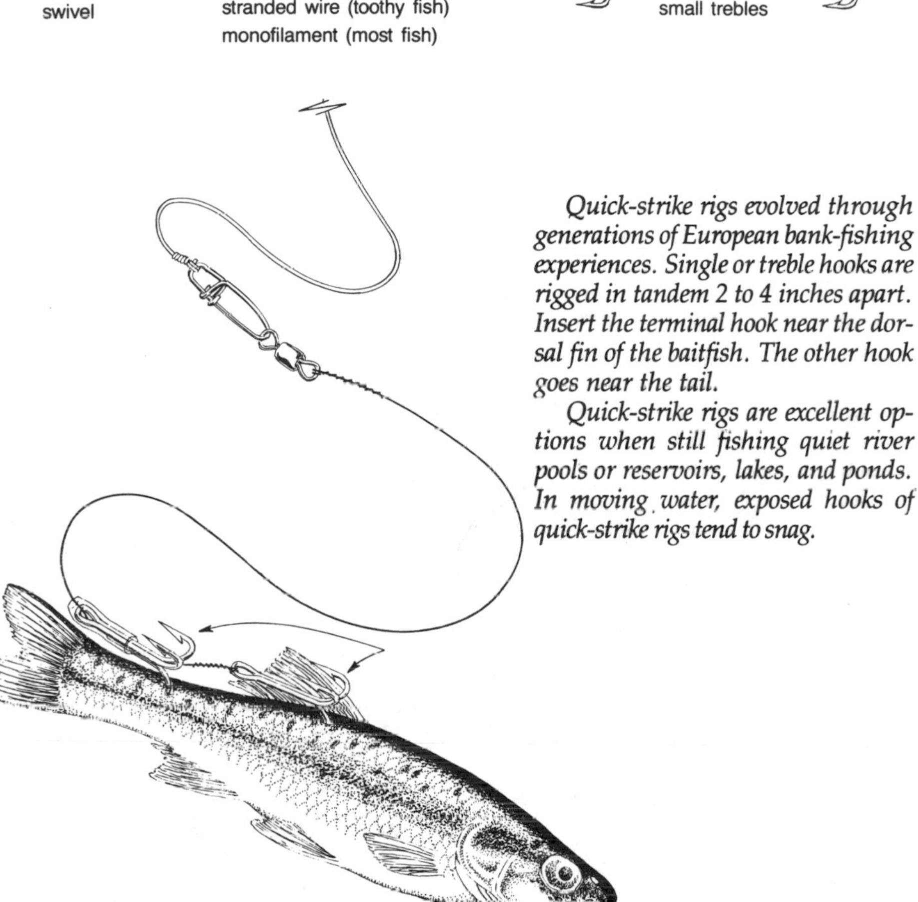

Quick-strike rigs evolved through generations of European bank-fishing experiences. Single or treble hooks are rigged in tandem 2 to 4 inches apart. Insert the terminal hook near the dorsal fin of the baitfish. The other hook goes near the tail.

Quick-strike rigs are excellent options when still fishing quiet river pools or reservoirs, lakes, and ponds. In moving water, exposed hooks of quick-strike rigs tend to snag.

lighter tackle. It takes a mighty stiff rod to sink the "shark hooks" used in conventional shiner fishing. The smaller and sharper hooks on quick-strike rigs set easier. It's still smart, though, to use a longer rod with a foregrip and a long butt. But instead of 30- or 40-pound line, 20-pound is fine for all but the most demanding situations.

A quick-strike rig is made with a pair of special double hooks called VB hooks. A tiny single hook is welded to the back of the shank of the main hook. VB hooks are imported from Partridge, an English hookmaker. When the small hook is embedded in your bait, the larger hook is exposed on the outside of the bait.

The hooks are snelled from 3 to 4½ inches apart on 15- to 20-pound monofilament. That gives an exposed hook in the nose of your bait with a second exposed hook along the dorsal fin. The size of the larger hook runs from #8 to #2. Those sizes are small enough to fish a shiner or sunfish in weeds without excessive hangups, but they're amazingly effective for solid hookups when a bass strikes.

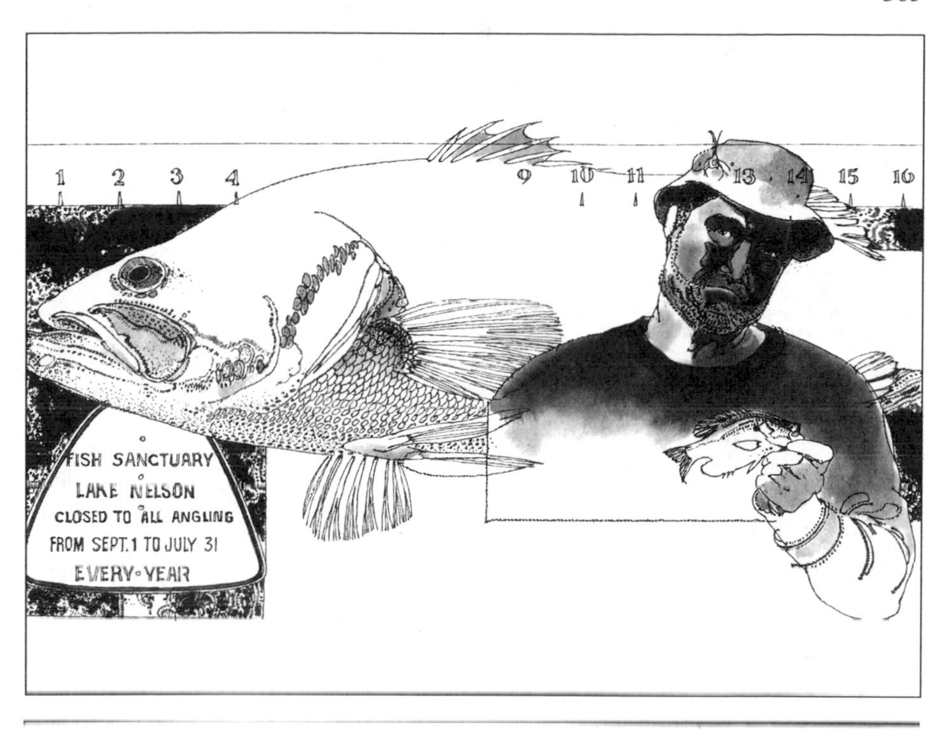

But now the sport is marred, and wott ye why? Fishes decrease, and fishers multiply. Thomas Bastard, 1599

Chapter 17

MANAGEMENT

Anglers have always looked longingly back to earlier times when fish were large and abundant. Fishing pressure isn't new, though radically new ramifications have developed.

Earlier, we mentioned a "horse race" between harvest pressures and management programs. On one hand, today's managers have the benefit of enormous amounts of accumulated research, improved technology, and increased manpower and funding. On the other hand, today's growing legions of anglers are armed with an enormous amount of knowledge and sophisticated fishing aids. Modern management is better than anything that has gone before, but it has to be. No wonder the past 20 years have marked such momentous changes in fisheries management.

CONSTRAINTS ON MANAGEMENT

Managers are limited in their attempts to sustain or restore fishing in the face of modern fishing pressure. Common constraints include:

• Inadequate funding limits every fisheries agency. Despite budget increases, there's never enough money to buy equipment and hire staff to conduct needed studies.

• Political pressures, including those from angler groups, sometimes force managers to make decisions that aren't justifiable on the basis of biological evidence.

• Managers don't readily admit this, but bureaucratic inefficiency and inertia sometimes stymie sound management. Too often, progressive managers are forced by their superiors to execute and defend outdated policies.

• Social traditions mold angler attitudes and it's often difficult to change the way anglers think and behave. In fact, fish often respond to new management programs better than fishermen.

• Managers sometimes have to settle for policies they consider second-best because of difficulties in enforcing regulations they believe are best.

Managers can work in three basic areas to influence fishing quality: environmental or habitat manipulation, stocking, and fishing restrictions. In each area, managers face limits.

While it's relatively easy to improve fishing by manipulating habitat in small waters, it's difficult and unpredictable in large lakes and reservoirs. Theoretically, an infertile lake could be fertilized to promote growth rates. But fertilizing a single large lake, let alone treating many lakes in a state, would be prohibitively expensive. And effects on preyfish or competitive species might confound the strategy.

Intensive weed management might benefit some lakes, but again the cost would be unreasonable. Severe water level fluctuations hurt bass populations, but fishery managers have limited influence on the agencies that control dam functions.

Money isn't the only problem. Modern managers also recognize that environmental alteration involves thorny political problems. No environmental manipulation has benefited bass fishing so much as the great boom of pond and reservoir construction during the mid-20th century. But radical increases in the amount of fishing water won't happen again, so we need to learn to take care of the waters we have.

Ultimately, the safest and most realistic habitat program is protecting water quality and habitat that bass and other species require. So rather than managing waters intensively for maximum production of bass, managers are challenged to maintain basic environmental quality.

Much the same is true of stocking. The better managers understand stocking, the more they see limitations that have thwarted management objectives in the past. Former stocking procedures sometimes wasted public dollars while actually degrading fishing quality. Supplementary stockings have sometimes skewed populations toward too many little bass or have been a waste of money because few of the introduced fish reached catchable size. As a result, stocking is primarily a tool to introduce bass into new

ANGLING PRESSURE MAKES A DIFFERENCE

The overharvest of adult fish ruins fishing quality. But is harvest the only problem? Or is high fishing pressure a concern even when anglers don't kill many fish?

Fishing pressure apparently does reduce fishing success even if the fish are released. A study done at the University of Illinois compared catch rates from identical ponds containing the same number of adult largemouth bass, but subjected to different amounts of fishing pressure. The catch rate dropped from 2.99 bass per hour in the pond under light pressure to 0.35 bass per hour in the pond under heavy pressure. The bass became harder to catch as they learned to avoid fishermen's offerings.

Researchers also compared the catch rates of ponds subjected to the same amount of pressure, but containing different densities (numbers) of bass. As expected, the catch rate increased from 0.11 bass per hour in the pond with the least bass to 1.61 bass per hour in the pond with the most bass. It takes a lot of "bass in the water" to provide good quality fishing.

Light pressure and dense fish populations combine to provide good fishing. Heavy pressure and low fish populations provide poor angling. Fishermen work against themselves by going where fish are dense and "naive," and fishing is fast. Pressure increases and fishing declines, particularly if harvest thins the population

Fisheries managers thus face a paradox. If they make fishing better, a body of water draws more pressure and fishing quality declines. But each body of water can eventually reach a point where population density and pressure are balanced. Further management efforts may not produce obvious improved results. Don't expect more than is possible, given the productivity of the water and the number of anglers who use it.

Mankin, P.C., D.P. Burkett, P.R. Beaty, W.F. Childers, and D.P. Philipp. 1984. Effects on population density and fishing pressure on hook-and-line vulnerability of largemouth bass. Trans. Ill. Acad. Sci. 77(3-4):229-240.

waters or increase bass populations where reproduction is severely limited by environmental problems.

Research has taught managers to consider the genetic impacts of stocking. Since native fish are usually the most genetically appropriate fish for a given region, attempts to improve bass fishing through stocking imported fish may destroy the genetic strength of native populations. Stocking to produce a few spectacular trophies can even cause long-term genetic damage.

Since fishery managers generally have slight control over environmental factors and since native spawning bass are the most efficient stockers, fishing regulations to restore angling quality are often the most effective form of management.

HOW MANY BASS?

Curious about the waters you fish? How many fish are there? These questions are more than idle curiosity for fisheries biologists, for the answers often are the basis for fish management decisions.

Task: Find the number of adult largemouth bass in a 5-acre pond.

First step: Collect a sample of fish.

With an electrofishing boat or seine, say they collect 21 bass that are tagged and released to mix with untagged fish. A few days later they make another collection, this time catching 25 bass, of which 5 had been tagged on the first occasion. Use this formula to estimate the total number of adult bass in the pond.

$$\text{Number of Fish} = \frac{\begin{pmatrix}\text{Number marked,} \\ \text{first occasion}\end{pmatrix} \times \begin{pmatrix}\text{Number collected,} \\ \text{second occasion}\end{pmatrix}}{\text{Number recaptured, second occasion}}$$

Verify this sampling method with a penny jar. Grab a handful of coins and mark them. Put them back, shake the jar, grab another handful, and count the marked coins. Use the formula.

Count the entire collection and you'll be surprised how close your estimate is. The more pennies you mark, the closer it will be.

Sampling means looking at a small portion of a population and making accurate inferences about the whole population. It's not always so simple when working in nature. But more complicated equations are available for more complicated situations.

TRADITIONAL MANAGEMENT PERSPECTIVES

Reservoir studies in the 1960s contradicted the belief that warmwater fisheries couldn't be damaged by hook and line. Many of today's managers were taught that fish populations are a renewable resource that can and should be exploited. While this concept is basically correct, managers have recognized that even a moderate amount of fishing can damage bass populations.

Early managers followed the principle of "maximum sustainable yield." This guideline fostered management activities geared to generate the largest harvest a fish population could sustain. In those terms, every harvested fish was evidence that things were going well. Released fish were "wasted" fish, poor use of a renewable resource. Creel surveys, which counted fish removed from the water, were the best measure of a fishery's productivity and therefore the success of a management program.

Stocking was sometimes used to replenish a gamefish population that seemed to be sagging. And stocking was always popular with anglers. It indicated that managers were doing something positive for the fishery. And few anglers understood that biologically unsound stockings could actually hurt a fishery.

AGING FISH

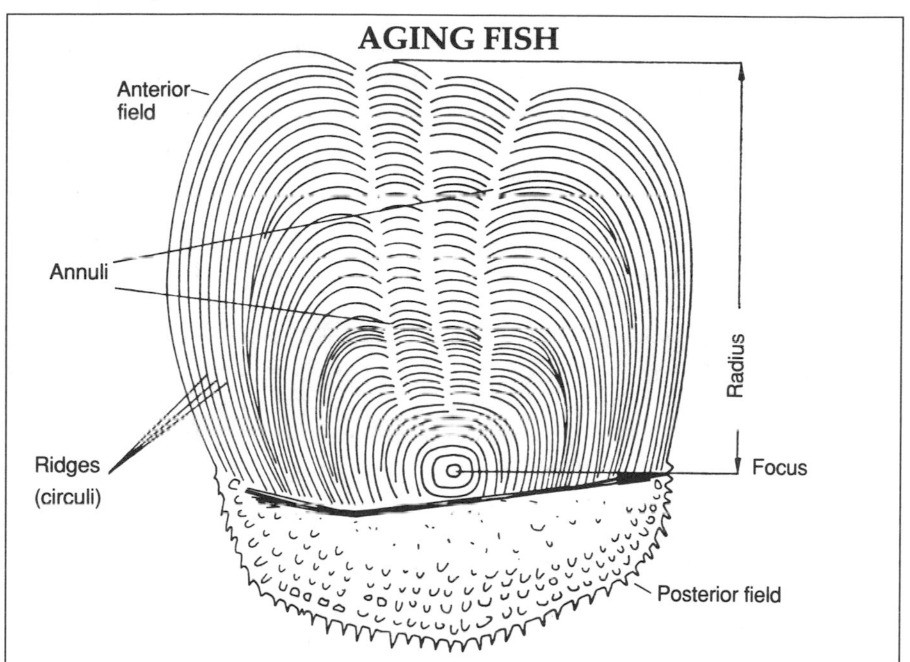

Determining the age of fish has been an important tool in fishery management since 1898 when scales were found to be good age indicators. Biologists calculate growth rates of populations by aging a sample of fish and calculating the average annual increments in length. This information helps managers determine the most appropriate harvest regulations, or if any are needed.

Scales have been the most widely used indicator of fish age because they're easily removed and can be read with simple equipment. In temperate climates, rings on scales (circuli) are more widely spaced during peak growth and narrower in winter when growth slows.

The shift from narrow to wider spacing is called an annulus or year mark, which is similar to marks on cross sections of tree trunks. Age determination with scales can be difficult for old fish that grow very little and tropical fish that grow all year. Other structures used for age determination include fin rays, vertebrae, and otoliths (ear bones).

Drawing adapted from T. Bagenal, 1978. Methods For Assessment of Fish Production in Fresh Waters, Blackwell Scientific Publications, Oxford, England.

THE PROBLEM OF QUALITY

As fishing pressure increased, anglers found they had to work harder to catch smaller and smaller bass, and they complained to managers. But anglers and managers sometimes had trouble communicating about fishing conditions and management goals.

As managers began to probe into the concept of fishing quality, it became clear that many anglers weren't just interested in catching or harvesting fish. They wanted an opportunity to catch big fish or to fish in a wilderness setting.

Philosophers have argued about the meaning of "quality" for centuries, but we use a simple definition that most bass fishermen can accept: A fine-quality bass fishery provides a fair chance to catch a number of good-size bass, with the possibility of hooking an occasional lunker.

As managers have accepted the responsibility of creating or restoring fine-quality fishing, they've had to change strategies. Instead of maximum sustainable yield, which emphasized high harvest and often contributed to low-quality fishing, managers began to talk about "optimum sustainable yield."

As visionary biologist Dr. Richard O. Anderson noted, optimum yield was a more challenging and demanding goal than maximizing yield because it involved social and economic as well as biological benefits. Yet it's optimum sustainable yield that steers most modern fishery management programs. Managers and knowledgeable anglers recognize that a healthy fishery contains a balance of predators and prey. And each predator species should be balanced with an appropriate number of large, intermediate, and small fish. Management for high harvest produced numbers of fish at the expense of a healthy balanced ecosystem and encouraged the removal of the most desirable fish. Optimum yield management promotes the health of fish populations, sometimes at the expense of harvest.

New perspectives were also necessary when managers confronted evidence from a number of sources that modern angling pressure is a major threat to bass populations. One was In-Fisherman's Perch Lake study conducted in the late 1970s. Perch is typical of bass-panfish lakes in the upper Midwest, though it received limited fishing pressure because of the lack of a good public access. The Minnesota Department of Natural Resources (DNR) granted permission for In-Fisherman staff to fish Perch Lake during the usual February through May closed season that protects prespawn and some spawning bass. All fish were to be tagged and carefully released.

The study was to determine whether angling pressure could threaten the bass population in such a lake. By the DNR's estimate, 250-acre Perch Lake contained 1,600 bass over 12 inches. Three In-Fisherman staffers caught about 1,100 of those bass—nearly 70 percent of the lake's entire population of adult bass! Most of the bass were caught during the prespawn period. This proved that a handful of skillful anglers could wipe out the bass in a lake like Perch in one season if they kept their fish and if bass in the prespawn and spawn period weren't protected.

Other studies confirmed this. Missouri fishery biologist Lee Redmond

CAN BASS CATCHABILITY BE MANAGED?

A study in Illinois showed some bass are nearly impossible to catch, while others are caught repeatedly. Researchers compared catches made under an 18-inch size limit with earlier no-limit fishing results in a 4-year investigation at Ridge Lake*.

About 15 percent of all bass longer than 8 inches were not caught. The remaining 85 percent were caught at least once, and some were taken 8 or more times. The average bass over 8 inches was hooked between 2 and 3 times a year, and a few exceptionally eager ones were released between 16 and 20 times. Over the 4-year period, 1,774 bass were recaptured a total of 6,969 times, or an average of 4 times each.

More than 90 percent of bass over 10 inches long were caught at least once, and all bass over 14 inches were caught at least once. Without the 18-inch limit, the lake would have contained far fewer bass, and most would have been very small.

While the lake may not have been "fished out," it clearly would have been severely "fished down" if the 18-inch limit hadn't forced catch and release. The strict size limit severely restricted bass harvest, but left many fish in the water for others to enjoy. The study shows that many bass are highly vulnerable to anglers, but some are harder to catch. Nevertheless, persistent pressure by skilled anglers eventually gets even the most skittish fish.

The researchers suggest that "catchability" may be inherited. A heavy harvest of easy-to-catch fish leaves only the hard-to-catch bass to spawn. Eventually, the result could be hard-to-catch bass.

Strict limits and catch-and-release tactics keep easy-to-catch fish in the breeding pool. As a result, bass may not get too smart to catch.

Fisheries managers also should know how "catchable" the fish they stock are. It's not enough to choose between northern or Florida-strain largemouth bass or smallmouth bass for stocking. Different habitats and angling conditions may require bass with different "catchability quotients."

**Burkett, D.P., P.C. Mankin, G.W. Lewis, W.F. Childers, and D.P. Philipp. 1986. Hook-and-line vulnerability and multiple recapture of largemouth bass under a minimum total-length limit of 457 mm. No. Amer. J. Fish. Mngt. 6(1): 109-112*

documented the 4-day catch of about 70 percent of the total bass population in a small impoundment. In another Missouri study, 1,550 bass were caught and released from a lake with an estimated population of 1,300 bass.

Some biologists believed these studies weren't pertinent to larger bodies of water, but those myths were soon dismissed. On Missouri's 7,800-acre Pomme de Terre Reservoir, biologists confirmed an annual harvest of 50 percent of the bass population. When West Point Reservoir on the Georgia-Alabama border opened to fishing in 1976, it had an excellent population of young bass. Biologists who studied the effects of liberal fishing regulations found that within two years, West Point's virgin bass fishery had been decimated.

Modern angling pressure is a reality that must be addressed. Can it hurt fishing quality? You bet!

DOWNFISHING

Traditionally, "overharvest" has referred to a fish population so badly reduced that the total harvest in pounds of fish drops significantly. "Downfishing" refers to the selective removal of larger fish. Lakes affected by downfishing are "fished down." Downfishing and the resulting reduction in fishing quality takes place long before a condition of overharvest can be documented. Overharvest is a term stemming from the strategy of managing for high harvest. "Downfishing," on the other hand, implies concern for fishing quality.

PROPER RELEASE

Harvesting bass is a traditional part of the angling experience and doesn't damage populations if practiced in moderation. Yet increasing fishing pressure on bass means most anglers must release most of the legally harvestable bass they catch, most of the time, if fishing quality is to be maintained.

These guidelines help ensure that released bass survive:

- Minimize the time bass are held out of water.
- Grip bass by the lower jaw between your thumb and fingers, which prevents them from struggling and injuring themselves. Do not squeeze fish around the abdomen or gill plates.
- Hold heavy bass vertically so their weight doesn't tear jaw tissues.
- There are several options for landing bass: Lead them boatside, then grab them by the lower jaw; lift smaller fish directly from the water with the rod; or use a net with nonabrasive mesh, such as coated nylon or rubber. Don't let fish bounce on a boat deck.
- Carefully remove hooks to avoid unnecessary injury. Don't try to remove deeply embedded hooks. Instead, cut the line close to the hook.
- A nicked gill may bleed profusely, but fish blood clots quickly following release, and most bass survive such injuries.
- Gently release bass at the surface; don't drop fish, particularly large ones.

CATCH AND RELEASE

The first Catch-and-Release Symposium was held at Humboldt State University in 1977. At the conference, several scientists argued that managers had to address the growing problem of downfishing and proposed that catch-and-release regulations might sustain good fishing in the face of heavy fishing pressure.

Catch and release had been practiced by European fishermen and to an extent by some North American trout and salmon anglers. To combat criticism from local anglers who resented tournament anglers coming in to kill "their" fish and to foster a conservation ethic, the Bass Anglers Sportsman Society initiated catch-and-release bass tournaments in 1971.

But the success of catch-and-release management of warmwater fish like largemouth bass hadn't been demonstrated sufficiently. So the first Catch-and-Release Symposium ended with an urgent call for research. Only a decade later, at the second Catch-and-Release Symposium, biologists revealed abundant data on the topic.

The first issue explored was whether bass could survive the trauma of being caught, unhooked, and released. Studies showed that bass are hardy. Those caught on artificial lures and promptly returned to the water have at least a 95-percent survival rate.

Research has also proven that regulations mandating catch and release can improve bass fishing quality. Specifically, the right catch-and-release policy or size limit regulation can increase the numbers of catchable bass, boost catch rates, balance preyfish populations, and increase potential for trophy-size fish. Catch-and-release regulations have been successful on large and small lakes in many regions of the country. In many cases, voluntary release by concerned anglers has also helped maintain good fishing.

WE'RE HOLDING AND RELEASING BASS WRONG!

David Campbell, biologist in charge of spawning the 13-pound-plus lunkers donated by anglers to the Texas Parks and Wildlife Department's Share a Lone-Star Lunker program, says he's received several bass with damaged jaws. Jaws were broken or cartilage torn so badly that bass couldn't eat. Eventually the fish starved. Damage apparently is due to the way bassers display fish for friends and cameras, while holding them by the lower jaw.

The jaw grip immobilizes bass, makes them easier to handle, and doesn't remove protective fish slime. Small bass aren't usually harmed when held by the jaw. But as bass grow, weight increases faster than the strength of thin jaw tissues. When compared to the strength of jaw bones and muscles, the weight of small fish is proportionally much less than that of larger fish. By the time bass reach lunker size, their weight can damage jaw tissue if they're held horizontally with one hand.

When large bass are lip-landed and held by the jaw, they must be held absolutely vertical until the weight of the tail can be supported by the angler's other hand. The jaw should never be forced into a full-open position. It should point forward, not down when bass are held horizontally for pictures. Anglers must support the weight of the body and tail.

Unfortunately, we've been holding bass wrong for years. Television stars routinely display bass by bending jaws down for prerelease pictures. Outdoor magazines have used hundreds of photos showing improper bass holds because we haven't known better. Hopefully, this will end.

You may also see anglers swish fish back and forth in the water before release. Allegedly, this re-oxygenates the gills. But gill filaments are designed to stream with a flow from only one direction. Filaments are attached at only the forward end and backward currents can bend, bruise, or break them. In addition, too much forward movement can force excess water into the fish's stomach Simply releasing fish is best if they're strong enough to swim away.

Don't use a bass's jaw as a lever. Let it hang straight down.

While holding bass by the jaw, keep the fish vertical and in a natural posture.

To display a fish, support its weight with both hands, and don't distort the jaw.

LENGTH LIMITS

Fishing regulations based on concern for numbers of fish (maximum harvest) usually limited the number of bass an angler could take in a day. Bag limits were intended to spread available fish among anglers. Concern for angling quality obliged managers to consider fish size as well.

Length limits that restrict the size of fish anglers can harvest expose some sizes of bass to harvest pressure while protecting others. Length limits have become the most effective management tool for maintaining high-quality fisheries in the face of high fishing pressure.

Length limits can take three forms: A minimum length limit means releasing all bass below a designated size. This type of regulation protects bass populations with poor "recruitment," the process by which fish hatch and grow to catchable size. One example might be a strip pit with ample food, but little spawning habitat.

A maximum length limit means releasing bass over a certain size. This protects trophy fish where angling pressure has targeted them. This regulation, however, has rarely been tried on bass.

A slot limit requires releasing certain size ranges of bass. Much recent length limit research has dealt with slot limits, potentially the most flexible tool for managing bass populations.

A commonly chosen slot protects 12- to 15-inchers, but that's not the best regulation for all lakes. In lakes with high recruitment, a slot of 11 to 14 inches might be best. On lakes where anglers seem unwilling to harvest small bass, slots protecting 13- to 17-inch fish are better. For slot limits to work, the bulk of the harvest must be bass below the low end of the slot, since reducing numbers of small fish increases growth rates. Angler reluctance to harvest small bass can turn a slot limit into a functional minimum length limit.

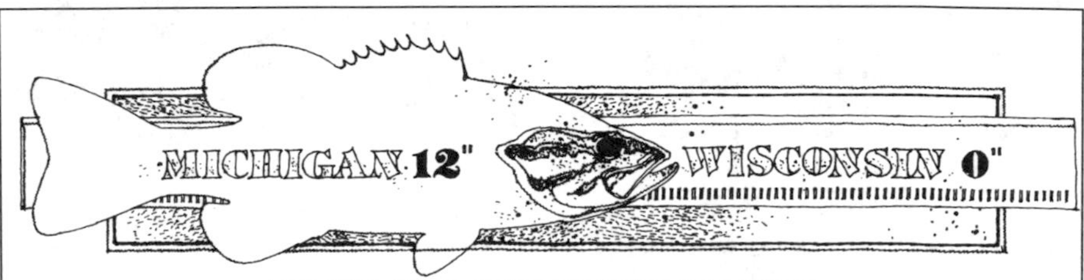

HIGH SLOT LENGTH LIMITS

High slot length limits differ from 12- to 15-inch or similar slot limits used to improve the quality of high-density largemouth bass populations. For example, Texas Parks and Wildlife Department has used 15- to 21-inch slot regulations to protect an existing high-quality largemouth bass population. The bass population developed before fishing occurred, so 15- to 21-inch (and longer) bass were in the lake when the regulation was applied.

The intent of the regulation is to *maintain* high-quality bass fishing. Harvest of smaller fish ensures that bass growth doesn't slow. But if a 15- to 21-inch slot limit was applied to an overharvested or downfished bass population, few bass would ever reach 15 inches to be protected.

SELECTIVE HARVEST ™

Emphasis on catch and release doesn't mean that fish shouldn't be harvested and eaten. The best policy for the future is a practice we call "selective harvest™." Fishing has traditionally involved keeping and eating fish. That tradition is entirely compatible today if anglers learn to make sound decisions about which fish to keep—species, size, and the body of water those fish come from.

We base our approach on relative numbers and size of fish. Top predators like pike, muskies, walleyes, and bass usually are the largest, yet least numerous species. Panfish like bluegills, perch, bullheads, and crappies are smaller and more numerous than top predators.

Large predators are the best candidates for release because they're targeted by many fishermen and are worth so much more in the water than in the freezer. That idea seems clear to many fishermen.

But segments of panfish populations are vulnerable, too. The odds of an individual crappie or perch getting large is slight. Larger panfish are a unique commodity and should be candidates for release, a thought that hasn't been accepted by enough fishermen.

Our selective harvest™ rule is to (1) keep more numerous panfish before less-abundant larger predators; and (2) keep smaller, more abundant fish of a species before larger less-abundant ones.

BASS SEASONS

Scientific consensus is lacking on one crucial area of harvest management: Should bass be protected during the prespawn and spawn periods? As we've noted, bass are especially vulnerable then. During the In-Fisherman Perch Lake study, two anglers in one boat caught and released 80 prespawn bass in less than three hours. It's common for 50 percent of the annual bass harvest to take place during spring (February through April in the South, March through May farther North).

Large bass are most vulnerable when they're shallow early in the year. A

PROTECTING THE SPAWN

Some catch-and-release fishermen release fish to give them a chance to spawn again. But the number of spawners has only indirect influence on the quality of fishing.

Shortages of breeding fish may limit the number of fry that grow (recruit) to adult size under special circumstances. But adverse weather, poor water quality, food shortages, competition, and predation usually determine how many fry and fingerlings survive. When these physical and biological factors limit recruitment, the number of spawners has little importance. When these factors are favorable, a few spawners can produce more fry than the water can support.

Almost all fish eggs, fry, and fingerlings become food for predators or die from other causes; only one or two fry per nest must survive to adulthood to sustain a bass population.

After the spawn, the number of fry and fingerlings is usually near a lake's capacity to hold tiny bass. That's one reason why stocking young bass into established populations usually doesn't improve bass fishing. If small bass aren't scarce, stocked fish are surplus "fish food." Once the number of fry and fingerlings reach capacity, additional recruits can't be forced through the system.

To improve or sustain good fishing, *adult* bass must be stocked (or returned to the water) if a lake is producing its maximum number of juveniles and is still short of adults. The number of spawners and fry only affects fishing quality when reproduction, growth of juvenile fish, and recruitment to adult size are well below the capacity of the lake to produce and hold recruits.

The mortality rate of adults is most important to fishing quality. If adults are fished down, anglers get fewer hits. In most waters, fishing is the main cause of adult mortality, so catch and release reduces adult mortality. Increased spawning or stocking often doesn't increase the abudance of adult bass.

Texas report of the 50 largest bass ever caught showed that 58 percent were caught in February or March. Florida guides who once guaranteed 10-pound bass by targeting big spawners are all out of business because they removed too many trophies that require a decade to replace under optimal environmental conditions. But even professional managers and biologists disagree about the desirability of protecting bass in spring.

Because of the short growing seasons in the North, it takes about 12 years to produce a 5-pound bass. Under ideal circumstances, that same fish can be produced in six years in southern waters. Competent biologists contend that fast growth rates in the South allow bass to replenish themselves without the protection of a closed season, and that climate conditions don't make bass as vulnerable as they are in northern waters.

Should prespawn and spawning bass be protected from angling pressure and harvest? Evidence seems to indicate that they should be protected in most northern regions, although spring catch-and-release seasons are experimental on some waters. We join with concerned anglers who believe trophy bass need more protection in states such as Florida. But it would be difficult or impossible to close the season in states that have never had a closed season. It's also possible that such a restriction wouldn't help keep big bass abundant.

TROPHY BASS

One theme in modern bass management is the importance of large fish. Because anglers often target and sometimes selectively harvest large bass, management plans must consider strategies to keep large bass in bass

IS BIGGER BETTER?

A bass population that's genetically well adapted isn't necessarily one that grows fast or lives long. Ever wonder why bass don't get as big as sharks, or tuna, or muskies?

Larger size doesn't increase the overall fitness of bass. Fish are compromises of many different selective forces. A 50-pound bass wouldn't have to worry about being eaten by an otter. And it could produce millions of eggs. But how many shiners would it have to eat each day? And could it catch any in a stump field or weedbed?

The mosquito fish ***(Gambusia)*** *is very "successful" by any account. It grows, multiplies, and colonizes new waters. But they're rarely over 1 1/2 inches long.*

Alabama is known for producing lots of big bass. But in the lower Alabama River, there's a population of largemouths that are fat and healthy, but don't grow large. Apparently, these characteristics are advantageous in that environment, but no one knows why. We probably won't see them stocked anywhere else.

Understanding fish genetics is the key to stocking the best possible fish, fish that will thrive and produce the best possible fishing.

populations. That's a rather new idea. Managers once encouraged the harvest of trophy bass to prevent wasting the resource by releasing fish near the end of their lifespan. It was also incorrectly assumed that big bass weren't as important to spawning efforts as were mid-size bass.

Progressive managers and anglers now have a new perspective. Trophy bass have demonstrated exceptional ability to resist disease, avoid predators, and grow. They're fish that have successfully beaten incredible odds, and they're not quickly or easily replaced.

The glamor of big bass has encouraged a number of states to stock Florida-strain bass or conduct genetic experiments to create a "superbass." These programs aren't necessarily bad, but they represent a quick-fix approach to the challenge of managing for trophy bass. Trophy bass management should never detract attention from the basic need to manage for overall bass fishing quality. And the best way to manage for trophy bass is not to create them artificially, but to improve habitat conditions and protect large bass that develop naturally so they can achieve giant size. They are the true "superbass!"

TOURNAMENTS

Because tournaments are a sensitive topic, the impact of tournaments on bass fishing quality is probably one of the best-researched areas of bass fishing. Dozens of studies have dealt with the subject in one way or another.

With little disagreement, studies have concluded that tournaments don't harm fisheries. But that doesn't mean they don't produce adverse effects. While promoters claim successful releases of 96 to 98 percent, careful research suggests that even the best-run tournaments may inflict a mortality rate of about 10 percent. That's not bad, and it again suggests that work in areas other than tournaments is necessary to improve overall fishing quality.

Still, tournaments concentrate pressure on already pressured resources, and many could be run better to further reduce mortality. Livewells are no longer the "death wells" they once were, but they can and should be better. Tournaments need tighter regulations to limit holding times, minimize fish handling, and penalize contestants who bring in fish that will die shortly after being released. In some areas, scheduling events during cooler months can reduce conflicts among user groups and minimize bass mortality.

The most important step tournaments can make toward minimizing negative impacts—and associated public criticism—is to adopt a "fish for inches" format. Using standardized measuring boards, partners record fish lengths and immediately release bass at the catch location. Because fish aren't held in livewells or weigh-in bags or transported long distances, survival rates are maximized and tournament effects minimized. For high-profile or big-money events, however, "paper tournaments" present obvious drawbacks.

Tournaments will remain a major factor in modern bass fishing. In most regions, tournament fishing is increasingly popular. Fortunately, tournament anglers generally lead other anglers in understanding the need for more and better fisheries management.

As we noted in Chapter 2, many bass fishermen enjoy the competition and social aspects that tournaments provide. Following the lead of the Bass Anglers Sportsman Society, almost all events attempt to release bass alive after they've been weighed and assess a weight penalty for each dead bass.

*Hooking, handling, holding in livewells, and the weigh-in process are all damaging experiences for fish. These stresses can kill fish in livewells or several days following release. It's imperative that tournament anglers study factors that cause mortality and work to minimize them. For the most complete coverage of this topic, we recommend **Live Release of Bass, A Guide for Anglers and Tournament Organizers**, available for $2.00 from Bass Research Foundation, 1001 Market St., Chattanooga, TN 37402.*

CUSTOMIZED MANAGEMENT

No single management formula can be applied to every body of water. Regulations ideal for Florida will not necessarily work in Montana. In fact, an ideal management strategy for one lake can be detrimental to a neighboring lake.

Why? In addition to environmental conditions, two key variables are recruitment and growth rates. Growth rates are determined by food supply, lake fertility, genetics of the fish population, harvest rates, and the length of the growing season. Recruitment depends on spawning habitat and factors that determine how many young bass survive to adulthood. Factors like soil characteristics, the size and shape of the basin, the nature of the water supply, types of weeds present, and the composition of the fish community affect growth and recruitment and vary among waters. Waters with differing rates of growth and recruitment may require different size limits to promote high-quality fishing.

A major thrust of progressive management has been to reject focusing on a single species. That is, rather than simply trying to manipulate bass numbers, managers study the whole lake community before attempting to

DIFFERENT RULES FOR DIFFERENT WATERS

At the 1987 Catch-and-Release Symposium, Dr. William Davies reported the findings of his Auburn University (Alabama) research team that studied 187 bass and bluegill ponds for more than 10 years. They concluded that harvest rates should be varied according to the productivity and nature of each pond.

A limited harvest was appropriate for some ponds and not others. The need for catch and release depended on water fertility and the potential for bass recruitment.

Bass ponds with low fertility and high recruitment required moderate harvest to stay productive, but infertile waters with poor recruitment held no extra bass and required total release.

Fisheries with high fertility and high recruitment supported a fairly high harvest of young adult bass; but fertile waters that held many gizzard shad had no surplus bass. Shad outcompeted bass fry for food, resulting in low recruitment rates for bass. There were never enough bass to keep shad checked.

Davies studied ponds, but evidence suggests similar relationships between fertility, recruitment, and the need for harvest or release of predators in larger lakes and reservoirs, though the relationships are more complex. Placing a blanket size limit on Davies' ponds would help some and harm others. We need different rules for different waters.

alter population or size relationships. Management policies that impact one species in a lake affect all other species.

Fishing pressure must also be a consideration in management decisions. A lake near a large metropolitan area requires a different management plan than a remote water.

Thus each body of water is unique and so presents unique management challenges. In some cases, regulations specifically designed for individual bodies of water would maximize angling opportunities while also protecting bass populations. Notification problems and law enforcement would be challenging, however.

SOCIOLOGICAL MANAGEMENT

As managers pondered what their programs should accomplish, they began asking anglers what they expected from management. They learned that anglers don't agree on what they expect management to accomplish.

Generally, specialist anglers who prefer fishing for one species of fish favor catch and release and put high premium on a chance to catch trophy fish. Occasional anglers are typically content to catch small fish and favor liberal bag limits and intensive stocking. Many anglers have attitudes and preferences somewhat between these two extremes.

ANGLER DIVERSITY

For years, most fisheries agencies lumped fishermen when they surveyed the attitudes of anglers. Recently, however, biologists and sociologists have divided anglers into groups that want different things from fisheries agencies.

For example, Brian Chipman and Dr. Lou Helfrich of Virginia Polytechnic Institute* surveyed fishermen on two Virginia rivers. They found six distinct groups of anglers ranging from unskilled generalists who sought anything that would bite, to skilled generalists who could successfully catch many species, to skilled specialists who were

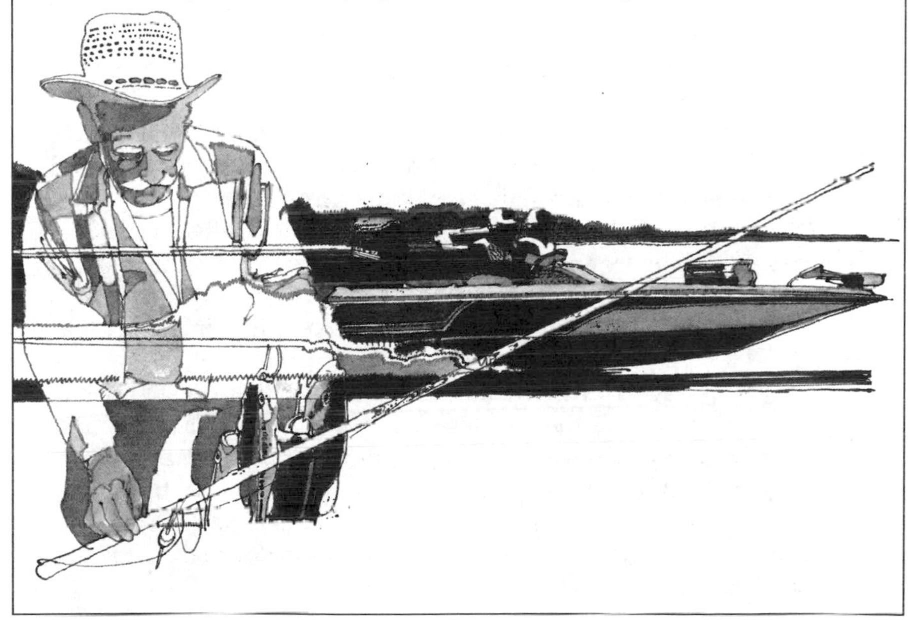

interested in specific species taken with specific techniques or tackle.

Skilled specialists emphasized angling ability, fished frequently, and wanted fisheries to hold some trophy-size fish of their target species. They preferred catching and releasing large fish over catching and keeping smaller fish and favored restrictive harvest regulations.

Fishermen with underdeveloped skills sought escape from the work-a-day world, fished infrequently, placed emphasis on activity with family and friends, and emphasized luck as a reason for success. These anglers were pleased if they caught a few small fish of any species and favored liberal harvest rules.

Between these groups were anglers with increasing amounts of skill who fished primarily for food. They desired large catches, preferred liberal limits, and felt fish stocking was the most important management tool.

Other studies have shown similar results. Skilled specialists have different management goals than skilled generalists, and each group differs from unskilled anglers.

Unskilled, casual anglers rarely fish and value fishing quality less than social benefits. They prefer an occasional, relaxing, hassle-free trip over a good catch. They may resist strict limits if politically aroused, but seldom read fishing magazines and often don't understand complex fishery management issues. Most anglers fall into this unskilled casual angler category.

At any given time, however, skilled anglers who fish frequently are more likely to be fishing. These anglers may be few in number, but create a large share of fishing pressure.

Experts read more about fishing and fisheries, care more about the quality of fisheries, and are more likely to try to influence management policies. If experts are more interested, more knowledgeable, and more concerned, should they have more influence on fisheries policies than anglers who don't care?

Expert specialists differ distinctly from skilled generalists in attitude toward catch-and-release fishing, regulations, stocking policies, and species preferences. Should managers try to satisfy both groups?

So far, most angler surveys haven't measured the relative catch rates and harvest of different angler groups. Some biologists assume most of the harvest is made by casual anglers because there are so many of them. Others suspect that skilled anglers making multiple trips take more fish.

Fisheries managers must create a variety of fishing possibilities to respond to the needs of these different groups. Managers need more information about different types of anglers. And they need an effective way to inform casual anglers about management options.

**Chipman, B.D. and L.A. Helfrich. 1988. Recreational specializations and motivations of Virginia river anglers. No. Amer. J. Fish. Mngt. 8(4):390-398.*

At first, variability of anglers might seem too problematical to managers. But instead of problems, management based on public preferences offers new opportunities.

Because different lakes have different qualities, and because different angler groups have different expectations, the future of bass management is sure to involve special regulations that create a variety of angling experiences. Some lakes might be fly-fishing only. Others might be managed for trophy bass. Others might be managed to produce many small bass for fast, easy fishing.

THE FUTURE

Catch and release, often involving length limit regulations, is a primary management program for the future. If anglers accept limits on which fish they may harvest, they can continue to enjoy excellent bass fishing.

There are two alternatives, however, to accepting catch and release. The

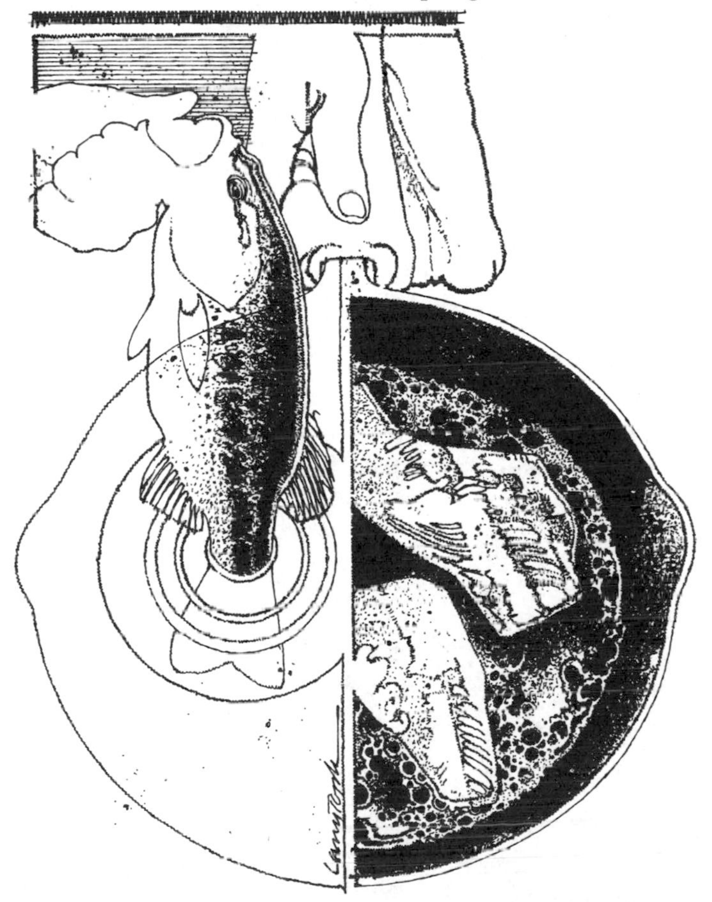

Selective Harvest™ will have an important impact on the future of fishing. We need to continue a tradition of eating some fish, while we learn to release those fish that can sustain good fishing.

obvious one is to accept a continual decline in fishing quality. If catching bass becomes increasingly more difficult, and if the bass caught are too small to be interesting, bass fishing itself will become endangered because the rewards won't justify the effort. Many people contend that this has already happened in some regions.

The other alternative is: If it becomes clear that bass fishing is damaging bass populations, managers might be forced to impose harsh limits on anglers' access to the resource. Unless anglers support progressive regulations, managers might be forced to reduce the amount of fishing pressure bass populations are exposed to. For example, a fishing license in the future might entitle an angler to 15 days of fishing.

We love to fish, so we don't want to even contemplate the prospect of severe limits on fishing opportunity. Ultimately, it seems far more desirable for anglers to accept sound harvest limitations.

Fisheries management, especially bass management, changed more in the last 20 years than during the previous 100. Does that mean biologists have answers to all the important questions? No! The need for research remains as great as ever.

Another trend that must continue if managers are to meet the challenges of providing fine-quality fishing in the future is the increase in cooperation among fishery managers, other regulatory authorities, and angler groups. For example, although managers can't force the Corps of Engineers or other agencies to regulate water flows to enhance fisheries, respectful communication has increased voluntary cooperation. Many cooperative projects have been launched between managers and fishing clubs, community groups, or private businesses to improve fishing. We badly need more of this.

Achieving better mutual respect and communication between anglers and managers is one of the most urgent missions of In-Fisherman. The progress we've already seen is one of the most promising indications that good bass fishing will be available for future generations.

GLOSSARY

Definitions of Select Terms Used In This Book

Action: Measure of rod performance that describes the elapsed time between flexion and return to straight configuration; ranges from slow to fast; also refers to gearing of reels.
Adaptation: Biological adjustment that increases fitness.
Adapted: Capable of thriving in a habitat.
Algae: Simple plant organisms.
Alkalinity: Measure of the amount of acid neutralizing bases.
Amp: Measure of electrical current.
Amp Hour: Storage capacity measurement of a deep-cycle battery obtained by multiplying the current flow in amps by the hours that it's produced.
Anal Fin: Fin located on the ventral side of most fish between the urogenital pore and caudal fin.
Angler: Person using pole or rod and reel to catch fish.
Antireverse: System that prevents reels from spinning in reverse.

LARGEMOUTH BASS ANATOMY

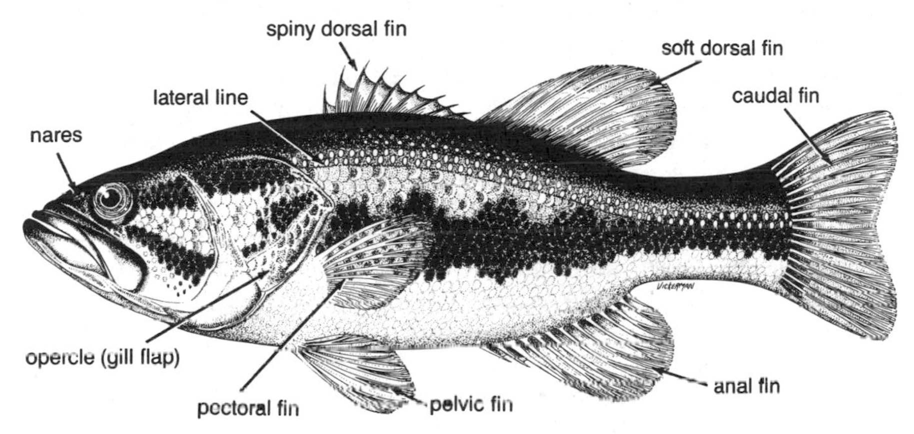

Aquaculture: Commercial production of fish for food.
Aggregation: Group of one species of fish within a limited area.
Backlash: Tangle of line on a baitcasting reel due to spool overrun.
Backwater: Shallow area off a river.
Bag Limit: Restriction on the number of fish that an angler may harvest in a day.
Baitfish: Small fish often eaten by predators.
Bar: Long ridge in a body of water.
Bay: Major indentation in the shoreline of a lake or reservoir.
Bell Sinker: Pear-shaped sinker with brass eye on top.
Blank: Fishing rod without grip, guides, or finish.
Brackish: Water of intermediate salinity between seawater and freshwater.

Break: Distinct variation in otherwise constant stretches of cover, structure, or bottom type.
Breakline: Area of abrupt change in depth, bottom type, or water quality.
Buzzbait: Lure composed of a leadhead, rigid hook, and wire that supports one or more blades; designed for surface fishing.
Buzzing: Retrieving spinnerbaits or buzzbaits along the surface so they splash water.
Cabbage: Any of several species of submerged weeds of the genus *Potamogeton*.
Canal: Manmade waterway for navigation.
Carrying Capacity: Maximum density of organisms that a body of water can sustain.
Catchability: Measure of the willingness of fish to bite lures or bait.
Caudal Fin: Fish's tail.
Channel: The bed of a stream or river.
Chemical: Combination of molecules.
Chugger: Topwater plug with a cupped face designed to make a splash when pulled sharply.
Cline: Vertical or horizontal section of a body of water where water characteristics change abruptly.
Community: Group of interacting organisms within an area.
Contaminant: Toxic substance in the environment.
Coontail: Submerged aquatic plant of the hornwort family typically found in hard water; characterized by stiff, forked leaves.
Countershaded: Color pattern consisting of dark back and light belly.
Cove: An indentation along the shoreline of a lake or reservoir.
Cover: Natural or manmade objects on the bottom of lakes, rivers, or impoundments, especially those that influence fish behavior.
Crankbait: Lipped diving lure.
Creel Limit: The number of fish of a species or species group that an angler can retain or harvest in a day.
Crustacean: Hard-shelled, typically aquatic invertebrate.
Current: Water moving in one direction.
Dam: Manmade barrier to water flow.
Dark-Bottom Bay: Shallow, protected bay with a layer of dark organic material on the bottom that warms quickly in spring.
Debris: Natural or manmade objects in water.
Deep-Cycle Battery: Battery with thick lead plates, designed to be repeatedly drained and recharged.
Dissolved Oxygen: Oxygen molecules dispersed in water.
Diurnal: Occurring within a 24-hour daily period.
Dorsal Fin: Fin located on center of fish's back.
Downfishing: Level of fishing pressure that reduces fishing quality and abundance of large fish.
Drag: System for allowing fish to pull line from reel while antireverse switch is engaged.
Drainage: The area drained by a river and all its tributaries.
Drop-Off: An area of substantial increase in depth.

Eddy: Area of slack water or reversed current in a stream or river.
Egg Sinker: Tapered, oblong sinker with a hole from end to end.
Electrophoresis: Lab procedure for identifying proteins used to identify genetic stocks.
Epilimnion: Warm surface layer of a stratified lake or reservoir.
Estuary: Area where a river meets saltwater and has characteristics of freshwater and marine environments.
Euro-Style: Similar to fishing tackle designed in Europe, especially floats, rods, rigs.
Euryhaline: Organism that's tolerant of a broad range of salinity.
Eutrophic: Highly fertile waters characterized by warm, shallow basins.
Extirpated: Eliminated from former habitat.
Farm Pond: Small manmade body of water.
Fecundity: Number of eggs produced by a female in a season.
Feeder Creek: Tributary to a stream.
Feeding Strategy: Set of behaviors used for capture and metabolism of prey.
Fertility: Degree of productivity of plants and animals.
Fertilizer: Natural or synthetic materials added to water or land to increase productivity.
Filamentous Algae: Type of algae characterized by long chains of attached cells that give it a stringy feel and appearance.
Fingerling: Juvenile fish, usually from 1 to 3 inches long.
Fish Culture: Production of fish in hatcheries.
Fished Down: Fish population adversely affected by fishing pressure.
Fisherman: Person catching fish by any means.
Fishery: Group of fish that support fishing.
Fishery Biologist: Person who studies interaction of fishermen and fisheries.
Fishing Pressure: Amount of angling on a body of water in a period of time, usually measured in hours per acre per year; its effects on fish populations.
Fitness: Ability of an animal to survive and reproduce.
Flat: Area of lake, reservoir or river characterized by little change in depth.
Flipping: Presentation technique for dropping lures into dense cover at close range.
Flipping Stick: Heavy action fishing rod, 7 to 8 feet long, designed for bass fishing.
Float: Buoyant device for suspending bait.
Float Stop: Adjustable rubber bead or thread, set on line above float to determine fishing depth.
Fluorescent: Emits radiation when exposed to sunlight.
Forage: Something eaten; the act of eating.
Freeze-Out Lake: Shallow northern lake subject to fish kills in late winter due to oxygen depletion.
Freeze-Up: Short period when ice first covers the surface of a body of water.
Frequency: Number of cycles in a unit of time, usually a second.
Front: Weather system that causes changes in temperature, cloud cover, precipitation, wind, and barometric pressure.
Fry: Recently hatched fish; cooking method using heated oil.

Gamefish: Fish species pursued by anglers.
Gear Ratio: Measure of a reel's retrieve speed; the number of times the spool revolves for each complete turn of the handle.
Genetics: The study of mechanisms of heredity.
Gradient: Degree of slope in a stream or riverbed.
Graph: Sonar unit that draws underwater objects on paper.
Habitat: Type of environment in which an organism usually lives.
Harvest: Remove fish with intent to eat.
Hole: Deep section of a stream or river.
Home Range (Area): Defined area occupied by an animal for most activities over an extended time period.
Hybrid: Offspring of two species or subspecies.
Hypolimnion: Deep, cool zone below the thermocline in a stratified lake or impoundment.
Ice-Out: Short period during which ice on a body of water completely melts.
Ichthyologist: Scientist who studies the biology or taxonomy of fish.
Impoundment: Body of water formed by damming running water.
Invertebrate: Animal without a backbone.
Jig: Lure composed of leadhead with rigid hook, often with hair, plastic, rubber, or other dressings.
Jigworm: Plastic worm rigged on an open-hook jighead.
Jonboat: Flat-bottom aluminum boat with low gunnels.
Jump Bait: Cigar-shape topwater plug designed to move erratically when retrieved.
Key: Systematic classification of species characteristics to aid identification.
Lake: Confined area where water accumulates naturally.
Larva: Immature form of an organism.
Lateral Line: Sensory system of fish that detects low frequency vibrations in water.
Ledge: Sharp contour break in a river or reservoir.
Length Limit: Regulation that prohibits harvest of fish below, above, or within specified lengths.
Livebait: Any living animal used to entice fish to bite.
Livewell: Compartment in boat designed to keep fish alive.
Location: Where fish position themselves in response to the environment.
Management: Manipulation of biological system to produce a fishery goal.
Melanophore: Skin cell capable of changing color.
Mesotrophic: Waters of intermediate fertility between eutrophic and oligotrophic.
Metalimnion: Term for thermocline.
Migration: Directed movement by large number of animals of one species.
Minnow Bait: Long, thin, minnow-shape wood or plastic lure designed to be fished on or near the surface.
Monofilament: Fishing line made from a single strand of synthetic fiber.
Mottled: Blotchy coloration.
Nares: Nostrils of fish or other aquatic vertebrates.
Native: Naturally present in an area.

Natural Selection: Process of differential survival and reproduction among individuals that affects the genetic makeup of subsequent generations.
Niche: The role of an organism in an ecological community.
Nymph: Larval form of an insect.
Olfaction: Sense of smell.
Oligotrophic: Infertile waters; geologically young; characterized by deep, cool, clear oxygenated waters and rocky basins.
Omnivore: Organism that eats a wide variety of items.
Opportunistic: Feeding strategy in which items are eaten according to availability.
Otolith: Ear bone of fish.
Overharvest: A level of fish harvest from a body of water that substantially reduces abundance of catchable fish, particularly large fish.
Overwintering Area: Area where fish hold during winter, particularly in cold climates.
Oxbow: A U-shaped bend in a river.
Panfish: Group of about 30 small warm-water sportfish; not including bullheads or catfish.
Pattern: A defined set of location and presentation factors that consistently produce fish.
Pectoral Fin: Paired fin usually located on fish's side behind the head
Pelagic: Living in open, offshore waters.
Pelvic Fin: Paired fin usually located on lower body.
Pesticide: Substance applied to kill undesirable plants, insects, or animals.
pH: A measure of hydrogen in concentration.
Phosphorescent: Ability to glow in the dark after exposure to a light source.
Photoperiod: Interval during a day when sunlight is present.
Photosynthesis: Process in which green plants convert carbon dioxide and water into sugar and oxygen in the presence of sunlight.
Phytoplankton: Tiny plants suspended in water.
Pit: Area excavated for mining operations that fills with water.
Pitch: Sound determined by the frequency of sound waves.
Pitching: Presentation technique in which worms or jigs are dropped into cover at close range (15 to 30 feet) with an underhand pendulum motion, using a 6 ½- to 7 ½-foot baitcasting rod.
Plankton: Organisms drifting in a body of water.
Plug: Solid-bodied wood or plastic lure.
Point: Projection of land into a body of water.
Polarized: Capability of breaking up sunlight into directional components.
Pollution: Material generated by human activity that negatively affects the environment.
Pond: Small natural or manmade body of water.
Pool: Deep section of a stream or river.
Population: Group of animals of the same species within a geographical area that freely interbreed; level of abundance.
Postspawn: Period immediately after spawning; In-Fisherman calendar period between Spawn and Presummer.

Pound Test: System for measuring the strength of fishing line; the amount of pressure that will break a line.
Predator: Fish that often feed on other fish.
Presentation: Combination of bait or lure, rig, tackle, and technique used to catch fish.
Prespawn: Period prior to spawning; In-Fisherman calendar period between Winter and Spawn.
Prey: Fish often eaten by other fish species.
Prop Bait: Topwater plug with one or more propellers at the front or back.
Push Pole: Long (12- to 16-foot) wood, fiberglass, or graphite pole used for propelling a boat through shallow water or dense aquatic weeds.
Quick-Strike Rig: European-style system for hooking live or dead baits; includes 2 hooks and allows hooks to be set immediately following a strike.
Radio Tag (Transmitter): Device emitting high-frequency radio signals which when attached to an animal indicates its location.
Range: Area over which a species is distributed.
Rattlebait: Hollow-bodied, sinking, lipless crankbaits that rattle loudly due to shot and slugs in the body cavity.
Ray: Bony segment supporting a fin.
Reservoir: Large manmade body of water.
Recruitment: Process by which fish hatch and grow to catchable size.
Reeds: Any of several species of tall, emergent aquatic weeds that grow in shallow zones of lakes and reservoirs.
Reef: Rocky hump in a body of water.
Resting Spot: Location used by fish not actively feeding.
Rhizome: Rootlike stem of plants that sends up vertical shoots.
Riffle: Shallow, fast flowing section of a stream or river.
Rig: Arrangement of components for bait fishing, including hooks, leader, sinker, swivel, beads.
Riprap: Large rocks placed along a bank.
Riverine: Having characteristics of a river.
Run: Straight, moderate-depth section of a stream or river with little depth change.
Salinity: Concentration of salts in a liquid.
School: Group of fish of one species that move in unison.
Sedentary: Residing within a restricted area.
Seiche: Oscillation of water level in a large lake or reservoir caused by strong directional winds.
Selective Harvest™: Deciding to release or harvest fish, based on species, size, and relative abundance.
Sensory Organ: Biological system involved in sight, hearing, taste, smell, touch, or lateral line sense.
Set Rig: Rig that's cast or drifted into position on the bottom to await a strike.
Shot: Small, round sinkers pinched onto fishing line.
Silt: Fine sediment on the bottom of a body of water.
Sinkers: Variously shaped pieces of lead used to sink bait or lures.

Slip Float: Float with a hole from top to bottom for sliding freely on line.
Slip Sinker: Sinker with a hole for sliding freely on line.
Slop: Dense aquatic vegetation matted on the surface.
Slough: Cove or backwater on a reservoir or river.
Slot Limit: Type of regulation that prohibits harvesting fish within a specified length range.
Slow Roll: Spinnerbait presentation in which the lure is retrieved slowly through and over cover objects.
Snag: Brush or tree in a stream or river.
Solitary: Occupying habitat without close association to other animals.
Sonar: Electronic fishing aid that emits sound waves underwater and interprets them to depict underwater objects.
Spawn: Reproduction of fish; In-Fisherman calendar period associated with that activity.
Species: Group of potentially interbreeding organisms.
Spine: Stiff, sharp segment of fin.
Spoon: Any of a wide variety of metal, plastic, or wood lures with a generally spoonlike shape and a single hook.
Sportfish: Fish species pursued by anglers.
Stock: Place fish in a body of water; population of animals.
Stress: State of physiological imbalance caused by disturbing environmental factors.
Strike: Biting motion of a fish.
Strike Window (Zone): Conceptual area in front of a fish within which it will strike food items or lures.
Structure: Changes in the shape of the bottom of lakes, rivers, or impoundments, especially those that influence fish behavior.
Stumpfield: Area of an impoundment where stands of timber have been cut prior to impoundment, leaving stumps below the surface.
Substrate: Type of bottom in a body of water.
Suspended Fish: Fish in open water hovering considerably above bottom.
Swim (Gas) Bladder: Organ of most bony fish that holds a volume of gas to make them neutrally buoyant at variable depths.
Tailwater: Area immediately downstream from a dam.
Taxonomist: Scientist who studies the classification of organisms.
Temperature Tolerant: Able to function in a wide range of temperatures.
Terminal Tackle: Components of bait fishing system including hooks, sinkers, swivels, leaders.
Thermal Effluent: Hot water discharged from a power plant.
Thermocline: Layer of water with abrupt change in temperature, occurring between warm surface layer (epilimnion) and cold bottom layer (hypolimnion).
Topwaters: Lures designed to be worked on the surface.
Toxic: Capable of causing illness or death.
Tracking: Following radio tagged or sonic-tagged animals.
Trailer: A plastic skirt, grub, pork rind, live bait, or other attractor attached to a lure to entice fish.

Trailer Hook: An extra hook attached to the rear hook of a lure to catch fish that strike behind the lure.

Transducer: Electronic part of a sonar unit that emits and receives sound impulses and converts them to visual images.

Tributary: Stream or river flowing into a larger river.

Trigger: Characteristics of a lure or bait presentation that elicit a biting response in fish.

Trolling: Fishing method in which lures or baits are pulled by a boat.

Trolling Motor: Electric motor positioned on the bow or transom to push or pull a boat.

Trophic: Relating to the fertility of a body of water.

Turbid: Murky water discolored by suspended sediment.

Turbulence: Water disturbed by strong currents.

Twitch Bait: Long, thin, minnow-shape lure of wood or plastic, designed to be fished on or near the surface.

Ultraviolet (UV) Light: Radiation with wavelengths shorter than 4,000 angstroms; beyond violet in the color spectrum.

Waterdog: Immature salamander possessing external gills.

Watershed: The region draining runoff into a body of water.

Weed: Aquatic plant.

Weedline (Weededge): Abrupt edge of a weedbed caused by a change in depth, bottom type, or other factor.

Wetland: Areas covered by water at least part of each year.

Wing Dam: Manmade earth or rock ridge to deflect current.

Winterkill: Fish mortality due to oxygen depletion under ice in late winter.

Year Class: Fish of one species hatched in a single year.

Zooplankton: Tiny animals suspended in water.

IN-FISHERMAN MASTERPIECE SERIES

- **WALLEYE WISDOM:** A Handbook of Strategies
- **PIKE:** A Handbook of Strategies
- **SMALLMOUTH BASS:** A Handbook of Strategies
- **LARGEMOUTH BASS:** A Handbook of Strategies
- **CRAPPIE WISDOM:** A Handbook of Strategies
- **CHANNEL CATFISH FEVER:** A Handbook of Strategies
- **BIG BASS MAGIC**
- **FISHING FUNDAMENTALS**
- **ICE FISHING SECRETS**

Each masterpiece book represents the collaborative effort of fishing experts. The books don't represent a regional perspective or the opinions of one good angler. Each masterpiece book is species specific, but teems with information application to all areas of the country and to any fishing situation.

In-Fisherman

7819 Highland Scenic Road, Baxter MN 56425 • 218.829.1648

In-Fisherman®
COMMUNICATIONS NETWORK

ICE FISHING GUIDE
AN IN-FISHERMAN PUBLICATION

In-Fisherman®
LIBRARY SERIES

The In-Fisherman Library Series is but part of the In-Fisherman Communications Network, a multifaceted, multi-media organization, teaching how to catch fish while striving to maintain a healthy fishing resource for future generations.

The In-Fisherman Communications Network began in 1975 with **In-Fisherman** magazine, which continues as the core of the network. Publishing the latest, most comprehensive information about fish, their world, and how to catch them, In-Fisherman magazine satisfies anglers' needs for practical, innovative, and fascinating information.

In addition to **In-Fisherman** magazine and the **In-Fisherman Library Series,** the In-Fisherman Communications Network publishes the **In-Fisherman Masterpiece Book Series,** species specific books representing the collaborative effort of several fishing experts; and the **Walleye Guide** and **Walleye In-Sider** magazines—North America's leading sources for walleye information.

And that's only print media. **In-Fisherman TV Specials** are hailed as the most informative fishing shows on television. **In-Fisherman Radio** plays on 400 stations nationwide, reaching over a billion listeners annually. **In-Fisherman Video Club** presents a treasury of angling wisdom on a variety of fish species from a large library of videos, with 6 to 8 new releases each year. The **Professional Walleye Trail** pits the world's best walleye anglers in run-and-gun fishing competition across North America.

For information on any area of the In-Fisherman Communications Network, write In-Fisherman, 7819 Highland Scenic Road, Baxter, MN 56425, 218.829.1648

In-Fisherman® VIDEO

In-Fisherman® TELEVISION

In-Fisherman® RADIO